Curriculum and Teaching Dialogue

Volume 25, Numbers 1 and 2

Curriculum and Teaching Dialogue

Edited by

Chara Haeussler Bohan
Georgia State University

Associate Editor

John L. Pecore
University of West Florida

Assistant Editor

Franklin S. Allaire
University of Houston–Downtown

Graduate Research Assistants

Abbey Hortenstine
Georgia State University

INFORMATION AGE PUBLISHING, INC.
Charlotte, NC • www.infoagepub.com

Library of Congress Cataloging-in-Publication Data

CIP record for this book is available from the Library of Congress
http://www.loc.gov

DOI Number: 10.52966

ISSN Number: 1538-750X

ISBNs: 979-8-88730-364-2 (Paperback)

979-8-88730-365-9 (Hardcover)

979-8-88730-366-6 (ebook)

Copyright © 2023 Information Age Publishing Inc.

All rights reserved. No part of this publication may be reproduced, stored
in a retrieval system, or transmitted, in any form or by any means, electronic,
mechanical, photocopying, microfilming, recording or otherwise, without written
permission from the publisher.

Printed in the United States of America

American Association for Teaching and Curriculum Leadership for 2022–2023

President
Crystal Howell, University of Northern Colorado

President Elect
Christy McConnell, University of North Florida

Executive Council

Taryn Robertson
University of San Diego

Joseph Flynn
Northern Illinois University

Franklin A. Allaire
University of Houston-Downtown

Todd Hodgkinson
Drake University

Benjamin Ingman
University of Denver

Cristy Sellers Smith
Pacific University

Caroline Conner
Kennesaw State University

Corey Nagle
University of West Florida/
Bristol (CT) Public Schools

Michelle Tenam-Zemach
Nova Southeastern University

Executive Secretary
Aubrey Southall, Aurora University

Web Liaison
Linda Conn, Minot State University

Dana K. Haraway
Historian, James Madison University

Editorial Review Board

Donna Adair Breault, PhD
Ashland University

Kimo Alexander Cashman, PhD
University of Hawai'i at Mānoa

David Callejo Pérez, PhD
Saginaw Valley State University

Robert Donmoyer, PhD
University of San Diego

David J. Flinders, PhD
University of San Diego

Lyn C. Forester, EdD
Doane University

Sandra Guzman Foster, PhD
University of the Incarnate World

Alan W. Garrett, PhD
Eastern New Mexico University

Kate Kauper, PhD
Cornell College

Amy L. Masko, PhD
Grand Valley State University

Pardess Mitchell, EdD
William Rainey Harper College

Christy McConnell Moroye, PhD
University of Northern Colorado

Wesley Null, PhD
Baylor University

Chyllis E. Scott, PhD
University of Nevada, Las Vegas

Bruce Uhrmacher, PhD
University of Denver

Bill White, EdD
James Madison University

Christine Woyshner, EdD
Temple University

CONTENTS

Acknowledgments ....*xi*

2022 KEYNOTE ADDRESS

Presidential Address—Seeking Solidarity
  Crystal D. Howell *3*

VOLUME 25, NUMBER 1

**Editorial Remarks—Back to the Future: Culture Wars, Education
  Legislation, Book Bannings, and Fake News**
  Chara Haeussler Bohan *13*

**AATC Keynote Address—Seeking Solidarity: Defining Self-
  Interest in the Context of Capitalism as a Global Social System**
  Lois Weiner *19*

  1. Racial and Cultural Pedagogies in Education: A Retrospective
     Antonio J. Castro, Yeji Kim, and Mary Adu-Gyamfi *33*

  2. Legislate to (Un)educate: Examining the Impact of Divisive
     and Dehumanizing Education Policies
     Gregory Samuels, Amy Samuels, and Brandon J. Haas *51*

  3. Writing a Love Letter to Educators in the Wake of Anti-CRT
     Efforts
     Alexandra Allweiss, Scott Farver, and Anne-Lise Halvorsen *69*

viii CONTENTS

4. Making Sense of the Message: The Perceptions and Impact of State Legislation That Challenges the Teaching of Hard History
Debby Shulsky, Sheila Baker, and Renée E. Lastrapes 87

5. Attacking Antisemitism: Investigating How Museum-Led Professional Development Affects Preservice Teachers' Preparedness to Teach the Holocaust
Caroline Conner and Andrea Miskewicz 115

6. Factors Shaping Teacher Education Graduates' Abilities to Impact Students' Learning and Development During Induction
Joyce E. Many, Carla L. Tanguay, and Ruchi Bhatnagar 135

7. The Fluid Curriculum: Reinvigorating the Role of the Teacher as Curriculum Maker
Bradley Conrad, Christy McConnell, Sarah Campbell, and P. Bruce Uhrmacher 155

VOLUME 25, NUMBER 2

Editorial Remarks—The Teacher Shortage and Rapidly Increasing Virtual Schools
John L. Pecore 173

AATC Keynote Address— Finding and Sustaining Solidarity
Jen Johnson 177

1. How Veteran Teachers Are Impacted by Administrators: A Case Study
Sarah Campbell 187

2. Ideological Foundations, Curricular Models, and the Path of Bilingual Education
Leah Davis 203

3. Bespoke Learning: Using the Evidence Continuum to Design Learner-Centered Curriculum and Teaching
Robyn Thomas Pitts 217

4. The Lived Experience of Female K–12 Teachers During the COVID-19 Pandemic: A Phenomenological Study
Sarah Campbell, Rebecca Reinhardt, Mallori Sage, and Emily Strong 233

Contents ix

5. Ninth-Grade Students With Disabilities' Math Efficacy and Teachers' Instructional Efficacy
   John M. Palladino 249

6. Narcissistic or Overwhelmed? Divergent Pathways to Academic Entitlement
   Elizabeth J. Pope, Monica K. Erbacher, and Lauren Pierce 263

OUTTAKES

1. The Tensions and Intentions of Researching Ongoing Holocaust Education Legislation
   Rebecca C. Christ and Brandon J. Haas 283

2. Grappling With the Exit From a Community of Research Participants
   Juan Manuel Gerardo 287

3. Mama Scholarship: Tackling the Motherlode
   Robyn Thomas Pitts 291

4. "Everyone is a Math Person": How Findings of Positive Math Identity Derailed My Study but Enhanced My Teaching
   Stephanie B. Purington 297

5. The Metacognition of a Reader: An Unexpected Co-Journey Towards Growth and Self-Discovery
   Mallori Sage 301

6. It's Not Always Black and White: Reflections on Research Design, Participant Recruitment, and Data Collection
   Ryan B. Warren 305

7. Time Zones, Pandemic, and War, Oh My! The Challenges of Conducting an International Virtual Exchange
   Jie Zhang, Mariana Sokol, and Cynthia Boyer 309

BOOK REVIEWS

1. *Reimagining School Discipline for the 21st Century Student: Engaging Students, Practitioners, and Community Members* by John A. Williams III and Chance W. Lewis
   Reviewed by Lizette Burks 315

x CONTENTS

2. *Looking Like a Language, Sounding Like a Race* by Jonathan Rosa
Reviewed by Derek Gottlieb *319*

3. *Teaching as a Human Activity: Ways to Make Classrooms Joyful and Effective* by J. Amos Hatch
Reviewed by Katherine Perrotta *325*

4. *Teaching Resilience and Mental Health Across the Curriculum* by Linda Yaron Weston
Reviewed by Naomi Jeffery Petersen *329*

5. *Reconstructing Care in Teacher Education after COVID-19: Caring Enough to Change* by Melanie Shoffner and Angela W. Webb
Reviewed by Jess Smith *333*

6. *Bringing History and Civics to Life* by Karalee Wong Nakatsuka and Laurel Aguilar-Kirchoff
Reviewed by Aubrey Brammar Southhall *337*

About the Authors *339*

ACKNOWLEDGMENTS

The editors want to extend a very special thanks to the following individuals for their editorial review service to *Curriculum and Teaching Dialogue*: William White, Mahnoor Ahmad, Alan Garrett, Amy Corp, Cristy Sellers, LaBotta Taylor, Robyn Thomas Pitts, Sonja Varbelow, Sandra Guzman Foster, Derek Gottlieb, Pardess Mitchell, Alexander Butler, Paul Parkison, Mandi Leigh, Wesley Null, Michelle Tenam-Zemach, Dana Haraway, Todd Hodgkinson, Crystal Howell, Amy Masko, Aaron Zimmerman, Joseph Flynn, Matthew Clay, Kate Kauper, Bruce Uhrmacher, Daniel Conn, Kimo Cashman, Joe Zajdel, Christine McConnell, Tony Castro, Bradley Conrad, Steve Camicia, Taryn Robertson, Corey Nagle, Chyllis Scott, Colleen Eddy, Robert Donmoyer, Ellen Edeburn, Ben Ingman, Leah Davis, Ervin Sparapani, Christine Woyshner, Hyeri Hong, Vicki Boley, Katherine Perrotta, Matthew Clay, and Jennifer Deets.

The editors would like to share their recognitions and deep appreciation to the committee members of the Francis P. Hunkins Distinguished Article Award: John Pecore (Associate Editor & Committee Chair), Sandy Watson, Louise Allen, and William White. Their commitment to *Curriculum Teaching and Dialogue* and AATC provides an example of why we should continue our good work in the fields of teaching and curriculum.

Curriculum and Teaching Dialogue,
Volume 25, Numbers 1 & 2, pp. xi–xi
Copyright © 2023 by Information Age Publishing
www.infoagepub.com
All rights of reproduction in any form reserved.

2022 KEYNOTE ADDRESS

PRESIDENTIAL ADDRESS DELIVERED TO THE AMERICAN ASSOCIATION FOR TEACHING AND CURRICULUM (AATC) ANNUAL CONFERENCE AT THE CHICAGO CULTURAL CENTER ON OCTOBER 6, 2022, CHICAGO, ILLINOIS

SEEKING SOLIDARITY

Crystal D. Howell
Randolph College

Good evening, friends and colleagues. I am delighted to be speaking with you tonight, here in downtown Chicago. When we began planning this year's conference—now nearly two years ago—I knew immediately that I wanted us to come together here. I was then and remain outraged and inspired by the historical and contemporary labor movement at work in the city.

Chicago has been a hub for labor activities for nearly 200 years. Its history—and that of Illinois altogether—is indelibly bound up with that of organized labor. In the early years of statehood, Illinois's economy relied mostly on agriculture, and in comparison to more industrialized states in the Northeast, it experienced little labor unrest. But, as the nineteenth century progressed and the state became more industrialized, it grew more and more antipathetic toward workers. In 1861, miners in the southern coalfields of the state harnessed the demand created by the Civil War and together with miners from Missouri formed the American Miners'

Curriculum and Teaching Dialogue,
Volume 25, Numbers 1 & 2, pp. 3–10
Copyright © 2023 by Information Age Publishing
www.infoagepub.com
All rights of reproduction in any form reserved.

4   C. D. HOWELL

Association, the first national miners' union. Shortly thereafter in 1863 the legislature retaliated by passing the La Salle Black Law, which

> prohibited any person from preventing any other person from working at any lawful occupation on any terms he might see fit and from combining for the purpose of depriving the owner or possessor of property of its lawful use and management. (Beckner, 1929, p. 180)

Just two years later, the Iron Molder's International Union—which historian Robert Sampson (n.d.) called "the most powerful union then in existence" ("Early Years" section)—met in Chicago in the "largest convention of workingmen of one craft ever held on the continent" (Social Sciences, Health, and Education Library Resources in Labor & Employment Relations, n.d., "1865" section). By 1867, organized labor had regained enough political power to pressure the legislature into passing an eight-hour workday law, but employers would not obey it and the state would not enforce it. The 1870s and early 80s saw strikes around the city and continued calls for a real eight-hour workday, culminating in 1886's Haymarket Tragedy and, less than a decade later, the Pullman Strike. Throughout its history, Chicago has been home to both the antagonists—such as the Pinkerton National Detective Agency—and protagonists—such as the International Workers of the World—of the United States' labor story.

I signed the contract to come to Chicago in December 2020. Like the rest of the world, I had spent the last several months in varying degrees of isolation, watching the world from my windows and computer screen. I was revising the final (okay, almost final) draft of a paper about the #55strong movement in West Virginia (WV) and their use of a secret Facebook group to organize before, during, and after their historic strike in February and March 2018. Their nine-day statewide work stoppage inspired similar actions in Oklahoma, Arizona, Colorado, California, Kentucky, North Carolina, South Carolina, Tennessee, Virginia, and, of course, Chicago, where in October 2019, teachers, paraprofessionals, and service personnel fought for not only salary and benefit increases but also reduced class sizes and more social workers, school nurses, and librarians.

I was—I am—a member of the WV teachers' Facebook group, and during that first very hard COVID winter, I frequently observed conversations in the group. They were focused on the state's COVID numbers and its complicated, frequently changing system for figuring out when it was safe to go to school. Most of the 55 counties had gone back in person for at least part of that fall, and members shared color-coded county maps nearly daily as they monitored whose infection and community spread rates were too high, forcing them back to totally online instruction. They talked about what that would mean for students who needed school breakfasts and lunches, for students who did not have internet or adults at home. They talked about the vaccine rollout and whether teachers should get it with other frontline workers like doctors and nurses but before the elderly members of their community—many of whom were raising school-age children as a result of the opioid epidemic. They talked about the lack of high-speed internet (or any internet at all) in many remote communities, making virtual learning days *un*learning days. The breadth of these concerns—and many of those articulated by teachers in the other states I mentioned—fits into the framework of *social justice unionism*, a contemporary term used by Dr. Lois Weiner (2012) and other scholars (e.g., Dandala, 2019; Maton, 2016) to call attention to the entanglement of teachers' work and students' experiences with broader social issues like racism and classism. This form of unionism finds teachers fighting not only for pay and benefits but also for students' access to things like affordable nutritious food, stable housing, and healthcare.

What has motivated teachers around the United States to demand more for one another and for their communities in recent years? What brought together workers from the Southern coalfields of this state with the city's ironworkers and meatpackers and machinists during the nineteenth century? Solidarity—that elusive thing we are, according to the cover of our program, seeking together right now. Perhaps, after Dr. Weiner's keynote and several more sessions throughout the day, we will feel it together as well. Tonight, I want to spend my time with you working toward a better understanding of solidarity as a scholarly concept and then consider what is required of a *practical solidarity*.

In his article "Solidarity: Concept, Conceptions, and Contexts," Rainer Forst (2021) begins with a dozen or so questions about solidarity. Is it a value or a virtue? Can criminals have it—that is, is solidarity always in the service of the good? For example, is what members of organized crime families have solidarity? Is solidarity just a feeling, or is it something humans can rationally conjure? Can it be institutionalized, or must it arise spontaneously? "In short," he summarizes,

> the very nature of solidarity—its grounds, motives, content, scope, and form—is the subject of numerous disagreements, not just in light of the different histories and trajectories of the concept but also in light of the different uses we make of it in our normative vocabulary. (p. 2)

As a former language teacher, I often begin my scholarly investigations with word study. The term *solidarity* comes from the Latin *solidum*, a term itself used in Roman law. *Obligatio in solidum*—which literally means binding into a solid—referred to "the unlimited liability of each individual ... member within a family or other community to pay common debts"

6   C. D. HOWELL

(Bayertz, 1999, p. 3). Smith et al. (1890) offer a fuller description of this particular sort of bond:

> Solidarity is mainly passive: one creditor is entitled against two or more debtors by different obligations; but these obligations, though different from one another, have one and the same act or forbearance as their object: so that when that object is once attained by the performance of one of them, all the having no longer any object, cease *ipso facto* to exist. (para. 17)

They explicate this legalese with a helpful example:

> For instance, where two persons jointly commit a delict—e.g., break a man's windows—the obligation to make compensation ... is of this nature: as soon as one has paid for mending the windows, the other's liability is at an end. (para. 17)

This understanding of solidarity is, like other obligations under Roman law, personal and pragmatic; it is a *description of* not a moral or ethical *judgment about* how equilibrium may be restored after a debt has been incurred. In other words, it is how we pay what we owe, together.

Our more contemporary understanding of solidarity as akin to fraternity or community spirit did not emerge until the 1800s, after appearing in Napoleon's Civil Code. The term was then adapted from its legal use by the French philosopher Charles Fourier and others, and by the turn of the next century, solidarity had taken on its contemporary meanings. Within the academy, our use of the term comes in part from the work of Émile Durkheim, one of the foundational scholars in the field of sociology. Durkheim (1893/1933) argued that societies are held together by what he called *social solidarity*, writing that "men cannot live together ... without tying themselves together with strong, durable bonds" (p. 228). In his book *The Division of Labor in Society*, Durkheim asserted that pre-industrialized societies experience what he calls *mechanical solidarity*, a sort of solidarity that stems from members' homogeneity, particularly in their work. In a small, pre-industrialized community, for instance, Durkheim purported that members would feel bound to one another by labor such as farming or animal husbandry done by every or almost every community member. In contrast, he believed, larger industrialized societies experience *organic solidarity*. Organic solidarity emerges in societies where members do many kinds of labor yet continue to rely on one another. Such societies are held together by members' interdependence.

Since then, Kurt Bayertz (1999) notes, the concept of solidarity has come to "share the same fate as other central concepts within ethical and political terminology, namely that of not being defined in a binding manner, and consequently of being used in very different and sometimes contradictory ways" (p. 3). He then considers several uses of solidarity. First, its most general use: "the tie which binds all of us human beings to one big moral community" (p. 5). He traces this use back to the Ancient Greek idea of the *polis* through to Christianity's principle of brotherhood or brotherly love. Second, he describes a narrower conception in which solidarity "does not refer to the tie binding humanity as a whole, but to the cohesion of a narrower and more limited community, including the resulting (particular) obligations" (p. 9)—in other words, a society. A third important use, he writes, is "wherever individuals form a group in order to stand up for their common interests" (p. 16). This use is most relevant to our conversations about workers' organizations. Bayertz notes that this form of solidarity, unlike the first two he describes, "has a *positive* component, which results from the goals ... those involved are keen to realize with the help of their solidary actions" (p. 16). "This type of solidarity," he continues, "is particularly needed where institutionalized mechanisms for the production and maintenance of justice do not exist or fail" (p. 17). In other words, this use of solidarity is explicitly normative and contextual.

Thus far, the other scholars I have cited have been considering solidarity in a conceptual sense from the perspective of their respective fields, including law, sociology, and philosophy. But as Dr. Weiner reminded us in her keynote address, our domains are curriculum and instruction. Our domains are schools. We work in and for classrooms, students, and teachers, contexts and actors often ignored by our colleagues in other disciplines.

With this in mind, I return to scholars who *do* consider our discipline. I return also to my time studying West Virginia teachers' secret Facebook group. As a part of this project, I led a focus group with the group's mods and admins, and from their conversation along with a survey administered to group members broadly, I aimed to understand better the group's overt and covert functions. I'm happy to share the resulting article with you—because I really did finish that draft!—but for tonight I wanted to conclude by revisiting that conversation to try to understand how West Virginia's teachers made solidarity real, how they took a normatively motivated sense of mutual attachment and obligation and turned it into a practical solidarity.

First, their practical solidarity required imagination—specifically, a social imagination, which Maxine Greene (1995) describes as "the capacity to invent visions of what should be and what might be in our deficient society, on the streets where we live, in our schools" (p. 5). In my conversation with West Virginia teachers, imagining something different happened again and again. The four participants in the focus group imagined and described a different physical environment—one without water poisoned by mine runoff: one with clean, welcoming school facilities in good repair and accessible to all community members. Participants imagined school

8 C. D. HOWELL

systems where teachers, service personnel, bus drivers, students, and community members supported one another's goals. Participants imagined what their classrooms might be like if their students had the material, social, and emotional resources they needed to thrive. And participants imagined a future for themselves in which they were respected.

Second, their practical solidarity required action. Greene (2010) later writes that neither imagination nor intent are sufficient. "There must be a transmutation of goodwill," of what she calls "*wide-awakeness* into action" (p. 1), citing Paulo Freire's (1970) "conscientization" (p. 221). And this action must be ongoing. Geographer and prison abolitionist Ruth Wilson Gilmore describes solidarity in the film *Geographies of Racial Capitalism* as "something that is made and remade and never just is ... this radical dependency ... is about life, and living, and living together" (Castle & Card, 2020). Big, public collective action was, of course, critical to the West Virginia teachers' movement. Their work stoppage and presence at the state capital, in legislative chambers, and on picket lines in their communities were vital to the success of their movement, as were superintendents' decisions to close schools rather than discipline striking teachers. But practical solidarity also requires smaller-seeming action. Participants described, for instance, how community members beyond school staff brought them food on the picket line. How people shared their cause via word of mouth as well as social media. How community members called their legislators and at times stood with them on picket lines. These intentional actions reflected a practical solidarity, among *and with* West Virginia's teachers.

Finally, their practical solidarity required love. I mean this in multiple ways. Participants talked about loving their students and communities and engaging in the #55strong movement as a result of this love. I think this kind of love is real and important. But we were reminded in Dr. Weiner's keynote that too often teaching is regarded and talked about as women's work. As bell hooks (2004) writes in her book *The Will to Change: Men, Masculinity, and Love*, the patriarchy wants us to believe that women have some greater capacity for love and "emotional caretaking" (p. 96), and this is why the teaching force is overwhelmingly women. School boards in the United States have used this lie to hire and pay women—and men who decide to do this supposed women's work—less than their similarly educated and credentialed peers for more than two hundred years. Instead, I suggest that, as hooks (2001) wrote earlier in *All About Love*, "with love at the center of our lives, work could have a different meaning and focus" (p. 162). Hooks (2001) names ways that we express love, including the "generous sharing of resources," such as "time, attention, material objects, skills, [and] money" (p. 163). Participants were angry at West Virginia's leaders for denying them those expressions of love. Mary, a music teacher with a decade of experience, said, "I'm a mother, I'm part of this community, I'm a West Virginian, and you continue to let that ripple out, I'm working class, I'm poor ... [in] West Virginia we have one billionaire, he's the governor, and all the rest of us are working class and poor." All participants echoed her description of how elected state leaders had consistently ignored teachers' and students' needs. In contrast, participants described how local leadership and union members were generous with what they had, sharing strategies and material resources. They described how they loved one another.

Imagine. Act. Love. Some attendees tonight may criticize this as too simple a summary of practical solidarity. But do not mistake simple for easy. Right now, it is not easy to imagine a world where women have full bodily autonomy. It is not easy to act, doing work like knocking on doors for candidates who support public school teachers and respect their expertise in the classroom. It is not easy to love our neighbors and colleagues enough to give them our time and attention when we need love and time and attention ourselves. But that is the work I leave here tonight attempting to carry out, and that is the work I encourage our organization to do as well. Thank you.

REFERENCES

Bayertz, K. (1999). Four uses of "solidarity." In K. Bayertz (Ed.), *Solidarity* (pp. 3–28). Springer.

Beckner, E. R. (1929). *A history of labor legislation in Illinois*. University of Chicago Press.

Castle, T. (Producer), & Card, K. (Director). (2020). *Geographies of Racial Capitalism* [Film]. The Antipode Foundation. https://antipodeonline.org/geographies-of-racial-capitalism/

Dandala, S. (2019). Teacher social justice and the field of industrial relations in the United States. *Labor and Society, 22*, 571–584. https://doi.org/10.1111/wusa.12426

Durkheim, E. (1933). *The division of labor in society* (G. Simpson, Trans.). The Free Press of Glencoe, Illinois. (Original work published 1893)

Forst, R. (2021, February). *Solidarity: Concept, conceptions, and contexts* [Working Paper]. Normative Orders Research Centre of Goethe University Frankfurt am Main. https://publikationen.ub.uni-frankfurt.de/frontdoor/index/index/docId/60890

Freire, P. (1970). The adult literacy process as cultural action for freedom. *Harvard Educational Review, 40*(2), 205–225. https://www.hepg.org/her-home/issues/harvard-educational-review-volume-40,-issue-2/herarticle/_1026

Greene, M. (1995). *Releasing the imagination: Essays on education, the arts, and social change*. Jossey-Bass.

Greene, M. (2010). Prologue to art, social imagination and action. *Journal of Educational Controversy, 5*(1), Article 2.

hooks, b. (2001). *All about love: New visions*. William Morrow.

hooks, b. (2004). *The will to change: Men, masculinity, and love*. Atria Books.

Maton, R. (2016). WE learn together: Philadelphia educators putting social justice unionism principles into practice. *Workplace, 26*, 5–19. https://doi.org/10.14288/workplace.v0i26

Sampson, R. (n.d.). *"Fight like hell for the living": A brief sketch of working people's history in Illinois*. Social Sciences, Health, and Education Library (SSHEL) Resources in Labor & Employment Relations. University of Illinois. https://www.library.illinois.edu/sshel/laboremployment/laborinillinois/history/

Smith, W., Wayte, W., & Marindin, G. E. (1890). Obligationes. In *A dictionary of Greek and Roman antiquities*. John Murray. http://www.perseus.tufts.edu/hopper/text?doc=Perseus%3Atext%3A1999.04.0063%3Aalphabetic+letter%3DO%3Aentry+group%3D1%3Aentry%3Dobligationes-cn

Social Sciences, Health, and Education Library (SSHEL) Resources in Labor & Employment Relations. (n.d.). *Chronology of Illinois labor history (1819–1996)*. https://www.library.illinois.edu/sshel/laboremployment/laborinillinois/chronology/

Weiner, L. (2012). Social movement unionism: Teachers can lead the way. *Race, Poverty, & the Environment, 19*(2), 37–40. https://www.reimaginerpe.org/19-2/weiner-fletcher

VOLUME 25, NUMBER 1

EDITORIAL REMARKS

BACK TO THE FUTURE

Culture Wars, Education Legislation, Book Bannings, and Fake News

Chara Haeussler Bohan
Georgia State University

Happy 25th anniversary *Curriculum and Teaching Dialogue*. As noted in the editors' call for manuscripts, anniversaries are times of reflection on the past, present, and possibilities for the future. As editors, we sought manuscripts for a special issue that focused on trends in teaching and/ or curriculum over the past 25 years, as well as research papers and conceptual essays concerned with the current trend of legislative attacks and interference. Thus, the editors sought reflection about this past quarter century of research on teaching and curriculum as well as appraisals of the current state and future of education. As editor of the issue with this special focus, I also contemplated how my own 35 years of work in education equipped me for the current climate. In the morning, as I sip a cup of warm coffee with almond milk and stevia, I often read about educational affairs in the daily newspaper on some form of electronic device. From this privileged vantage point, recent school news has not been overwhelmingly positive, I must confess.

Reflecting on my formative years as a Reagan-era "baby," the current situation is both similar to and different from the fall of 1987 when I began

Curriculum and Teaching Dialogue,
Volume 25, Numbers 1 & 2, pp. 13–18
Copyright © 2023 by Information Age Publishing
www.infoagepub.com
All rights of reproduction in any form reserved.

14   C. H. BOHAN

a preservice teacher placement in an alternative school in Ithaca, New York—work that began my foray into teaching. Notably, four years earlier, the National Commission on Excellence in Education published *A Nation at Risk* (1983), and it was a clarion call to action. Nowadays, I joke that my fellow 17-year-olds and I were part of the "risk," as I was a high school junior in the spring and senior in the fall of 1983. The wording in the opening paragraphs of the *Nation at Risk* report was certainly meant to shock: "If an unfriendly foreign power had attempted to impose on America the mediocre educational performance that exists today, we might have viewed it as an act of warfare" (p. 9).

So the culture wars were beginning when I entered the teaching profession in the early 1990s. The American Association for Teaching and Curriculum (AATC) was founded around the same time as a scholarly organization devoted to the study of teaching and curriculum. In that era, polarization abounded in politics and academia. The conservative political commentator Rush Limbaugh gained popularity with his nationally syndicated radio show; in academia, Arthur Schlesinger (1991) in *The Disuniting of America: Reflections on a Multicultural Society* argued that multiculturalism served to fragment American society. Schlesinger's writing stood in stark contrast to James Banks's (1997/2007) work on multiculturalism in his book *Educating Citizens in a Multicultural Society*. So are educators today facing a similarly polarized world that is gathering at a different "bat time" but on the same "bat channel?"[1]

Similar pronouncements that contemporary students' academic learning is in decline abound, just as appeared in newspapers in the 1980s at the start of the standards movement. Have you heard of pandemic learning loss? Consider a recent headline in *The New York Times*: "It's Not Just Math and Reading: U.S. History Scores for 8th Graders Plunge" (Mervosh, 2023). Think about politicians like Ron DeSantis and media personalities such as Tucker Carlson who advocate against all things "WOKE" while making false claims about ballot machines. Critics on the left, however, such as Alexandria Ocasio-Cortez (AOC), the first female member of the Democratic Socialists of America elected to Congress, engage in polemics and diametrically opposite positions. For example, AOC supports abolishing U.S. Immigration and Customs Enforcement altogether.

What are the differences between the early 2020s and three decades ago? Social media is one new wrinkle. The power of the multitudes and rapid dissemination of ideas cannot be underestimated. Algorithms have led to living in a world of echo chambers rather than learning to engage in civil discourse, particularly with those who hold differing points of view. In addition, not all sources on the internet are credible, so students need to be taught to evaluate the trustworthiness of sources. This task becomes extremely difficult when news stations and commentators provide false information to the public. Tucker Carlson is not the first media personality known to lie; Dominion Voting Systems won a $787 million settlement against Fox News thanks in part to Carlson's misinformation, that is, "fake news" (Bowden, 2023). Recall CBS fired four executives in 2005, and Dan Rather had already planned to step down over false reports that George W. Bush had received preferential treatment while in the Texas Air National Guard (Kiehl & Zurawik, 2005). Even *The New York Times* and *USA Today* have had top editors resign after reporters were found to have fabricated stories. Thus, it becomes imperative to teach students a healthy bit of skepticism and to evaluate sources for bias and authenticity, as well as to develop historical thinking skills of sourcing, contextualizing, corroborating, and questioning (Bohan et al., 2022). The challenge for teachers becomes more difficult; in the past two years, there has been a barrage of state legislation aimed at limiting academic freedom (so called "divisive concepts" or "anti-CRT" laws) as well as laws in support of banning books. How can students evaluate the credibility of a source if they are not permitted to read it?

In this special issue, several articles address the challenges that educators face given the spread of recent state legislation aimed at limiting what can be taught in classrooms. In last year's editorial, I noted that 42 states had considered varying iterations of this kind of law (the number has now risen to 44), and now anti-diversity, equity, and inclusion laws, aimed particularly at higher education, are forming a similar wave (Bohan, 2022). Not all states enacted these laws, but 18 states have passed them as of February 2023 (Stanley, 2023). Indeed, Jason Stanley titled his opinion piece on the topic "Banning Ideas and Authors is not a 'Culture War'—It's Fascism."

Volume 1 begins with Keynote Speaker Lois Weiner's address to the 2022 AATC Conference in Chicago, "Seeking Solidarity: Defining Self-Interest in the Context of Capitalism as a Global Social System." Weiner, Professor Emerita, New Jersey City University, has spent her career researching teachers' work and teacher unions. In the opening article, "Racial and Cultural Pedagogies in Education: A Retrospective," Antonio Castro, Yeji Kim, and Mary Adu-Gyamfi take a retrospective view of the development of three theoretical ideas related to race and culture in education within the last 25 years: culturally relevant and sustaining pedagogies, critical race theory, and racial literacies. The authors highlight key innovations related to curriculum and instruction, as well as identify persistent challenges to inclusive teaching. They conclude by advocating for teaching strategies to promote a more just and equitable world amidst turbulent times. In the second article, "Legislate to (Un)educate: Examining the Impact of Divisive and Dehumanizing Education Policies," Gregory Samuels, Amy Samuels, and Brandon J. Haas explore recent education policies that ban the teaching of critical race theory, restrict teaching race-related topics,

16 C. H. BOHAN

and prohibit conversations about divisive concepts. They problematize the impact of silencing complex issues, especially those that limit, prohibit, or intimidate conversations about race and racism in the United States. The authors explore the perceptions of educators related to these anti-CRT bills. Exploring the impact of this legislation on teacher education at the university level, Alexandra Allweiss, Scott Farver, and Anne-Lise Halvorsen describe three first-hand experiences with university tensions and limits in "Writing a Love Letter to Educators in the Wake of anti-CRT Efforts." The authors were part of collective efforts to respond to proposed anti-critical race theory legislation in the state of Michigan. Strikingly, these efforts faced abandonment from administrators, yet this is not surprising in an era where state purse strings can dictate policy. In the fourth article, "Making Sense of the Message: The Perceptions and Impact of State Legislation that Challenges the Teaching of Hard History," Debby Shulsky, Sheila Baker, and Renée E. Lastrapes explore the impact of anti-CRT legislation in the state of Texas. In particular, they explore the limitations and challenges social studies teachers in Texas face and how the legislation, known as Texas Senate Bill 3, has influenced social studies teachers' classroom pedagogy.

In the last three articles in Volume 1, the authors focus on how educators can engage in hopeful strategies to disrupt and reinvigorate the role of teachers. Caroline Conner and Andrea Miskewicz examine the problem of anti-semitism and offer advice in "Attacking Antisemitism: Investigating How Museum-Led Professional Development Affects Preservice Teachers' Preparedness to Teach the Holocaust." Utilizing an instructional model of historical empathy, researchers designed a virtual Holocaust education workshop for preservice teachers. Results highlight the power of partnerships between preservice teacher educators and museum educators to train teachers and the power of eyewitness testimony to evoke empathy. In the sixth article, Joyce E. Many, Carla L. Tanguay, and Ruchi Bhatnagar examine novice urban teachers' abilities to impact student learning and development. Their article, "Factors Shaping Teacher Education Graduates' Abilities to Impact Students' Learning and Development During Induction," revealed the importance of (a) connecting with learners and (b) receiving support. Successful teacher education programs prepare graduates to set high expectations, use culturally responsive strategies, and meet diverse learners' needs. In the final article, "The Fluid Curriculum: Reinvigorating the Role of the Teacher as Curriculum Maker," Bradley Conrad, Christy McConnell, Sarah Campbell, and Bruce Uhrmacher advocate for a "fluid curriculum," one that empowers teachers to create an equitable, culturally relevant curriculum that is responsive to students, relevant to students' lives, and adaptable to the local context in which it is enacted. Because a fluid curriculum places the teacher as creator and students as engaged actors, it may address both the teacher retention and equity issues in U.S. schools. Thus, Volume 1 ends on a hopeful note and offers an optimistic response to recent "divisive concepts," "anti-CRT," and "anti-DEI" state legislation.

As editor of *Curriculum and Teaching Dialogue*, these past 6 years, I have had the privilege to serve the AATC community and the delight to read the research that its members and others create. This volume is the culmination of that work. It has been a wonderful opportunity to read current research, help authors improve their writing, and think about possibilities for teaching and curriculum. O. L. Davis, Jr., was my mentor at The University of Texas at Austin, and he worked as an editor of the ASCD journal, *Journal of Supervision and Curriculum*, for a dozen years from 1993–2005. Thus, editorship was an academic family responsibility given my proclivity to emulate my mentor by engaging in the heavy use of a red pen. In all seriousness, I was able to undertake the position because of the support from the CTD team. John Pecore helped despite a heavy schedule of grant administration and departmental responsibilities, and I am certain that the journal would not have become a well-oiled machine without his organizational skills. Franklin Allaire brought the outtakes and book review sections to new heights by recruiting broadly from the membership. And a series of Georgia State University graduate research assistants (GRAs) engaged in the bulk of moving manuscripts back and forth from authors to editors, copy editors, and the publisher. GRAs include current members of AATC, Cristy Sellers (Smith) who was the first, followed by Susan Ophelia Cannon, Julia (Stikeleather) Bearden, and Abbey Hortenstine. The journal will be in good hands moving forward. Bradley Conrad, Capital University, has assembled a fantastic team of scholars including Crystal Howell, Randolph College, and the former journal GRA Cristy Sellers, Pacific University. Cristy Sellers created the Google forms and documents that are used to complete the behind-the-scenes work for blind reviews, manuscript evaluations, and so on. Life has a way of coming full circle. Au revoir. Adiós. Baibai. Slán. Yasou. Au wiedersehen. Adeus. Shalom. Ka ọ dị. Sayōnara. Arrivederci. Do pobachennya. Aloha.

REFERENCES

Banks, J. A. (2007). *Educating citizens in a multicultural society*. Teachers College Press. (Original work published 1997)

Bohan, C. H. (2022). 42 reasons to be concerned about the status of teaching and curriculum. *Curriculum and Teaching Dialogue, 24*(1), 13–17.

Bohan, C. H., Baker, H. R., & King, L. J. (2022). *Teaching enslavement in American history: Lesson plans and primary sources*. Peter Lang.

Bowden, J. (2023, May 7). Tucker Carlson 'preparing for war' against Fox News in order to be released from contract early. *The Independent.* https://www.independent.co.uk/news/world/americas/us-politics/tucker-carlson-fox-news-contract-b2334535.html

Kiehl, S., & Zurawik, D. (2005, January 11). CBS fires 4 executives, producers over Bush-National Guard Report. *Baltimore Sun.* https://www.baltimoresun.com/entertainment/tv/bal-te.to.cbs11jan11-story.html

Mervosh, S. (2023, May 4). It's not just math and reading: U.S. history scores for 8th graders plunge. *The New York Times.* https://www.nytimes.com/2023/05/03/us/us-history-test-scores.html

National Commission on Excellence in Education. (1983). *A nation at risk: The imperative for educational reform.* U.S. Government Printing Office. http://edreform.com/wp-content/uploads/2013/02/A_Nation_At_Risk_1983.pdf

Schlesinger, A. (1991) *The disuniting of America: Reflections on a multicultural society.* W.W. Norton & Co.

Stanley, J. (2023, February 14). Banning ideas and authors is not a 'culture war'—it's fascism. *The Guardian.* https://tinyurl.com/yfd6myw5

NOTE

1. This popular culture reference to the 1960s Batman television show, where Adam West played the main character, might only be understood by Americans over 50 years of age.

KEYNOTE ADDRESS GIVEN AT AATC ANNUAL
CONFERENCE OCTOBER 6, 2022, IN
CHICAGO, ILLINOIS

SEEKING SOLIDARITY

Defining Self-Interest in the Context of Capitalism as a Global Social System

Lois Weiner
New Jersey City University

Seeking solidarity, the conference theme, means being mindful of how direct and indirect effects of individual and collective efforts help create a more just, equal, humane world. In that regard I begin my remarks by noting your invitation to speak on this theme has helped me rethink ideas I have addressed in Chapters 1 and 2 of my new book, and Chapter 3, on occupational identity, forthcoming (Weiner, 2022a, 2022b). Thanks for the invitation and the spark.

I think we need to start any discussion of solidarity to create and nurture alliances for social justice by acknowledging the complicity of the labor movement and the entire education establishment, including teachers' unions, higher education, and teacher education in sustaining a socially and racially segregated, unequal, unjust system of public education (Rothstein, 2014). There is no "golden age" to which we can return, so our task is to envision and make real a future with just, equal, democratic schools (Couture et al., 2020).

Curriculum and Teaching Dialogue,
Volume 25, Numbers 1 & 2, pp. 19–31
Copyright © 2023 by Information Age Publishing
www.infoagepub.com
All rights of reproduction in any form reserved.

Solidarity is often assumed to be altruistic, a subordination of one's immediate needs and desires. In contrast, I propose that building and sustaining relations of solidarity requires identifying and acting on our real needs. This process helps us see the inextricable connectedness of struggles to improve all dimensions of life, in the workplace and beyond. Our sense of self-interest is often obscured by taken-for-granted assumptions about what is possible, a problem exacerbated by geographical blinders or lack of knowledge about historical precedents. I suggest when we mistake what is now for what has been and may come, when we cast self-interest in a status quo presumed inevitable, we subvert possibilities of building alliances, of common struggle based on interests we share with others.

I will use a personal example that you may have experienced to illustrate how, in retrospect, the dominant perception of self-interest among full-time faculty was erroneous and allowed a damaging change in our work and program quality—"adjunctification" of teaching, the massive replacement of full-time faculty lines with contingent labor. As Robert Ovetz (2020) explains, massive increase in use of adjunct faculty to teach has been accompanied by faculty disempowerment about curriculum, working conditions, and governance—the hallmarks of corporatization of higher education. Ovetz identifies how the corporate university has used educational technology to separate teaching, assessment, and curriculum development. His recommendations about pushing back on this danger exemplify a point I discuss later, why critical analysis, idealism (often found in work of scholars), and collective action (found more often in the labor movement) are all essential in building and sustaining solidarity.

ADJUNCTIFICATION, NEOLIBERALISM, AND TEACHER PREPARATION

When I started as a teacher educator at what was Jersey City State College in 1990, full-time education faculty also supervised student teachers as part of our teaching load. The administration preferred hiring adjuncts, mainly retired teachers, asserting they brought more recent classroom experience. When pressed the administration noted this was also a method to cut costs; adjunct faculty were paid an hourly wage, translated into time a supervision required, and received no benefits. Many teacher education faculty did not consider this an issue of importance to them or our students. Others saw the change as being in their professional self-interest. Diminishing responsibility for on-site supervisions, which were more time-consuming than teaching classes on campus, increased time for other activities, like research, which had more status. A few full-time faculty argued change in workload that dropped on-site supervisions would likely damage program quality because full-time faculty were the primary institutional connection between the program, college, and schools, most of them urban, that helped us prepare student teachers and often hired our graduates. Adjunct faculty, who had no voice or authority about our program offerings, could not serve this role.

In contract negotiations, our faculty union attempted to protect the load for supervision for full-timers but had little support from those directly affected. The union could have but did not try to protect adjunct faculty who took over supervision by providing them with equivalent authority, pay, and working conditions. Reduced "load" for supervision soon translated into less load—and fewer lines—for full-time faculty, resulting in hiring even more adjunct faculty, now to teach regular courses. A process begun in the education program spread to the rest of the college. Required "area" courses for freshmen and sophomores that were the most labor-intensive were given to adjunct faculty, paid by the teaching hour, with no responsibility or authority for advising or office hours. With this shift, students who needed the most support were denied access to faculty who held office hours required by their full-time position.

This example illustrates how discerning our real self-interest often requires seeing how actions that seem to benefit us immediately actually do long-term harm to our professional well-being. One antidote to this is a critical lens about how these micro decisions fit into the huge picture of social, economic, political, and cultural aspects of society, in other words, our social system. Growth in use of contingent labor in higher education coincided with and reflected other neoliberal reforms, pushed nationally and globally, to downsize public institutions of higher education. Key in this project was displacing university-based teacher education with privatized alternate route programs, and relying on standardized tests to control who entered and exited the profession (Weiner, 2007). These policies along with many others identified as neoliberal, have been advanced globally with rhetoric about improving educational outcomes for low-income children of color, rectifying inequality (Benavot & Smith, 2020). Some right-wing supporters of high-stakes standardized tests to measure student, teacher, and school performance have acknowledged they failed to ameliorate inequality and have actually worsened it. Yet, the testing, based on international standards over which those most affected have no voice, continues (Gacoin, 2019; Klees et al., 2019). One reason is that testing is inseparable from new, invasive forms of control and privatization with educational technology (National Education Policy Center, 2021; Williamson & Hogan, 2020), a focus of my new book.

UNDERSTANDING CAPITALISM AS A SOCIAL SYSTEM

Democracy is often assumed to mean "liberal democracy" and associated with capitalism, an economic system. Another conceptualization of their relationship is that capitalism is a social system that can include liberal democracy (Capitalism can also adopt other political forms, such as fascism.) Understanding capitalism as a social system is not new but went out of favor when "neoliberalism" was accepted in critical theory as capitalism's latest stage. Rustin (2012) argues for reviving the "antiquated" idea of capitalism as a social system, "an ensemble of interrelated elements (modes of production, distribution, social control, socialization, communication, military power, etc.)" (p. 84). Although Rustin does not make this argument, I suggest a theoretical advantage of seeing capitalism as a social system is that it explains that social oppression in all its forms—racism, patriarchy, anti-immigrant sentiment, heteronormativity, and ableism—are not only "baked into" capitalism's development, but evolve with it, alongside other elements of the ensemble. Indeed, the Right's newest attacks on curricula that expose truths about social oppression in our nation's history demonstrate capitalism's capacity to adapt its stance towards forms of social oppression.

The social system frame also explains the unique location and role of unions and labor activism in capitalism. Capitalism depends on control of work and workers for profit, which is what drives the system. This system gives workers in their role at the workplace a unique strategic power—not to be mistaken for a moral or political superiority—in challenging the status quo. Moreover, workers must act collectively to make significant improvements in their conditions and pay, hence the reason "solidarity" is often identified as a labor concept. When they flex their labor muscles to control business and profit, regardless of whether they are conscious of the implications of their actions, workers challenge capitalism's control over their lives. They also challenge the economic and political assumptions about competition and individualism—capitalism's pseudo-Darwinian, survival of fittest, ethos.

While it is better if workers understand organizing at the workplace as a challenge to capitalism's ethos and class power, regardless of whether they do, the fact of their organizing creates a new kind space at work and in society. Real unions, and in this I exclude gangster or sweetheart organizations that have no mechanism for members to exert control over what is negotiated in their name, introduce the idea of democracy into the workplace—and beyond. Even if unions try to wall off the workplace from the society, they find they must have a relationship with politics, with the state, because workers' rights to organize on the job are inseparable in a liberal democracy from the state's role in protecting capitalism and profit.

However, unions are stuck in a contradictory role in liberal democracy in capitalism. They must try to protect workers' rights but are caught in a political system that constrains their power and authority (Find one significant protection workers have won from the government, from the 40-hour week to occupational safety, that has not been hard-fought, paid for by great sacrifices, even of life itself). Dealing with this contradiction of being a foe of capitalism's driving engine—profit and control over work—while having to exist within the system creates conservatizing pressures to which no union officer or organization is immune. Unions' institutional stability comes from a steady source of income, members' dues, as well as laws that protect collective bargaining and give the union more legal power. Yet these same laws often inhibit robust self-activity. One example is organizing a walkout in solidarity with a worker who has been unfairly disciplined when the contract, which is a truce in class warfare, has a "no strike" clause.

These same legal restrictions affect workers' consciousness of and capacity to use their labor power to defend social movements. Yet, as activists defending social justice take to the streets, we see unions and union members finding creative ways to use contract campaigns to fight for demands—political, economic, and social—that go beyond the legal restrictions imposed by collective bargaining. The first example of this situation in recent history occurred here in Chicago, when the reform leadership of the Chicago Teachers Union developed its landmark program for The Schools Chicago's Students Deserve, naming apartheid as the problem and embedding economic demands in proposals for restoring teachers of "special" subjects to schools, along with hiring counselors and social workers to support students' social and emotional well-being (Nuñez et al., 2015).

The great challenge in building solidarity within unions, among unions, and between unions and movements struggling against social oppression, is educating members about how their self-interest depends on connecting economic demands to aims of social movements outside the workplace, and in the case of teacher unions, outside the school walls. One obstacle which should not surprise us, since bigotry is systemic, is that social hierarchies reflecting oppression in society infect and permeate social relations at the workplace and workers' consciousness on the job. Because these social attitudes undercut solidarity and collective action, unions have a very practical stake in making our society more just and equal, although too many do not realize this goal is in their self-interest. Ironically, when unions contend that workers' economic well-being is the union's first or only responsibility, they adopt capitalism's mindset: workers have no value beyond what they give the boss.

Yet, when workers are mobilizing to improve their economic situation, they begin a process that opens possibilities for new understandings, for political education. As we saw in the state-wide walkouts in "red states," economic demands quickly became focused on politics, with teachers learning that legislators for whom they voted were their opponents. Especially in cities, teachers' natural supporters were parents and community activists who had been struggling for increased school funding, more equal allocation of funds, and many times, equal educational opportunity (Dyke & Muckian-Bates, 2020).

While struggle can educate, not all experiences are equally educative. That is why we need curriculum and instruction—and teachers. And who better to help unions with political education that strengthens democracy and builds solidarity than educators? So, to conclude my remarks I want to describe a recent experience I had in helping the National Education Union (NEU), the largest union of education workers in the United Kingdom and Wales to "flip the switch" in how union organizing occurs in academies, the U.K. equivalent of charter schools, which now include one-half of all schools in the U.K.

The director of organizing, D., who has read my work, contacted me to help with supporting the NEU's national staff responsible for organizing academy chains to develop rank-and-file, that is member, "ownership" of mobilizing, unionizing drives, and contract enforcement. The original plan was for me to give a speech, as would a well-known journalist. Then participants would ask questions and discuss it. After hearing his plan, I suggested an alternative format because from a pedagogical perspective what was planned did not align with the aim. The scheduled events duplicated and reinforced the problem we wanted to reverse: national staff telling people what to do, and those they were telling, doing it. We needed an activity—constructing knowledge together—that helped national staff experience the difference between the "transmission model" of education, teacher-centered instruction, and a student-centered mode. Appendix A contains a detailed description of the workshop, whose format I think you will recognize as jigsaw, a staple of small-group instruction, informed by research on classroom discourse and small-group activities. When we recall this research was a response to the civil rights movement and efforts in the 1970s and 1980s to desegregate the schools, de-track classrooms, and increase educational outcomes for underserved students, we can see why it would be so useful to support union members to think and act as if they are equals to union staff. An evaluation form that the national union mandates for all its staff development activities indicated the participants thought the activity was helpful. The more persuasive evidence about the workshop's usefulness was participants' requests to D. for my lesson plan, so that they can do this activity with the district organizers whom they supervise.

One question D. and I discussed following the student-centered activity was members' resistance to empowerment, to "owning" the union, telling staff what they needed and organizing on their own. This mindset puts a brake on challenging hierarchical relations in the school—relations permeated by classism, racism, patriarchy, ableism, and heteronormativity, so it has far-reaching negative effects in terms of building solidarity. I thought back to Dewey's explanations in *How We Think* and *The Child and Curriculum* about why students may prefer being told what to do, rather than doing the work of learning by doing themselves. I include excerpts in Appendix B. Briefly what I found most applicable in terms of political education was Dewey's observation that even when a condition is oppressive, people become used to their chains. Change becomes more frightening and difficult than passive acceptance of what is familiar. Teachers may live with loss of professional autonomy and blame, even abuse, for students' underachievement because the alternative, mobilizing to resist, is frightening or unimaginable. Another factor Dewey (1906) notes is teachers may allow their charm and personal warmth to substitute for "psychologizing" (p. 38) the material, discovering the intrinsic motivation that can drive independent learning. Students may be pleased and passive. A lively, animated organizer or union president makes the teacher-centered union meeting, dominated by instructions and orders, palatable. The other factor Dewey identifies is social conditioning, the student's willingness, even desire, to please a person in authority, providing answers the teacher (or, I would add, the test or software) expects.

BEING A CRITICAL FRIEND TO TEACHERS UNIONS

We have much to offer teachers unions and teachers struggling to transform their unions, to make them democratic, creating space for teachers to unpack what their real self-interest demands and how to win it in alliances with other social justice movements. Elsewhere I describe that role as a critical friend (Weiner, 2021). Being a friend means showing up for struggles, asking "How can I help?" and doing it. Being critical demands that we look objectively at mistakes and weaknesses in our friends' actions and analysis. I suggest the more pointed and public our critique, the more explicit and strong must be the support.

Seeking solidarity begins with recognizing our respective strengths and weaknesses as well as our mutual needs and concerns. Unions need us and we need them. Our opponents realize the power of solidarity, which is why they undercut its possibility by telling and showing us so often "there is no alternative" to their exercise of power and control. I think good teachers have to believe we have the power to change lives. What they may not realize is that our power can extend to altering our society.

Dr. Weiner can be reached by email at drweinerlo@gmail.com.

REFERENCES

Benavot, A., & Smith, W. C. (2020). Reshaping quality and equity: Global learning metrics as a ready-made solution to a manufactured crisis. In A. Wulff (Ed.), *Grading goal four: Tensions, threats, and opportunities in the sustainable development goal on quality education* (pp. 238–261). Brill.

Couture, J.-C., Grøttvik, R., & Sellar, S. (2020, September). *A profession learning to become: The promise of collaboration between teacher organizations and academia.* UNESCO. https://unesdoc.unesco.org/ark:/48223/pf0000374156

Dewey, J. (1910). *How we think.* D.C. Heath & Co.

Dyke, E., & Muckian-Bates, B. (2020). *Rank-and-file rebels: Theories of power and change in the 2018 education strikes.* Colorado State University Open Press. https://press.colostate.edu/

Gacoin. (2019, October). *Navigating the Global "Transformation" of Education.* BCTF Research Department. Accessed September 19, 2020.

Klees, S. J., Stromquist, N. P., Samoff, J., & Vally, S. (2019, 11 January). The 2018 World Development Report on Education: A critical analysis. *Development and Change, 50*(2), 603–620.

National Education Policy Center. (2021, 28 January). 'Dataveillance," algorithmic bias, and other concerns about learning management systems. 2021. *National Education Policy Center Newsletter.* Retrieved February 5, 2021, from National Education Policy Center: https://nepc.colorado.edu/publication/newsletter-dataveillance-012821

Nuñez, I., Michie G., & Konkol, P. (2015). *Worth striking for: Why education policy is every teacher's concern. Lessons from Chicago.* Teachers College Press.

Ovetz, R. (2020, September). The algorithmic university: Online education, learning management systems, and the struggle over academic labor. *Critical Sociology, 47*(7–8), 1–20. https://doi.org/10.1177%2F0896920520948931

Rothstein, R. (2014, March 25). Segregated housing, segregated schools. *Education Week.* Retrieved May 19, 2018, from https://www.edweek.org/ew/articles/2014/03/26/26rothstein_ep.h33.html

Rustin, M. (2012). The crisis of a social system. In J. Rutherford & S. Davison (Eds.), *The neoliberal crisis* (pp. 80–87). Soundings. https://indefenceofyouthwork.files.wordpress.com/2012/03/the_neoliberal_crisis.pdf

Weiner, L. (2021, April 10). Heads up! Chins down! Resisting the new bipartisan neoliberal project in education. *New Politics.* https://newpol.org/heads-up-chins-down-resisting-the-new-bipartisan-neoliberal-project-in-education/.

Weiner, L. (2022a, April 19). Capitalism and the changing classroom. Education "reforms" through the neo-liberal lens. *Tempest.* https://www.tempestmag.org/2022/04/capitalism-and-the-changing-classroom/

Weiner, L. (2022b, Winter). Education reforms and capitalism's changes to work: Lesson for the Left. *New Politics, 18*(4). https://newpol.org/issue_post/education-reforms-and-capitalisms-changes-to-work/

Weiner, L. (2007, May/June). A lethal threat to U.S. teacher education. *Journal of Teacher Education, 58*(4), 274–286. https://doi.org/10.1177/0022487107305603

Williamson, B., & Hogan, A. (2020). *Commercialisation and privatisation in/of education in the context of Covid-19.* Queensland University of Technology.

APPENDIX A

National Education Union Workshop Outline

Introduction: This activity, which I developed and led for the National Education Union in the U.K. and Wales, aims to support union staff to make the members feel and be empowered, teaching them by modeling what it means to "own" the union's organizing. It disrupts the transmission model of training and with it the hierarchy of the business union.

In curriculum and instruction this format would be identified as "student-centered instruction" relying on small groups. It uses a format of

a. participants meeting together to receive the same information,
b. brainstorming together for ideas, then
c. breaking up into small groups that are given a task and roles to encourage full participation by all in the group, then
d. having each group share its ideas with the entire workshop, taking comments and questions as time allows.
e. It ends with an overview in which the organizer explains how the format has been intended to model members' feelings of empowerment and confidence in leadership of their own struggles.

I think it differs from other models of union organizing because it assumes that members, even those who are very new, have much to teach one another—and staff running the workshops. It relies on the workshop leader being very knowledgeable about the issues and being able to let participants "own" their ideas.

When I used a similar format in UTLA, a longtime staff person told me it was the most dynamic, exciting organizing workshop he had ever seen.

1. Start by having people introduce themselves to the entire group or if it is too big for that in small groups. This heightens the possibility of people volunteering ideas. [We know from classroom research that if people do not volunteer to speak in the first or second class, the chance they will ever offer an idea, unsolicited by the teacher/instructor/workshop leader, plummets to almost zero.]
2. Provide an overview of the big political picture, why organizing and their involvement in the union matter—but make it very brief. Allow some time for people to ask and answer questions, limiting their time for speaking so as to maximize participation.
3. Introduce the workshop activity: Today we are going to brainstorm for the most important issues our members think they face

28   L. WEINER

and generate ideas for campaigns that they can organize to solve these problems, or at least improve the situation.

4. Ask people what they think members' greatest concerns are and why and put these ideas on a list visible to all. (Paper flip chart or electronic screen.) As people name issues, the new ideas should be folded into the previous issues, when possible, with the workshop leader checking with people about whether this merger is acceptable. Is this idea really a separate idea? Or is it a subset or even overarching issue. [This is why the workshop leaders MUST have deep knowledge of the situation in the schools, from the members' perspective.]

    It is essential the workshop organizer "check in" with participants consistently: *"Does my wording capture your idea? Do you agree with how I have combined these? Let me know. You are the experts here."* In doing this the workshop leader reinforces participants' "ownership" of the ideas and campaigns and also learns from them about conditions in the schools.

    Also, problems should be phrased so as to encourage progressive solutions. Example: *"How do we deal with students who misbehave and are violent when the administration doesn't do its job?"* is rephrased to *"How do we organize to identify, create and reinforce a school culture that supports academic achievement and classroom norms that make all teachers and students feel respected and valued?"* [The former leads to blaming students, "othering" misbehavior in ways that invites racist explanations. It recapitulates the "law and order" sentiment fanned by the Right. The latter points to pro-active possibilities for helping to alter the systemic issues that underlie misbehavior, including teaching behaviors that are not conducive to building trust with students.

5. After you have collected several issues, the issues are grouped so as to have topics broad enough to be generalizable to more than one school or chain but not so general as to be amorphous and not readily actionable. Here again, the deep knowledge of the person leading the workshop is key. Participants should help the workshop organizer in this process. Each topic becomes the responsibility of a small group.

6. The workshop leader asks people to self-select to join these groups to generate ideas/campaigns/proposals about how members can address the problem. Members can ask the union (staff) for specific assistance and information, BUT the project/campaign has to be carried out by members themselves, along with members at another branch, school, LEA and activist groups from the community.

The group decides who will be the *chair*, *reporter*, the *timekeeper*, and the *recorder*. The more public job, reporter, should preferably be from groups underrepresented in union leadership. The recorder should not be a woman—who are generally given or take the role of secretary. Someone else the chair, making sure no one speaks more than once until everyone has had a chance to speak once about a particular idea.

It is important that everyone feels their problem/challenge has been recognized. If an issue does not belong in any groups, then take time before breaking into the groups to brainstorm about where the person could seek assistance. [This process models valuing all ideas and the people who propose them.]

During this time the organizer circulates to make sure the group is on task, no one person is dominating, and perhaps to make suggestions about connections to community and social justice activists who are not involved in education matters.

7. All the groups come together, and the reporter is given time (strictly enforced) to explain what they have decided. The organizer or someone helping writes down these solutions. Time is allowed for questions and comments from the entire group. Perhaps changes are made, but they must be accepted by the group who has spent time figuring this out. Later the ideas are distributed to everyone in the workshop, along with names of members of the group. The participants in each group should be identified (if they so wish) as "experts" who can be called upon for assistance by other participants who have a question or face this problem and want advice.

8. Final discussion: How did the workshop format differ from typical staff-led workshops—or union meetings at schools? What is gained in this format? What is sacrificed? Given this tradeoff, when is it most effectively used? How did the solutions change as the group discussed them? Did you see connections to community activists immediately? If not, how did they emerge?

APPENDIX B

Excerpts From John Dewey

From Dewey's (1910) *How We Think*:

(b) Teachers—and this holds especially of the stronger and better teachers—tend to rely upon their personal strong points to hold a child to his work, and thereby influence to substitute their personal influence for that of subject-matter as a motive for study. The teacher finds by experience that his own personality is often effective where the power of the subject to command attention is almost nil; then he utilizes the former more and more, until the pupil's relation to the teacher almost takes the place of his relation to the subject. In this way the teacher's personality may become a source of personal dependence and weakness, an influence that renders the pupil indifferent to the value of the subject for its own sake.

c) The operation of the teacher's own mental habit tends, unless carefully watched and guided, to make the child a student of the teacher's peculiarities rather than of the subjects that he is supposed to study. His chief concern is to accommodate himself to what the teacher expects of him, rather than to devote himself energetically to the problems of subject-matter. "Is this right?" comes to mean "Will this answer or this process satisfy the teacher?"—instead of meaning, "Does it satisfy the inherent conditions of the problem?" It would be folly to deny the legitimacy or the value of the study of human nature that children carry on in school; but it is obviously undesirable that their chief intellectual problem should be that of producing an answer approved by the teacher, and their standard of success be successful adaptation to the requirements of another. (pp. 49–50)

From Dewey's (1906) *The Child and the Curriculum*:

If the subject-matter of the lessons be such as to have an appropriate place within the expanding consciousness of the child, if it grows out of his own past doings, thinkings, and sufferings, and grows into application in further achievements and receptivities, then no device or trick of method has to be resorted to in order to enlist interest. (pp. 34–35)

Three aspects of this recourse to outside ways for giving the subject-matter some psychological meaning may be worth mentioning. Familiarity breeds contempt, but it also breeds something like affection. We get used to the chains we wear, and we miss them when removed. Tis an old story that through custom we finally embrace what at first wore a hideous mien. Unpleasant, because meaningless, activities may get agreeable if long enough persisted in. *It is possible for the mind to develop interest in a routine or mechanical procedure if conditions are continually supplied which demand that mode of operation and preclude any other sort.* (pp. 35–36)

The second substitute for living motivation in the subject- matter is that of contrast-effects; the material of the lesson is rendered interesting, if not in itself, at least in contrast with some alternative experience. To learn the lesson is more interesting than to take a scolding, be held up to general ridicule, stay after school, receive degradingly low marks, or fail to be promoted. (p. 37)

Human nature being what it is, however, it tends to seek its motivation in the agreeable rather than in the disagreeable, in direct pleasure rather than in alternative pain. And so has come up the modern theory and practice of the "interesting," in the false sense of that term. The material is still left; so far as its own characteristics are concerned, just material externally selected and formulated. (pp. 37–38)

The legitimate way out is to transform the material; to psychologize it that is, once more, to take it and to develop it within the range and scope of the child's life. But it is easier and simpler to leave it as it is, and then by trick of method to *arouse* interest, to *make* it *interesting*; to cover it with sugar-coating; to conceal its barren ness by intermediate and unrelated material; and finally, as it were, to get the child to swallow and digest the unpalatable morsel while he is enjoying tasting something quite different. (p. 38)

CHAPTER 1

RACIAL AND CULTURAL PEDAGOGIES IN EDUCATION

A Retrospective

Antonio J. Castro, Yeji Kim, and Mary Adu-Gyamfi
University of Missouri-Columbia

ABSTRACT

This article traces the development of three theoretical ideas related to race and culture in education within the last 25 years: culturally relevant and sustaining pedagogies, critical race theory, and racial literacies. The review highlights key innovations related to curriculum and instruction, as well as identifies persistent challenges to inclusive teaching. The authors hope this retrospective will allow opportunities to reconsider and recommit efforts toward promoting a more just and equitable world amidst turbulent times.

In 1995, Gloria Ladson-Billings published her groundbreaking article "Toward a Theory of Culturally Relevant Pedagogy" in the *American Educational Research Journal*, which introduced the concept of culturally relevant pedagogy. In the same year, Ladson-Billings and Tate (1995) established the theoretical basis for critical race theory (CRT) in the field of education in their article "Toward a Critical Race Theory of Education" in the *Teachers College Record*. These ideas laid the groundwork for extensive scholarship

Curriculum and Teaching Dialogue,
Volume 25, Numbers 1 & 2, pp. 33–49
Copyright © 2023 by Information Age Publishing
www.infoagepub.com
All rights of reproduction in any form reserved.

centered on issues of race, equity, and inclusion, as well as the expansion of theories in pursuit of racial justice, which include but are not limited to culturally relevant and sustaining pedagogies, CRT, and racial literacies.

Now, 27 years since these publications, changes in the demographic, educational, and sociopolitical landscape of schooling have made racial and cultural pedagogies vital necessities for the typical classroom. First, the number of migrants in the United States has doubled since 1990 and have consequently increased racial, ethnic, cultural, and linguistic diversity in U.S. schools. Between 2000 and 2017, the percentage of U.S. school-age children and youth coming from racially or ethnically minoritized backgrounds increased 11%, constituting 49% of the total student population (de Brey et al., 2019). As of 2019, emergent bilingual students enrolled in public schools across the United States composed 10.4% of the student population, and that number is continuously growing (National Center for Education Statistics, 2022).

Furthermore, in the early 2000s, policies such as the No Child Left Behind Act and the Common Core State Standards enforced accountability and standardization and led to an unprecedented priority on scripted, standardized curricula; assessment-driven teaching; and high-stakes testing. In sacrifice of neoliberal ethos, pedagogies that promote diversity, justice, and racial equity have been largely marginalized (Royal & Gibson, 2017).

Recently, a "re-emergence of white[1] supremacism and of intensified racial conflict" (Pei, 2017, p. 592) threatens the political and social landscape. Although the United States has a longstanding history of racism and racist policies, the presidency of Donald Trump led to a surge in white racism and nationalism. As exemplified in the violent "Unite the Right" rally in Virginia and the rising hate crimes targeting racially and ethnically minoritized communities, the discourses of white supremacy have intensified (Pei, 2017; Yacovone, 2022).

On the political front, several states seek to enact legal bans against the teaching of CRT and, in some cases, race and equity itself (Bissell, 2023). In her interview with Gloria Ladson-Billings for *Education Week*, Madeline Will (2022) noted how some conservatives conflated CRT with culturally relevant teaching and other equity-oriented approaches. Ladson-Billings reported that she laughed at the outrageous ways in which some lumped ideas like social and emotional learning and feminism under the critical race banner. "The attack on anything that allows more participation and moves us toward equity is going full force," she concluded (Will, 2022, para. 19). Indeed, the widespread anti-CRT campaigns have instilled fear into schools; prevented teachers from fostering discussions on racism, sexism, or systematic inequalities in the United States; and produced more confusion among teachers and the public about "what CRT is (and is not)" (Bissell, 2023, p. 228).

These shifts in demographic, educational, and sociopolitical circumstances call for more attention to racial and cultural pedagogies in education. In this article, we trace some of the developments of educational theories related to racial justice and equity and explore how these theories have shaped research and practice in the field of education. While acknowledging several important areas of social justice and asset-based pedagogies, here we focus on three dominant scholarships: culturally relevant and sustaining pedagogies, CRT, and racial literacies. This retrospective review offers opportunities to reconsider and recommit researchers' and educators' efforts toward promoting a more just and equitable world amidst turbulent times.

CULTURALLY RELEVANT AND SUSTAINING PEDAGOGIES

The notion that schools function as a socializing institution to Americanize and assimilate immigrants and racially and ethnically minoritized students runs deep within U.S. history (Graham, 2005). For many, *American* denotes white, middle class, American-born, native-speakers of English (Spring, 2021). By positioning historically minoritized students as failing, deviant, culturally deprived, or culturally disadvantaged compared to the dominant "American" white culture, the U.S. education system prioritized "eradicating the linguistic, literate, and cultural practices many students of color brought from their homes and communities and to replace them with what were viewed as superior practices" (Paris, 2012, p. 93). Generally speaking, culturally relevant and sustaining pedagogy frameworks contradict this long-standing assimilationist and deficit paradigm in U.S. education and instead take asset-based approaches to historically minoritized students. Culturally relevant and sustaining pedagogy approaches attempt to validate and center the rich and distinctive cultures, languages, and identities that many students possess and bring to the classrooms by incorporating their lives and experiences into their learning.

Ladson-Billings (1994) first called attention to the importance of culturally relevant and sustaining pedagogy in her seminal work *The Dreamkeepers: Successful Teachers of African American Children*. Ladson-Billings conducted an ethnographic study to explore exemplary teaching practices and pedagogical beliefs of teachers hailing from different racial backgrounds who worked with African American students. She discovered three major domains of the teachers' work, which she later termed *culturally relevant teaching* in journal publications. Ladson-Billings (1998) explained that culturally relevant teaching rests on three central tenets: "(a) students must experience academic success; (b) students must develop and/or maintain cultural competence; and (c) students must develop a critical consciousness through which they challenge the status quo of the current social order" (p. 160). In other words, teachers practicing culturally relevant teaching challenge students with rigorous academic activities and uphold and affirm their cultural beliefs, practices, and backgrounds while encouraging them to notice and engage in the critique of inequality. Ladson-Billings (1994) characterized culturally relevant teaching as a theoretical framework that aims to "empower students intellectually, socially, emotionally, and politically by using cultural referents to impart knowledge, skills, and attitudes" (p. 21).

The literature on culturally relevant pedagogy has proliferated across multiple subject areas (e.g., Brown et al., 2019; Walker & Hutchison, 2021) and cultural contexts (e.g., Koh, 2020; Lee, 2010; Watson et al., 2016). In addition, other scholars, such as Gay (2010) and Paris and Alim (2014), have expanded and enriched the theory. For example, Geneva Gay (2010) offered a broader conception of culturally responsive teaching, which is defined as "using the cultural knowledge, prior experiences, frames of reference, and performance styles of ethnically diverse students to make learning encounters more relevant to and effective for them" (p. 31). Six characteristics of culturally responsive teaching include: setting high expectations for all students; engaging cultural, experience, and personal knowledge of students; bridging gaps between home and school cultures; practicing a holistic educational approach; leveraging student strengths; and questions and challenging normative school practices (Gay, 2010).

Similarly, Paris and Alim (2014) adapted culturally relevant teaching and expanded into culturally sustaining pedagogy. According to Paris and Alim (2014), culturally relevant teaching is often implemented in schools in superficial, static, and reductive ways that solely focus on "racial and ethnic difference(s) … without attending to the dynamic enactments of our equally important present or future" (p. 92). This shift in terminology illuminates that the focus of teaching and learning should move beyond the relevance of students' heritage cultures and towards sustaining students' "linguistic, literate, and cultural pluralism as part of the democratic project of schooling" (p. 93). In other words, culturally sustaining pedagogy seeks to support the heritage practices of racially and ethnically minoritized students while also fostering multifaceted, complex, and flexible cultural and linguistic practices among youth in this increasingly diverse and globalized world.

Despite its growing prominence as an asset-based approach, culturally relevant and sustaining pedagogy faces a crisis of marginalization spurred on by current neoliberal school policies (e.g., Brown et al., 2022; Sleeter & Cornbleth, 2011). For example, Royal and Gibson (2017) studied narratives of Black teachers in Philadelphia and found that the context of neoliberal school reform contributed to "disempowering the efforts of culturally relevant educators and making high test scores the sole focus of schooling" (p. 1). They noted that the neoliberal school reform, marked with "hyperaccountability and hyperstandardization" (Royal & Gibson, 2017, p. 3) created a culture of compliance and conformity among educators, which threatened their autonomy and agency to implement more student-centered and culturally relevant and sustaining pedagogy for their students. Coupled with issues of school funding, many teachers ended up adhering to prescribed, standardized instruction that prepared their students for multiple-choice tests and data-driven learning instead of paying attention to and drawing on diverse and dynamic cultures, languages, and communities among their students.

CRITICAL RACE THEORY

In 2023, many states witnessed attempts to legally ban CRT from public schools. As a result, in some schools educating about race and racism can lead to reprimands or termination. Although this current attack on CRT arises from a conversative and white-supremacist reaction to the growth of Black Lives Matter, worldwide protests in the wake of the death of George Floyd, and the shifting racial demographics of the United States (see Yacovone, 2022); early critiques of the use of CRT in the field of education came from well-meaning, diversity-focused scholars.

According to Busey et al. (2022), Ladson-Billings and Tate (1995) encountered some resistance when they shared draft copies of their soon-to-be-published landmark work "Toward a Critical Race Theory in Education" at the American Educational Research Association conference. Ladson-Billings (2013) reflected, "our focus on race as a primary tenet of inequality violated the sacred rule of maintaining the race, class, and gender triumvirate" (p. 34). The "friendly fire" of critique came from multiculturalists, social justice advocates, and liberal educators who, as noted by Busey and colleagues (2022), "conceptualized education as nice, neutral, and colorblind" (p. 7). Howard and Navarro (2016) explained that CRT diverged from multicultural education approaches, which "did not explicitly critique systems of oppression, such as racism and capitalism … [and] were overlooking structural inequality" (p. 257). Hence, CRT pushed for deeper analysis of race as central to the educational experience and challenged most broad-based views on equity and social justice. Still, some critical theorists worried that the use of race as a "central category of analysis" (Darder & Torres, 2004, p. 97) detracted from a larger critique of capitalism (see Ledesma & Calderon, 2015).

Taylor (2016) defined CRT as a subdivision of critical legal studies (CLS), which grew as a response to the persistent inequity found in society, especially after decisions in landmark legal cases meant to increase equity for people of color and women. Early critical race theorists "openly criticize[d] the role of law in the construction and maintenance of racially based social and economic oppression," and sought, "to formulate new strategies to affect transformation" (Taylor, 2016, p. 2). Influential scholars included Derrick Bell, Charles Lawrence, Richard Delgado, Lani Ganier, and Kimberlé Crenshaw. These scholars and others met frequently to discuss issues and define a theoretical stance. For example, Brown and Jackson (2021) described one meeting of critical legal scholars at Madison, Wisconsin, in 1989. The workshop prompted debate about the entrenchment of white supremacy and the loss of gains for educational equality since the U.S. Supreme Court Case *Brown v. Board of Education* (1954). They coined the term *interest convergence*, which characterized racial reform as being moved forward only when that reform coincided with the interests of the white majority and their intentions to retain legal, social, and material superiority. For example, according to Bell (1980), the landmark *Brown v. Board of Education* case benefited white Americans to a greater degree than it did African Americans, because *Brown v. Board of Education* helped build America's international reputation as a country concerned with civil rights and equality during the post-World War II fight for global democracy. Other concepts, such as race as property, intersectionality, racial realism, and counter-storytelling evolved from these initial dialogues (Brown & Jackson, 2021).

In 1995, Ladson-Billings and Tate (1995) described three propositions arising from CLS: (a) race is the significant factor in determining inequality, (b) inequality is bound by property rights, and (c) the intersection of race and property offer analytical tools to examine inequity in education. Since then, the various tenets of CRT have informed scholarship in teaching and learning. For example, Busey et al. (2022) traced seven tenets (e.g., centrality of race, interest convergence, counter-storytelling) and nine principles and themes (e.g., racial realism, critique of colorblind ideology, whiteness as property, material determinism). In this manuscript, we focus on the development of two concepts from CRT that have had a significant impact on teaching and curriculum: counter-storytelling and critical race pedagogy and praxis.

Counter-Storytelling

Ladson-Billings and Tate (1995) wrote that the "theme of 'naming one's own reality' or 'voice' is entrenched in the work of critical race theorists" (pp. 56–57). Ladson-Billings (1998) elaborated that "story provides the necessary context for understanding, feeling, and interpreting.... People of color speak with experiential knowledge about the fact that our society is deeply structured by racism" (p. 13). Creating these stories can serve to preserve and reaffirm the lived experience of people of color and other marginalized groups. The stories, once created, can also serve as counter-narratives that can speak back to members of the dominant group, shedding light on the often-unseen practices of oppression (Dixson & Anderson, 2018). According to Solorzano and Yasso (2008), "counter-stories can shatter complacency, challenge the dominant discourse on race, and further the struggle for racial reform" (p. 32). As a result, the process of creating counter-stories and counter-narratives has been employed as both a research methodology (e.g., Solorzano & Yosso, 2008) and as a pedagogical tool (Miller et al., 2020). Miller et al. (2020) described how counter-narratives can be used with K–12 students in two ways: having students create their own counter-stories (see Stovall, 2006a, 2006b) and using already constructed counter-narratives to challenge deficit views and colorblindness found in school texts and majoritarian stories within society.

Critical Race Praxis

Lynn and Parker (2006) defined critical race pedagogy and praxis as involving "a critique of racism as a system of oppression and exploitation that explores the historical and contemporary constructions and manifestations of race in our society" (p. 282). Expanding on this definition, Ledesma and Calderon (2015) added that critical race pedagogy works to "empower students of color while dismantling notions of colorblindness, meritocracy, deficit thinking, linguicism, and other forms of subordination" (p. 208). In this process, Ledesma and Calderon (2015) supported the notion to also "teach Whites to understand themselves through the history of the other" (p. 209) and by disrupting their own whiteness and white privilege in the class by challenging majoritarian narratives with counter-stories.

Similar to culturally relevant and anti-racist pedagogies, critical race pedagogy and praxis requires the development of racial consciousness for classroom teachers. However, Howard and Navarro (2016) observed that consciousness "cannot be taught in a superficial way that reduces racial awareness to simplistic dos and don'ts, but requires a deep level of analysis, self-reflection, and understanding of racial realities both past and present" (p. 261). Leonardo and Boas (2013) offered this set of considerations for teachers:

- Critically reflect on racialized and gendered histories and how you are implicated in them.
- Make race and race history part of the curriculum and fight for its maintenance in it.
- Teach race as a structural and systemic construct with material, differential outcomes that are institutionally embedded not reducible to identities.
- Work to understand and teach race not as a personal crusade but as a sociohistorical construct through which we are all (unequally) produced (p. 322).

Several of these considerations speak to the development of a curriculum designed to analyze race and racism within society. Such a curriculum according to Yasso (2002) ought to: (a) explore the role of racism, sexism, classism, and other forms of subordination within institutional structures; (b) challenge majoritarian narratives and cultural assumption about people of color and/or colorblindness and meritocracy; (c) draw on counter-narratives, such as stories, biographies, testimonies of lived experiences from cultural informants; and (d) engage in historical and contemporary analysis of educational inequity and access.

Despite advances in the development and practice of CRT in education stemming from Ladson-Billings and Tate's (1995) landmark article, CRT faces strong political opposition. Efforts by right-wing conservatives led by Chris Rufo and others to legislate against the use of CRT have resulted in several states proposing restrictive bills on the teaching of antiracism. An article published in *The New Yorker* reported on how Rufo invented the CRT attack, calling the concept "the perfect villian," because "its connotations are all negative to most middle-class Americans" (Wallace-Wells, 2021, para. 6). In fact, Rufo explained his goal for distorting the public meaning of CRT in a 2021 tweet, writing "We have decodified the term and will recodify it to annex the entire range of cultural constructions that are unpopular" (Blow, 2023, para. 4). This purposeful attempt to create misconceptions about what CRT is has opened up the doorway to censor all forms of equity-oriented teaching. For example, Rufo recently tweeted in 2023 against the terms diversity, equity and inclusion (DEI), writing, "We've won the debate against CRT; now it's time to dismantle DEI" (Blow, 2023, para. 2). When interviewed by Charles Blow (2023) of *The New York Times*, Kimberlé Crenshaw lamented, "They started with CRT. They moved to 'Don't Say Gay.' Now they're moving to all Black students. It's not going to be long before they include all ethnic studies" (Blow, 2023, para 16). Crenshaw concluded, " I believe that this is the battle for the next century" (Blow, 2023, para. 19). Her words echoed W.E.B. Du Bois's (1903) statement that race would be the central problem of the 20th century.

RACIAL LITERACIES

Despite the resurgence of neoliberal ethos and white supremacy, racial literacies have emerged as a new approach for educating students to understand how racism is constructed and manifested in societies. The origin of the term racial literacy can be traced to the work of two scholars: legal scholar Lani Guinier and sociologist France Winddance Twine. First, Guinier (2004) argued legal advocates must move beyond racial liberalism, which saw the problem of racism as interpersonal and psychological. Instead, racial literacy served as a mechanism through which people identify the contextual nature of race, the role of race and power in perpetuating racism, and the intersectionality of race and "explanatory variables" (p. 115). Hence, Guinier's ideas sought to expose the systemic and structural nature of race and racism.

While Guinier situated her theory of racial literacy as an analytical tool in the legal field, Twine (2004) investigated the skills and practices utilized by transracial parents with their multiracial children. In her seven-year ethnographic case study of white transracial birth parents in Britain, she attended to the "labour that white parents perform as they translate and transform the meaning of whiteness, blackness, and racism in their families" (p. 881). For example, parents engaged in frequent discussion and evaluation of the child's experiences with race by providing consistent opportunities for their children to develop their race cognizance (by practicing how they "critically evaluate media and textual representations of black people"; Twine, 2004, p. 885). Secondly, race cognizant parents provided access to privileged cultural knowledge by encouraging social relationships with Black adults and families whether through informal or formal (i.e., supplementary schools) settings. By examining these practices, Twine (2004) developed a theory of how these parents fostered certain skills (i.e., confidence, self-esteem, analytical skills) of racial literacy in their children. Her study focused on parents who were, or were not, "racism-cognizant" (p. 885) and traced family discussions about the children's experiences with race. Results from the study illustrated that those who were more cognizant asked their children to critically recognize, evaluate, and respond to racial inequalities; these parents also provided supplementary cultural opportunities in which the children formed relationships among interracial groups.

According to Twine and Guinier, racial literacy is both a mechanism through which people can identify the contextual nature of race, the role of race and power in perpetuating racism, and the intersectionality of race (Guinier, 2004) as well as the skills and practices employed by people in teaching others about race and racism (Twine, 2004). Stevenson (2014) drew on these two perspectives in his review of scholarship about racial socialization in schools. He defined racial socialization as "the transmission and acquisition of intellectual, emotional, and behavioral skills to protect and affirm racial self-efficacy by recasting and reducing the stress that occurs during racial conflicts with the goal of successfully resolving those conflicts" (p. 18). While he recognized that the school is an extension of the systemic nature of race and racism (Guinier, 2004), he also envisioned teachers and administrators as partners in disrupting racism through racial literacy practices (Twine, 2004). Thus, his work is unique in that it revolved around, first, acknowledging and reflecting on oneself as having a racial identity and position, then engaging in relationships to navigate racially stressful situations to lessen psychological damage. Ultimately, Stevenson (2014) moved Twine's and Guinier's work forward by positioning racial literacy as a capacity to be developed, practiced, and internalized in order to "read, recast, and resolve racially stressful encounters" (p. 27).

Beyond Stevenson's scholarship, other scholars apply racial literacy as a framework to analyze the practices of parenting (An, 2020), students in English language arts (Grayson, 2017), preservice teachers (King, 2016), and mixed racial groupings (Skerrett, 2011); as models of racial literacy as a progression toward racial reconciliation (Horsford, 2014); or as an ongoing process of development in teacher education (Sealey-Ruiz, 2021). Three new developments within racial literacy scholarship promise a significant impact on teaching and curriculum: (a) considering racial literacy as a journey of continuous development, (b) bridging theory and practice, and (c) pushing beyond the Black/white binary.

First, scholars now focus on how racial literacy is developed and learned over time. Laughter et al. (2021), in their recent review of the literature on racial literacy, found that the majority of studies they found center on the idea of "becoming" (p. 12) literate, a process that is continual and cyclical. Likewise, Nash et al. (2018) observed that racial literacy is learned over time and in diverse contexts, but not without contradictions. In addition, Rolón-Dow et al. (2020) refused to place participants on a "developmental continuum" (p. 14), but instead, positioned their teacher candidates as learners and accepted that the outcome of engaging with race and racism "will vary in depth, speed, and clarity" (p. 14) within the group. This attention to racial literacy as a learned skill (much like reading literacy) opens up doorways to explore both pedagogies and context associated with racialized knowledge and socialization.

Second, scholars bridge theory and practice by considering steps involved in the development of racial literacies. For example, Sealey-Ruiz (2020) offered a step-by-step approach to developing racial literacy. Her more general principles of racial literacy are to question assumptions, engage in critical conversations, and practice reflexivity (Price-Dennis & Sealey-Ruiz, 2021, p. 286). These three principles are largely resonant with

Stevenson's (2014) attention to reflection on racial selves and engaging in dialogue in relationships. However, she added a heuristic for developing racial literacy that outlined six components (not necessarily in linear order), which included: interruption, archaeology of self, historical literacy, critical reflection, critical humility, and critical love (Sealey-Ruiz, 2021). These six guiding principles provide a blend of Guinier's focus on the institutional and systemic levels and Stevenson's focus on personal story, all within what Sealey-Ruiz named as her attempt at bringing theory and practice together.

Third, one specific characteristic understood to be inherent in the intersectional nature of racial literacy is the attention paid to all racialized groups. However, this nuanced attention to race has not always been explicitly stated in the literature, which naturally led many scholars in the U.S. context to limit racial literacy to a Black/white binary. Such a view rejects the racialization of other historically marginalized groups (i.e., Indigenous peoples). Oto and colleagues (2022) highlighted this push toward acknowledging geographical factors as a more recent development in racial literacy scholarship. They explained that "place is a significant aspect of understanding how race is constructed for local refugee communities" (p. 107). Considering how refugees are often "collapsed into legible racial forms such as Black or Asian" (p. 107), it is important to think of racial literacy as incorporating more than the binary (i.e., anti-Indian racism, anti-Asian racism). Thus, the plural form of the term—racial literacies—has been taken up more recently to attend to this plurality of racialization and racial formations in the United States' past and present.

With these developments in racial literacies, researchers, teachers, and students can lean on Sealey-Ruiz's process components to scaffold their ongoing development toward greater educational equity and more explicitly acknowledge racial literacies as extending beyond the Black/white binary to all historically and intersectionality marginalized communities.

RACIAL AND CULTURAL PEDAGOGIES IN HARD TIMES

This review highlights the developments of culturally relevant and sustaining pedagogies, CRT, and racial literacies, paying particular emphasis to the criticisms of and promising features of these theories. Although efforts by educators to promote racial and cultural pedagogies in their classrooms and affirm the racial and cultural backgrounds of children and families are continuously hampered by the shifting educational and sociopolitical landscape—such as the rise of the neoliberal education system, white supremacy and anti-CRT movements—the turbulent times we are currently experiencing paradoxically signal the necessity and appropriateness of advocating for and implementing these theories and pedagogies.

Each of these theoretical perspectives offer unique strengths and possibilities for addressing issues of equity. Culturally responsive and sustaining pedagogies champion an asset-based, student-affirming stance for classroom teachers and schools. Here teachers are called upon to not only affirm, but also sustain the lived cultural experiences of students and integrate their cultural funds of knowledge when crafting a relevant curriculum. CRT applied to education and learning attends to structural inequity and the role that schools play to both reinforce and challenge such inequity. Educators guide students to unpack institutional racism, such as inequitable school funding, school resegregation, and the school-to-prison pipeline, and also to name and work against social structures and ideologies that justify racism, such as colorblindness, meritocracy, privilege, and white supremacy. Finally, racial literacies blend aspects of both culturally relevant and sustaining pedagogies and tenets of CRT. As King (2016) noted, "racially-literate people understand racism as a persistent problem and consider its various manifestations, socio-historical, socio-economic, and socio-political structures, as salient racial apparatuses" (p. 1). In this way, racial literacies seek to dismantle structures of racism. Yet still, racial literacies also offer personal and psychological tools to help individuals not just decipher racism and its grammar but respond to it. The tools of racial literacies can be "used to describe, interpret, explain and act on the constellation of practices (e.g., historical, economic, psychological, interactional) that comprise racism and anti-racism" (Mosley & Rogers, 2011, p. 126). As Twine (2004) described, such tools might involve discussions with youth about race and police violence or how to cope with microaggressions.

Across these three theories, a set of common teaching practices emerge which might inform teachers, teacher educators, and curriculum developers who adopt equity-oriented pedagogies. These practices include: honoring the cultural and community assets of students; making curriculum relevant for all students; raising critical consciousness and awareness of race and racism; tracing and challenging racist political, economic, and social structures; and challenging racism through counter-storytelling. Adopting such practices requires educators to be race-cognizant and to hold a stance of critical humility needed for them to reflect on their own privilege and racial literacies development.

Scholarly efforts should be directed towards theoretical development and empirical validation of culturally relevant and sustaining pedagogies, CRT, and racial literacies. Researchers should carry out future exploration comparing these three theories, further identifying their implication on policies, curriculum, and teaching. In doing so, the voices and experiences of teachers should not be left out but be placed at the center. As Sleeter (2011) asserted, to advance racial and cultural theories it is necessary to strengthen "research that both elaborates on what it looks like in classrooms, and that connects its practices with impacts on students" (p. 20). Researchers should investigate how teachers navigate the neoliberal, white supremacist ideologies that dominate education and strategically adopt and implement culturally relevant and sustaining pedagogies, CRT and racial literacies for their students despite these constraining circumstances. As Ladson-Billings (1994) demonstrated in her landmark study, *The Dreamkeepers*, researchers can learn much from teachers themselves. Perhaps the next decade of research for racial justice might very well depend on how scholars listen to and learn from educators as they practice equity-oriented pedagogies in today's troubling political climate.

REFERENCES

An, S. (2020) Learning racial literacy while navigating white social studies. *The Social Studies, 111*(4), 174–181. https://doi.org/10.1080/00377996.2020.1718584

Bell, D. (1980). Brown v. Board of Education and the interest convergence principle. *Harvard Law Review, 93*, 518–533. https://doi.org/10.2307.1340546

Bissell, T. (2023). Teaching in the upside down: What anti-critical race theory laws tell us about the first amendment. *Stanford Law Review, 75*(1), 205–259. Retrieved May 1, 2023, from https://review.law.stanford.edu/wp-content/uploads/sites/3/2023/01/Bissell-75-Stan.-L.-Rev.-205.pdf

Blow, C. M. (2023, Feb 22). America, right-wing censors and the 'battle for the next century'. *The New York Times*. https://www.nytimes.com/2023/02/22/opinion/america-right-wing-censors.html

Bohan, C., Baker, H. R., & King, L. J. (2022). *Teaching enslavement in American history: Lesson plans and primary sources*. Peter Lang.

Brown, B. A., Boda, P., Lemmi, C., & Monroe, X. (2019). Moving culturally relevant pedagogy from theory to practice: Exploring teachers' application of culturally relevant education in science and mathematics. *Urban Education, 54*(6), 775–803. https://doi.org/10.1177/0042085918794802

Brown, C. P., Ku, D. H., Puckett, K., & Barry, D. P. (2022). Preservice teachers' struggles in finding culturally sustaining spaces in standardized teaching contexts. *Journal of Early Childhood Teacher Education*, 1–21. https://doi.org/10.1080/10901027.2022.209932

Brown, K., & Jackson, D. D. (2021). The history and conceptual elements of critical race theory. In A. D. Dixson, & M. Lynn (Eds.), *Handbook of critical race theory in education* (pp. 9–22). Routledge.

Du Bois, W. E. B. (1903). *The souls of Black folks: Essays and sketches*. A. C. McClurg & Co.

Busey, C. L., Duncan, K. E., & Dowie-Chin, T. (2022). Critical what what? A theoretical systematic review of 15 years of critical race theory research in social studies education, 2004–2019. *Review of Educational Research*. Online First. https://doi.org/10.3102/0034654321105551

de Brey, C., Musu, L., McFarland, J., Wilkinson-Flicker, S., Diliberti, M., Zhang, A., Branstetter, C., & Wang, X. (2019). *Status and trends in the education of racial and ethnic groups 2018* (NCES 2019-038). U.S. Department of Education. https://nces.ed.gov/pubs2019/2019038.pdf

Darder, A., & Torres, R.D. (2004). *After race: Racism after multiculturalism*. New York University Press.

Dixson, A. D., & Anderson, C. R. (2018). Where are we? Critical race theory in education 20 years later. *Peabody Journal of Education, 93*(1), 121–131. https://doi.org/10.1080/0161956X.2017.1403194

Gay, G. (2010). *Culturally responsive teaching: Theory, research, and practice* (2nd ed.). Teachers College Press.

Graham, P. A. (2005). *Schooling American: How the public schools meet the nation's changing needs*. Oxford University Press.

Grayson, M. (2017). Race talk in the composition classroom: Narrative song lyrics as texts for racial literacy. *Teaching English in the Two Year College, 45*(2), 143–167. Retrieved May 1, 2023, from https://library.ncte.org/journals/TETYC/issues/v45-2/29428

Guinier, L. (2004). From racial liberalism to racial literacy: *Brown v. Board of Education* and the interest-divergence dilemma. *Journal of American History, 91*(1), 91–118. https://doi.org/10.2307/3659616

Horsford, S. D., (2014). When race enters the room: Improving leadership and learning through racial literacy. *Theory Into Practice, 53*, 123–130. https://doi.org/10.1080/00405841.2014.885812

Howard, T. C., & Navarro, O. (2016). Critical race theory 20 years later: Where do we go from here? *Urban Education, 51*(3), 253–273. https://doi.org/10.1177/0042085915622541

King, L. (2016). Teaching black history as a racial literacy project. *Race Ethnicity and Education, 19*(6), 1303–1318. https://doi.org/10.1080/13613324.2016.1150822

Koh, Y. (2020). Achieving joy through community-based culturally relevant art education: A case study of Korean-American elementary students in the Midwest. *Journal of Cultural Research in Art Education, 37*(1). https://doi.org/10.2458/jcrae.4754

Ladson-Billings. G. (1994). *The dreamkeepers: Successful teaching for African-American students*. Jossey-Bass.

Ladson-Billings, G. (1995). Toward a theory of culturally relevant pedagogy. *American Educational Research Journal, 32*(3), 465–491. https://doi.org/10.2307/1163320

Ladson-Billings, G. (1998). Just what is critical race theory and what's it doing in a nice field like education? *International Journal of Qualitative Studies in Education, 11*(1), 7–24. https://doi.org/10.1080/095183998236863

Ladson-Billings, G. (2013). Critical race theory—what it is not! In M. Lynn & A. D. Dixson (Eds.), *Handbook of critical race theory in education* (pp. 34–47). Routledge.

Racial and Cultural Pedagogies in Education   47

Ladson-Billings, G., & Tate, W. F., IV. (1995). Towards a critical race theory of education. *Teachers College Record, 97*(1), 47–68. https://doi.org/10.1177/016146819509700104

Laughter, J., Pellegrino, A., Waters, S., & Smith, M. (2021): Toward a framework for critical racial literacy, *Race Ethnicity and Education, 26*(1), 73–93. https://doi.org/10.1080/13613324.2021.1924130

Ledesma, M. C., & Calderon, D. (2015). Critical race theory in education: A review of past literature and a look to the future. *Qualitative Inquiry, 21*(3), 206–222. https://doi.org/10.1177/1077800414557825

Lee, J. S. (2010). Culturally relevant pedagogy for immigrant children and English language learners. *Teachers College Record, 112*(14), 453–473. https://doi.org/10.1177/016146811011201408

Leonardo, Z., & Boas, E. (2013). Other kids' teachers: What children of color learn from white women and what this says about race, whiteness, and gender. In M. Lynn & A. D. Dixson (Eds.), *The handbook of critical race theory in education* (pp. 313–324). Routledge.

Lynn, M., & Parker, L. (2006). Critical race studies in education: Examining a decade of research on US schools. *The Urban Review, 38*, 257–290. https://doi.org/10.1007/s11256-006-0035-5

Miller, R., Liu, K., & Ball, A. F. (2020). Critical counter-narrative as transformative methodology for educational equity. *Review of Research in Education, 44*(1), 269–300. https://doi.org/10.3102/0091732X20908501

Mosley, M., & Rogers, R. (2011). Inhabiting the "tragic gap": Pre-service teachers practicing racial literacy. *Teaching Education, 22*(3), 303–324. https://doi.org/10.1080/10476210.2010.518704

Nash, K., Howard, J., Miller, E., Boutte, G., Johnson, G., & Reid, L. (2018). Critical racial literacy in homes, schools, and communities: Propositions for early childhood contexts. *Contemporary Issues in Early Childhood, 19*(3), 256–273. https://doi.org/10.1177/1463949117717293

National Center for Education Statistics. (2022). *English learners in public schools: Condition of education*. U.S. Department of Education, Institute of Education Sciences. https://nces.ed.gov/programs/coe/indicator/cgf

Oto, R., Rombalski, A., & Grinage, J. (2022). The role of racial literacy in US K-12 education research: a review of the literature. *Race Ethnicity and Education, 26*(1) 94–111. https://doi.org/10.1080/13613324.2022.2047635

Paris, D. (2012). Culturally sustaining pedagogy: A needed change in stance, terminology, and practice. *Educational Researcher, 41*(3), 93–97. https://doi.org/10.3102/0013189X12441244

Paris, D., & Alim, H. S. (2014). What are we seeking to sustain through culturally sustaining pedagogy? A loving critique forward. *Harvard Educational Review, 84*(1), 85–100. https://doi.org/10.17763/haer.84.1.9821873k2ht16m77

Pei, S. (2017). White supremacism and racial conflict in the Trump Era. *International Critical Thought, 7*(4), 592–601. https://doi.org/10.1080/21598282.2017.1405665

Price-Dennis, D., & Sealey-Ruiz, Y. (2021). *Advancing racial literacies in teacher education: Activism for equity in digital spaces.* Teachers College Press.

Rolón-Dow, R., Flynn, J., & Mead, H. (2020). Racial literacy theory into practice: Teacher candidates' responses. *International Journal of Qualitative Studies in Education, 34*(7), 663–679. https://doi.org/10.1080/09518398.2020.1783013

Royal, C., & Gibson, S. (2017). They schools: Culturally relevant pedagogy under siege. *Teachers College Record, 119*(1), 1–25. https://doi.org/10.1177/016146811711900108

Sealey-Ruiz, Y. (2021). The critical literacy of race: Toward racial literacy in urban teacher education. In T. Howard & H. Milner (Eds.), *Handbook for Urban Education* (pp. 281–295). Routledge.

Skerrett, A. (2011). English teachers' racial literacy knowledge and practice. *Race Ethnicity and Education, 14*(3), 313–330. https://doi.org/10.1080/13613324.2010.543391

Sleeter, C. E. (2011). An agenda to strengthen culturally responsive pedagogy. *English Teaching: Practice and Critique, 10*(2), 7–23. Retrieved May 1, 2023, from https://edtechbooks.org/-uGyt

Sleeter, C. E., & Cornbleth, C. (2011). *Teaching with vision: Culturally responsive teaching in standards-based classrooms.* Teachers College Press.

Solorzano, D. G., & Yasso, T. J. (2002). Critical race methodology: Counter-storytelling as an analytical framework for education research. *Qualitative Inquiry, 8*(1), 23–44. https://10.1177/107780040200800103

Spring. J. (2021). *Deculturalization and the struggle for equality.* Routledge.

Stevenson, H. (2014). *Promoting racial literacy in schools: Differences that make a difference.* Teachers College Press.

Stovall, D. (2006a). We can relate: Hip-hop culture, critical pedagogy, and the secondary classroom. *Urban Education, 41*(6), 585–602. https://doi.org/10.1177/0042085906292513

Stovall, D. (2006b). Where the rubber hits the road: CRT goes to high school. In A. D. Dixson & C. K. Rousseau (Eds.), *Critical race theory in education* (pp. 231–240). Routledge.

Taylor, E. (2016). The foundations of critical race theory in education: An introduction. In E. Taylor, D. Gillborn, & G. Ladson-Billings (Eds.), *Foundations of critical race theory in education* (pp. 1–30). Routledge.

Twine, F. W. (2004). A white side of Black Britain: The concept of racial literacy. *Ethnic Racial Studies, 27*(6), 1–30. https://doi.org/10.1080/0141987042000268512

Walker, S., & Hutchison, L. (2021). Using culturally relevant pedagogy to influence literacy achievement for middle school Black male students. *Journal of Adolescent & Adult Literacy, 64*(4), 421–429. https://doi.org/10.1002/jaal.1114

Wallace-Wells, B. (2021, Jun 18). How a conservative activist invented the conflict over critical race theory: To Christopher Rufo, a term for a school of legal scholarship looked like the perfect weapon. *The New Yorker.* https://www.newyorker.com/news/annals-of-inquiry/how-a-conservative-activist-invented-the-conflict-over-critical-race-theory

Watson, W., Sealey-Ruiz, Y., & Jackson, I. (2016). Daring to care: The role of culturally relevant care in mentoring Black and Latino male high school students. *Race Ethnicity and Education, 19*(5), 980–1002. https://doi.org/10.1080/13613324.2014.911169

Will, M. (2022, Apr 20) What should culturally relevant teaching look like today? Gloria Ladson-Billings explains. *Education Week*. https://www.edweek.org/leadership/what-should-culturally-relevant-teaching-look-like-today-gloria-ladson-billings-explains/2022/04

Yacovone, D. (2022). *Teaching white supremacy: America's democratic ordeal and the forging of our national identity.* Penguin Random House.

Yasso, T. J. (2002). Toward a critical race curriculum. *Equity & Excellence in Education, 35*, 93–107. https://doi.org/10.1080/713845283

NOTE

1. In this article, we will capitalize "Black" but not "white" (unless the words are capitalized differently from authors we quote directly. We follow the example of Bohan and colleagues (2022), who wrote that "to capitalize 'Black' in America in 2022 is to recognize a people who have struggled historically for recognition *as a people* in a society with a troubled history and legacy of white supremacy" (pp. 7–8).

CHAPTER 2

LEGISLATE TO (UN)EDUCATE

Examining the Impact of Divisive and Dehumanizing Education Policies

Gregory Samuels
University of Montevallo

Amy Samuels
University of Montevallo

Brandon J. Haas
University of North Georgia

ABSTRACT

Authors explore recent education policies that ban the teaching of critical race theory, restrict teaching race-related topics, prohibit conversations about divisive concepts, and problematize their impact in further silencing (and potentially erasing) complex issues about race and racism and other forms of oppression in historical and sociocultural contexts. This article highlights legislative efforts and examines findings and implications from a study designed to explore perceptions of educators related to the anti-critical race theory bills.

Curriculum and Teaching Dialogue,
Volume 25, Numbers 1 & 2, pp. 51–68
Copyright © 2023 by Information Age Publishing
www.infoagepub.com
All rights of reproduction in any form reserved.

Over the last few years, many state legislatures and school boards have introduced bills that ban the teaching of critical race theory (CRT) in K–12 schools and higher education. As explained by *Education Week* (Schwartz, 2023), as of February 2023, 44 states introduced bills or took other steps that would restrict teaching CRT or limit how educators can discuss racism and sexism. Further, 18 states have imposed these bans and restrictions either through legislation or other avenues. Such actions were inspired by Executive Order 13950 (2020) issued by President Trump, which was later revoked by President Biden, that banned federal contractors from conducting antiracist professional learning that is informed by CRT or other "race-based ideologies." We argue these divisive education policies are designed to restrict teaching race-related topics and limit conversations about race, racism, and other forms of oppression by appealing to emotionality through inaccuracy and misrepresentation. Consequently, such legislation upholds narratives of white supremacy and continues to silence narratives, voices, and contributions of Black, Indigenous, and people of color (BIPOC) individuals and communities. Additionally, restrictive education policies perpetuate an inaccurate view of history and disregard deeper issues around oppression and marginalization, including historical implications of racism and other forms of oppression, such as gender identity, national origin, religion, and sexual orientation. We note that even though white is generally capitalized in formal writing, we will use lower-case white throughout the article as a means of decentering white narratives in history, an approach commonly used by CRT scholars.

While the bills are collectively referred to as CRT bills, most do not mention CRT and inaccurately interpret the academic framework. Furthermore, the language in the policies is often vague, thereby encouraging misinterpretation and resulting in unfounded complaints or actions. For example, parents in Alabama reported violations of the state school board policy because their children's schools were celebrating Black History Month (Bella, 2022). In addition, Ron DeSantis, Governor of Florida, drew upon such legislation to restrict implementation of an Advanced Placement African American Studies course in schools across the state, proclaiming "it lacks educational value" and "it is a vehicle to a political agenda" (*Wall Street Journal* Editorial Board, 2023). As Bohan et al. (2022) emphasize, "Black history isn't an uncomfortable topic *per se*," but topics such as slavery cause "the white students to squirm" and often result in discomfort (p. 2). In addition, "Teaching the history of slavery," or Black history in general, "is sometimes seen as an attack on American civic values and can arouse the anger of parents, administrators, and school boards" (Bohan et al., 2022, p. 3) like the actions demonstrated in Alabama and Florida.

Since race continues to be a significant factor that influences access, opportunities, and outcomes, as authors, we contest the rejection of racialized views of the United States. Educators have a responsibility to encourage students to examine how race operates in thoughts, conceptualizations, and actions, and evaluate how racist and oppressive laws, ordinances, and policies shape current disparities and inequalities. Therefore, we actively challenge the existence of divisive and dehumanizing education policies that restrict educators' ability to foster and sustain educational experiences that explore historical truths. Educators must commit to facilitate learning that is not only historically accurate and inclusive, but also promotes critical understandings about people and their lives, especially those who have traditionally been placed on the margins. Additionally, it is critical to consider that teachers are professionals—professionals who are credentialled and trained in their craft. As such, as highlighted by Bohan (2022), we should "leave the work of determining how and what to teach to professionals who have dedicated their careers to education and not to scare tactics targeted at a political base" (p. 15).

In this research, we explore related education policies and problematize their intended and unintended impacts, which further silence complex issues about the role of race in historical and sociocultural contexts, as well as the impact of racism and other forms of oppression. Many anti-CRT education policies propose negative consequences for educators and institutions who violate the bills, including loss of state funding, termination of employment, monetary fines, or criminal charges for educators (Young & Friedman, 2022). In addition, educators who are on the front lines are responsible for aligning their work to ensure adherence to the policies, even when such policies are in direct conflict with state curriculum standards or educator preparation requirements. As such, this study is designed to examine the perceptions of educators related to the legislative efforts, actions, and impacts of anti-CRT bills.

OVERVIEW OF THE RESEARCH

Critical Race Theory

CRT has origins within critical theory. Consequently, it serves as a framework that considers the dynamics of power and oppression and explores strategies to advance society in a more equitable way. This theory functions by examining power relations and exploring nuanced questions related to how power is utilized to maintain current social standings (Lynn et al., 2006). Delgado and Stefancic (2017), prominent legal scholars, explained, "The critical race theory (CRT) movement is a collection of activists and scholars engaged in studying and transforming the relationship among race, racism, and power" (p. 3). Lynn and Jennings (2017) highlighted the claims of early legal scholars, noting CRT challenges the dominant narrative as the normative standard; recognizes and addresses the ingrained nature of racism in political and legal structures; and offers a framework for engineering the use of literary knowledge and storytelling to counter the omnipresent social construction of race. Moreover, CRT is a theoretical perspective that systematically examines the construct of race by establishing racism as a structural precursor to legal oppression and identifying race as the key component in social inequalities (Crenshaw, 2019; Delgado & Stefancic, 2017; Lynn et al., 2006). Ladson-Billings (1998) emphasized that "Critical race theory begins with the notion that racism is normal in American society" (p. 7) as it was created and upheld by legal principles (Crenshaw, 2019; Delgado & Stefancic, 2017; Ladson-Billings, 2021). Additionally, critical race theorists argue race is an influential and significant factor in examining and understanding inequalities in the United States and internationally, because the disparities and inequalities are "logical and predictable results of a racialized society in which discussions of race and racism continue to be muted and marginalized" (Ladson-Billings, 2021, p. 17).

While CRT is interdisciplinary, it is valuable in educational contexts because it can be used to analyze various disparities and provides a framework to challenge the dominant discourse on race, racism, and cultural deficit theories (Solórzano & Yosso, 2001). Seeking to disrupt educational patterns that often perpetuate racialized disparities for BIPOC students, CRT establishes a foundation comprised of six central tenets (a) racism is endemic; (b) race is socially constructed; (c) racialized concepts change over time; (d) interest convergence is advantageous for social progress; (e) inclusion of counterstories is critical for underscoring alternative perspectives; and (f) intersectionality supports understanding how various identity components such as race, ethnicity, gender identity, and sexuality influence experiences, perceptions, and positionings (Abrams & Moio, 2013). CRT has been applied to explore experiences of both BIPOC teachers and students, while calling attention to racist classroom practices and further uncovering various critical pedagogies to address race and racism in educational spaces.

The application of CRT in educational research began in the mid-1990s through the work of Gloria Ladson-Billings and William F. Tate IV (Ladson-Billings, 1998; Ladson-Billings & Tate, 1995). They argued that race remained untheorized in education and saw CRT as a framework that "provided a robust theoretical understanding of race" (Ladson-Billings, 2021, p. 3). Utilizing CRT in educational discourse places race and racism, as well as the voices and experiences of BIPOC teachers and students, at the center of the discussion. It also positions race as central in the analysis of educational inequalities (Ladson-Billings, 2021; Lynch, 2006). As emphasized by Solórzano and Yosso (2000):

> CRT in education is defined as a framework or set of basic perspectives, methods, and pedagogy that seeks to identify, analyze, and transform those structural, cultural, and interpersonal aspects of education that maintain the marginal position and subordination of African American and Latino students. CRT asks such questions as: What role do schools, school processes, and school structures play in the maintenance of racial, ethnic, and gender subordination? (p. 42)

When considering analysis of curriculum, instruction, assessment, school funding, disproportionality, or desegregation, applying tenets of CRT accounts for educational inequalities in access, opportunities, and outcomes, because "it exposes the seeming neutrality of societal norms that must be addressed if we are to reach the full equality promised by the Constitution" (Ladson-Billings, 2021, p. 3). In relation to curriculum:

> It is not just the distortions, omissions, and stereotypes of school curriculum content that must be considered, it also is the rigor of the curriculum and access to what is deemed "enriched' curriculum via gifted and talented courses and classes. (Ladson-Billings, 1998, p. 18)

In addition, CRT can be applied in research to examine why instruction of African American students is often centered around the idea that students are academically deficient and takes a remedial approach (Ladson-Billings, 1998; Solórzano & Yosso, 2001). As Ladson-Billings (1998) argued, "Adopting and adapting CRT as a framework for educational equity means that we will have to expose racism in education and propose radical solutions for addressing it" (p. 22).

"Critical race scholarship has also articulated the need to use racial position as an epistemological perspective from which to better apprehend the reality of all topics, not just 'race-relevant' ones" (Crenshaw, 2019, p. 15). The theory establishes racism as endemic in the United States and encourages educators to evaluate the impact of race laws and policies on systems and structures, not simply the attitudes, mindsets, and behaviors of individuals or groups. The focus lies not only on merit or individualism, but rather CRT considers current access, opportunities, and outcomes and examines how historical laws, policies, and norms impacted current access, opportunities, and outcomes. CRT challenges practitioners and policy makers to explore those who were granted and/or denied access and opportunities, both historically and currently, which then inspires the question: how does (did) that access and those opportunities impact outcomes?

In Derrick Bell's early work in critical legal studies, he argued, "Diversity is not the same as redress ... it could provide the appearance of equality while leaving the underlying machinery of inequality untouched" (as cited by Cobb, 2021, para. 15). This idea can be expanded to inform understanding of continued racial disparities and inequalities in educational contexts. While attempts have been made that suggested the appearance of equality, for example school desegregation as a result of *Brown v. Board of Education* (1954), when those attempts were retracted the foundation of the inequality was left undisturbed, thereby allowing the inequalities and disparities to persist (Delgado & Stefancic, 2017; Ladson-Billings, 2021). To genuinely address the issue and influence systemic change, it is not only the disease that must be addressed, but the symptoms as well. As a result, it is necessary to consider the impact of laws and policies throughout history and reimagine approaches to transform racist and inequitable sociopolitical spaces and foster more equitable access and opportunity-bound structures, systems, and institutions.

Overview of Divisive Education Policies

In *The Souls of Black Folk* (1903/2014), W. E. B. Du Bois contended, "the problem of the Twentieth Century is the problem of the color line" (p. 3). While he presented this idea in 1903, deeply embedded implications of racial oppression and injustice persist today, which are evidenced through educational opportunity gaps, employment discrimination, wage gaps, wealth disparities, ownership of property, access to health care, mass incarceration, and police brutality (Hannah-Jones, 2021; Sensoy & DiAngelo, 2017). However, despite overwhelming evidence of historical and current implications of how race has shaped and continues to structure society in oppressive and unequal ways, increased awareness of racism and racialized disparities and injustices continues to be challenged and denied. By appealing to emotionality, individuals in positions of power have introduced censorious legislation to silence discussions and critiques about the impact of racism and other forms of oppression on history and society, further empowering those who want to ignore or refuse to look into the "Veil" (Du Bois, 1903/2014, p. 3)

As of February 2023, 44 states have introduced legislation or official policies that ban teaching CRT or related concepts in K–12 schools (Schwartz, 2023). While many of the policies do not explicitly name critical race theory, the related commentary underscores the academic theory. For example, in Alabama, the resolution titled "Preservation of Intellectual Freedom and Non-Discrimination in Alabama Public Schools" states:

> Concepts that impute fault, blame, a tendency to oppress others, or the need to feel guilt or anguish to persons solely because of their race or sex violate the premises of individual rights, equal opportunity, and individual merit, and therefore, have no place in professional development for teachers, administrators, or other employees of the public educational system of the State of Alabama, and WHEREAS, for the same reasons, such concepts should not be taught to students in the public educational system of the State of Alabama. (Alabama State Board of Education, Action Item G.2.o)

The resolution continues by proclaiming, "that the Alabama State Board of Education affirms that we will not support, or impart, any K–12 public education resources or standards intended to indoctrinate students in social or political ideologies that promote one race or sex above another" (Alabama State Board of Education, Action Item G.2.o). Similarly, Florida's Stop the Wrongs to Our Kids and Employees (W.O.K.E.) Act, signed into law in 2022, prohibits schools and publicly funded workplaces from "subjecting any student or employee to training or instruction that espouses, promotes, advances, inculcates, or compels such individuals to believe specified concepts constitutes discrimination based on race, color, sex, or national origin" (Florida S.B. 148, 2022).

Anti-CRT legislation such as what was passed in Alabama and Florida, also known as divisive concepts bills, and often referred to as anti-truth laws, were inspired by the Executive Order issued by President Trump in September 2020 that banned federal contractors from conducting antiracist professional learning or racial sensitivity training that drew on critical race theory or other "race-based ideologies" or promoted the idea that "the United States is an inherently racist or evil country or that any race or ethnicity is inherently racist or evil" (Executive Order No. 13950, 2020). Executive Order 13950 (2020) underscored principles of merit and individualism; rejected racialized views of the United States or any consideration of how race operates in thoughts, conceptualizations, and actions; and disregarded how racist laws, ordinances, and policies shaped (and continue to shape) current disparities and inequities. The resulting impact was the reification of the national fantasy (Berlant, 1991; Helmsing, 2022) that falsely represents the United States as the land of opportunity that equally extends access to all who live there.

Current efforts to ban or prohibit discussions of certain topics is not new. PEN America (Friedman & Tager, 2022) describes the thoughts of Jeet Heer who proclaimed, "these attacks follow an 'old script, one where the name of the bogeyman changes but the basic storyline is always the same: sinister, alien forces are trying to corrupt children'" (p. 5). Accordingly, attempts to incite fear are created and heightened further by mischaracterizations of CRT as a Marxist, un-American ideology that is strategically taught in schools; threatens American values; and indoctrinates children into liberal, evil, and toxic mindsets (Bump, 2021).

While many divisive education policies are vague and sweeping in nature and do not explicitly name critical race theory or concepts related to diversity, equity, and inclusion, the deliberate ambiguity further problematizes the issue because policies "will be applied broadly and arbitrarily, threatening to effectively ban a wide swath of literature, curriculum, historical materials, and other media, and casting a chilling effect over how educators and educational institutions discharge their primary obligations" (Friedman & Tager, 2022, p. 4). Furthermore, this vague and sweeping nature begs the question of who has the power to decide what is deemed uncomfortable or offensive or what will result in feelings of guilt or shame.

OVERVIEW OF THE STUDY

This study, which was approved by the Institutional Review Board (IRB), was designed to explore the perceptions of K–20 educators related to anti-CRT bills and utilized both qualitative and quantitative methods. Using an online survey, composed of 16 questions, we collected data from 18 educators over a six-week period and explored participants' opinions of (a) the policies and legislative efforts, (b) their views on how the policies and legislative efforts will (or will not) impact their teaching, (c) their ideas on how the policies and legislative efforts will impact equity initiatives in educational settings, (d) their insights about the impact of the policies and legislative efforts on teaching about race and racism in history, and (e) their beliefs about how the policies and legislative efforts will impact inclusive representation of diverse stories and experiences in the curriculum. The survey included Likert-scale questions as well as open-ended free response questions.

The opportunity to participate in the study was advertised via social media and national educational organizations in which teachers and teacher educators are largely represented. We invited in-service educators to participate to express their experiences and perceptions on issues related to proposed and recently passed anti-CRT legislation. Eighteen participants completed the survey. Respondents self-identified as practicing K–20 educators; specifically, 44% were university educators, 39% taught in grades 7–12, and 17% were elementary educators. Ninety-five percent of participants identified as currently working in a state that has introduced or passed legislation being referred to as a CRT Bill or that restricts or censors teaching about race or racism. The majority of participants work in educational settings in the South (90%); however, educators from the Northeast were also represented (10%) in the study. While the survey was widely shared, limitations to the study were a small sample size ($n = 18$), as well as responses that largely focused on educators in the South. Limitations could be addressed by extending the study to explore the experiences and perceptions of educators to include more geographically diverse representation, as well as conducting focus groups or individual interviews to allow for more in-depth exploration of the research questions.

DATA COLLECTION AND ANALYSIS

We collected and analyzed data from an online survey that was created and disseminated via Google Forms. For open-ended responses, we employed Rubin and Rubin's (2012) steps of interview data analysis. We used coding procedures to determine themes and to transition from raw data to overarching concepts. The process involved recognition, examination, coding, sorting, and synthesis. Recognition, examination, and coding required preparing the data. Sorting and synthesis involved analyzing the data. Recognition entailed the process of reading, reviewing, and studying the survey responses in relation to the research questions to determine conceptual themes important for understanding the research. Examination involved carefully exploring concepts and themes to clarify meaning and understanding. Coding called for designating and employing a system of color-coded highlighting to readily retrieve and examine conceptual themes across the surveys using NVivo software. The primary themes revealed in the data were (a) preserving power and status, (b) democracy at risk, and (c) glimmers of hope. Participants are represented by pseudonyms in the manuscript.

FINDINGS

Drawing from the Likert-scale responses, the majority of participants were concerned with divisive education policies. When asked about their opinion of the legislation being referred to as a CRT Bill, or legislation that restricts or censors teaching about race or racism, 72% of participants strongly disagreed and 22% disagreed with the legislative efforts. Regarding impacts on teaching, 53% of participants reported they believe proposed and existing policies will have an overall negative impact and, more specifically, 72% of respondents believe legislative efforts will have a negative impact on equity initiatives in their educational settings. In addition, 94% of participants expressed the policies and legislative efforts will have a negative impact on teaching content related to race and racism, while 67% of respondents believe it will have a negative impact on the representation of diverse stories and multiple perspectives in the curriculum.

Preserving Power and Status

It remains a perplexing reality that many people continue to view racism as an issue of the past, which was eradicated by the civil rights movement and the election of President Barack Obama as the nation's first African American President. These beliefs persist despite the continuous and irrefutable examples of racism's existence, examples that were revealed long before the 2016 presidential campaign that commenced with the comparison of Mexicans to rapists. During this same time period, the horrific murders of Ahmaud Arbery, George Floyd, Breonna Taylor, Atatiana Jefferson, Stephon Clark, Botham Jean, Philando Castile, Alton Sterling, Freddie Gray and countless others continued to place race(ism) at the forefront of public discourse. While racialized violence and protests are not new:

> What is new is that a larger percentage of Americans recognize the protestors were motivated by longstanding concerns about the treatment of Black people in the United States. These same people were calling for more Black history in schools to help them understand the histories behind policing, oppression, and resistance. (Bohan et al., 2022, p. 2)

Still, amid a nationwide outcry for justice and reform, a different movement took root simultaneously, which resulted in the passage of divisive education policies and related legislation that restrict, or prohibit, discussions of race, racism, and divisive concepts. Additionally, the 2022 midterm elections saw 50% of gubernatorial candidates in the South having signed or supported restrictions on classroom teaching about race (Richard, 2022), which further indicated the desire of many people to protect the status quo that minimizes or silences multiple perspectives and inclusive history that accurately examines oppression, marginalization, racial successes, and struggles.

Participants in the study underscored how these policies demonstrate the emotional protection for select students—privileged students. Participant "Ryan" stated, "This leads to greater concern about protecting the 'emotions and feelings' of white students at the expense of being forthright and honest with all students, especially to the detriment of validating the experiences and histories of students of color." This idea is further complicated by the fact that white students in the United States no longer comprise the majority of the PK–12 population, indicating a societal shift that will continue until minoritized populations in the United States constitute the majority.

This demographic shift has paved the way for more people of color to be in positions of power, a trigger for what Anderson (2016) has termed "white rage" (p. 1). It is this phenomenon, and related emotions and fears, that kickstarted the flurry of laws that sought to protect and defend "the master narrative," which Woodson (2017) defined as "the social mythologies that mute, erase, and neutralize features of racial struggle in ways that reinforce ideologies of White supremacy" (p. 317). The suggestion that "only one experience and story is valued when CRT, race and racism is prohibited from curriculum; and it's not the one of my students," demonstrates how this concept manifests in the classroom, limits curricular decision making, omits experiences of diverse groups, and further advances a decontextualized and whitewashed representation.

Emotion plays a central role in the function of society by connecting national identity and one's feelings (Fortier, 2010). Zembylas (2014) defines "governing through affect," (p. 7) as "the prescription of one's feelings for the nation and for those who are deemed 'similar' or 'different'" (Zembylas, 2014, p. 7). Currently, legislators are "governing through affect" (Zembylas, 2014, p. 7) by creating policies that appeal to people's emotions, in order to establish control over classroom practices by restricting curricular content, instructional resources, and pedagogical approaches. Participants emphasized a variety of emotions when describing their feelings of fear, nervousness, and stress that can impact their curricular decision making. Participant "Taylor" expressed concern about the impact of "fear of retribution from parents, administrators, community" that could influence classroom practice.

Literature demonstrates the importance of emotion in education (Boler, 1999; Zembylas, 2009) and in social studies specifically (Garrett, 2017; Sheppard et al., 2015), providing insight into the contemporary culture wars taking place over curriculum, which "castigate schools as bastions of liberal indoctrination" (Bohan, 2022, p. 13). Boler (1999) described a pedagogy of discomfort as an invitation to critical examination that brings into focus the role of emotion in defining "how and what one chooses to see, and conversely, not to see" (p. 177). Policy then acts as a barrier or guide rail to coerce students into having the "proper feelings" (Zembylas, 2014) that usher society in particular directions. The current legislative efforts further demonstrate those in positions of power are maneuvering in an effort to preserve their power and status, as well as structure the educational narratives to preserve the power and status of people who are similar to themselves.

Democracy at Risk

The United States, like many other nations, is at a crossroads and how the nation moves forward will pave a path for future policies and practices throughout the democracy. In the study, participants raised concerns regarding how this trend of legislation would not only impact the classroom, but society writ large. Participants' responses continually suggested these laws would negatively impact our democratic society as a whole and outlined fear about the future of the nation, implicitly questioning whether democracy was at risk. Participant "Ashley" asked pointedly, "If we cannot discuss racism, sexism, the term 'genocide,' or societal bias in our laws—then where does that leave our students and our country?"

History is complex and students need to have opportunities to grapple with these complexities through historical analysis that draws from diverse and multiple perspectives. Instead, corporate curriculum has long since manipulated curriculum to mislead and misrepresent the realities of the past (Loewen, 2007) and present information in such a way that "conceals pain and injustice, masks racism, and demeans our Black students" (Watson et al., 2018, p. 9). Such censorship of content was a central concern for participants, who wish to accurately portray history as more than a single, one-dimensional story. Respondents posed questions such as "how can we have honest debate around the history of Supreme Court cases without being able to discuss racism?"

Anti-CRT legislation further complicates classroom practice by lacing the teaching of multiple perspectives and diverse experiences with fear. The policies limit, or in some cases prohibit, discussion of topics deemed "divisive," which then restricts how teachers can approach the teaching of history. Participant "Jo" stated, "I am frustrated by the current political climate … I also understand how this is related to power and the null and hidden curriculum in schools." A poignant message is sent to teachers and students alike when curriculum is censored or manipulated, particularly when educators consider who has the power to define what is deemed divisive or controversial. Consequently, censorship sets the stage for trauma and *curriculum violence* (Ighodaro & Wiggan, 2010), which is defined as "deliberate manipulation of academic programming," which, "compromises the intellectual or psychological well-being of learners" (p. 2). Curriculum violence considers the impact, not the intent, because the actions do not have to be strategic or deliberate to result in trauma or harm. For example, omission of certain histories from the curriculum is also a form of curriculum violence, because it harms how students learn history and see themselves represented in it (Jones, 2020).

Underscoring the ideas of power and decision making, as well as the need to include teacher voices in the conversation, participant "Jo" stated,

"I think the two sides need to talk to each other more." The lack of discourse between different ideas and approaches further shifts censorship from content to the individual self, as participant "Chad," who was critical of CRT noted, "I've witnessed first-hand how students self-censor in order to please teachers who are critical scholars, and to please other students who are motivated by critical theory." This participant continued by admitting, "I wouldn't answer this survey if it weren't anonymous. It would damage my standing with critical scholars and their fellow-travelers in my profession." Comments like this demonstrate the problematic duality of failed discourse that impacts both the classroom and spaces beyond. Since public discourse, which includes critical analysis and debate, is imperative to the preservation of democracy, it is important to consider how vague restrictions, censorship, and curricular misrepresentation not only impact the knowledge to which students have access but the far-reaching impact of these restrictions.

Glimmers of Hope

Despite the frightening barrage of policy censoring curriculum, there is hope for continued resistance. The 2022 midterm elections yielded the second highest midterm voter turnout for 18–29-year-old voters (29%) in history. Ideally, this trend will continue to spark the glimmers of hope related to civic participation that were revealed in our study. Participants spoke of how young students make meaningful connections that promote empathy and good citizenship. Participant "Jane" spoke of their kindergarten class:

> We recently read Malala's Magic Pencil in my kindergarten classroom and my students were so engrossed by her story. They asked thoughtful questions about her hijab and about the Taliban. We kept it age appropriate, but imagining not having those kinds of empathy-building conversations in my classroom makes my stomach turn. When we discussed how she is an activist who stands up for what's right and fights for the rights of others, my students instantly brought in their learning about MLK Jr. and the indigenous people we read about in *Water Protectors*. These stories matter and representation of our students matters.

Another participant argued that:

> Teaching the Truth is necessary for an informed, empathetic, inclusive society. Failure to teach about racialized identities and racism results in citizens who are not equipped to recognize and advocate for necessary changes to protect the lives of the global majority.

Abolitionist teachers can take back classrooms through action (Love, 2019). Resistance to divisive education policies might focus on respect and commitment to doing what is in the best interest of students. As participant "Anthony" explained, "I will not dishonor my students, profession, or self by allowing unjust restrictions to be placed on my classroom discussions or content." It is clear that such legislative efforts have invoked an emotional/affective response, but is it also evident that the responses have led to both resistance and action. As researchers, we wonder if these policies—which are rooted in fear, misinformation, and hatred—further provide opportunities for teachers to consider how to craft lessons that tease out the humanity in all of us through age-appropriate critical thinking and reflection, as described in the anecdote from the kindergarten class.

IMPLICATIONS

Shaping school curriculum in a way that intentionally omits or marginalizes diverse voices, contributions, and perspectives enacts a null curriculum that perpetuates issues currently embedded throughout all levels of society. Love (2019) asked, "How do you matter to a country that would rather incarcerate than educate you?" (p. 2). Current legislative efforts codify and reinforce curriculum violence (Ighodaro & Wiggan, 2010) against BIPOC students and communities in ways that white people cannot grasp. These impacts extend beyond curriculum, which is evidenced through the school to prison pipeline that indisputably impacts students of color disproportionately to white students (Haas et al., 2020). This legislation erects yet another barrier to overcoming oppressive and inequitable systems and structures by impeding learning by further mispresenting, marginalizing, and excluding the voices and experiences of minoritized students and communities.

Hammond (2015) pointed to neuroscience research when discussing the reality that all students are "wired for expansive learning, high intellectual performances, and self-determination" (p. vi). To activate this potential, learners search and connect to what is meaningful, which is "based on [their] cultural frame of reference" (p. vi). Relevance further provides opportunity for affective responses, such as empathy, that encourages agency for students as they grow and consider their place in the world (Endacott & Brooks, 2018). A primary purpose for education is to develop students to be thoughtful and engaged citizens. However, Starkey (2008) argued that "racism is a barrier to citizenship and is the antithesis of democracy" (p. 329). Therefore, policy that restricts content and curricula that positions students against making these connections works against education and will have dire consequences.

CONCLUSION

Derrick Bell (2002), considered by many to be the father of CRT, proclaimed that "racism lies in the center, not the periphery; in the permanent, not the fleeting; in the real lives of black and white people, not in the caverns of the mind" (p. 37). As we continue to witness the current culture wars, where one side is vehemently resisting historical truths and mandating a culture of silence on racial dialogue, it is clear that racism remains at "the center." Systematic omission, misrepresentation, or distortion of the experiences of BIPOC students and communities in educational experiences encourages a belief, either implicit or explicit, that infers people of color are insignificant in the historical and economic development of the United States (King, 2020; Takaki, 2008). As King (2014) stated, "The African proverb, 'Until the lions have their historians, tales of the hunt shall always glorify the hunter,' is used to metaphorically describe how dominant groups inscribe power through historical narrative" (p. 2). Consequently, to disrupt exclusionary historical narratives focused on Eurocentric perspectives, that exclude or victimize people of color, educators must both expose and examine how racism is operationalized and systematically engrained in individuals, systems, and institutions. We must problematize and strategically confront the permanence of racism and encourage honest reflection about how people see (or selectively choose not to see) race and racism; because avoiding, denying, or silencing this reality is not only inaccurate and incomplete but also serves to perpetuate institutionalized racism and white supremacy.

REFERENCES

Abrams, L., & Moio, J. (2013). Critical race theory and the cultural competence dilemma
in social work education. *Journal of Social Work Education*, 45(2), 245–261. https://doi.org/10.5175/JSWE.2009.200700109

Alabama State Board of Education (2021, August 12). *Preservation of intellectual freedom and non-discrimination in Alabama public schools*. Action Item G.2.o. https://www.alabamaachieves.org/wp-content/uploads/2021/08/ALSBOE-Resolution-Declaring-the-Preservation-of-Intellectual-Freedom-and-Non-Discrimination-in-AL-Public-Schools.pdf

Anderson, C. (2016). *White rage: The unspoken truth of our racial divide*. Bloomsbury.

Bell, D. (2002). Learning the three "I's" of America's slavery heritage. In P. Finkelman (Ed.), *Slavery and the Law* (pp. 29–42). Rowman & Littlefield.

Bella, T. (2022, February 4). Black History Month is not critical race theory, Alabama educator says in response to complaints. *The Washington Post*.

Berlant, L. (1991). *The anatomy of national fantasy: Hawthorne, utopia, and everyday life*. University of Chicago Press.

Bohan, C. H. (2022). 42 reasons to be concerned about the status of curriculum and teaching. *Curriculum and Teaching Dialogue, 24*(1 & 2), 13–17. https://www.infoagepub.com/products/Curriculum-and-Teaching-Dialogue-Vol-24

Bohan, C. H., Baker, H. R., King, L. J., & Morris, W. H., Jr. (2022). *Teaching enslavement in American history: Lesson plans and primary sources*. Peter Lang.

Boler, M. (1999). *Feeling power: Emotions and education*. Routledge.

Bump, P. (2021, November 4). Tucker Carlson is very mad at 'evil' critical race theory, whatever it is. *The Washington Post*. https://www.washingtonpost.com/politics/2021/11/04/tucker-carlson-is-very-mad-evil-critical-race-theory-whatever-it-is/

Brown v. Board of Education (1954). 347 U.S 483, 492.

Cobb, J. (2021, September 13). The man behind critical race theory. *The New Yorker*. https://www.newyorker.com/magazine/2021/09/20/the-man-behind-critical-race-theory

Crenshaw, K. W. (2019). *Seeing race again: Countering colorblindness across the disciplines*. University of California Press.

Delgado, R., & Stefancic, J. (2017). *Critical race theory: An introduction* (3rd ed.). New York University Press.

Du Bois, W. E. B. (2014). *The souls of Black folk*. Millennium. (Original work published 1903)

Endacott, J., & Brooks, S. (2018). Historical empathy: Perspectives and responding to the past. In S. Metzger, & L. McArthur Harris (Eds.), *The Wiley international handbook of history teaching and learning* (pp. 203–226). Wiley Blackwell.

Executive Order No. 13950, 3 C. F. R. 60683–60689 (2020, September 22). https://www.federalregister.gov/documents/2020/09/28/2020-21534/combating-race-and-sex-stereotyping

Florida Senate Bill 148. (2022, July 1). https://www.flsenate.gov/Session/Bill/2022/148

Fortier, A. M. (2010). 'Proximity by design? Affective citizenship and the management of unease', *Citizenship Studies 14*(1), 17–30. https://doi.org/10.1080/13621020903466258

Friedman, J, & Tager, J. (2022). *Educational gag orders: Legislative restrictions on the freedom to read, learn, and teach*. PEN America. https://pen.org/report/educational-gag-orders/

Garrett, H. J. (2017). *Learning to be in the world with others*. Peter Lang.

Haas, B., Samuels, A., & Samuels, G. (2020), Higher learning: Race and the school-to-prison pipeline. In D. Mackey, & K. Elvey (Eds.), *Society, ethics, and the law: A Reader* (pp. 277–289). Jones and Bartlett Learning.

Hammond, Z. (2015). *Culturally responsive teaching & the brain: Promoting authentic engagement and rigor among culturally and linguistically diverse students*. Corwin.

Hannah-Jones, N. (2021). *The 1619 project*. The New York Times Company.

Helmsing, M. E. (2022). Teaching beyond racialized national fantasies for anti-racist curriculum: A portrait of a high school civics course. *Curriculum and Teaching Dialogue 24*(1), 67–81. https://www.infoagepub.com/products/Curriculum-and-Teaching-Dialogue-Vol-24

Ighodaro, E., & Wiggan, G. A. (2010). *Curriculum violence: America's new civil rights issue*. Nova Science Publishers.

Jones, S. P. (2020). Ending curriculum violence. *Learning for Justice*. https://www.learningforjustice.org/magazine/spring-2020/ending-curriculum-violence

King, L. J. (2014). When lions write history: Black history textbooks, African-American educators, & the alternative Black curriculum in social studies education, 1890–1940. *Multicultural Education*, *22*(1), 2–11. https://eric.ed.gov/?id=EJ1065311

King, L. J. (2020). Black history is not American history: Toward a framework of Black historical consciousness. *Social Education*, *84*(6), 335–341. https://www.socialstudies.org/social-education/84/6/black-history-not-american-history-toward-framework-black-historical

Ladson-Billings, G. (1998). Just what is critical race theory and what's it doing in a nice field like education? *Journal of Qualitative Studies in Education*, *11*(1), 7–24. https://doi.org/10.1080/095183998236863

Ladson-Billings, G. (2021). *Critical race theory in education: A scholar's journey*. Teachers College Press.

Ladson-Billings, G., & Tate, W. F., IV. (1995). Toward a critical race theory of education. *Teachers College Record*, *97*(1), 47–68. https://doi.org/10.1177/016146819509700104

Loewen, J. (2007) *Lies my teacher told me: Everything your American history textbook got wrong*. Atria Books.

Love, B. (2019). *We want to do more than survive: Abolitionist teaching and the pursuit of educational freedom*. Beacon Press.

Lynch, R. V. (2006). Critical-Race educational foundations: Toward democratic practices in teaching "other people's children" and teacher education. *Action in Teacher Education*, *28*(2), 53–65. https://doi.org/10.1080/01626620.2006.10463410

Lynn, M. & Jennings, M. (2017). Power, politics, and critical race pedagogy: A critical race analysis of Black male teachers' pedagogy. In A. Darder, R. D. Torres, & M. P. Baltodano (Eds.), *The critical pedagogy reader* (pp. 535–556). Routledge.

Lynn, M., Williams, A. D., Park, G., Benigno, G., & Mitchell, C. (2006). Critical theories of race, class, and gender in urban education. *ENCOUNTER: Education for Meaning and Social Justice*, *19*(2), 17–25. https://doi.org/:10.1007/s11256-006-0035-5

Richard, A. (2022, October 31). *Half the candidates for governor in South favor restrictions on teaching about race, SEF profiles show*. Southern Education Foundation. https://southerneducation.org/in-the-news/half-the-candidates-for-governor-in-the-south-favoring-restrictions-on-teaching-about-race/

Rubin, H., & Rubin, I. (2012). *Qualitative interviewing: The art of hearing data* (3rd ed.). SAGE.

Schwartz, S. (2023, February 27). Map: Where critical race theory is under attack. *Education Week*. https://www.edweek.org/policy-politics/map-where-critical-race-theory-is-under-attack/2021/06

Sensoy, O., & DiAngelo, R. (2017). *Is everyone really equal: An introduction to key concepts in social justice education*. Teachers College Press.

Sheppard, M., Katz, D., & Grosland, T. (2015). Conceptualizing emotions in social studies education. *Theory & Research in Social Education, 43*(2), 147–178. https://doi.org/10.1080/00933104.2015.1034391

Solórzano, D., & Yosso, T. (2000). Towards a critical race theory of Chicano and Chicana education. In C. Tejada, C. Martinez, & Z. Leonardo (Eds.), *Charting new terrains in Chicana(o)/Latina(o) education* (pp. 35–66). Hampton Press.

Solórzano, D., & Yosso, T. (2001). From racial stereotyping and deficit discourse toward a critical race theory in teacher education. *Multicultural Education, 9*(1), 2–8. https://www.researchgate.net/publication/234647460_From_Racial_Stereotyping_Toward_a_Critical_Race_Theory_in_Teacher_Education

Starkey, H. (2008). Antiracism. In J. Arthur, I. Davies, & C. Hahn (Eds.), *The SAGE Handbook of education for citizenship and democracy* (pp. 329–341). SAGE.

Takaki, R. (2008). *Different mirror: A history of multicultural America.* Back Bay Books.

Wall Street Journal Editorial Board. (2023, January 27). Ron DeSantis, Black history and CRT Florida has a point in rejecting AP African-American Studies. *Wall Street Journal.* https://www.wsj.com/articles/ron-desantis-ap-african-american-studies-curriculum-florida-education-critical-race-theory-11674831789

Watson, D., Hagopian, H., & Au, W. (2018). *Teaching for Black lives.* Rethinking Schools.

Woodson, A. N. (2017). "There ain't no white people here": Master narratives of the civil rights movement in the stories of urban youth. *Urban Education 52*(3), 316–342. https://doi.org/0042085915602543

Young, J. C., & Friedman, J. (2022, August 17). *America's censored classrooms.* https://pen.org/report/americas-censored-classrooms/

Zembylas, M. (2009). Affect, citizenship, politics: Implications for education. *Pedagogy, Culture & Society, 17,* 369–384. https://doi.org/10.1080/14681360903194376

Zembylas, M. (2014). Affective citizenship in multicultural societies: Implications for critical citizenship education. *Citizenship Teaching & Learning, 9*(1), 5–18. https://doi.org/10.1386/ctl.9.1.5_1

CHAPTER 3

WRITING A LOVE LETTER TO EDUCATORS IN THE WAKE OF ANTI-CRT EFFORTS

Alexandra Allweiss, Scott Farver, and Anne-Lise Halvorsen
Michigan State University

ABSTRACT

This conceptual essay explores three "moments" related to our collective efforts as white teacher educators to respond to proposed anti-critical race theory legislation in Michigan. These moments made visible institutional tensions and limits related to taking a stand against racist policies. We explore how we might obstruct flows of power in our roles as faculty through our institutional, teaching, and curriculum engagements.

"I share your concerns, but ..." was a refrain we heard over and over as we created a collective space for faculty to engage in and deepen their anti-racist pedagogy, and wrote a letter of love and solidarity for teachers to encourage our college to make a statement against efforts to restrict teaching and learning about race, histories, and justice in our state (Michigan) and across the United States. The statement that followed the "but" took different forms—variously referring to timing, tone, accountability to donors, fears of retaliation, political impacts, not wanting to

---

Curriculum and Teaching Dialogue,
Volume 25, Numbers 1 & 2, pp. 69–86
Copyright © 2023 by Information Age Publishing
www.infoagepub.com
All rights of reproduction in any form reserved.

"offend" or make (white, wealthy, privileged) people uncomfortable–but ultimately they all worked to shift away from the shared response; and we argue that each "but" worked to constrain accountability to Black and Indigenous peoples and communities and other communities of color in our college and beyond.

In this article, we explore three moments in our collective work as three white teacher educators committed to developing and enacting anti-racist pedagogy and curriculum at our public university that made visible institutional limits, or "walls" (Ahmed, 2012, p. 129), and efforts to constrain and contain justice to make it palatable and "safe." Both of the limits and efforts to contain worked to uphold the flows of white institutional power and raised questions for us about the role of higher education amidst anti-critical race theory (CRT) legislation, as well as other restrictive policies being rolled out across the country. In our work, we draw on the concepts of anti-racist pedagogy and academic freedom and are informed by frameworks of CRT, decoloniality, and critical whiteness studies (CWS). In doing so, this piece engages with Patel's (2018) call to think about what happens when framings of justice are molded to uphold whiteness and institutional power dynamics. We conclude by considering the implications of these framings and institutional flows of power and think about what it looks like to be obstructions within flows of power (Ahmed, 2012) as we think about how we might obstruct flows of power in our roles as faculty through our own institutional, teaching, and curriculum engagements.

While the moments we describe are located within a particular educational setting, we argue that these moments have transference to other contexts; these tensions are not unique to our educational space. Our goal is to situate our experiences within broader challenges in higher education related to academic freedom, anti-racist pedagogy, and the role of white educators in this ongoing hostile political environment. We share these experiences from our vantage points—as faculty members without administrative responsibilities. As with all storytelling, perspective influences one's worldview.

CONCEPTUAL FRAMEWORKS

This article, which focuses on a particular, localized, curricular tension, is grounded in two conceptual frameworks: anti-racist pedagogy and academic freedom. These two frameworks help explain both the rationale for these three moments highlighted in this article and the tensions we faced as faculty seeking ways to take collective action in support of teachers. They also help connect these tensions to larger educational patterns and systems.

Anti-Racist Pedagogy

Our work, particularly that within the university, is grounded in a commitment to anti-racist pedagogy. Anti-racist pedagogy is a broad framework that includes CRT, de-/anti-colonial frameworks, culturally sustaining pedagogy, and CWS among other theories and approaches (e.g., Gillborn, 2006; Ladson-Billings, 1995, 2009, 2014; Paris, 2012; Paris & Alim, 2014; Will, 2022). It also entails critical reflection on social positioning and commitments to confronting internalized racial oppression and superiority (Kishimoto, 2016). Our work specifically draws on CRT, decoloniality, and CWS.

CRT, as a framework applied to education, is used to analyze the role of racism in everyday life, including educational spaces and policies (see Delgado & Stefancic, 2012; Ladson-Billings & Tate, 1995). In this article, we use the framework of CRT to explore understandings (and misunderstandings) about CRT in K–12 settings. CRT focuses on actions and outcomes, and not just intent. In particular, we draw on two tenets of CRT most relevant to our experiences to guide our analysis. The tenet that lays out an understanding of racism as ordinary and a central part of U.S. life and the tenet on interest convergence (i.e., white people will support racial justice as long as they benefit) help us see the racial logics undergirding the moments described here.

Furthermore, our location as the first "land grab" institution (Lee & Ahtone, 2020), in particular, requires a reckoning with the interconnected ways land grab and white supremacist settler violence continue to be perpetuated by, sustain, and permeate our institution (Grande, 2018; paperson, 2017). Decolonial theories make visible and disrupt the interconnected forms of racialized colonial violence and ways modern/colonial power structures persist materially and epistemically through ongoing acts and processes of conquest (e.g., King, 2019; Quijano, 2000). Decolonial frameworks push us to work and imagine education otherwise (e.g., Andreotti, 2021).

CWS centers the urgent demands to disrupt and dismantle whiteness and white supremacy, and like CRT and decoloniality, demands epistemic and material transformations. CWS offers a transdisciplinary analytic lens for "unmask[ing] the everyday presence of whiteness … and examin[ing] how whiteness operates in ways that deleteriously impact people of Colour and how this sadomasochism ultimately also dehumanises whites" (Matias & Boucher, 2021, p. 8). In education, CWS scholars have discussed the ways whiteness is embedded and enacts violence in and through curriculum, teaching, teacher education, and institutionalized white ignorance (e.g., Baldwin, 1963/1998; Leonardo, 2009; Matias, 2013, 2016; Sleeter, 2017).

Academic Freedom

One of the many privileges of academia, and in fact a hallmark, is academic freedom, which has been vigorously defended for decades by the American Association of University Professors (AAUP), beginning with a 1915 Declaration of Principles on Academic Freedom and Academic Tenure for faculty at both public and private institutions. Academic freedom is not easily defined and is interpreted differently across different contexts. In this manuscript, we draw on Reichman's (2019) conception of academic freedom which,

> guarantees to both faculty members and students the right to engage in intellectual inquiry and debate without fear of censorship or retaliation. It grants considerable scope to the consciences of individual teachers and researchers, but it functions ultimately as the collective freedom of the scholarly community to govern itself in the interest of serving the common good in a democratic society. (p. 4)

Academic freedom protects faculty and students' freedom of speech with the broader goal of fighting against the damaging effects of anti-intellectual attacks on expertise, knowledge, and truth (Reichman, 2019, p. 5). Restricting free and open dialogue is antithetical to both democracy and the advancement of knowledge. In 1970, the AAUP revised the original 1915 statement (which had also been revised in 1940) to make clear that extramural speech should not be disciplined unless it has bearing on professional competence, which is in the faculty's jurisdiction (Reichman, 2019, p. 53).

Yet, in practice, how is academic freedom protected? In what ways is it curtailed, even indirectly? It is important to examine cases to understand the extent to which it is and is not fully protected. For example, in 1970, Angela Davis, an Assistant Professor of Philosophy, was fired from the University of California, Los Angeles for her membership in the Communist Party for using "inflammatory rhetoric" in speeches. Davis's example highlights the tensions of scholars taking stances that universities do not support—especially stances that might upset donors or disrupt the white neoliberal status quo (Gordon, 2020). When Dr. Sunera Thobani, a professor at the University of British Columbia, spoke out about the September 11 attacks, her remarks were mobilized by the media and political leaders and a "hate crime" investigation was publicly launched against her and she was framed as anti-American because of the criticism of the United States

(Thobani, 2003). Thobani's (2003) experience further highlights the ways academic freedom is individualized and couched within neoliberal imperialist settler colonial interests and ideologies (Jeppesen & Nazar, 2012). These attacks on the academic freedom of Scholars of Color have a history that is deeply rooted in racism.

It is a fallacy to assume that faculty constitute a uniform "special interest group." As Reichman (2019) argued:

> As any faculty member will readily attest, the notion that "the faculty" is a uniform "special interest group" is at best an aspiration of some. Faculty members are divided by discipline, rank, and employment category (tenured, contingent, etc.), as well as by race, age, gender, and, of course, political leanings. If we are an interest group, we are a pretty fractured one. (p. 106)

Faculty have diverse backgrounds, commitments, and scholarly interests; yet faculty members tend to share a vested interest in the actions and commitments of their institution and may take a collective stance toward a policy, event, financial stance, or personnel decision. A point of debate exists around the question of whether academic freedom extends to institutions, or if it only applies to individuals (see the Kalven Report, 1967; Lu, 2022). The individual focus assumes that institutional neutrality is possible and laudable and not, in fact, a political choice and decision. The fallacy of neutrality is clearly laid bare through the role of donors and funding that support certain research agendas and work to frame particular stances as "political" and others as "neutral."

METHODOLOGY

This article uses poetic (Parsons & Pinkerton, 2022) and scholarly personal narrative approaches (Mawhinney, 2012; Nash, 2019; Nash & Viray, 2013), which center personal narratives, memories, and stories and breaks from "academic" writing that distances the scholar from/in the writing. Nash and Viray (2013) explained scholarly personal narrative "puts the self of the scholar front and center ... use[s] the personal insights gained in order to draw larger conclusions for readers, possibly even to challenge and reconstruct older political or educational narratives" (p. 4). Thus, this approach can take different forms and allows the writer to story themselves and their experiences and connect them to larger processes (Nash, 2019). We bring our narrative prose approach together with poetic frameworks that "make use of aural, visual, and conceptual poetic elements and lean on poetic structures such as stanzas, line breaks, and white space to meaningfully ... communicate essential themes" (Parsons & Pinkerton, 2022, p. 120).

Together these approaches allowed us to recreate our experiences in the moments we share here.

To reconstitute moments and feelings from our shared experiences, we drew on our notes, emails, text messages, and memory. The three of us texted before, during, and after the moments centered here and met virtually several times to rehash what we had seen, felt, and experienced. In this article, we use a colloquial and poetic style of remembering that does not adhere to dominant academic conventions and voice in order to paint a picture of how we were feeling in those moments. We each wrote our own sections, and then had our co-authors add to them as we collectively remembered the experience from three different angles. Since these moments are recreations, we want to be clear that we do not use direct quotations for words that come from people other than ourselves. Writing in this style helped us make sense of what happened and allowed us to paint a broader picture for others to see and hopefully feel and connect to our experiences, since, while specific, our experiences also reflect larger themes. Before sharing these experiences, we share our state's political context that motivated our efforts.

CONTEXT SETTING: MICHIGAN HOUSE & SENATE BILLS

On May 20, 2021, a group of eight Republican state representatives introduced Senate Bill 460, "The revised school code," that required of school boards the following: (a) prohibit CRT, *The 1619 Project*, or any "anti-American" and "racist" theories; (b) withhold funds of 5% to school districts in violation of (a); and (c) report which districts and schools were in violation of (a).

The following month, on June 23, 2021, State Representative Andrew Beeler introduced House Bill 5097 to prohibit the teaching of CRT in K–12 schools. Beeler's (2001) framing of CRT was that it promoted race or gender "stereotyping":

> Students go to school to learn, and our curriculum should not be teaching students to stereotype each other based on race or gender or to view themselves or their country poorly as a result.... My plan will promote respect among Michigan students and patriotism for the United States and the opportunity it provides to all, regardless of one's background. (Beeler, 2021)

Opposition was swift. Two Democratic senators walked out of the House committee meeting before the bill was introduced, calling the bill "anti-truth." The State Superintendent of Michigan, Dr. Michael Rice (2021), declared in a statement about CRT:

Race and racism, integral parts of our country's history, should most assuredly be part of a comprehensive social studies curriculum. Educators have not just the right but the responsibility to teach the breadth of our history, and this history includes race and racism. (para. 4)

At the November 9, 2021, Detroit Public Schools Community District School Board Meeting, Superintendent Nikolai Vitti vigorously defended CRT in Detroit schools:

We were very intentional about creating a curriculum, infusing materials and embedding critical race theory within our curriculum…. Because students need to understand the truth of history, understand the history of this country, to better understand who they are and about the injustices that have occurred in this country. (Schemmel, 2021, para. 3)

The following year, the Michigan Education Association also expressed a stance against the anti-CRT legislation (Gustafson, 2022). Educators were largely united in their stances but many expressed concerns and fears related to this proposed legislation.

While we focus here on the events in Michigan, these anti-CRT bills are similar to ones introduced and passed in many states across the country. As of September 28, 2022, 44 states have taken steps toward limiting the discussion of racism in schools; 17 of those have enacted laws or legally binding action (Bissell, 2023; Schwartz, 2021). There is an anti-CRT wave across the country, leaving teachers vulnerable and restricting their autonomy and ability to teach full truths and histories in ways that are attentive to the knowledges, experiences, histories, and needs of students in their classrooms. This begs the question of how teacher educators might support teachers in K–12 classrooms as they do this critically important work?

WRITING A LOVE LETTER

In this section, we describe three moments in which we attempted to take action reflective of our institution's curricular framings and commitments: the founding of a university-sponsored learning community focused on anti-racist education, the process and challenges of taking a stand on proposed anti-CRT legislation through a "love letter," and the politics surrounding distributing the "love letter" to educators.

Founding of a Learning Community

In 2021, following calls for "real change" (from doctoral students in our department) in addressing whiteness and white supremacy in our department, college, and university, and building on prior accountability efforts through racial caucus groups, we worked together to form and develop an anti-racist learning community for faculty in our department. We imagined it as a collective space of joint responsibility and accountability work, directly responding to the concerns expressed by doctoral students related to harm enacted on doctoral Students of Color. These students, like many before them, called on white faculty to do better and be better; to reflect on how our actions uphold white supremacy; and to take action to educate ourselves, listen, and enact material changes at both individual and institutional levels.

We decided to formalize our efforts by applying for a "Learning Community" for the 2021–2022 academic year. Learning Communities at our institution provide spaces for complicated discussions about leadership and pedagogy; they are supported with a $500 grant and with opportunities to collaborate and learn from other Learning Communities. They are autonomous and run by the faculty leaders who propose and lead them. They can take a range of formats and operate with no administrative oversight. As the Learning Communities program director explained, "It's a space we designed to maximize autonomy and academic freedom" (Teachout, n.d.). All faculty were invited to participate in our Learning Community although we specifically targeted faculty identifying as white, as an affinity group, so that we could learn, grow, and hold each other without burdening Peers of Color with our missteps, ignorance, and microaggressions that white educators are prone to do.

During our monthly meetings, we read and analyzed letters and statements by students (often, but not entirely, by students of color) across departments at our institution and other universities to understand the harms being done and their specific demands for action. We shared strategies for centering anti-racist approaches into our courses (particularly through diversifying readings, rethinking what is considered "foundational," and revising course activities and assignments), considered ways to mentor and support students into the doctoral program and assistantships, among other ideas—with the hopes of working alongside other department members identifying as white to disrupt and re/imagine curricula, pedagogies, and frameworks rooted in whiteness, harm, and domination. At one meeting, a member expressed concern about the current proposed anti-CRT legislation in Michigan and together we realized that taking a stance was exactly the kind of work we should be leading. We began brainstorming action steps which included writing a love letter to educators

Writing a Love Letter to Educators in the Wake of Anti-CRT Efforts 77

(both aspiring and current) in the wake of proposed anti-CRT legislation. Our writing of a love letter was inspired and guided by the history of critical scholars and activists writing love letters of care and solidarity in the face of overwhelming oppression and political injustice (e.g., Baldwin, 1962; Coates, 2015; Dunn, 2021; Paris, 2020; Shalaby, 2017).

In the midst of this work, we faced an external threat that, in many ways, made even more evident how critical these efforts were. In December 2021, we learned that our learning community was referenced in an article with inaccurate information, in a conservative media outlet. The author argued that Learning Communities at our institution were funded with $1 million in taxpayer dollars. Our institution's response was to focus on the inaccurate and inflated amount of dollars ("the egregious overstatement of funding") rather than the heart of the issue, which was that our institution was being criticized for efforts related to anti-racist education and decentering whiteness. We believe that our institution, and institutions in general, *should* be standing behind and putting more money toward this work. As we continued our work, we saw how a focus on funding and moves away from taking a direct stance against systems of oppression and was indicative of what was to come.

~~Writing~~ and Editing the Love Letter.

What. The. F$&@!

I (Scott) muttered it once to myself as I read the text, and again out loud when I opened my laptop, and a third time, much louder, as I watched what was happening in real time. I hoped my kiddos didn't hear me.

It was after dinner, and I thought we had our draft in a good place. We had worked on it a long time, thinking about word placement, terms, flow, and overall message. But a colleague had let me know that a different (*senior*) colleague was in our document at this moment in time, changing wording. The texter wondered if I knew what was going on.

I didn't.

What. The. F$&@!

I tried to turn off editing access, angrily jabbing at my laptop keys, but it was no use–I didn't have access to the permissions due to an oversight. I couldn't change anything, so I sat there and watched helplessly as our words were highlighted and deleted and replaced and *erased*. It was painful to watch all of the meetings, conversations, and thought be struck and replaced so quickly.

But it wasn't the deleting and replacing itself that was a problem. As a member of the *academe* I am used to wordsmithing sessions and feedback and editing so that we can "move the work forward." What I didn't like about what was happening on the screen in front of me was the way our message was getting watered down and essentially *erased*.

Our group had been working hard to speak back to problematic education legislation that was being proposed in our state, and we wanted to take a strong stand in support of our teachers. We wrote a letter of love to teachers, detailing how we stand with them against things like ~~white supremacy~~ differences of opinions, ~~racism~~ hate, and ~~the specific bills that were being proposed~~ moves to potentially limit speech. We wanted to let them know that we as faculty would support them as they continued to teach ~~CRT~~ about diversity in their classrooms across the state. We wanted teachers to know that ~~the university stood with them~~ they were not alone.

The muttering and swearing was because of this watered-down whitewashing of the message we had set out to send. I immediately thought about the conversations we had in our last meeting.

We don't want to make too many waves …

We have to think about who will read this …

We need to be as broad as possible …

What. The F$&@!

The muttering continued a few days later in meetings with university administrative officials. The message was similar.

You can take a stand as individuals, but you see why we can't do this as a university …

We just don't want to get too political …

We have to think about all of our students and alumni …

The Dissemination of the Letter

Ugh…

I (Alex) opened my email. I knew what it was going to say before I even began reading. It was about our letter. It said that there were "implications" that we had to take into account before we could even think about making a collective statement from an institutional body. The email went on to explain that we could always share the letter as individuals.

There was a line being drawn and it was frustrating, but not surprising. And it sure hurt.

I teach foundations classes with Scott that are based around a stated commitment to justice and critical race and anti-colonial frameworks. Our letter of love was just a request that the college stand behind our curriculum and our graduates who teach in the ways we prepare them. And we were getting shut down. We wrote in our letter:

> As individuals working in the number one-ranked programs in elementary and secondary education…. We commit to continue teaching tenets of CRT in our teacher preparation and graduate courses, and will continue to provide resources to teachers like you on antiracist teaching…. And we know this is not enough, and we will continue to find ways to do better as we stand by your side in this work…

This was work we had committed to doing in our department. It was in our core curriculum. This should be a College statement. We were not some ragtag group of misfits; this work came from our scholarship, teaching, and what we thought was a shared commitment from the university. Besides, a statement is a small thing. Or so we thought.

While I anticipated *hesitancy* towards sending out this public letter, when we met virtually the next month with administrators, I was surprised by the entrenched *resistance*. My heart was pounding. As I signed into the virtual meeting.

Breathe.

Black boxes. On the hour, faces appeared. I held my breath. Then the words flowed just as we knew they would.

You are welcome to take stances as individuals …

But it would be hard to support this from a collective position …

We need to be mindful of donor s…

We should think about institutional dynamics …

What about the timing of this?

This seems very political …

It didn't seem to matter that CRT was the core of our courses and the work of many scholars in the college. That we prepare our students to understand that all teaching is political. Or that our Learning Community was explicit in sharing that we were going to do this work.

At one point we were asked to maybe lead a webinar instead of sharing the letter and I angrily texted my colleague "I guess they think we can webinar our way out of white supremacy."

After 30 minutes, we finally got to respond to their objections.

The timing was exactly when it had to be.

We shouldn't be beholden to donors.

Our institution needs to support our stances and Students of Color in general.

We had taken political stances before.

This is political and we need to take a stand on this.

We had written a letter of love to teachers because the work of anti-racism and decoloniality is rooted in love. Through the void of Zoom, it was made abundantly and absolutely clear that the college would not put out the statement; we would have to do it on our own, because of "academic freedom." As we texted back and forth during the meeting and debriefed afterwards, it clear that the idea of academic freedom that we were being given was a "lackey" (Patel, 2018) standing on firmly neoliberal grounds; we would be (reluctantly) supported as individuals in our statement, but the institution would not support a collective work, framing, and statement— that was too dangerous or political.

Breathe.

What. The F$&@!

LESSONS LEARNED AND IMPLICATIONS FOR CURRICULUM

In thinking about the intersections between anti-racist pedagogies and academic freedom, we are struck by the irony of what it means to do anti-racist work under the guise of academic freedom without support from or in opposition to the institution. Taken together, the three moments we presented illuminate how the framework of academic freedom provided by the university was not about protecting *faculty* doing anti-racist work, but rather protecting the *institution* from having to take a stand on the work it was paying faculty to do in order to appear "safe" and "neutral" for white students and donors. CRT scholars critique notions of objectivity and neutrality and make clear the ways such logics that work to frame the world as good, just, and "rational" and racism as an individual, rather than a systemic, issue uphold and maintain white supremacy (Crenshaw et al., 1995; Delgado 1983, 1992; López, 2003). Race neutral language, like that with which we were confronted, has an actively exclusionary effect (Haney-López, 2000). We were not sure if the specter of the donors was based on particular donors' political stance, or a feeling that wealthy donors invested in the institution as it is; either way this discourse worked as a mechanism to resist change and uphold white settler claims to the university space and knowledge and supports Grande's (2018) theorization of the university "as an arm of the settler state—a site where the logics of elimination, capital accumulation, and dispossession are reconstituted" (p. 47). Together, the three moments make visible how these played out through silences and silencing to reveal the ways such logics continue to undergird our land-grab institution.

Theories like CRT and CWS make visible the ways the pushback we received in explicit and implicit forms from our institution are connected to and illustrative of larger patterns and structures of power and oppression (Gillborn, 2005; Harris, 1993; Leonardo, 2004). They also show us that the "racialized script of silence" we encountered is often found within large institutions such as ours—especially as they use those scripts to maintain the status quo of power (Valiavska & Meisenbach, 2023, p. 1). The hesitance of the institution to stand behind anti-racist work and take a stance worked to "protect the idea of a neutral social order" (López, 2003, p. 69) and demonstrates the "political power of Whiteness" (Matias & Mackey, 2016, p. 35) found within the institution. This understanding has led scholars to question if the university is "beyond reform" (Grande, 2018, p. 49). While we were aware of these in theory, we experienced these things in action in a new way–perhaps a nod to our own limitations and experiences as white educators, as we are also complicit and complacent within these larger systems due to our own whiteness (Allen, 2004)—and this was exactly why we were engaging in this work in the first place.

However, when we pushed to move these messages outside the proverbial walls of the university, the institution was not prepared to take a collective stance, revealing its foundational commitments. Instead, the institution offered us academic freedom to do what we wanted as *individuals*. Faculty could be activists, but the university needed to remain neutral with regard to particular legislation. The question of whether, and if so how, institutions should take a stand on controversial issues is unresolved (Lu, 2022). However, we question why institutions do not align themselves with policies and laws that reflect their *own* values and missions and disavow those that do not. The courses at the university we teach center CRT; the

Learning Community was developed and sanctioned by the university; our department's core principles explicitly center social justice. We strive to enact anti-racist pedagogy, de-/anti-colonial frameworks, and CWS not only in our coursework and scholarship but also in our service.

These particular politics of institutional neutrality draped in claims of academic freedom are connected to neoliberal ideals of accountability to money, power, and white ignorance; they also raise questions about not just who has access to academic freedom (Jeppesen & Nazar, 2012), but what (and for whom?) is academic freedom even for? And what counts as "too political?" These processes made clear the harmful attempts to bifurcate love and politics (e.g., Ahmed, 2013; hooks, 2001; Lanas & Zembylas, 2014). The doublespeak of academic freedom is that the institution is permitted to claim that faculty have autonomy to do and say what they want, while also allowing that claim to release them from protecting the individuals doing the work already being sanctioned by the same institution. If universities are not willing to collectively take a stand about racist education policies, what are the consequences for classroom teachers?

CONCLUDING THOUGHTS

The political climate in Michigan is not as hostile toward educators as it is in other states. While anti-CRT legislation has been proposed, it is guaranteed to dead-end with the Democratic governor, at least for now. However, the threat of anti-CRT legislation has sent a chill down the spines of educators across the country: nearly 25% of teachers report changing their lesson plans in the wake of anti-CRT laws (Woo et al., 2022). As teacher educators committed to anti-racist teaching, we are unnerved as we think about how we are preparing our students for their own future classrooms where our work might not be condoned by the university.

Institutions of higher education need to reconcile their commitments to students, particularly those from marginalized backgrounds, with their policies that impose curricular violence on students. Whereas many professional academic and community organizations have expressed direct opposition to these kinds of education policies, many institutions including ours have remained silent. And to be clear, the sharing of a statement of support in this situation is the *absolute bare minimum* required to do the work. A support statement is the first necessary step towards real change— it is not in and of itself the end of the work that needs to be done.

What happened with the dissemination attempts regarding our letter is not unique. The problems we highlight here extend beyond our own institution and call attention to the kinds of pressures individual faculty and public institutions face regarding taking a political stance. In the end, we collected over 70 signatures from faculty, staff, and students, but as individuals, rather than as a collective. Our struggles made visible various institutional limits, or walls (Ahmed, 2012), including concerns about alienating donors and being too political. While it is powerful to have a collective of individual voices showing love and demanding change, the lack of support from the institution was troubling, particularly as we think about how the weaving of the two stances (individual and institutional) can bring systemic change. One without the other on its own will not lead to the necessary systemic change towards justice. Protecting students from harm and standing behind our anti-racist ideals should not be dismissed as too political—it is authentic, honest, and necessary for justice. It is what our students, particularly those embarking on a career in education, deserve.

REFERENCES

Ahmed, S. (2012). *On being included*. Duke University Press.

Ahmed, S. (2013). *The cultural politics of emotion*. Routledge.

Allen, R. L. (2004). Whiteness and critical pedagogy. *Educational Philosophy and Theory*, 36(2), 121–136. https://doi.org/10.1111/j.1469-5812.2004.00056.x

Andreotti, V. D. O. (2021). Depth education and the possibility of GCE otherwise. *Globalisation, Societies and Education*, 19(4), 496–509. https://doi.org/10.1080/14767724.2021.1904214

Baldwin, J. (1962, January 1). A letter to my nephew. *The Progressive*. https://progressive.org/magazine/letter-nephew/

Baldwin, J. (1998). A talk to teachers. In T. Morrison (Ed.), *Baldwin: Collected essays* (pp. 678–686). The Library of America. (Original work published 1963)

Beeler, M. (2022). Rep. Beeler introduces plan to prohibit critical race theory in K–12 curriculum. https://gophouse.org/posts/rep-beeler-introduces-plan-to-prohibit-critical-race-theory-in-k-12-curriculum

Bissell, T. (2023). Teaching in the upside down: What anti-critical race theory laws tell us about the first amendment. *Stanford Law Review 75*, 205–259. https://review.law.stanford.edu/wp-content/uploads/sites/3/2023/01/Bissell-75-Stan.-L.-Rev.-205.pdf

Coates, T. N. (2015). *Between the world and me*. Spiegel and Grau.

Crenshaw, K., Gotanda, N., Peller, G., & Thomas, K. (Eds.). (1995). *Critical race theory: The key writings that formed the movement*. The New Press.

Delgado R. (1983). Imperial scholar: reflections on a review of civil rights literature. *University of Pennsylvania Law Rev.*, *132*(3), 561–578. https://doi.org/10.2307/3311882

Delgado R. (1992). The imperial scholar revisited: How to marginalize outsider writing, ten years later. *University of Pennsylvania Law Rev.*, *140*(4), 1349–1372. https://doi.org/10.2307/3312406

Delgado, R., & Stefancic, J. (2012). *Critical race theory: An introduction*. New York University Press.

Dunn, A. H. (2021). *Teaching on days after: Educating for equity in the wake of injustice*. Teachers College Press.

Gillborn, D. (2005). Education policy as an act of white supremacy: Whiteness, critical race theory and education reform. *Journal of Education Policy, 20*(4), 485–505. https://doi.org/10.1080/02680930500132346

Gillborn, D. (2006). Rethinking white supremacy: Who counts in "whiteworld." *Ethnicities, 6*(3), 318–340. https://doi.org/10.1177/1468796806068323

Gordon, D. (2020). The firing of Angela Davis at UCA, 1969-1970: Communism, academic freedom, and freedom of speech. *Culture and Society, 57*, 596–613. https://doi.org/10.1007/s12115-020-00554-8

Grande, S. (2018). Refusing the university. In E. Tuck & K. W. Yang (Eds.), *Toward what justice?: Describing diverse dreams of justice in education* (pp. 47–65). Routledge.

Gustafson, A., (2022). *Senate Republicans advance anti-CRT bill that educators say will censor teachers*. Michigan Advance. https://michiganadvance.com/2022/06/07/senate-republicans-advance-anti-crt-bill-that-educators-say-will-censor-teachers/

Haney-López, I. F. (2000). Institutional racism: Judicial conduct and a new theory of racial discrimination. *Yale Law Journal, 109*(8), 1717–1884. https://doi.org/10.2307/797509

Harris, C. I. (1993). Whiteness as property. *Harvard Law Review, 106*(8), 1707–1791. https://doi.org/10.2307/1341787

hooks, B. (2001). *All about love: New visions*. Harper Perennial.

Jeppesen, S., & Nazar, H. (2012). Beyond academic freedom: Canadian neoliberal universities in the global context. *TOPIA: Canadian Journal of Cultural Studies, 28*, 87–113. https://doi.org/10.3138/topia.28.87

Kalven, H., Franklin, J., Kolb, G., Stigler, G., Getzels, J., Goldsmith, J., & White, G. (1967). Kalven committee: Report on the University's role in political and social action. *The University of Chicago Record, 1*(1). https://provost.uchicago.edu/sites/default/files/documents/reports/KalvenRprt_0.pdf

King, T. L. (2019). *The Black shoals: Offshore formations of Black and Native studies*. Duke University Press.

Kishimoto, K. (2018). Anti-racist pedagogy: from faculty's self-reflection to organizing within and beyond the classroom. *Race Ethnicity and Education, 21*(4), 540–554. https://doi.org.10.1080/13613324.2016.1248824

Ladson-Billings, G. (1995). Toward a theory of culturally relevant pedagogy. *American educational research journal, 32*(3), 465–491. https://doi.org/10.2307/1163320

Ladson-Billings, G. (2009). *Dreamkeepers* (2nd ed.). Jossey-Bass.

Ladson-Billings, G. (2014). Culturally relevant pedagogy 2.0: a.k.a. the remix. *Harvard Educational Review, 84*(1), 74–84. https://doi.org/10.2307/1163320

Ladson-Billings, G., & Tate, W. F. (1995). Toward a critical race theory of education. *Teachers College Record, 97*(1), 11–30. https://doi.org/10.1177/01614681950970010

Lanas, M., & Zembylas, M. (2014). Towards a transformational political concept of love in critical education. *Studies in Philosophy and Education, 34*(1), 31–44.

Lee, R., & Ahtone, T. (2020, March). *Land-grab universities*. High Country News. https://www.hcn.org/issues/52.4/indigenous-affairs-education-land-grab-universities

Leonardo, Z. (2004). The color of supremacy: Beyond the discourse of 'white privilege'. *Educational Philosophy and Theory, 36*(2), 137–152. https://doi.org/10.1111/j.1469-5812.2004.00057.x

Leonardo, Z. (2009). *Race, whiteness, and education*. Routledge.

López, G. R. (2003). The (racially neutral) politics of education: A critical race theory perspective. *Educational Administration Quarterly, 39*(1), 68–94. https://doi.org/10.1177/0013161X02239761

Lu, A., (2022). The apolitical university: Should institutions remain neutral on controversial issues? Is that even possible? *The Chronicle of Higher Education*. https://www.chronicle.com/article/the-apolitical-university

Matias, C. E. (2013). Check yo'self before you wreck yo'self and our kids: Counter-stories from culturally responsive white teachers?... To culturally responsive white teachers! *Interdisciplinary Journal of Teaching and Learning, 3*(2), 68–81.

Matias, C. E. (2016). *Feeling white: Whiteness, emotionality, and education*. Brill.

Matias, C. E., & Boucher, C. (2021). From critical whiteness studies to a critical study of whiteness: Restoring criticality in critical whiteness studies. *Whiteness and Education, 8*(1), 64–81. https://doi.org/10.1080/23793406.2021.1993751

Matias, C. E., & Mackey, J. (2016). Breakin' down whiteness in antiracist teaching: Introducing critical whiteness pedagogy. *Urban Review, 48*(1), 32–50. https://doi.org/10.1007/s11256-015-0344-7

Mawhinney, L. (2012). Othermothering: A personal narrative exploring relationships between black female faculty and students. *Negro Educational Review, 62/63*(1–4), 213–232.

Nash, R. (2019). *Liberating scholarly writing: The power of personal narrative*. Information Age Publishing.

Nash, R. J., & Viray, S. (2013). The who, what, and why of scholarly personal narrative writing. *Counterpoints, 446*, 1–9. https://www.jstor.org/stable/42982209

Paperson, l. (2017). *A third university is possible*. University of Minnesota Press.

Paris, D. (2012). Culturally sustaining pedagogy: A needed change in stance, terminology, and practice. *Educational Researcher, 41*(3), 93–97.

Paris, D., & Alim, H. S. (2014). What are we seeking to sustain through culturally sustaining pedagogy? A loving critique forward. *Harvard Educational Review, 84*(1), 85–100. https://doi.org/10.17763/haer.84.1.982l873k2ht16m77

Paris, R. (2020). How "An open letter of love to Black students: # BlackLivesMatter" came to be. In A. Eagle Shield, D. Paris, R. Paris, & T. San Pedro (Eds.), *Education in movement spaces* (pp. 119–132). Routledge.

Parsons, L. T., & Pinkerton, L. (2022). Poetry and prose as methodology: A synergy of knowing. *Methodological Innovations, 15*(2), 118–126. https://doi.org/10.1177/20597991221087150

Patel, L. (2018). When justice is a lackey. In E. Tuck & K. W. Yang (Eds.), *Toward what justice?* (pp. 101–112). Routledge.

Quijano, A. (2000). Coloniality of power and Eurocentrism in Latin America. *International Sociology, 15*(2), 215–232. https://doi.org/10.1177/02685809000150020

Reichman, H. (2019). *Understanding academic freedom.* Johns Hopkins University Press.

Rice, M. F. (2021, August 10). *Reflections on critical race theory, race, racism, other isms, and the teaching of history.* State Board of Education Meeting. https://www.michigan.gov/-/media/Project/Websites/mde/Year/2021/08/10/Race_and_Racism_August_2021.pdf?rev=d6626b10e32d42f09c07ca41a2f70c2a

Schemmel, A., (2021). Detroit superintendent says district was 'intentional' about 'embedding' CRT in schools. *Komo News.* https://komonews.com/news/nation-world/detroit-superintendent-says-district-was-intentional-about-embedding-crt-into-schools

Schwartz, S. (2021). Who's really driving critical race theory legislation? An investigation. *Education Week.* https://www.edweek.org/policy-politics/whos-really-driving-critical-race-theory-legislation-an-investigation/2021/07

Shalaby, C. (2017). *Troublemakers: Lessons in freedom from young children at school.* The New Press.

Sleeter, C. E. (2017). Critical race theory and the whiteness of teacher education. *Urban Education, 52*(2), 155–169. https://doi.org/10.1177/00420859166689

Teachout, G. (n.d.). *MSU Learning communities are spaces to explore ideas in education, teaching, and learning.* https://iteach.msu.edu/iteachmsu/groups/iteachmsu/stories/1085?param=post

Thobani, S. (2003). War and the politics of truth-making in Canada. *International Journal of Qualitative Studies in Education, 16*(3), 399–414. https://doi.org/10.1080/0951839032000086754

Valiavska, A & Meisenbach R. (2023) Racialized scripts of silence: How whiteness organizes silence as a response to social protest about racism in the United States, *Journal of Applied Communication Research*, 1–20. https://doi.org/10.1080/00909882.2023.2169888

Will, M. (2022). What should culturally relevant teaching look like today? Gloria Ladson-Billings explains. *Education Week.* https://www.edweek.org/leadership/what-should-culturally-relevant-teaching-look-like-today-gloria-ladson-billings-explains/2022/04

Woo, A., Wolfe, R. L., Steiner, E. D., Doan, S., Lawrence, R. A., Berdie, L., Greer, L., Gittens, A. D., & Schwart, H. L. (2022). *Walking a fine line—Educators' views on politicized topics in schooling.* RAND Corporation. https://www.rand.org/pubs/research_reports/RRA1108-5.html

CHAPTER 4

MAKING SENSE
OF THE MESSAGE

The Perceptions and Impact of State
Legislation that Challenges the Teaching
of Hard History

Debby Shulsky, Sheila Baker, and Renée E. Lastrapes
University of Houston–Clear Lake

ABSTRACT

In December 2021, Texas lawmakers passed a bill related to the national debate and politicization of critical race theory (CRT). Texas Senate Bill 3 seemingly limits the teaching of "sensitive" topics. These perceived limitations may present challenges for social studies teachers in the state. This study examines the knowledge and perspectives of social studies educators regarding Texas SB 3 and its impact on Texas 6-12 social studies teachers' classroom pedagogy.

American politics is rooted in a history of eras in which polarized beliefs caused division among the citizenry. From our early years as a nation, our leaders were in conflict over the foundational structures of the American government. Additional dissension is evident across the timeline of

---

Curriculum and Teaching Dialogue,
Volume 25, Numbers 1 & 2, pp. 87–114
Copyright © 2023 by Information Age Publishing
www.infoagepub.com
All rights of reproduction in any form reserved.

American history. This includes events such as the Civil and Vietnam Wars and issues regarding the integration of American institutions and the country's immigration policies. In most recent history, the political culture of America has become exceedingly divisive over the course of the last three presidential campaigns and elections. This discordant environment has been further complicated by the prevalence of the "widespread use and circulation of misinformation" (Kahne & Bowyer, 2017, p. 7). Within this milieu, controversy has emerged around the definition, tenets, and pervasiveness of critical race theory (CRT). As a reaction to this public debate, legislation banning CRT within schools' curricula has been passed across the nation.

In September 2020, under the direction of President Donald Trump, the Office of Management and Budget issued a memo to federal agencies with the concluding sentence: "The divisive, false, and demeaning propaganda of the critical race theory movement is contrary to all we stand for as Americans and should have no place in the Federal government" (Office of Management and Budget, 2020, p. 2). This memo was the catalyst for subsequent declarations regarding the presence of CRT within institutions across the nation.

In 2021, the University of California Los Angeles (UCLA) School of Law's Critical Race Studies Program (CRS) began the CRT Forward project in an effort to "address the current attacks on Critical Race Theory while also highlighting the past, present, and future contributions of the theory" (UCLA Law, n.d.a, para. 1). The data presented within the CRT Forward project reports that "since September of 2020, a total of 203 local, state, and federal government entities across the United States have introduced 619 anti-Critical Race Theory (anti-CRT) bills, resolutions, executive orders, opinion letters, statements, and other measures" (UCLA Law, n.d.b, para. 1). Specific to the field of education, 35 states filed 137 bills in 2022 that restrict what teachers are allowed to teach (Sachs, 2022).

Like other states across the nation, in 2020, Texas lawmakers introduced numerous anti-CRT legislation and passed Senate Bill 3 (SB 3) in December 2021. The intent of Texas Senate Bill 3, as noted in its Author/ Sponsor's Statement of Intent, is to "update civics and social studies curriculum and instruction and prohibit the teaching of critical race theory and its elements" (The Texas Senate, 2021, p. 1). Many elements of SB 3 positively impact social studies curricula (e.g., development and attention to civics education). However, other elements of the legislation are considered by some as censorship of curricula within the social studies disciplines. SB 3 (2021) prohibits teachers from: (a) being compelled to discuss current events or controversial issues; (b) awarding grades or extra credit for work or service with any organizations involved in lobbying, social or public advocacy, or political activism (does not include service in nonpartisan, community-based projects); (c) being required to participate in training centered around race or sex stereotyping; and (d) teaching that one race or sex is superior or to be blamed or made to feel guilty for past actions against others.

The passage of this bill fueled contradicting narratives regarding the purpose and meaning of the bill as well as the curricular and teaching implications for the educational community in Texas. These contradicting narratives resulted from a vaguely written bill that allows for a breadth of interpretations of its intent and meaning. This quote from the Texas AFT, the state chapter of the American Federation of Teachers, illustrated the contradicting narratives surrounding the bill.

> The bill is part of a national movement by conservatives trying to sow a narrative of students being indoctrinated by teachers. Our members rightfully have expressed outrage against this insult of their professionalism to provide balanced conversations with students on controversial issues. (McGee, 2021, para. 11)

The author of the bill, Republican Senator Bryan Hughes explained, "Our classrooms should be places for fostering a diverse and fact-based discussion of various perspectives.... They're not for planting seeds for a divisive political agenda" (KVUE News Staff, 2021, para. 9). Ironically, Hughes said classrooms are not places for divisive political agendas; however, SB 3 grew out of a political agenda focused on making CRT a political and divisive issue.

Nearly a year after SB 3 was enacted, those impacted by the law were struggling to make sense of the bill. In an effort to offer clarification and guidance centered around the bill, Senator Hughes appeared before the Texas State Board of Education to explain the law he authored:

> That bill is not an attempt to sanitize or to teach our history in any other way than the truth—the good, the bad and the ugly—and those difficult things that we've been through and those things we've overcome. (Lopez, 2022, para. 4)

The Senator went on to say,

> We still teach that really bad things were done by people of particular races, and it may be that in teaching those things, students may feel guilty about that.... What we're saying is you don't say, "Little Johnny, little Jimmy, you should feel bad because of what your forebears did." (Lopez, 2022, para. 8)

In his attempt to try to clarify things, the senator, inadvertently, insulted the professionalism of Texas teachers while failing to clarify how teachers are to teach critical analysis of all perspectives within the constraints of a vaguely worded piece of legislation. Texas Board of Education member, Aicha Davis, seemed to understand the fears and frustrations of Texas teachers, "We always talk about teachers leaving in droves and this was one of the reasons.... Teachers were literally scared to teach even the TEKS (Texas Essential Knowledge and Skills) that existed because of this" (McGee, 2021, para. 13). This presents a challenge among teachers given that the TEKS are the state standards that Texas teachers are expected to address within their curriculum. How to approach the teaching of these standards is a real obstacle to demystifying the intentions of SB 3.

The impact of public discourse regarding the legislation led to a state of confusion for all stakeholders. The politicization of CRT within national politics further complicated public understanding of the bill and promoted the misinformed notion that CRT is being taught in Texas schools. This led to ensuing controversy and divisiveness. Within this context, no clear path for educators on the front line exists to help them understand and integrate the tenets of SB 3 into their teaching practice. As a result of the vague and contradictory information encompassing SB 3, we explored the level at which Texas social studies teachers understood SB 3. Therefore, the purpose of this study was to examine the knowledge and perspectives of social studies educators regarding Texas SB 3 and its impact on Texas 6–12 social studies teachers' classroom pedagogy.

In light of similar legislation across the nation, this study will offer insight for social studies teachers nationwide regarding their understanding of similar legislation within their own states and, most importantly, how these laws impact their teaching and curricular decisions. Legislation enacted as a result of the politicization of CRT is prevalent within a majority of states in America. Understanding the impact of such laws on the curricula decisions of teachers is important. Lawmakers need to understand the positive and negative repercussions of legislation directed toward educational institutions. Educational leaders require insight into how they can support teachers in maintaining best practices in social studies education while still upholding such laws. As a result of SB 3, Texas social studies teachers are navigating the complex and uncertain impact this bill has had on their approach to teaching social studies. To determine if social studies teachers understand SB 3 and how it will impact their practice, this study was guided by the following research questions:

1. To what extent do Texas 6–12 Social Studies teachers understand SB 3?
2. To what extent does the passage of SB 3 directly impact Texas social studies teachers' pedagogy related to the teaching of

sensitive/controversial topics and what supports have teachers received?

3. Is there an association between gender and level of comfort teaching controversial topics since the passage of SB 3?
4. Is there an association between political identity and comfort in teaching controversial topics since the passage of SB 3?
5. What are the participants' responses to the open-ended survey questions regarding their comfort levels in teaching sensitive topics and the impact of SB 3 on curricular choices and teaching?

LITERATURE REVIEW

Historically, matters centered upon the education of American children have garnered national attention and debate (Teitelbaum, 2022). In the late 1930s and early 1940s, conservatives opposed the use of Harold Rugg's progressively centered social studies textbook series (Evans, 2007). Conservatives labeled Rugg's work as "un-American." Rugg understood that his texts may be viewed as controversial; however, placating his critics would ensure that American children would be educated by texts that "suppresse[d] facts about controversial questions" (Dorn, 2007, p. 469).

In the 1970s, a humanities teaching program, Man: A Course of Study (MACOS), based on the theories of Jerome Bruner spurred controversy (Teitelbaum, 2022). The curriculum was criticized for its emphasis on questioning aspects of the American tradition (Evans, 2011).

Another debate occurred after the development of the Common Core State Standards Initiative in 2009, which established a new set of national standards in English language arts and mathematics (Teitelbaum, 2022). Opponents of the Common Core claimed the standards failed in several ways, including supporting students with special needs; lacking rigor compared to previous standards; broad and vague language; an increased value placed on standardized test performance; and inequity in discipline standards (Meador, 2018).

The latest controversy is centered around anti-CRT bills that have been enacted in states across the nation. These bills impose a variety of forms of censorship upon teachers, including limitations on what social studies teachers can teach; the banning of certain topics related to sex, gender, race, religion, sexual orientation or gender identity; limiting classroom discussions on controversial topics; banning any curriculum that creates feelings of "discomfort or guilt" (p. 1); and banning any materials that contradict certain approved versions of U.S. history (Greene, 2022, New Mexico section). The following is a review of the literature in the areas of teacher responses to anti-CRT legislation and the nature of the social studies curriculum.

Teacher Responses to Anti-CRT Legislation

When implementing a new policy, one's perception of the policy may be more important than the policy itself (Wronowski, 2018). The perceptions of a policy can have a direct impact on how it is implemented. In the case of anti-CRT legislation, implementation of the laws is even more complicated due to the vagueness and political narrative surrounding such state mandates. Educators across the nation have responded to anti-CRT legislation in a variety of ways.

In 2022, the *State of the American Teacher Survey* and the *State of the American Principal Survey* highlighted early reaction to the intent of anti-CRT legislation. The surveys indicated that 54% of teachers and principals believed classroom discussions about race and other contentious topics should not be restricted (Woo et al., 2022). In 2022, the RAND Corporation surveyed over 8,000 educators across the country about state mandated classroom censorship policies and the impact on teacher curricular decisions. Interestingly, the study found that roughly one-fourth of participants surveyed did not know if they were impacted by the restrictions imposed by such laws (Lehrer-Small, 2023). In states where censorship laws were enacted, fewer than one third of educators knew the laws had been passed.

The findings of the 2022 *American Instruction Resources Survey* indicated one in four educators aware of anti-CRT laws in their state altered their curricula in order to avoid parents' and officials' potential judgment that their curricula is controversial (Woo et al., 2023). This survey highlights that teachers in states without restrictive laws are also impacted by this national legislative trend. In states that do not have censorship bills, 22% of teachers are reconsidering their resources and modifying their instructional practices. Comparatively, 28% of teachers in states with enacted restrictions have done the same. More specifically, 50% of social studies teachers in states with restrictive bills have reconsidered their approaches to their practice. In states free of such curricula limitations, 38% of social studies teachers have shifted their curricula choices (Woo et al., 2023). Overall, participants indicated concern about the impact of the legal constraints on their curricula and student learning.

Woo et al. (2023) noted that nearly one in five teachers integrate topics related to race or gender within their lessons. Roughly one third of teachers admitted they strongly emphasize such topics "because or in spite of" the directives of restrictive legislation (Woo et al., 2023, p. 22). In states where there was no such legislation, teachers felt the need to create a safe learning environment for their own students. Consequently, these teachers have become more deliberate about using diverse materials as well as censored materials deemed "dangerous" in states with laws limiting curriculum (Woo et al., 2023, p. 22). Regardless of the state in which educators teach, 8,679 have signed the Zinn Education Project's (2022) "Pledge to Tell the Truth," proclaiming:

> We the undersigned educators will not be bullied. We will continue our commitment to develop critical thinking that supports students to better understand problems in our society, and to develop collective solutions to those problems. We are for truth-telling and uplifting the power of organizing and solidarity that move us toward a more just society. (p. 1)

The common factor among teachers who outwardly ignore the anti-CRT laws is their commitment to diversity, honoring their students' identities, and providing a safe learning environment for all. As these types of restrictive laws continue to be enacted, teachers face an environment compounded by multiple perspectives and directives from a variety of stakeholders on which they must make decisions about how to navigate their daily work as a teacher (Woo et al., 2023).

Nature of the Social Studies Curriculum

Undergirding the anxiety and confusion around SB 3 is the nature of the social studies curriculum. Social studies consist of various disciplines centered on the exploration of social relationships and societal functions. Undoubtedly, the disciplines under the social studies umbrella are fraught with topics that may be labeled as hard. As Charles Beard (1929) explained about the discipline of social studies:

> It will be said that the growth of social studies places on teachers an impossible burden, it compels them to deal with controversial questions.... They are in a different position from that of a teacher of Latin or mathematics.... The subject matter of their instruction is infinitely difficult and it is continually changing. (p. 372)

Hard History

Hard history is a reality for social studies educators and includes such difficult topics as equal rights, nuclear warfare, and the treatment of Native Americans. These topics may be labeled *hard*, meaning they are hard to teach due to the uncomfortable revelations and inquiries they present.

Goldberg (2020) explained, "Difficult histories expose learners to historical suffering and victimization that constitute a collective trauma. The difficulty stems from the strong emotional reactions or ethical responses learners may evince, undermining their trust in security and morality of this world" (p. 130). The challenge in identifying hard history topics is caused by the lens through which one approaches these topics based on their lived experiences and perspectives. A topic considered difficult by one may not be considered difficult by another (Goldberg, 2020). As one would expect, perspectives differ based on positionality, identity, and background schema (Zembylas & Loukaidis, 2021), all of which can solicit emotional reactions to topics from some that others would interpret as simply facts (Baker et al., 2022; Gross & Terra, 2018).

The passage of SB 3, as well as its predecessor Texas House Bill 3979, has caused confusion regarding the manner in which hard history should be approached. This confusion was publicly exposed when a school district in the Dallas metropolitan area made the national news (Hixenbaugh & Hylton, 2021). At a district-wide training regarding the curation of classroom libraries, teachers were guided to include multiple perspectives within their literature selections. In an effort to provide an example of which books teachers can have in classroom libraries, the school district's executive director of curriculum and instruction directed teachers to provide students with access to books that contain opposing views. After being provided with the Holocaust as an example, one teacher asked how one might include other perspectives on such a horrific event as the Nazi annihilation of approximately six million Jews. This led to others' concerns about the need for the removal of historical novels told from the singular perspective when books with a counter perspective are not available. The dialogue that emerged from this training illustrates the lack of clarity regarding the interpretation of such legislative directives and the concerns of educators who are expected to adhere to curricular mandates.

Controversy

In its simplest form, controversy is a prolonged heated debate resulting from a disagreement on a given topic. Diana Hess (2009) further distinguished controversy as "contention that emerges from real-life—authentic—topics" (as cited in Lintner, 2018, p. 14). Hess and McAvoy (2015) suggested that the controversy of an issue can be considered as either open or settled. An open issue requires many evidenced-based viewpoints and is highly and publicly debated, "appearing on ballots, in courts, within political platforms, in legislative chambers, and as part of political movements" (Hess & McAvoy, 2015, pp. 168–169). A settled issue is one that has moved beyond controversy, as those in debate have reached a general agreement with the discussants providing rational justification for their decision. Given hindsight, controversial topics may shift from being a settled issue to an open issue and back again, depending on the zeitgeist of the time (Hess & McAvoy, 2015).

As already established, hard history is a natural component of the social studies curriculum. This notion, coupled with the erratic nature of what topics are deemed controversial, places social studies teachers in a precarious situation regarding what current controversial issues they will address in their classrooms and how they will approach the exploration of such topics. This is and has been, a prevailing struggle for many social studies educators. Literature on the teaching of controversial issues highlights a host of justifications for the challenges teachers face when addressing such charged topics with their students (Hess, 2005; Journell, 2013a). The reasons for teachers' trepidation and, most often, avoidance of addressing contentious issues within their classrooms include a lack of knowledge and training (Hinde, 2004; Journell, 2013b; Lintner, 2018; Oulton et al., 2004; Philpott et al., 2011) and fear of repercussions and pressure from stakeholders (Byford et al., 2009; Journell, 2017; Lintner, 2018). Other barriers that impact teachers' willingness to speak about controversial issues may include their level of self-awareness and regulation of bias (Hinde, 2004), lack of exposure to teaching practices that promote discourse on hard topics, fidelity to a standards-based curriculum (Hinde, 2004), consideration of student sensitivity, and fear of unintended offense towards others (Journell, 2017; Philpott et al., 2011).

SB 3 addresses the teaching of controversial issues directly in Sec. 28.0022. CERTAIN INSTRUCTIONAL REQUIREMENTS AND PROHIBITIONS.

> (a) For any course or subject, including an innovative course, for a grade level from kindergarten through grade 12: (1) a teacher may not be compelled to discuss a widely debated and currently controversial issue of public policy or social affairs; (2) a teacher who chooses to discuss a topic described by Subdivision (1) shall explore that topic objectively and in a manner free from political bias. (A Bill to be Entitled, 2021, p. 7)

At face value the guidance within the bill seems straightforward—you can choose to teach a charged issue or not. However, labeling an issue as controversial is not a straightforward process (Hess & McAvoy, 2015; Shulsky & Baker, 2022). It can be subjective and is most often impacted by the community context and, most recently, the divisive political climate. In the end, there can be significant dissension about labeling an issue as controversial. The impact of this complex identification process may further justify Texas teachers' complete avoidance of teaching contentious topics.

As Hinde (2004) noted, teachers avoid engagement with controversial issues due to distrust in their ability to constantly identify and monitor their own biases. In deeply divisive times, what one says may be highly scrutinized to the point of villainization. Within such unforgiving environments, teachers may second guess their ability to effectively manage their political bias and decide to avoid placing themselves in such vulnerable positions. This is unfortunate since active engagement in the art of civil discourse is an essential skill for citizens in a healthy democracy, especially during contentious times (Lintner, 2018). Teachers' decisions to avoid opportunities to engage students in discussion on controversial issues inefficiently prepare students for the reality of living in a democratic society. Hess (2018) reiterated this point: "The stakes, after all, are exceptionally high: empowering young Americans to become active participants—and to co-exist peacefully—in a pluralistic society brimming with opposing views" (p. 306). This highlights the need for the development of civic literacy in our schools and is emphasized by the inclusivity of civic education in SB 3. On this point, a lack of clarity regarding SB 3 may cause a curricular and pedagogical dilemma for social studies teachers.

Theoretical Framework

This study is framed within the sensemaking theory developed by Karl Weick in the 1970s and introduced to organizational studies in 1995 (Weick, 1995). Weick presented sensemaking as a multistep process by which one goes from a place of awareness to a place of understanding about a particular event or situation. Weick defined sensemaking, in its simplest form, as "the making of sense" (Weick, 1995, p. 4). Moore and Hoffman (2011) further defined sensemaking as "an approach that involves planning and replanning about how to make sense of an issue; foraging for, and harvesting sources of information; seeking to understand what they reveal; and communicating that knowledge to others" (p. 26).

Though Weick applied his theory to events that occur within organizations, for the purpose of this study, the theory is being applied to the event of the passage of SB 3 within the "organization" of education and social studies teachers' awareness and understanding of the law. The passage of SB 3 was an impactful event that necessitated teachers in the social studies disciplines to make sense of the law. The first step in the sensemaking process is for teachers to simply be aware of the passage of SB 3 and the narrative surrounding the bill. The next step is for teachers to read SB 3 with a critical lens in an attempt to understand what the bill is saying. The steps in this process require reading and rereading until one makes sense of the law. Included in this step would be consulting additional resources and discourse with other social studies teachers to gain multiple perspectives and levels of understanding. Critical reading of the bill and discussions about the bill would be repeated as one works toward gaining an understanding of SB 3. This study is positioned in stage one of the sensemaking process, examining the participants' levels of awareness and early interpretations of the law. This theory offers a lens through which to discover the levels at which the social studies teachers in this study understand SB 3 and how their interpretations, at this early stage, impact their practice.

METHODOLOGY

This IRB-approved mixed methods study was conducted with Grades 6–12 social studies teachers in the state of Texas. In order to discover trends in the opinions offered by social studies teachers across the state, as well as to delve into those opinions qualitatively, mixed methodology was used as the research design; we used a survey with both closed-ended and open-ended response categories (Creswell & Guetterman, 2019). The researchers developed this survey and social studies experts validated it. After a public information request from the Texas Education Agency (TEA, 2021) for the email addresses of Grades 6–12 social studies teachers, the researchers input the survey into Qualtrics and generated an anonymous link. Upon opening the anonymous survey link, participants were presented with an informed consent cover letter which stated that there was no threat of reprisal because their responses were anonymous, and the participants could withdraw at any time. The sample ($n = 411$) was majority male (53.3%), white (67.2%), and politically moderate (43.3%). Most of the respondents taught American History (35%), followed by World History (10.9%), Geography (10.7%), and Texas History (10.2%). Bachelor's degrees were held by 48% of participants and 44.4% had a master's degree. The average years of experience was $M = 13$, $SD = 9.2$ years with a median of 12 years.

Instrumentation

The survey consisted of demographic questions regarding the sample, as well as a series of questions regarding SB 3 and respondents' familiarity and comfort with the bill. The final four questions were qualitative, and participants were allowed to type in their responses. See Appendix A for the survey instrument.

RESULTS

To determine the distribution of responses to the question regarding the extent to which Texas social studies teachers have read and understood SB

3, percentages were calculated for each response item. The majority (74%) of respondents have read SB 3 and feel that prior to its passage, they were comfortable teaching sensitive or controversial topics. However, over a quarter reported not having read the bill at all. Since its passage, 61% have read the bill with critical analysis; and 74% understand the bill.

Regarding the impact of SB 3 on teachers' pedagogy related to the teaching of sensitive or controversial topics, respondents stated 53% believe it will impact their teaching. Greatly impacting teachers' pedagogy is the lack of guidance provided from those in administration. Respondents stated they had not received any guidance (43%), followed distantly by guidance from the Social Studies Coordinator (16%), Department Chair (7%), and Principal (6%). Of the guidance provided, 16% received guidance on what SB 3 denotes can and cannot be taught; 18% received guidance on the value of addressing sensitive or controversial topics appropriately and objectively; and 8% received guidance on how to address parent concerns regarding the teaching of American history. When asked to what extent respondents' comfort levels in teaching controversial topics have changed since the passage of SB 3, 40% indicated that their comfort levels have not changed; 24% have not changed much; 21% have somewhat changed; and 15% have changed very much.

Quantitative Results

Gender and Comfort Level

To ascertain whether there was an association between gender and level of comfort teaching controversial topics (RQ3) and whether there was an association between political identity and comfort teaching controversial topics since the passage of SB 3 (RQ4), four chi-square tests of association were performed. Chi-square tests of association are appropriate when comparing two nominal variables (Agresti, 2019). The variables for the first test were gender (male and female) and response to the prompt, "To what extent has your comfort level changed regarding the teaching of "sensitive" or "controversial" topics since the passing of SB 3?" Findings were significant ($X^2[3, N = 322] = 26.6, p < .001, phi = .29$), with twice as many males agreeing more to *not at all* as females. The association between gender and comfort level with teaching sensitive or controversial topics, "Prior to passage of Texas SB 3 were you uncomfortable teaching sensitive or controversial topics?" was not significant ($X^2[1, N = 329] = .08, p = .80$).

Making Sense of the Message   99

Political Affiliation and Comfort Level

The same two comparisons were made by political affiliation: *very liberal*, *liberal*, *moderate*, *conservative*, and *very conservative*. Similar results were found. The first comparison was significant, with those who identify as *very conservative* choosing *not at all* to the item at higher than the expected rate "To what extent has your comfort level changed regarding the teaching of 'sensitive' or 'controversial' topics since the passing of SB 3?" ($X^2[12, N = 334] = 38.5, p < .001, phi = .34$). Similar to the responses for gender, the second item "Prior to passage of Texas SB 3 were you uncomfortable teaching sensitive or controversial topics?" was not significant ($X^2[4, N = 342] = 1.9, p = .75$).

Qualitative Results

To analyze the qualitative data, the responses to the prompts were read through multiple times. The researchers took notes and developed an initial list of codes. Data were analyzed using an iterative process. After multiple cycles, we merged some codes to form themes (Creswell & Guetterman, 2019). The findings under each survey prompt are supported by quotes selected by the researchers as most representative of participant responses. All participants identified their gender and political affiliations and are reported with each participant.

Cause of Teachers' Discomfort Teaching Sensitive or Controversial Topics

Participants were asked, "What is the cause of your discomfort teaching sensitive or controversial topics?" The coding of the responses to this question highlighted backlash and politics as the overarching themes. Several respondents agreed that they had no discomfort in teaching controversial topics. Participant 63 (very liberal male) remarked on teaching history being uncomfortable, "I have no discomfort. If we are being true to the title of historian, history should be uncomfortable. History is filled with injustice, power struggles, class and racial struggles." Similarly, Participant 27, (liberal female) stated:

> I had no discomfort. As a multi-racial female, I know I have to teach history that at times can be considered sensitive. I teach the truth based on history, not my feelings and put the history into perspective for my students.

Additionally, Participant 38 (liberal female) noted:

> I'm comfortable right now teaching history the way it happened. I've never had a white[1] student say they felt bad learning about slavery or Jim Crow. If anything, my students feel righteous indignation over the way people of color were treated.

Overwhelmingly, participants of this study feared backlash in its many forms. Parent backlash was a dominant fear within the responses, as expressed by this participant:

> Well, there is always the possibility of being recorded or taken out of context. Last year I covered the January 6 insurrection and linked it to past rebellions in history, discussed the causes of anti-government extremism, etc. I had three students walk out of my class in protest and their parents attempted to have me disciplined for teaching "something I had no business talking about in class." (Participant 115, liberal male)

Students misconstruing the discussions and content presented by the teacher was noted as an area of concern, as some students often fuel parents' upset. Participant 140 (very liberal male) stated:

> The language of the law is vague, so any student/parent can accuse the teacher of wrongdoing for teaching anything. Teachers (including me) will self-censure being afraid of how the facts might make people uncomfortable. I still teach the things from the TEKS, but I'm definitely aware of how I'm one student away from a big fiasco.

Another emerging concern evident in the data was the lack of confidence in administrative support when complaints were made. One participant indicated, "The idea that someone with a grudge could report me teaching sensitive topics with no basis in truth. I fear the administration would rather support the unsubstantiated report and abandon the teacher rather than investigate the allegation" (Participant 198, conservative male).

The foundational source of discomfort in teaching controversial issues was the possibility of being fired. Respondents held concern that their jobs, credentials, and reputations could be at risk. Participant 196 (liberal male) articulated this fear expressed by many: "being accused of being in violation of the law and thereby dragged into a controversy that could threaten my position, license, reputation, and as a result, my chosen profession and livelihood."

Politics emerged as a common umbrella regarding the discomfort of participants. The political leanings of the communities in which respondents teach surfaced as a source of discomfort regarding controversial issues within the curriculum. Participant 27 (moderate female) referred to the political leanings of both sides, "that either too conservative pushback is going to silence me, or too liberal pushing is going to silence me."

The encroachment of politics into the educational system was expressed in a number of ways within the responses. A catalyst for respondents' discomfort was the intrusion of politics in education, with many noting politicians' lack of expertise in education:

> SB 3 interferes with the social studies curriculum, mandating content be taught that may not be the best use of class time, or that may not allow for appropriate accommodations. Instructional decisions should be made by trained educators, not politicians. (Participant 25, moderate female)

Another concern regarding politics highlighted in these data was politicians' use of the bill as a political pawn connected to the national rhetoric surrounding CRT; a respondent reported, "State governments, usually all three branches, are getting into public school curriculum and educational personnel because they need new boogeymen to drive fearful voters. It's not just here in Texas" (Participant 5, moderate male).

Overall, respondents noted the negative impact such politicization has on their comfort level with teaching publicly debated topics.

> I am very troubled that politicians are making political points (or performing political theater) by targeting teachers and public education. I worry that it intimidates or affects my fellow teachers. I don't like that it specifically excluded the 1619 project[2] [*sic*], whether or not I would teach that in my class. (Participant 49, liberal male)

A trend of note in the responses was the language of SB 3. Respondents directly addressed the vague and unclear messages of the bill as a point of major concern guiding their discomfort as they navigate teaching in compliance with the legislation.

> I am concerned with what could be considered "controversial." It seems far too vague and very much in the eye of the beholder.... It's hard to know what might make a student "feel discomfort, guilt, anguish" [quoting from SB3] etc. over historical events. The bill is far too vague. (Participant 116, moderate male)

Teachers' Concerns About SB 3 and Its Impact on Their Teaching

Participants were asked, "What are your concerns about SB 3 and its impact on your teaching choices?" Some of the same concerns echoed the reasons for teachers' discomfort around the teaching of controversial issues (i.e., backlash and politics). However, the responses to this question suggest distinct additional overarching themes that include curriculum content and pedagogy, lack of freedom, student civic readiness, and those who have no concerns.

Respondents expressed significant concern about teaching the content of their discipline accurately and truthfully.

> Though the law keeps intact verbiage that insists on impartiality in covering controversial topics, the specific items that were removed from the curriculum requirements having to do with racial and gender inclusion, directly calling out the 1619 project [*sic*], and the addition of language that directly prohibits discussion of systemic racism makes the law's intent clear in prohibiting a genuinely inclusive curriculum and tying the hands of educators that might otherwise wish to include historically ignored or undervalued narratives, while also prohibiting the discussion of uncomfortable stains on the national fabric of racial history. (Participant 216, liberal male)

In addition, pedagogical matters were raised by respondents.

> I don't agree with the 1619 Project [*sic*] thesis, but the project brought a host of primary and secondary sources and some interesting analysis. My major concern is teachers fearing to use primary sources to engage uncomfortable issues for our students. (Participant 120, moderate male)

A second theme that emerged in this study was the frustration surrounding a perceived lack of freedom. More specifically, respondents consistently mentioned censorship. "I very much watched what I said. I was extremely careful when I used the term 'white.' In other words, I censored myself. At times in lectures, I held back hard truths about how Blacks have been treated" (Participant 144, liberal male).

Another concern for respondents was the development of the dispositions within students that cultivate critical thinking and civic literacy. Participant 204 (liberal male) states,

> My main concern is that SB 3 will create a chilling effect among teachers who haven't read or don't understand the law, and now will be afraid to engage students in the types of conversations that are crucial for developing engaged, informed citizens.

A number of respondents expressed no concern for the bill or its impact on their classroom practice.

> I won't adjust the critical way in which I teach history. If we aren't willing to think critically about our successes and failures, then there's no reason to

learn the subject. If I end up losing my job for that, then so be it. (Participant 196, liberal male)

SB 3's Impact on Curriculum or Teaching Choices

Respondents were asked, "What difference, if any, has SB 3 had on your curriculum or teaching choices?" A majority of respondents expressed that SB 3 has made no difference in how they approach their curriculum or their teaching choices. Participant 170 (conservative male) stated, "None. Students, like adults, that live in a democracy should learn to hear all opinions and have those opinions stand in the light of open debate with respect and civility." Those who have shifted their curricular approach indicated "I glossed over or skipped some topics this year and instead chose the hills I was willing to defend" (Participant 119, liberal female).

DISCUSSION

The findings of the current study support trends in the national data illuminated in the 2022 *American Instructional Resources Survey* (Woo et al., 2023). Both studies showed that there is a gap in teachers' knowledge and awareness pertaining to the anti-CRT legislation. The teachers were either unaware of the passage of the legislation, were aware and had not read it, or had read it and did not recognize the implications regarding their practice. Regardless, the spectrum of awareness and knowledge about the content of these legislative mandates indicates that teachers are at the beginning stages of the sensemaking process (Weick, 1995). Without awareness and a true understanding of the legislation, implementation can be complex and inconsistent in social studies classrooms within districts and states.

The concerns that surfaced from the responses expressing discomfort align with the literature, noted earlier, regarding the challenges teachers face when addressing controversial issues within the social studies curriculum (Hess, 2005; Journell, 2013a). Although the concerns of social studies teachers around controversial issues have been present in the field, the current highly politicized context has created increased trepidation in teachers regarding if and how they approach controversy within their classrooms (Byford et al., 2009; Journell, 2017; Lintner, 2018; Shulsky & Baker, 2022).

The exploration of sensitive and controversial topics is a part of the social studies curriculum and the data from this study highlight the key role that discussion on these topics plays in the cultivation of the skills required of the next generation of citizens (Justice & Stanley, 2016; National Council for the Social Studies [NCSS], 2017). Teachers' perceptions of censorship and the containment of discussions in the classroom poses a dilemma in fulfilling this goal and making sense of what teachers believe this bill is requiring them to do (Hinde, 2004; Shulsky & Baker, 2022).

Notably, our data show that men responded more in depth than women to the qualitative prompts. On average, 18.5% of the women in this study provided comments to the open-ended questions, whereas men provided 81.5%. This data is unusual since research has shown that women are more likely to respond to online surveys (Wu et al., 2022). Similarly, respondents who identified as conservative or very conservative stated they had not changed their teaching of sensitive topics at all, while liberal and moderate respondents reported having censored their teaching practices. All respondents echoed their commitment to the end goal of social studies education—the preparation of future citizens (NCSS, 2017). Regarding the impact of the legislation on teaching choices, teachers are treading carefully through their curricular decisions. This includes resource selection, the framing of topics, and teachers' willingness to justify certain curricular decisions.

The catalyst for this study was that we, as teacher educators, understand how SB 3 would impact our own teaching practice. We realized our own limited understanding and misinterpretation of the bill was constructed by the public narrative. In total, the tone of the qualitative data gathered in this study is an example of the discourse within the public arena. Many of the responses were passionately centered on political identity—moderate, conservative, or liberal. These polarized views are parallel to the contradictory public narrative noted in the media quotes addressed within this research. This alignment reiterates the need for clear articulation of the expectations for educators regarding the implementation of the bill. The multiple interpretations and clear misinterpretations of the bill indicate there is no clear or consistent guidance on the meaning and implementation of the legislation.

Laws offer a common ground for citizens to navigate society. In this case, this law offers no clear touchstone for districts across the state as they attempt to fulfill the intent of this legislation. As such, the bill could weaken the disciplines of social studies when teachers decide to teach the "safe" way as they interpret the bill. This lack of clarity exposes flaws in the development and implementation of this bill—it was created by legislators and not by or in collaboration with educators. Critical public conversation about the intent of the bill and how its contents should be implemented into Texas classrooms has the potential to support teachers in their sensemaking process and strengthen their classroom pedagogy. Such clarity could have a positive effect on the pedagogy of social studies teachers. The current level of misunderstanding of SB 3 is negatively impacting how social studies is approached in Texas classrooms. In addition, such public discourse could educate the public about SB 3 and best practices in social studies education.

LIMITATIONS AND IMPLICATIONS

The findings of this study should be considered in light of the following limitations. The data were collected in the summer of 2022 in a very conservative state during the midst of a media frenzy regarding anti-CRT legislation. Our sample was majority male, white, and less than half identified as politically moderate, which does not generalize to the nation at large. Similarly, we only collected open-ended response survey data which were analyzed qualitatively. Future studies should conduct interviews or mixed-political affiliation focus groups.

Teachers and school administrators need professional development on how to implement and supervise instruction in light of these laws. The development of state-wide focused, intentional professional development for teachers and administrators is critical in supporting educators across the state and the nation as they navigate government mandates. Teachers are the frontline of the implementation of SB 3. As Wronowski (2018) suggested, the success of policies rests on the implementers' interpretations of the policy. Supporting teachers in their sensemaking of SB 3 would bring clarity to the actions required of teachers and positively impact the implementation process (Weick, 1995).

This study was our attempt to explore how other educators were perceiving the bill and how it was impacting their practice. Responses have revealed a spectrum of reactions to SB 3 from those who are unfazed by the bill to others who indicate fear of backlash, curriculum constraints, censorship, and ultimately, loss of credentials. This spectrum suggests very diverse interpretations of the law indicating the need for deep discussion and clarification on how the legislation is to be accurately interpreted by teachers and how its ideas and intentions should be manifested in the classrooms of teachers across the state. In the words of a Texas social studies educator,

> I will continue teaching knowing that my skills on understanding the complexities of American history and our nation's founding are vastly superior to elected officials and individuals who incorrectly believe that a balanced approach is not being conducted in Texas classrooms. (Participant 92, male moderate)

NOTES

1. The authors acknowledge APA 7 Bias-Free Language guidelines regarding capitalization of ethnic or racial groups. However, this is a direct written statement from a participant, and we wanted to maintain the consistency of the quote.
2. *The 1619 Project* referred to by this participant is a *New York Times Magazine* initiative that aims to reframe American history by centering the consequences of slavery and the contributions of Black Americans with the national narrative (Hannah-Jones et al., 2019).

REFERENCES

A Bill to be Entitled: An Act relating to the social studies curriculum in public schools. Texas S.B. 3, 87th Legislative Second Special Session. (2021). https://capitol.texas.gov/tlodocs/872/billtext/pdf/SB00003F.pdf

Agresti, A. (2019). *An introduction to categorical data analysis* (3rd ed.). John Wiley & Sons.

Baker, M., Robinson, H. T., & Joseph, M. (2022). The fear of harm: The challenges preservice urban teachers have with historical perspective recognition when discussing difficult histories. *Texas Education Review, 10*(1), 30–48. https://doi.org/10.15781/680y-je53

Beard, C. A. (1929). The trend in social studies. *Social Studies, 20*(8), 369.

Byford, J., Lennon, S., & Russell, W. B. III. (2009). Teaching controversial issues in the social studies: A research study of high school teachers. *Clearing House: A Journal of Educational Strategies, Issues and Ideas, 82*(4), 165–170. https://doi.org/10.3200/TCHS.82.4.165-170

Creswell, J. W., & Guetterman, T. C. (2019). *Educational research: Planning, conducting, and evaluating quantitative and qualitative research* (6th ed.). Pearson.

Dorn, C. (2007). "Treason in the textbooks": Reinterpreting the Harold Rugg textbook controversy in the context of wartime schooling. *Paedagogica Historica, 44*(4), 458–479

Evans, R. W. (2007). *This happened in America: Harold Rugg and the censure of social studies*. Information Age Publishing.

Evans, R. W. (2011). *The tragedy of American school reform: How curriculum politics and entrenched dilemmas have diverted us from democracy*. Palgrave Macmillan. https://doi.org/10.1057/9780230119109_6

Goldberg, T. (2020). Delving into difficulty: Are teachers evading or embracing difficult histories? *Social Education, 84*(2), 130-136.

Greene, P. (2022). Teacher anti-CRT bills coast to coast: A state by state guide. *Forbes*. https://www.forbes.com/sites/petergreene/2022/02/16/teacher-anti-crt-bills-coast-to-coast-a-state-by-state-guide/?sh=1df79c6a4ff6

Gross, H. M., & Terra, L. (2018). What makes difficult history difficult? *Phi Delta Kappan, 99*(8), 51–56.

Hannah-Jones, N., Elliott, M., Hughes, J., & Silverstein, J. (2019). The 1619 project: New York Times magazine. *The New York Times.* https://www.nytimes.com/interactive/2019/08/14/magazine/1619-america-slavery.html

Hess, D. E. (2005). How do teachers' political views influence teaching about controversial issues? *Social Education 69*(Jan/Feb), 47–48.

Hess, D. E. (2009). *Controversy in the classroom: The democratic power of discussion.* Routledge.

Hess, D. E. (2018). Teaching controversial issues: An introduction. *Social Education, 82*(6), 306

Hess, D. E., & McAvoy, P. (2015). *The political classroom: Evidence and ethics in democratic education.* Routledge.

Hinde, E. (2004). Bones of contention: Teaching controversial issues. *Social Studies and the Young Learner, 17*(2), 31–32. https://doi.org/10.1080/1356251042000216624

Hixenbaugh, M., & Hylton, A. (2021, Oct.14). *Southlake school leader tells teachers to balance Holocaust books with 'opposing' views.* NBC News. https://www.nbcnews.com/news/ us-news/southlake-texas-holocaust-books-schools-rcna2965

Journell, W. (2013a). Learning from each other: What social studies can learn from the controversy surrounding the teaching of evolution in science. *The Curriculum Journal, 24*(4), 494–510. https://doi.org/10.1080/09585176.2013.801780

Journell, W. (2013b). What preservice social studies teachers (don't) know about politics and current events—and why it matters. *Theory & Research in Social Education, 41*(3), 316–351. https://doi.org/10.1080/00933104.2013.812050

Journell, W. (2017). Framing controversial identity issues in schools: The case of HB2, bathroom equity, and transgender students. *Equity & Excellence in Education, 50*(4), 339–354. https://doi.org/10.1080/10665684.2017.1393640

Justice, B., & Stanley, J. (2016). Teaching in the time of Trump. *Social Education, 80*(1), 36–41. https://www.socialstudies.org/social-education/80/1/teaching-time-trump

Kahne, J., & Bowyer, B. (2017). Educating for democracy in a partisan age: Confronting the

challenges of motivated reasoning and misinformation. *American Educational Research Journal, 54*(1), 3–34. https://doi.org/10.3102/0002831216679817

KVUE News Staff (2021, July 16), *Critical race theory bill SB3 passes in Texas Senate by 18–4 vote.* KVUE-ABC. https://www.kvue.com/article/news/politics/texas-legislature/ critical- race-theory-senate-texas-legislature/269-9e40d158-a700-437b-8bf0-8d8a2aaeec92

Lehrer-Small, A. (2023, January 25). *National Study Reveals 1 in 4 Teachers Altering Lesson Plans Due to Anti-Critical Race Theory Laws.* The 74. https://www.the74million.org/ article/national-study-reveals-1-in-4-teachers-altering-lesson-plans-due-to-anti-critical-race-theory-laws/

Lintner, T. (2018). The controversy over controversy in the social studies classroom. *SRATE Journal, 27*(1), 14–21.

Lopez, B. (2022, August 1). Author of "critical race theory: Ban says Texas schools can still teach about racism. *The Texas Tribune.* https://www.texastribune.org/2022/08/01/texas-social-studies-curriculum/

McGee, K. (2021, June 15). Texas "critical race theory" bill limiting teaching of current events signed into law. *The Texas Tribune.* https://www.texastribune.org/2021/06/15/abbott-critical-race-theory-law/

Meador, D. (2018). What are some pros and cons of the Common Core State Standards. *ThoughtCo. Updated.* https://www.thoughtco.com/common-core-state-standards-3194603

Moore, D. T., & Hoffman, R. R. (2011). Sensemaking: A transformative paradigm. *American Intelligence Journal, 29*(1), 26–36.

National Council for the Social Studies (NCSS). (2017). *National standards for the preparation of social studies teachers.* https://www.socialstudies.org/standards

Office of Management and Budget. (2020). *Memorandum for the heads of executive departments and agencies: Training in the federal government.* Russell Vought. https://www.whitehouse.gov/wp-content/uploads/2020/09/M-20-34.pdf

Oulton, C., Day, V., Dillon, J., & Grace, M. (2004). Controversial issues—Teachers' attitude and practices in the context of citizenship education. *Oxford Review of Education, 30*(4), 489–507. https://www.jstor.org/stable/pdf/4127162.pdf

Philpott, S., Claybough, J., McConkey, L., & Turner, T. N. (2011). Controversial issues: To teach or not to teach? That is the question! *Georgia Social Studies Journal, 1*(1), 32–44.

Sachs, J. (2022, February 3). Teachers could face penalties for lessons on race, gender, politics (Interview by T. Gross) [Radio broadcast]. In Gross (Executive Producer), Fresh air. https://www.npr.org/2022/02/03/1077959482/teachers-could-facepenalties-for-lessons-on-race-gender-politics

Shulsky, D., & Baker, S. (2022). The three Cs of teaching within contentious times. In D. Vesperman, A. Aydinian-Perry, M. T. Missias, & W. G. Blankenship (Eds.), *Out of Turmoil: Catalysts for Re-learning, Re-teaching, and Re-imagining History and Social Sciences* (pp. 91–108). Information Age Publishing.

Teitelbaum, K. (2022). Curriculum, conflict, and critical race theory. *Phi Delta Kappan, 103*(5), 47–53. https://kappanonline.org/curriculum-conflict-critical-race-theory-teitelbaum/

Texas Education Agency. (2021). *Senate Bill 3, 87th Texas Legislature, Second Called Session—Update to Instructional Requirements and Prohibitions.* https://tea.texas.gov/about-tea/news-and-multimedia/correspondence/taa-letters/senate-bill-3-87th-texas-legislature-second-called-session-update-to-instructional-requirements-and-prohibitions

The Texas Senate. (2021, July 14). *Senate Research Center—Bill Analysis.* https://capitol.texas.gov/tlodocs/871/analysis/pdf/SB00003I.pdf#navpanes=0

UCLA Law. (n.d.a). *CRT Forward.* https://crtforward.law.ucla.edu/

UCLA Law. (n.d.b). *The UCLA Law CRT Forward Tracking Project.* https://law.ucla.edu/academics/centers/critical-race-studies/ucla-law-crt-forward-tracking-project

Weick, K. E. (1995). *Sensemaking in organizations.* SAGE.

Woo, A., Wolfe, R. L., Steiner, E. D., Doan, S., Lawrence, R. A., Berdie, L., Schwartz, H. L. (2022). *Walking a fine line—Educators' views on politicized topics in schooling: Findings from the state of the American teacher and state of the American principal surveys* (Report No. RR-A1108-5). RAND Corporation. https://doi.org/10.7249/RRA1108-5

Woo, A., Lee, S., Tuma, A. P., Kaufman, J. H., Lawrence, R. A., & Reed, N. (2023). *Walking on eggshells—teachers' responses to classroom limitations on race-or gender-related topics: Findings from the 2022 American instructional resources survey* (Report No. RR-A134-16). *RAND Corporation*. https://eric. ed.gov/?redir=https%3a%2f%2fdoi.org%2f10.7249%2fRRA134-16

Wronowski, M. (2018). *De-professionalized and demoralized: A longitudinal examination of teachers' perception of their work and teacher turnover during the accountability era in the United States* [Doctoral dissertation, University of Oklahoma]. https://shareok.org/bitstream/handle/11244/299887/2018_Wronowski_Meredith_Dissertation.pdf?sequence=6

Wu, M. J., Zhao, K., & Fils-Aime, F. (2022). Response rates of online surveys in published research: A meta-analysis. *Computers in Human Behavior Reports, 7*, 1–11. https://doi.org/10.1016/j.chbr.2022.100206

Zembylas, M., & Loukaidis, L. (2021). Affective practices, difficult histories and peace education: An analysis of teachers' affective dilemmas in ethnically divided Cyprus. *Teaching and Teacher Education, 97*, 1–11.

Zinn Education Project. (2022, January 15). *Pledge to teach the truth.* https://www.zinnedproject.org/news/pledge-to-teach-truth

APPENDIX A

Texas Legislation Survey

Greetings

Currently, more than half the states in the nation have passed legislation that addresses how our nation's history is taught (Kaplan & Owings, 2021). This wave of legislation is, presumably, directly related to the national debate and politicization of Critical Race Theory (CRT). Within this national context, Texas lawmakers passed Senate Bill 3 (SB3) in December 2021.

The purpose of this survey is to examine the thoughts of Social Studies educators regarding Texas SB3 and its impact on classroom pedagogy. The response to this survey should take approximately 5–10 minutes to complete. Please try to answer all the questions.

Completing the attached survey is entirely voluntary, but answering each response will make the survey most useful. Your answers will be completely anonymous. We will use your responses to gain insight into Social Studies teachers' knowledge and perspectives on the impact of SB3. No obvious undue risks will be endured, and you may stop your participation in completing the survey at any time. You will not benefit directly from your participation in the study beyond sharing your experiences related to SB3, providing invaluable insight into how you are navigating the teaching of Social Studies. Your willingness to participate in this study is implied if you proceed with completing the survey. Your completion of this survey is not only greatly appreciated, but invaluable.

If you have any further questions, please feel free to contact either researcher at any time.

Thank you!

Sincerely,

Please tell us a little bit about yourself.

How many years have you taught as a Social Studies teacher?

What region do you teach in Texas?

- o 1 – Edinburg (1)
- o 2 – Corpus Christi (2)
- o 3 – Victoria (3)
- o 4 – Houston (4)
- o 5 – Beaumont (5)
- o 6 – Huntsville (6)
- o 7 – Kilgore (7)
- o 8 – Mount Pleasant (8)
- o 9 – Wichita Falls (9)
- o 10 – Richardson (10)
- o 11 – Fort Worth (11)
- o 12 – Waco (12)
- o 13 – Austin (13)
- o 14 – Abilene (14)
- o 15 – San Angelo (15)
- o 16 – Amarillo (16)
- o 17 – Lubbock (17)
- o 18 – Midland (18)
- o 19 – El Paso (19)
- o 20 – San Antonio (20)

In which Social Studies discipline do you teach?

o World Cultures (4)
o Texas History (5)
o American History (6)
o World History (7)
o Geography (8)
o Government (9)
o Economics (10)
o Specialized Social Studies Elective (please note the class) (11)

Which grade level do you teach most frequently? (If more than one please pick the one you most identify with or enjoy most.)

o 6th (1)
o 7th (2)
o 8th (3)
o 9th (4)
o 10th (5)
o 11th (6)
o 12th (7)

What is your gender?

o Male (1)
o Female (2)
o Prefer not to say (3)
o Prefer to self-describe (4) _____

What is your level of education?

o Bachelor of Arts or Science (1)
o Master's degree (2)
o Education Specialist (4)
o PhD/EdD (3)
o Other (please indicate) (5) _____

What is your age?

How many years (including this year) have you taught?

What are your teaching certifications other than Social Studies?

o I do not have certifications other than Social Studies (1)
o My other certifications are ... (3) _____

What is your race/ethnicity? Please check all that apply.

❑ Asian (1)

❑ Black or African American (2)

❑ Native American or Alaskan Native (3)

❑ Latino(a) (4)

❑ White (5)

❑ Native Hawaiian or Other Pacific Islander (6)

❑ Biracial or Multiracial (7) _____

Where would you place yourself on the political spectrum?

❑ Very Liberal (1)

❑ Liberal (2)

❑ Moderate (3)

❑ Conservative (4)

❑ Very Conservative (5)

Directions: Please answer the following questions to the best of your ability.

I have read Texas SB3.

o Yes (1)
o No (2)

I have read SB3 with critical analysis.

o Strongly disagree (1)
o Disagree (2)
o Agree (3)
o Strongly agree (4)

I understand SB3.

- o Strongly disagree (1)
- o Disagree (2)
- o Agree (3)
- o Strongly agree (4)

I believe that SB3 impacts my pedagogy.

- o Strongly disagree (1)
- o Disagree (2)
- o Agree (3)
- o Strongly agree (4)

Who, if anyone, provided guidance regarding the impact of Senate Bill 3 on your teaching practice? (Please check all that apply.)

❑ Social Studies Coordinator (1)

❑ Principal (2)

❑ Department chair (3)

❑ No one (4)

❑ Other (5) _____

If guidance was provided, please check if any of the following were addressed.

❑ What SB3 says you can and cannot teach. (1)

❑ The value of discussing sensitive and controversial topics in classrooms appropriately and objectively. (2)

❑ How to address parent concerns regarding the teaching of American History. (3)

❑ None of the above. (4)

❑ Please add any additional guidance that was provided: (5) _____
_____

To what extent has your comfort level changed regarding the teaching of "sensitive" or "controversial" topics since the passing of SB3?

- o Not at all (1)
- o Not much (2)
- o Somewhat (3)
- o Very much (4)

Prior to the passage of Texas Senate Bill 3 were you uncomfortable teaching "sensitive" or "controversial" topics?

- o Yes (1)
- o No (2)

What is the cause of your discomfort teaching sensitive or controversial topics?

Since the passage of Texas Senate Bill 3 are you comfortable teaching "sensitive" or "controversial" topics?

- o Yes (1)
- o No (2)

What are your concerns about SB 3 and its impacts on your teaching?

What difference, if any, has SB3 had on your curriculum or teaching choices?

CHAPTER 5

ATTACKING ANTISEMITISM

Investigating How Museum-Led Professional Development Affects Preservice Teachers' Preparedness to Teach the Holocaust

Caroline Conner and Andrea Miskewicz
Kennesaw State University

ABSTRACT

This study examines how a museum-led professional development workshop impacts preservice teachers' perceived preparedness to teach the Holocaust. Utilizing an instructional model of historical empathy, researchers designed a virtual Holocaust education workshop for preservice teachers. Teacher candidates at three large universities were invited to attend. Survey findings demonstrate that participants' preparedness to teach difficult history improved. Results highlight the power of partnerships between teacher educators and museum educators and the power of eyewitness testimony to evoke empathy.

According to the Anti-Defamation League (ADL), antisemitic incidents in the United States reached an all-time high in 2021, with over 2700 incidents of assault, harassment, or vandalism reported—the highest rate

---

Curriculum and Teaching Dialogue,
Volume 25, Numbers 1 & 2, pp. 115–134
Copyright © 2023 by Information Age Publishing
www.infoagepub.com
All rights of reproduction in any form reserved.

since 1979, when the ADL began conducting annual audits (ADL, 2022). While antisemitism levels are high in the United States, Holocaust knowledge and awareness are low. The Claims Conference, an international nonprofit organization supporting Holocaust survivors, hired a consulting group to conduct a national study of Holocaust education in the United States. Researchers conducted over 10,000 interviews of Americans ages 18–29—at least 200 per state. Results demonstrate a shocking lack of basic Holocaust knowledge across the 50 states (Claims Conference, 2020). Sixty-three percent of respondents did not know that six million Jews were murdered; 48% could not name one concentration camp, death camp, or ghetto. Gideon Taylor, President of the Claims Conference, stated that while these results are disturbing, "we need to understand why we aren't doing better in educating a younger generation about the Holocaust and the lessons of the past. This needs to serve as a wake-up call to us all, and as a road map of where government officials need to act" (Claims Conference, 2020).

A lack of Holocaust knowledge may be exacerbated by the fact that teachers report feeling unprepared to teach the Holocaust and other traumatic events, broadly (Allgood & Shah, 2021; Rich, 2019). In a 2004 national survey conducted by the United States Holocaust Memorial Museum (USHMM), 52% of teachers cited their own high school coursework as their primary source of Holocaust knowledge, compared with 23% citing professional development (Donnelly, 2006). Museums and historic sites can serve as valuable resources for teachers who are grappling with difficult topics in history (Marcus et al., 2012). Difficult history is defined as past events of mistreatment, mass violence, suffering and trauma (Rose, 2016). Not only can museums and historic sites provide meaningful, curated experiences that can deepen teachers' understanding of historical events and the people who lived through them, but they can provide a model of historical empathy.

Teachers desire more support to teach difficult histories, and museums and historic sites have the potential to improve their preparedness (Baron et al., 2019b; Cohen, 2022; Kershaw, 2016). Prior research tends to focus on professional development of in-service teachers at historic sites rather than the development of preservice teachers at museums. Additionally, findings demonstrate the effectiveness of utilizing an instructional model of historical empathy to teach the Holocaust in K–12 classrooms (Conner & Graham, 2023; Haas, 2020; Metzger, 2012; Riley, 1998); yet research investigating the benefits of using historical empathy as a framework for museum-led professional development is lacking. Thus, the current researchers designed a Holocaust education workshop for preservice teachers using an instructional model of historical empathy. The researchers sought to answer the following research question: How does a museum-led professional development workshop utilizing an instructional model of historical empathy impact preservice teachers' perceived preparedness to teach the Holocaust?

LITERATURE REVIEW

History of Holocaust Education

Holocaust education in the United States did not begin immediately after the end of World War II. In fact, it emerged over a generation later. Following American political turbulence in the 1960s, social studies educators began to shift towards the notion of relevance (Evans, 2004). New concepts were introduced in social studies curricula including student activism and civil rights, and many educators were committed to helping their students explore the connections between individuals and society.

The impetus for Holocaust education was a grassroots movement of teachers responding to national concerns of a lack of relevance in the curriculum (Fallace, 2006). In the 1970s, organizations such as the ADL began to develop resources about the Holocaust for teachers and students to use in the classroom to help combat antisemitism (ADL, n.d.); to what extent this curriculum was used is unknown. Additionally, historians and other scholars began to engage with interested teachers, museum patrons, and libraries to share knowledge about this era through lectures and papers. Popular forms of media such as NBC's *Holocaust* miniseries and Steven Spielberg's film *Schindler's List* grew American consciousness of the Holocaust.

With this greater awareness, states began mandating that the Holocaust be included in the K–12 curriculum. The first state to require Holocaust education was New Jersey in 1994 (Echoes & Reflections, 2022). As of August 2022, 20 states in the United States legally require educators to teach *about* the Holocaust; however, many of these states do not offer educators training and/or funding to learn *how* to teach it (USHMM, n.d.b.; Yang, 2023). Some states include the Holocaust in their statewide curriculum even though it is not legally mandated. For example, Georgia currently requires Holocaust education through the Georgia Standards of Excellence (GaDOE, 2016). Despite such curricular requirements, Georgia was among the five states with the lowest Holocaust knowledge score (Claims Conference, 2020)—indicating that preservice teachers in Georgia may need more support in Holocaust education.

Scholarship in history education broadly emphasizes the importance of replacing traditional lecture and passive learning with student-centered, active learning strategies (Deslauriers et al., 2019). There is evidence that classroom strategies designed to get students to participate in the learning process produce better outcomes. Some of these engagement methods in a history education context include digital history games, movies, role playing, and simulations (Keller, 1975; McCall, 2016; Peters, 2020). However, these strategies may not be appropriate for Holocaust education and could trivialize the experience of those who suffered or even perpetuate trauma (Gaffney, 2019).

To teach the Holocaust specifically, however, less is known about strategies that teachers are using. Contemporary research about Holocaust education frequently focuses on what teachers know about the subject (Gray, 2014; Jedwab, 2010). Such findings corroborate the Claims Conference report, which found that teacher knowledge about the Holocaust is shockingly low. Prior research suggests that by studying the Holocaust, students can learn the dangers of prejudice, hatred, and discrimination, and understand the value of diversity and respect for human rights (Lee, 2021; Salmons, 2003). Preparing teacher candidates to effectively teach the Holocaust may help combat antisemitism.

Museum-Led Professional Development for Teachers

As more states pass laws to protect Holocaust education, teachers are turning to institutions such as Yad Vashem and the USHMM for professional development. Unfortunately, research related to the strategies such institutions provide and the extent to which they are effective is unknown. While research is limited in regard to museum-led Holocaust education, museums and historic sites have a history of supporting teachers when it comes to topics of historical trauma and controversy (Segall, 2014). Not only do museums in the United States spend more than \$2 billion a year on educational activities including professional development, but also, they are stewards of public trust (American Alliance of Museums, 2021). As trusted organizations, many museums have found that teacher professional development can "be an efficient means of reaching K–12 educators" (Bingmann, 2017, p. 117). Teachers not only benefit from museum-led professional development as adult learners, but the experience has the potential to involve students with the museum through field trips and other forms of community engagement.

Research-based best practices in teacher training have been developed over the last several decades. Successful forms of professional development are rooted in collaboration, active participation, and evaluation; moreover, effective programs focus on a specific subject matter (Cooper et al., 2018; Fishman et al., 2003; Van Driel & Berry, 2012). Research connecting American public history institutions and teacher training is far more limited. Overwhelmingly, prior research was conducted at historic sites rather than museums (Baron et al., 2019a, 2019b; Kornegay Rose et al., 2019). While there can be overlap between historic sites and museums, they can serve different purposes and have different approaches to preserving and interpreting history. A historic site is a place that has been recognized and preserved for its cultural, historical, or natural significance (U.S. General Services Administration, 2019). Unlike historic sites, museums typically focus on the collection and display of objects rather than the preservation of physical sites. Many educators walked away from their experiences at both museums and historic sites with benefits such as peer networks, empathy, reflective practice, community connections, and better understanding of historic materials (Baron et al., 2019b; Sheppard et al., 2019). These results help validate the continuation of museums and historic sites supporting professional development for teachers (Baron et al., 2019a; Baron et al., 2021).

Even fewer researchers consider the connection between historic sites and preservice teacher development; however, the limited research that has been conducted shows promise in helping future teachers build their historical thinking skills such as using primary sources, artifacts, and adopting an inquiry-based approach (Patterson, 2020; Patterson & Woyshner, 2016). Studies highlight the power of place to evoke understanding and empathy. Researchers further emphasize the importance of mentorship opportunities that museum professionals may provide for preservice teachers. However, the impact of museum-led professional development for preservice teachers when the power of place is missing is an area that has yet to be examined.

HISTORICAL EMPATHY FRAMEWORK

While historic sites such as Monticello can use the power of place to evoke affective connections, museums must rely on other methods (Baron et al., 2019a). Thus, museums have begun using the framework of historical empathy in their professional development opportunities. For example, The Museum of History and Holocaust Education at Kennesaw State University (MHHE) incorporates elements of historical empathy into their teacher workshops on teaching difficult history (Conner & Graham, 2023). Although historic sites and museums have incorporated elements of historical empathy in their professional development, research investigating the effectiveness of using a historical empathy framework is absent.

The definition of historical empathy (HE) is often debated by scholars who contend that it is either a cognitive act or an affective one. Current researchers embrace the conceptual framework that HE is a dual-dimensional cognitive-affective construct (Colby, 2008; Brooks, 2011; Endacott &

Brooks, 2013). Endacott and Brooks (2013) defined historical empathy as "the process of students' cognitive and affective engagement with historical figures to better understand and contextualize their lived experiences, decisions, or actions" (p. 41). They provided a conceptual framework of HE that involves three interconnected processes: (a) *Historical Contextualization*—understanding how social, political, and cultural norms of a time period impact historical actors; (b) *Perspective Taking*—understanding how a person's lived experiences impact their beliefs, thoughts, and behaviors; and (c) *Affective Connections*—recognizing how emotions impact people's actions both in the past and the present. Historical empathy allows students to contextualize the past rather than use contemporary standards (Perrotta & Bohan, 2018).

In addition to their conceptual framework, Endacott and Brooks (2013) designed an Instructional Model for Historical Empathy. The model includes four phases: (a) an introductory phase, (b) an investigation phase (c) a display phase, and (d) a reflection phase. In the introductory phase, teachers provide background information to help students understand the historical context in which the event(s) occurred. The investigation phase requires students to analyze a variety of sources from multiple perspectives. In the display phase, students demonstrate what they have learned—emphasizing how the thoughts, beliefs, and behaviors of historical actors are impacted by contextual factors. During the reflection phase, teachers provide ample opportunities for students to reflect on what they have learned, make connections between the past and the present, and consider how their perspectives may have changed. While a variety of instructional methods can be utilized to promote historical empathy, source work is essential (Brooks, 2011; Colby, 2008; D'Adamo & Fallace, 2011; Davis, 2001; Doppen, 2000; Jensen, 2008; Kohlmeier, 2006; Perrotta, 2018).

The instructional model of historical empathy aligns to the curricular goals in history and social studies education (Conner & Graham, 2023; Perrotta & Bohan, 2020). In fact, the goal of promoting historical empathy through social studies began during the progressive education movements of the twentieth century (Perrotta & Bohan, 2018). The term historical empathy is not always explicitly used; however, the national social studies curricula continue to promote inquiry-based instruction. For example, the National Council for the Social Studies (NCSS) College, Career, and Civic Life (C3) Framework encourages teachers to utilize primary sources to engage students in the process of identifying different perspectives to promote empathy (NCSS, 2013). Similarly, the National Council for History Education (NCHE, 2016) encourages the promotion of historical empathy through the process of perspective taking. Moreover, the Common Core Standards for social studies emphasize student analysis of multiple sources to determine historical contexts and perspectives (Perrotta & Bohan, 2018).

Research demonstrates the vast benefits of using historical empathy in social studies instruction. For one, historical empathy increases student engagement and fosters a deeper understanding of historical content (Colby, 2008; Conner & Graham, 2023; Endacott & Pelekanos, 2015; Kohlmeier, 2006). The instructional framework enhances students' ability to analyze sources, recognize past perspectives, and contextualize those perspectives within a given period (Doppen, 2000; Jensen, 2008; Kohlmeier, 2006; Yancie, 2022). The instructional model of historical empathy adds value beyond school by promoting students' level of care—their care that events occurred, their care to learn about such events, their care for people of the past, and their care to change the future by promoting the common good (Barton & Levstik, 2004). Furthermore, students are more likely to recognize how their own perspectives are shaped by context—promoting rational decision making (Doppen, 2000).

Recent scholarship demonstrates the power of using historical empathy to teach racism and social injustice (Yancie, 2022). While research on the effectiveness of utilizing this model to teach difficult histories in the classroom is limited, several studies demonstrate that using historical empathy to teach the Holocaust improves students' ability to contextualize traumatic events and empathize with people of the past (Conner & Graham, 2023; Haas, 2020; Metzger, 2012; Riley, 1998). Students were able to contextualize how "normal people" acted irrationally by analyzing the social, political, economic, and cultural factors that led to the rise of Nazi ideology. More importantly, students were able to empathize with victims of the Holocaust and expressed a desire to avoid future atrocities. Findings support the use of historical empathy in social studies instruction, but the impact of utilizing this framework in preparing educators to teach difficult history is unknown.

METHODOLOGY

Participant Recruitment

Researchers emailed preservice teachers enrolled at three large universities in Georgia a recruitment flyer to participate in a free virtual professional development workshop on Holocaust education. The flyer contained a link to register for the workshop and asked participants to select two breakout sessions based on their interests/needs. Students who registered for the workshop were emailed a Nearpod presentation developed by the MHHE to view in advance. Nearpod is an online education platform that allows users to engage with digital content at their own pace. This presentation introduced them to the USHMM's (n.d.a.) Guidelines for Teaching about the Holocaust, a brief overview of the historical context in which the Holocaust occurred, and the instructional model of historical empathy.

Participants

Approximately 106 students registered for the workshop and 87 attended. Of the 87 workshop participants, 64 agreed to participate in the survey (73.6% response rate) and 61 completed the survey in its entirety. The three individuals who started the survey but did not complete it were removed from the data. Survey participants overwhelmingly self-identified as female ($n = 56$, 91.8%), with four self-identifying as male (6.6%), and one indicating N/A. Out of 64 participants, 50 self-identified as White (82%), six as Hispanic/Latinx (9.8%), two as Asian (3.3%), one as African American (2%), and one as American Indian (2%); the remaining participant selected N/A. The majority indicated that upon graduation they would be certified in elementary education ($n = 43$, 70.5%), while nine reported they would be certified to teach middle grades (14.8%), and 11 stated that they would be certified to teach secondary grades (18%). Reflecting the gender and racial disparity that exists in the field of education, participants in the workshop were predominately White and female (National Center for Education Statistics, 2021). Therefore, further research is needed to determine the impact of museum-led professional development on a more diverse group of participants.

Workshop Overview

Kennesaw State University's (KSU) History and Philosophy Department, the University of North Georgia's (UNG) College of Education, and the MHHE at KSU, in cooperation with the USHMM, presented a virtual professional development workshop on Holocaust studies. The workshop provided teachers with resources and pedagogical approaches to teach the Holocaust using a model of historical empathy. Participants did not have to pay to attend, and they received books and resources from the USHMM for participation. A Holocaust survivor, Hershel Greenblat, was the keynote speaker.

Workshop Design

The workshop was designed using the Instructional Model for Historical Empathy (Endacott & Brooks, 2013) and the USHMM's (n.d.a.) Guidelines for Teaching about the Holocaust. The USHMM (n.d.a.) recommends adhering to the following guidelines when teaching the Holocaust:

1. Define the term "Holocaust."
2. The Holocaust was not inevitable.
3. Avoid simple answers to complex questions.
4. Strive for precision of language.
5. Strive to balance the perspectives that inform your study of the Holocaust.
6. Avoid comparisons of pain.
7. Avoid romanticizing history.
8. Contextualize the history.
9. Translate statistics into people.
10. Make responsible methodological decisions. (para. 1)

Researchers designed sessions that adhered to these guidelines—with an emphasis placed on 5 (balance of perspectives), 8 (contextualize the history), 9 (translate statistics into people), and 10 (make responsible methodological decisions). Each breakout session was deliberately designed to model how to create instructional activities that adhered to the guidelines. For example, the Photo Narrative session demonstrated how Holocaust photographs can be used to translate statistics into people. Likewise, presenters discussed the importance of avoiding graphic images (such as dead bodies) to make responsible methodological decisions.

Moreover, researchers designed the workshop to model how preservice teachers might design their own lessons utilizing Endacott and Brooks's (2013) instructional model for historical empathy, which includes four phases: (a) an introductory phase, (b) an investigation phase (c) a display phase, and (d) a reflection phase. The pre-conference Nearpod activity, opening workshop session, and guided virtual museum tour served as the introduction to the Holocaust and the context in which it occurred. The breakout sessions modeled how to guide students in investigating various primary sources and provided participants a chance to display their learning through activities such as a gallery walk. Following each breakout session as well as the survivor testimony, participants were given time to discuss what they learned and reflect on their experiences.

Due to the COVID-19 pandemic, the researchers modified the original workshop design significantly. For one, they shifted from an in-person experience to a virtual one. Because video conference exhaustion is a phenomenon that was exacerbated by the pandemic, the researchers also decided to shorten the workshop to a half day (Nesher Shoshan & Wehrt, 2021). The virtual format limited the amount of content that could be shared, necessitated logistical changes to some of the activities, and made it difficult for the researchers to gauge engagement and understanding. Moreover, the researchers had to modify the study design as participant observation during workshop activities was not possible. Despite these challenges, the virtual workshop drew twice as many participants as the in-person workshop in 2022.

Data Collection and Analysis

Following the workshop, participants were invited to complete a brief survey of 15 questions. The first survey items gathered self-reported demographic data such as participants' gender, race/ethnicity, years of teaching experience, and level of teacher certification. The next five questions were Likert-scale items that asked participants the degree to which they agreed/disagreed with statements such as "The workshop exposed me to multiple perspectives of people affected by the Holocaust." The last three survey items were open-ended questions that prompted written responses from participants such as "How did the Holocaust education workshop impact the way you will teach the Holocaust (if at all)?"

Survey data was analyzed qualitatively to determine the impact the workshop had on teachers' perceived preparedness to teach the Holocaust and their understanding of historical empathy. The researchers utilized open coding to analyze participants' written responses (Merriam & Tisdell, 2016). Each researcher read the survey responses several times and wrote words/phrases in the margins such as "content knowledge" to describe the key idea(s) described by the participant. A running list of codes was created by each researcher and then the lists were compared. A deductive chunking process illuminates recurring patterns in the data to help answer the research questions (Bogdan & Biklen, 2007). For example, researchers discussed and narrowed the final list of codes by condensing similar ones such as "photo narrative," "case studies," and "gallery walk" into overarching categories such as "pedagogy."

FINDINGS

Teacher Development

While all participants believed that teaching the Holocaust was important (98.25% strongly agreed; 1.75% agreed), many teacher candidates explicitly stated that their primary reason for attending the workshop was because they felt unprepared to teach it (49.18% strongly agreed; 29.5% agreed; 21.31% disagreed). The participants who disagreed tended to be secondary history education majors, who had a strong content knowledge in the Holocaust. Their particular motives for attending the workshop varied, but many emphasized the desire to hear from the Holocaust survivor. Survey data suggests that participation in the workshop improved participants perceived preparedness to teach the Holocaust. All participants reported that after the workshop, they felt better prepared to teach the Holocaust (77.25% strongly agreed; 22.75% agreed). The categories that emerged from the data were related to the development of teachers' content knowledge, pedagogy, and empathy.

Improved Content Knowledge

To teach the Holocaust effectively, preservice teachers must know the historical content; yet many participants, particularly early education majors, admitted a lack of foundational knowledge. As one teacher candidate noted, "my memories of Holocaust teachings are from the 80s in my own high school experience and from my daughter's middle school experience." For most elementary teacher candidates, the only history course they took in college was U.S. History (pre-Civil War or post-Civil War). Corroborating prior research conducted by the USHMM (Donnelly, 2006), the last time many teacher candidates learned about the Holocaust was in their high school history courses. Thus, they remarked that the workshop was a much-needed review of the events that occurred. While the workshop focused on effective pedagogy for teaching the Holocaust, sessions utilized historical content to model effective instructional practices.

As a result, participants stated that the workshop improved their content knowledge regarding the historical context in which the Holocaust occurred (84.2% strongly agreed; 15.8% agreed). Participants identified two activities in particular that improved their content knowledge. First, they cited the Nearpod, which provided a historical timeline and contained links to two USHMM documentaries that helped them contextualize the events of the Holocaust: *The Path to Nazi Genocide* and *Why the Jews: History of Antisemitism*. Several participants indicated that they plan to use both the Nearpod and the USHMM videos in their future classrooms to provide historical context for their own students. Second, participants noted that the interactive virtual museum tour activity reviewed key events of the period through the exploration of victims' personal accounts. Participants emphasized that they "forgot they were learning history" as they became so engrossed in the stories of survivors during the tour.

Responsible Pedagogy

In addition to content knowledge, the workshop had a profound impact on participants' pedagogical approach to the Holocaust. Most participants emphasized that they would utilize the USHMM's Guidelines for Teaching about the Holocaust. Most notably, the principle of "translating statistics into people" was referenced. Participants also stressed making "responsible methodological choices" by selecting images that humanized victims. As one participant explained:

> The ten principles presented were helpful to me and will make me stop to think before I present something to my class about the Holocaust. Promoting critical thinking for students without traumatizing them is effective teaching. The best example I can give is one of the picture scenarios given: would I show students the image of one mass grave, or would I show the picture of the pile of shoes outside the gas chamber? Though the mass grave tore my heart, the shoes tore my soul. The best explanation I can give is that the shoes picture made me want to know the stories behind the shoes. The picture of the mass grave made me want to turn away. I would show students the shoes rather than the bones to humanize the victims.

To avoid traumatizing students, participants remarked that they would avoid simulations and games that trivialize the horror. As one teacher candidate stated, "I will make sure to analyze and evaluate pictures and textbooks before using them to make sure that I am not dehumanizing or offending families and survivors. I will use the voice of victims to tell their own stories."

Participants further indicated that they would use Endacott and Brooks's (2013) instructional model of historical empathy to design their lessons on the Holocaust. As one participant explained, "I like the framework we were introduced to in the Nearpod. I plan to go through the phases we did [introduction, investigation, display, and reflection] with my future students." Participants listed a variety of teaching strategies they would consider using to introduce the Holocaust such as Nearpod and the USHMM documentaries. The instructional methods participants mentioned most frequently involved source work such as the virtual/in-person museum tour, photo analysis, case studies, literature circles, and survivor testimony. The use of political cartoons, diary entries, and literature such as *Night* and *The Diary of Anne Frank* was also referenced. To display student knowledge teacher candidates frequently indicated their plan to utilize museum exhibit activities, gallery walks, photo narratives, narrative writing assignments, or discussion. While reflection activities were not explicitly mentioned in surveys, candidates demonstrated the importance of allowing time for students to process what they learned. As one participant stated, "I was reminded that I must give my students time to process the horror. You can't just teach it and move on."

Enhanced Empathy

Findings further suggest that the workshop fostered the three inter-dependent processes of historical empathy: historical contextualization, perspective taking, and affective connections (Endacott & Brooks, 2013). As stated previously, participants indicated that the workshop improved their current understanding of the historical context in which the Holocaust occurred (84.2% strongly agreed; 15.8% agreed). They also stated that the workshop exposed them to multiple perspectives of people affected by the Holocaust (93% strongly agreed; 7% agreed). As one participant stated, "I think the different case studies used in the Oath and Opposition breakout and the virtual field trip are great ways to expose students to many different viewpoints from this time period." The greatest impact of the workshop, however, appeared to be the affective connections participants made to victims of the Holocaust. Teacher candidates indicated that the workshop significantly increased that their level of empathy for people affected by the Holocaust (96.7% strong agreed; 3.5% agreed). They emphasized the power of personal accounts and photographs. As one participant stated, "It [the workshop] definitely taught me how to be more empathetic with teaching the Holocaust. I think we as teachers have a habit of falling just to statistics, but this workshop really enlightened me on the more human aspect."

Participants had strong emotional responses to the workshop content, particularly to the Holocaust survivor's testimony. Four recurring affective connections that emerged were sadness, shock, anger, and inspiration. Some participants connected to his story on a personal level:

> I was able to emotionally connect with Hershel's stories because I am a minority, and my parents are immigrants. I know how hard it is to live in a place where we are looked down on. I agree when he illustrated that we should steer away from hate and learn to respect everyone regardless of the color of our skin.

While acknowledging the sadness and horror, participants also felt a compelling call to action. Participants were inspired to improve the way that the Holocaust is taught in schools:

> I felt a strong need to change how we have talked about the Holocaust in the past. Coming from an education where we are taught about statistics more often than the people who lived it and focusing on the people who were on the Nazi side rather than the survivors and victims, this makes me want to give the people who survived and perished justice. I want to talk about their stories, how they survived, their families, and make sure they are heard by the students I am teaching.

Moreover, participants felt a personal responsibility to tell the victims' stories:

> I got incredibly emotional listening to Hershel, but when he said that it is our role and responsibility as teachers to make sure that our students have a meaningful understanding of the Holocaust it struck me. As we lose more Holocaust survivors every year, it is up to us to tell their stories.

Overwhelmingly, participants stated that the workshop increased their confidence in teaching the Holocaust using an instructional model of historical empathy (80.3% strongly agreed; 19.67% agreed).

LIMITATIONS

The current findings are limited as they rely upon self-reported data from preservice teachers who voluntarily attended the workshop; however, attendance at professional development does not guarantee learning. Given the high response rate of workshop participants in the survey, the findings strongly suggest that the workshop positively impacted preservice teachers' perceived preparedness to teach the Holocaust. A follow-up study is needed to determine how museum-led professional development utilizing a model of historical empathy influences teachers' practice in the classroom.

The researchers acknowledge that this was a foundational study illuminating the effectiveness of using the model of historical empathy for training teachers about the Holocaust. Researchers plan to conduct a longitudinal study to determine the workshop's potential change in teaching practices once preservice educators enter the classroom. Additionally, the current researchers are gathering qualitative survey and interview data from preservice teachers in the state of Georgia to better understand their preparedness for teaching the Holocaust. Both studies will include additional data points such as, but not limited to, pre- and post-questionnaires and interviews.

IMPLICATIONS

Attacking Antisemitism

The best weapon to fight antisemitism is Holocaust education that promotes empathy. For the attack to be successful, however, preservice teachers must be adequately prepared to teach it. Corroborating prior research, the current findings suggest that preservice teachers have a deficit in content knowledge about the Holocaust and teaching difficult history more broadly (Allgood & Shah, 2021; Rich, 2019). As prior researchers attest, teachers want support—almost 100 preservice teachers were willing to participate in voluntary professional development on Holocaust education during a pandemic (Cohen, 2022; Kershaw, 2016). Moreover, participants expressed a desire to learn how to address Holocaust denial—a form of antisemitism, which is defined as the belief that the Holocaust is a myth or has been exaggerated (Claims Conference, 2020).

Participants frequently expressed concerns related to teaching difficult history—highlighting how the current debate over critical race theory has heightened the anxiety educators experience (López et al., 2021). Current political and socioeconomic issues concerning social justice "highlight the urgency in promoting historical empathy in the school curricula" (Perrotta & Bohan, 2020, p. 599). While prior research illustrates the benefits of using historical empathy to teach difficult history, the current study offers evidence that it may also be beneficial to museum educators as a framework for teacher development. Corroborating prior research in Holocaust education, the use of a historical empathy framework enhanced preservice teachers' ability to contextualize events of the Holocaust, recognize multiple perspectives, and make affective connections to people from the past (Conner & Graham, 2023; Metzger, 2012; Riley, 1998).

The Power of Partnerships

Building on prior research conducted at historic sites (Baron et al., 2019a; Kornegay Rose et al., 2019), current results suggest that museums are also effective locales for teaching difficult history. Moreover, the current project demonstrates the power of partnerships between museum educators and teacher educators preparing teacher candidates to teach difficult history. Museum staff and university faculty collaborated to raise funds, recruit participants, develop the workshop, and facilitate sessions. For example, the "Utilizing Photographs to Teach the Holocaust" breakout session was cofacilitated by a museum educator and a history education professor—who combined their expertise in public history and critical pedagogy. Illuminating the power of partnerships, this collaborative session was the most highly rated breakout session by participants. Furthermore, the fact that the workshop was virtual demonstrates how partnerships between teacher educators and museum educators need not be limited by geography.

The Power of Testimony

Overwhelmingly, participants felt that the survivor testimony was the most important factor in contributing to their level of historical empathy—

which raises concerns for future workshops. Workshop attendees were profoundly impacted by Hershel Greenblat's eyewitness testimony. His story fostered empathy as preservice teachers listened to his experience during the Holocaust and after as a refugee. The day is fast approaching when the world, let alone museums, will not have Holocaust survivor speakers who can participate in their programs. Some of the youngest survivors, like Mr. Greenblat, are already in their 80s. Many Holocaust museums have started to implement alternative strategies that may help visitors empathize with those who experienced the Holocaust including recordings of testimony, holograms/virtual reality, and second and third-generation testimony (Haas, 2020; Ulaby, 2022); however, further research is needed to determine if these methods are as effective in promoting empathy as a first-hand account.

CONCLUSION

As antisemitism rises in the United States, Holocaust education becomes increasingly important. This study illustrates how museum-led professional development utilizing a framework of historical empathy can positively impact preservice teachers' perceived preparedness to teach the Holocaust. It further highlights the profound impact of survivor testimony on participants' level of empathy for Holocaust victims—raising the question as to how to foster such empathy when survivors are no longer living. In order to attack antisemitism, K–12 teachers must be prepared to teach the Holocaust effectively in their classrooms. Partnerships between museums and educator preparer programs are critical to the fight.

REFERENCES

Allgood, I., & Shah, R. (2021). Preparing preservice teachers to implement Holocaust curriculum in elementary grades: A study that shows the effects on undergraduate students' cognitive, reflective, affective, and active domains. *Critical Questions in Education, 12*(1), 20–39. https://files.eric.ed.gov/fulltext/EJ1287248.pdf

American Alliance of Museums. (2021, September 30). *Museums and trust 2021.* https://www.aam-us.org/2021/09/30/museums-and-trust-2021/

Anti-Defamation League. (n.d.). *Toward justice for all.* https://www.adl.org/who-we-are/history

Anti-Defamation League. (2022, April 25). *ADL audit finds antisemitic incidents in United States reached all-time high in 2021.* https://www.adl.org/news/press-releases/adl-audit-finds-antisemitic-incidents-in-united-states-reached-all-time-high

Baron, C., Sklarwitz, S., Bang, H., & Shatara, H. (2019a). What teachers retain from historic site-based professional development. *Journal of Teacher Education*, *71*(4), 392–408. https://doi.org/10.1177/0022487119841889

Baron, C., Sklarwitz, S., Bang, H., & Shatara, H. (2019b). Understanding what teachers gain from professional development at historic sites. *Theory & Research in Social Education*, *46*(1), 76–107. https://doi.org/10.1080/009331 04.2018.1489927

Baron, C., Sklarwitz, S., & Coddington, N. (2021). Hidden in plain sight: Museum educators' role in teacher professional development. *Teacher Development*, *25*(5), 567–584. https://doi.org/10.1080/13664530.2021.1897659

Barton, K. C., & Levstik, L. S. (2004). *Teaching history for the common good*. Routledge.

Bingmann, M. (2017). Professional development for teachers. In A. Johnson, K. A. Huber, N. Cutler, M. Bingmann, & T. Grove (Eds.), *The museum educator's manual: Educators share successful techniques* (2nd ed., pp. 101–118). Rowman & Littlefield.

Bogdan, R., & Biklen, S. K. (2007). *Qualitative research for education: An introduction to theories and methods* (5th ed.). Pearson.

Brooks, S. (2011). Historical empathy as perspective recognition and care in one secondary social studies classroom. *Theory & Research in Social Education*, *39*(2), 166–202. https://doi.org/10.1080/00933104.2011.10473452

Claims Conference (2020). *First ever 50-state survey on Holocaust knowledge of American Millennials and Gen Z reveals shocking results*. https://www.claimscon.org/millennial-study/

Cohen, R. M. (2022, March 28). *Why teachers are afraid to teach history*. The New Republic. https://newrepublic.com/article/165598/teachers-afraid-teach-history

Colby, S. R. (2008). Energizing the history classroom: Historical narrative inquiry and historical empathy. *Social Studies Research and Practice*, *3*(3), 60–79. https://doi.org/10.1108/ssrp-03-2008-b0005

Conner, C. J., & Graham, T. (2023). Using an instructional model of historical empathy to teach the Holocaust. *The Social Studies*, *114*(1), 19–35. https://doi.org/10.1080/00377996.2022.2073582

Cooper, L., C. Baron, L. Grim, and G. Sandling. (2018). Teaching teachers onsite: Using evaluation to develop effective professional development programs. *Journal of Museum Education*, *43*(3), 274–282. https://doi.org/10.1080/10598 650.2018.1489196

D'Adamo, L., & Fallace, T. (2011). The multigenre research project: An approach to developing historical empathy. *Social Studies Research and Practice*, *6*(1), 75–88. https://doi.org/10.1108/ssrp-01-2011-b0005

Davis, O. L., Jr. (2001). In pursuit of historical empathy. In O. L. Davis, E. A. Yeager, & S. J. Foster (Eds.), *Historical empathy and perspective taking in the social studies* (pp. 1–12). Roman & Littlefield.

Deslauriers, L., McCarty, L. S., Miller, K., Callaghan, K., & Kestin, G. (2019). Measuring actual learning versus feeling of learning in response to being actively engaged in the classroom. *Proceedings of the National Academy of Sciences*, *116*(39), 19251–19257. https://doi.org/10.1073/pnas.1821936116

Donnelly, M. B. (2006). Educating students about the Holocaust: A survey of teaching practices. *Social Education, 70*(1), 51–54. https://eric.ed.gov/?id=EJ751146

Doppen, F. (2000). Teaching and learning multiple perspectives: The atomic bomb. *The Social Studies, 91*(4), 159–169. https://doi.org/10.1080/00377990009602461

Echoes & Reflections. (2022). *State by state: Holocaust education legislation.* https://echoesandreflections.org/interactive-map/

Endacott, J. L., & Brooks, S. (2013). An updated theoretical and practical model for promoting historical empathy. *Social Studies Research and Practice, 8*(1), 41–58. https://doi.org/10.1108/ssrp-01-2013-b0003

Endacott, J. L., & Pelekanos, C. (2015). Slaves, women, and war! Engaging midde school students in historical empathy for enduring understanding. *The Social Studies, 106*, 1–7. https://doi.org/10.1080/00377996.2014.957378

Evans, R. W. (2004). *The Social Studies Wars: What should we teach the children?* Teachers College Press.

Fallace, T. D. (2006). The origins of Holocaust education in American public schools. *Holocaust and Genocide Studies, 20*(1), 80–102. http://dx.doi.org/10.1093/hgs/dcj004

Fishman B. J., Marx, R. W., Best S., & Tal R. T. (2003). Linking teacher and student learning to improve professional development in systemic reform. *Teaching and Teacher Education, 19*, 643–658. https://doi.org/10.1016/S0742-051X(03)00059-3

Gaffney, C. (2019). When schools cause trauma. *Teaching Tolerance, 62.* https://www.learningforjustice.org/magazine/summer-2019/when-schools-cause-trauma

Georgia Department of Education [GaDOE]. (2016). *Social studies Georgia standards of excellence.* https://www.georgiastandards.org/Georgia-Standards/Pages/Social-Studies.aspx

Gray, M. (2014). *Contemporary debates in Holocaust education.* Palgrave Macmillan. http://dx.doi.org/10.1057/9781137388575

Haas, B. J. (2020). Bearing witness: Teacher perspectives on developing empathy through Holocaust survivor testimony. *The Social Studies, 111*, 86–103. https://doi.org/10.1080/00377996.2019.1693949

Jedwab, J. (2010). Measuring Holocaust knowledge and its impact: A Canadian case study. *Prospects, 40*(2), 273–287. https://doi.org/10.1007/s11125-010-9153-7

Jensen, J. (2008). Developing historical empathy through debate: An action research study. *Social Studies Research and Practice, 3*(1), 55–67. https://doi.org/10.1108/SSRP-01-2008-B0004

Keller, C. W. (1975). Role playing and simulation in history classes. *The History Teacher, 8*(4), 573–581. https://doi.org/10.2307/492668

Kershaw, A. (2016, January 24). *Teachers have been told they need training for Holocaust lessons.* The Independent. https://www.independent.co.uk/news/education/education-news/teachers-need-training-for-holocaust-lessons-mps-say-a6830726.html

Kohlmeier, J. (2006). "Couldn't she just leave?": The relationship between consistently using class discussions and the development of historical empathy in a 9th grade world history course. *Theory & Research in Social Education, 34*(1), 34–57. https://doi.org/10.1080/00933104.2006.10473297

Kornegay Rose, K., Cahill, S., & Baron, C. (2019). Providing teachers with what they need: Re-thinking historic site-based professional development after small-scale assessment. *Journal of Museum Education*, *44*(2), 201–209. https://doi.org/10.1080/10598650.2018.1539560

Lee, M. H. (2021). *Faith-based education and civic value formation* [Dissertation, University of Arkansas, Fayetteville]. https://scholarworks.uark.edu/etd/3952/

López, F., Molnar, A., Johnson, R., Patterson, A., Ward, L., & Kumashiro, K (2021, September 23). *Understanding the attacks on critical race theory.* National Education Policy Center. http://nepc.colorado.edu/publication/crt

Marcus, A. S., Levine, T. H., & Grenier, R. S. (2012). How secondary history teachers use and think about museums: Current practices and untapped promise for promoting historical understanding. *Theory & Research in Social Education*, *40*(1), 66–97. https://doi.org/10.1080/00933104.2012.649466

McCall, J. (2016). Teaching history with digital historical games: An introduction to the field and best practices. *Simulation & Gaming*, *47*(4), 517–542. https://doi.org/10.1177/1046878116646693

Merriam, S. B., & Tisdell, E. J. (2016). *Qualitative research: A guide to design and implementation* (4th ed.). John Wiley & Sons.

Metzger, S. A. (2012). The borders of historical empathy: Students encounter the Holocaust through film. *Journal of Social Studies Research*, *36*(4), 387–410. https://www.journals.elsevier.com/the-journal-of-social-studies-research

National Center for Education Statistics. (2021, May). *Characteristics of public school teachers*. Annual Reports and Information Staff (Annual Reports). https://nces.ed.gov/programs/coe/indicator/clr/public-school-teachers

National Council of History Education. (2016). *History's habits of mind.* https://ncheteach.org/

National Council for the Social Studies. (2013). *College, career, and civic life C3 framework for social studies state standards.* https://www.socialstudies.org/sites/default/files/c3/c3framework-for-social-studies-rev0617.pdf

Nesher Shoshan, H., & Wehrt, W. (2021). Understanding "zoom fatigue": A mixed-method approach. *Applied Psychology*, *71*(3), 827–852. https://doi.org/10.1111/apps.12360

Patterson, T. (2020). Historians, archivists, and museum educators as teacher educators: Mentoring preservice history teachers at cultural institutes. *Journal of Teacher Education*, *72*(1), 113–125. https://doi.org/10.1177/0022487120920251

Patterson, T., & Woyschner, C. (2016). History in other contexts: Pre-service history teachers' field placements at cultural institutions. *The History Teacher*, *50*(1), 9–31. https://doi.org/10.1177/0022487120920

Perrotta, K. A. (2018). Pedagogical conditions that promote historical empathy with "The Elizabeth Jennings Project". *Social Studies Research and Practice*, *13*(2), 129–146. https://doi.org/10.1108/SSRP-11-2017-0064

Perrotta, K. A., & Bohan, C. H. (2018). More than a feeling: Tracing the progressive era origins of historical empathy in the social studies curriculum, 1890s–1940s. *The Journal of Social Studies Research*, *42*(1), 27–37. https://doi.org/10.1016/j.jssr.2017.01.002

Perrotta, K. A., & Bohan, C. H. (2020). Can't stop this feeling: Teaching the origins of historical empathy during the Cold War Era, 1950–1980. *Educational Studies, 56*(6), 599–618. https://doi.org/10.1080/00131946.2020.1837832

Peters, W. (2020). Film in history education: A review of the literature. *The Social Studies, 111*(6), 275–295. https://doi.org/10.1080/00377996.2020.1757598

Rich, J. (2019). "It led to great advances in science": What teacher candidates know about the Holocaust. *The Social Studies, 110*(2), 51–66. https://doi:10.1080/0 0377996.2018.1515060

Riley, K. L. (1998). Historical empathy and the Holocaust: Theory into practice. *International Journal of Social Education, 13*(1), 32–42. http://ijse.iweb.bsu.edu

Rose, J. (2016). *Interpreting difficult history at museums and historic Sites.* Rowman & Littlefield.

Salmons, P. (2003). Teaching or preaching? The Holocaust and intercultural education in the UK. *Intercultural Education, 14*(2), 139–149. https://doi.org/10.1080/14675980304568

Segall, A. (2014). Making difficult history public: The pedagogy of remembering and forgetting in two Washington DC Museums. *Review of Education, Pedagogy, and Cultural Studies, 36*(1), 55–70. https://doi.org/10.1080/10714413.2014.8 66818

Sheppard, M., Kortecamp, K., Jencks, S., Flack, J., & Wood, A. (2019). Connecting theory and practice: Using place-based learning in teacher professional development. *Journal of Museum Education, 44*(2), 187–200. https://doi.org/1 0.1080/10598650.2019.1597598

Ulaby, N. (2022, April 10). *Museums turn to immersive tech to preserve the stories of aging Holocaust survivors.* NPR. https://www.npr.org/2022/04/10/1089652445/museums-turn-to-immersive-tech-to-preserve-the-stories-of-aging-holocaust-surviv

United States Holocaust Memorial Museum. (n.d.a.). *Guidelines for teaching about the Holocaust.* https://www.ushmm.org/teach/fundamentals/guidelines-for-teaching-the-holocaust

United States Holocaust Memorial Museum. (n.d.b.). *Holocaust Education in the United States.* https://www.ushmm.org/teach/fundamentals/where-holocaust-education-is-required-in-the-us

U.S. General Services Administration. (2019, May 20). *National register of historic places.* https://www.gsa.gov/real-estate/historic-preservation/historic-building-stewardship/national-register-of-historic-places

Van Driel, J. H., & Berry, A. (2012). Teacher professional development focusing on pedagogical content knowledge. *Educational Researcher, 41*(1), 26–28. https://doi.org/10.3102/0013189X11431010

Yancie, N. (2022). Exploring race issues at turn of the 20th century: A qualitative study. *Research Issues in Contemporary Education, 7*(3), 29–66. https://files.eric.ed.gov/fulltext/EJ1359408.pdf

Yang, M. (2023, February 8). *Teach US students about Holocaust, experts say, amid rise in antisemitism.* The Guardian. https://www.theguardian.com/education/2023/feb/08/us-education-holocaust-antisemitism

CHAPTER 6

FACTORS SHAPING TEACHER EDUCATION GRADUATES' ABILITIES TO IMPACT STUDENTS' LEARNING AND DEVELOPMENT DURING INDUCTION

Joyce E. Many, Carla L. Tanguay, and Ruchi Bhatnagar
Georgia State University

ABSTRACT

Our study examined novice urban teachers' abilities to impact student learning and development. We interviewed 19 graduates, collecting narratives of critical teaching incidents. Analysis revealed the importance of (a) connecting with learners and of (b) receiving support. Teacher education programs were helpful in preparing graduates to set high expectations, use culturally responsive strategies, and develop relationships to meet diverse learners' needs. Graduates also identified induction supports that helped or hindered effectiveness.

Teacher education programs are critical in preparing teacher candidates for the profession and in extending support for new teachers into the induction years (Bastian & Marks, 2017; Freedman & Appleman, 2009).

Curriculum and Teaching Dialogue,
Volume 25, Numbers 1 & 2, pp. 135–153
Copyright © 2023 by Information Age Publishing
www.infoagepub.com
All rights of reproduction in any form reserved.

Drawing on an understanding of their candidates' strengths and needs, teacher education faculty can provide focused coursework and supports geared toward effective clinical experiences, constructive mentoring by a university supervisor and a mentor teacher, and opportunities for growth stimulated by reflection (Bastian & Marks, 2017; Many et al., 2019). Extensive teacher preparation is significantly correlated with novices' self-efficacy, their focus on student learning, and retention (DeAngelis et al., 2013; Tait, 2008; Tricarico et al., 2015). After graduation, continued support makes a difference, with high-quality induction programs tempering teachers' desires to leave the profession (Warsame & Valles, 2018). Other researchers also emphasize a combination of effective teacher preparation and comprehensive school district induction supports help to increase retention (Ingersoll, 2012; Ingersoll et al., 2012; Ronfeldt & McQueen, 2017). In particular, having a mentor who teaches the same subject matter and the frequency of support in subject matter or grade level instructions, classroom management, technology use, and use of assessment are important predictors of teacher retention (Maready et al., 2021).

Induction initiatives typically aim to improve the quality of beginning teachers by providing on-site support and guidance which is especially critical during the first three years of teaching (Feiman-Nemser, 2001; Ingersoll, 2012). New teachers have a number of stressors in their professional lives and are simultaneously juggling teaching and other responsibilities, while learning to refine their classroom management and pedagogical skills (Feiman-Nemser, 2001). Investigating the many challenges that novice teachers face, researchers found some of the top issues include novices' abilities (a) to meet diverse student learning needs (e.g., students with individualized education programs [IEPs], English learners [ELs]), (b) to communicate effectively with parents, (c) to plan for instruction and assessment, and (d) to establish classroom management practices (Maready et al., 2021; Nielsen et al., 2007). Despite intense teacher preparation, a novice teacher learns some aspects of teaching only when serving as the teacher of record. At that time, they are fully entrusted with all the responsibilities of teaching, team planning, serving on committees, and completing paperwork for accountability and reporting (Tricarico et al., 2015).

While teacher education and school system induction supports are critical for novice development, retention in the profession, and impact on student learning, certain personal beliefs and dispositions also determine the success and resiliency of novice teachers in high-need contexts (Tait, 2008; Tricarico et al., 2015). Teachers' resilience may be influenced by their values, core beliefs, passion for improving student learning, and ability to proactively seek strategies and resources for effective teaching (Ladson-Billings, 2014; Tricarico, 2015). Tait's (2008) findings indicated that a beginning teacher's resilience to persevere and stay in the profession is related to personal efficacy and emotional competence. Teachers who demonstrate self-efficacy exemplify the ability to problem solve, rebound, learn from experience, take care of themselves, and maintain an optimistic spirit (Tait, 2008). Research has also shown that successful teachers in high-need urban contexts build relationships with students and families, demonstrate an ethic of care, hold high academic and behavioral expectations, act as warm demanders, develop a sociocultural consciousness and criticality, and affirm student identities (Bondy & Ross, 2008; Freedman & Appleman, 2009; Kohli, 2019; Ladson-Billings, 2014, Muhammad, 2020). Tricarico et al. (2015) add that teachers who have an impact on student learning possess a strong work ethic, find resources to improve pedagogy, demonstrate knowledge and skills to differentiate instruction, and pursue teacher leader opportunities. Thus, teachers' program preparation, professional experiences in schools, and personal beliefs and dispositions intersect and influence their ability to persevere, survive, or thrive in a challenging environment (Borman & Dowling, 2008; Tricarico et al., 2015).

Given the importance of teacher preparation and the initial years in the profession, it is important to understand from the novice teachers' perspectives which factors contributed to their effectiveness in the first two years and also the factors that hindered their success in improving student learning (Tricario et al., 2015). This information could help teacher education programs improve their preparation and work with school districts to come up with induction structures that support novice teachers in their initial years. Providing novices with needed supports may also ensure that they do not become overwhelmed and decide to exit the profession (Bastian & Marks, 2017; Ingersoll, 2012; Maready et al., 2021; Ronfeldt & McQueen, 2017).

In this research, three teacher educators explore narratives of novice teachers' experiences, described as *critical incidents*, where they attempted to impact student learning and development. Participants had been prepared by the institution where the authors served as administrative leaders for the educator preparation programs. After their graduation the participants were hired by urban partner school districts to teach in schools serving students from diverse ethnicities. The specific research question addressed in this inquiry was: What helps or hinders novice teachers' ability to impact student learning and development in an urban school district?

METHODOLOGY

The context for this study was a college of education and human development (CEHD), located in the heart of a large, southeastern city in an urban, research university. The college's mission is to prepare educators who are *informed* by research, knowledge, and reflective practice; *empowered* to serve as change agents; *committed* to and respectful of all learners; and *engaged* with learners, their families, schools, and communities. Teacher candidates graduating from this program were prepared to focus on culturally responsive pedagogy, and most of their clinical experiences were in ethnically and linguistically diverse, high-need schools (Bhatnagar et al., 2016).

The design for this inquiry was an exploratory case study (Yin, 2018) bounded by graduates who had completed their first or second year of teaching between 2018–2020 in one of three partnering urban school districts. The authors purposely selected three districts (labeled 100, 200, and 300), which hired the largest number of the institution's graduates the previous year. Invitations to participate were emailed to graduates in these systems, and teachers consenting to participate included 19 educators (10 White, 6 African American, 2 Hispanic, and 1 Asian) from across diverse programs leading to certification offered by our institution (undergraduate and Master of Arts in Teaching programs in art, career and technical education, early childhood education, English to speakers of other languages [ESOL], elementary education, health care science, health and physical education, history, middle level, and special education).

The primary data source for this study focused on participants' narratives of critical teaching incidents related to their effectiveness. Interviews were conducted in person, by telephone, or via internet and lasted 45–60 minutes. The semi-structured interviews and data analysis were based on the Butterfield et al.'s (2009) description of the critical incident technique first developed by Flanagan (1954) and which we had adapted based on our own use of the protocol in a previous study (Many et al., 2019). The interview began with a focus on the interviewee's teaching context and beliefs about their ability to impact students' learning and development in their classroom. Next the participants described particular occasions where they were able to impact learning and development, or they struggled to impact their students (see critical incident protocol in Figure 6.1). Researchers audio recorded and transcribed each interview verbatim using Otter.ai, and then edited each transcript for clarification.

The first step of data analysis was focused on the participants' perceptions of what it meant to "impact student learning and development" and their subsequent descriptions of critical incidents (CI) where they had an impact on student learning and development or were challenged in doing so. Additionally, graduates described the helping factor, or the hindering factor as related to each corresponding CI, and they identified the source of the helping and hindering factors as program, school/district, or personal. Researchers coded the CI and related factors using constant comparative analysis (Corbin & Strauss, 2008), looking for patterns in the data within and across districts. Two independent raters analyzed data and any disagreements were settled by consensus.

Factors Shaping Teacher Education Graduates' Abilities   139

Figure 6.1

Critical Incident (CI) Interview Protocol

Critical Incident—Impact on Students		
You described your ability to impact student learning and development as XXXX. Think of a specific occasion (CI) when you felt you made an impact on student learning and development.		
Example of CI	**Helpful Factor**	**Importance**
• What was the incident/ experience where you impacted learning and development? • What was the outcome?	• What was a factor which helped you to be effective in this situation? • Were there any other factors that helped?	• How did XXX help? • Tell me what it was about > > > that you found so helpful?
Can you think of another occasion where you were able to impact learning and development during your first year of teaching? * (repeat until no additional CI's are identified)		
Critical Incident—Difficulty Impacting Students		
Were there times when you found it difficult to impact student learning and development during your first year? Think of a specific occasion when this happened.		
Example of CI	**Hindering Factor**	**Importance**
• What was the incident/ experience where you struggled to impact learning and development? • What was the outcome?	• What was a factor which hindered your ability to be effective in this situation? • Were there any other factors that may have added to the difficulty?	• How did XXX hinder your ability? • Tell me what it was about > > > that you found challenging?
Change Over Time		
Have you changed over time in your views of your ability to impact student learning and development? If so, when did you change in your view? What happened that caused you to begin to feel more positive or less positive about your ability?		

RESULTS

Findings included 146 CI and descriptions of 72 helping factors and 74 hindering factors reported by graduates as influencing their impact on student learning and development. Graduates attributed their success to factors associated with their program (43%), with the school and/or district (28%), and with their own personal characteristics (29%; See Figure 6.2). While helping factors were attributed to all three of these areas, factors which hindered new teacher effectiveness were more notably associated at the school or district level (73%) and were rarely attributed to personal characteristics (3%).

Figure 6.2

Source of Factors Helping or Hindering Graduate Effectiveness

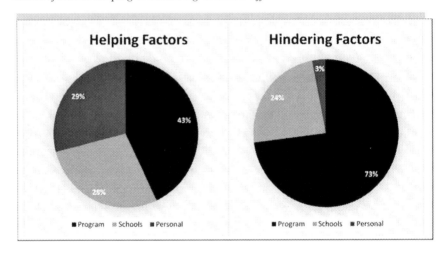

Two themes which shaped graduates' efforts to impact the learning and development of their students centered on the importance of (a) connecting with learners and (b) receiving support. These novice urban teachers described incidents where their teacher preparation programs were helpful in preparing them to focus on knowing their students to meet learners' diverse needs; however, graduates also identified their need for supports during their first and/or second years of teaching (i.e., induction), when teacher preparation was not enough. They also saw their effectiveness as related to the support or lack of support they received during their induction period.

Connecting With Learners

Graduates described CI that demonstrated their focus on connecting with their students to improve learning. In addition to the criticality of setting high expectations and teaching academically rigorous curriculum, novices described the importance of building relationships, advocating for students, and using culturally responsive classroom management strategies to create positive learning environments. Furthermore, these new teachers explained incidents where they were not as effective based upon hinderances related to the limited human capital to support diverse learner needs in their schools/districts (see Table 6.1).

Table 6.1

Factors Influencing Graduates' Ability to Connect to Learners

Source	Description
	Helping
Program	Set high expectations and academic rigor
	Developed student relationships and advocated for learners
	Used culturally responsive classroom management strategies and engaged students in positive learning environments
Personal	Learned from experiences through trial and error
	Used self-development strategies
	Hindering
School/District	Lack of support from resource personnel
Program	Needed more exposure to coursework and field experiences with diverse learners

How Novice Teachers Were Helped in Their Ability to Connect With Learners

Focusing on their ability to connect with learners in order to impact students' development, graduates cited program and personal factors as the sources of their success. New teachers credited the ways in which their preparation stressed drawing on the knowledge of the learner to build learning capacity as they described successful incidents where they set high expectations and academic rigor, advocated for learners, used culturally responsive classroom management strategies, and engaged students in positive learning communities. For example, one graduate attributed her success at *setting high expectations* for her learners to program coursework where she engaged in action research and learned what it meant to be a warm demander. Understanding the importance of the relation of students' efficacy and the affirmations they receive from teachers, she underscores that while she is pushes them to do what she expects them to do, she is going to love on them and reward them for their hard work.

Additionally, this elementary teacher explained that she learned in her program to *build student relationships* by using affirming language through her formative assessments. She noted the importance of providing immediate, direct feedback to improve student confidence and learning and to tell the students they are on the right track. She explained:

> I have one student in particular ... not only does she have a reputation for being a little bit of a mean girl, but then she struggles academically ... this last semester I began tutoring her and I've been able to see her confidence go up ... I give her that reassurance that she needs ... and I'm able to give her that direct feedback immediately so that she knows, ok I am on the right track.

Another novice explained how he learned in the CEHD program that by getting to know your learners and *advocating* for them, student learning will follow. This new ESOL high school teacher provided an example of an English learner who was interested, yet reluctant, to participate in school activities. Through this teacher's advocacy, the student was encouraged to take advantage of an opportunity to participate in creating the high school yearbook and apply the speaking and writing skills she was learning. He said:

> I kind of felt like [the yearbook] was an area where ESOL students kind of shied away from getting involved in school activities.... It'll push her into an environment ... [which] also helps her grow and also, I think it will help her represent another population of the school.... [My college coursework] talked a lot about advocating for ESOL students ... I didn't really realize ... they actually needed [for] people to advocate for them. So, [I] focus on that and encourage them, you know when they're a little bit too hesitant to do it for themselves.

Highlighting the criticality of building relationships with learners *to engage them in positive learning opportunities*, a middle-grades science teacher described the way her students' test scores "went through the roof" when she listened to her students' recommendations and changed the classroom to allow more active involvement and conversations.

> And I just had to like trust [the students'] opinion, like they are the people in the seats learning.... [Our college] used to tell us that like your kids are your customers, not their parents, not the school district. Your kids are

your customers and you are selling them your lesson. And if you can't sell it to them, they're not gonna buy it ... I got to figure out what my customers want. Yeah, they love it.

One kindergarten teacher used *culturally responsive classroom management strategies* and social and emotional supports learned during her preparation program as she worked with a new student who was struggling with behavior problems. The teacher explained that taking time to develop a close relationship with the learner and with her parents resulted in more classroom time for academic content:

It turned out she was just extremely anxious about school and extremely anxious about making new friends, and not really able to control everything. So, once I learned that, I was able to relay that to her parents and just have really, really strong relationship with her parents to make sure that she felt well prepared for kindergarten and that she felt supported socially and emotionally. And then we were able to focus on her academics.

As shown in Figure 6.1, graduates also highlighted CI that were made possible due to personal factors (i.e., reliance on self), such as *learning from their own experiences* as teachers or *engaging in self-development*. When graduates considered why they were effective at impacting learning and development, many cited the fact that they were continually *learning from experiences using trial and error*. One middle-grades social studies teacher (Interviewee 107) explained that seeing the difference in retention during lessons where she used a hands-on activity versus just talking to students was one example of how reflecting on what did or did not work in the classroom helped her learn what was effective. Other graduates indicated their ability to impact learners stemmed directly from their efforts at *self-development*. A special education teacher discussed the trauma, abuse, and violence her students were dealing with and explained how she highlights the ways in which she cares for herself to help students understand the importance of self-care:

And I talk to my kids all the time [about things I do for self-care] ... we're going to go on a trail hike, and it's going be great ... or I'm going to give myself a face mask.... We teach our kids, you need to take care of yourself like that.... And like how ... to set boundaries up in their lives.

Another novice explained how becoming an advocate for herself as a teacher who could make wise instructional decisions enabled her to also become an advocate for her students. This elementary teacher searched out and tried new strategies to support a student's needs, and she found it made a difference. She noted:

I really advocated for my students and for myself as an educator ... I was very proactive ... I completely adapted a new reading teaching model for this one child because, you know, like, I have to change things up for him. But just being flexible and willing, I think was the biggest ways that I was able to impact this child's life.

How Factors Hindered Novice Teachers' Ability to Connect With Learners

When reflecting on instances where they struggled to impact student learning, novice teachers expressed the need for specific resource personnel in their schools who could have stepped in to resolve situations or support them in more challenging environments. Some teachers also felt more exposure to coursework and field experiences with diverse learners (e.g., students with disabilities, ELs) in their programs could have been beneficial.

In terms of the school systems in which they worked, novices related occasions where requests for *specific resource personnel* (i.e., paraprofessionals, tutors, ESOL teachers, instructional and intervention specialists) were needed and not granted. One dual immersion teacher explained how primary classroom teachers had access to support staff, Response to Intervention (RTI), an intervention specialist, math coaches, and literacy coaches because instruction was in English. In contrast, because her dual immersion lessons were taught in Spanish, there was no assistance available to her in the classroom because the support teachers did not know Spanish. She stressed over the fact that the only way her students would have gotten support would be if they were pulled out of her classroom and be taught in English. The absence of support for English learners was also underscored as indicative of systemic inequality by another middle-school teacher who shared her frustration at being limited as a teacher when resources are not allocated equitably. She explained:

I'm very passionate and outspoken about the fact that our system is designed not for people that aren't from this country. And our system is designed for, like if we're truthful and honest, white students. And they're designed to promote a certain social order and I think that it's a system-wide issue, not just in [my school] not just in my county, but like in the United States. And I struggle with that because I don't know what to do, because I feel like my kids' voices aren't heard, and they're not cared about.

Lack of support from resource personnel in the school left teachers feeling frustrated and feeling that their students were being left behind because of a resource shortage. Other situations were described as being influenced not by a lack of resources, but rather a lack of administrative

Factors Shaping Teacher Education Graduates' Abilities   145

support. In talking about her students with learning needs, a middle-school teacher said students stuck at Level 3 for longer than a year should be recommended for an IEP, but there was not an adequate review process in place. She complained:

> To me that showed a real lack of support from the administration who really should be monitoring and checking in and looking at RTI on a consistent basis so that, particularly our students of color, who oftentimes don't have parent advocates, specifically in my school, are not getting lost and staying at Tier 3 for, you know, all of their middle-school career.

Finally, in thinking about their struggles, graduates expressed the need for *more exposure to coursework and field experiences with diverse learners*, a program factor. Multiple graduates commented on the need for more knowledge and hands-on opportunities to work with students with disabilities. For example, one elementary teacher shared that she had chosen an ESOL track in college rather than a special education track, so she was left lacking the knowledge and skills she felt she needed to work with a child with specific disabilities. She shared that although she had varied grade level and teaching situations with English language learners, she had never been "in a classroom where any behavior [was] even similar to this child … I didn't experience inclusion classes or what it looks like … when you have a student who might qualify for an inclusion class." This new educator was surprised and disconcerted by the experience because of her lack of preparation for teaching students with special behavioral needs.

Other novices called for more opportunities to be prepared for issues in the real world around poverty, trauma, and immigration as well as how to deal with problems teachers encounter that go far beyond teaching the curriculum. One middle-grades teacher explained:

> Like there are real issues, like social-work related issues that we have to be prepared to deal with, and I think even having like … social work training for teachers, where they know how to deal with kids emotionally grabbing kids [or] like attempting suicide at my school…. There's a lot more than just teaching and how to teach, but teachers need to be prepared for like ESOL and students' suicide and the impact of social media, that I don't think that education focuses on yet.

Despite the range of field experiences provided in their programs, the novice teachers called for more diverse experiences, namely teaching students with disabilities in collaborative inclusive settings, teaching English learners, and working with other school specialists to assist students dealing with trauma.

Receiving Support

Graduates also described CI where they felt they needed more assistance from their schools and districts to impact student learning and development. They saw their success, or their lack of success, as being due to whether they received support from colleagues and administrators at their schools. For an overview, see Table 6.2.

Table 6.2

Factors Effectiveness as Influenced by the Availability of Support

Source	Description
School/District Helping	
Support from colleagues	Other teachers—with instructional strategies
	Counselors, school psychologists—meeting cognitive, emotional, and behavioral needs of learners
Support from administrators	Feedback on practice based upon observation
	School culture inclusive of socioemotional learning
School/District Hindering	
Limited support from administrators	Challenging student behaviors
Lack of timely or accessible professional development	Needed classroom/behavior management strategies
	Needed strategies to support culturally responsive instruction for ELs
Lack of effective mentoring	Misalignment of grade level/subject area with mentor
	Conflicting schedule with mentor
	Unapproachable, intimidating mentor
	No mentor

How Colleague/Administrative Supports Helped Novice Urban Teachers

Many of our new teachers highlighted their *school colleagues as the primary source of human capital* within their schools and districts that contributed to their success. Graduates indicated that their colleagues provided the most support with instructional strategies (e.g., how to make instruction engaging, interactive, real-world applicable, useful for test preparation, and the incorporation of technology). One special education teacher noted she was supported by not only her department chair and science coach but also by the district science coordinator to understand how to plan and teach the curriculum to cover everything that would eventually be on the grade-level test. *Other teachers and school personnel* (e.g., counselors, school psychologists, other teachers) also provided support for graduates in meeting the cognitive, emotional, and behavioral needs of their students. One elementary teacher shared her positive experience of reaching out for assistance to colleagues, the school psychologist, and the school counselor. She underscored that she continually found her coworkers to be willing to help and that they "never seemed annoyed by it, they were always just like, 'Of course, what do you need?'"

Administrator support, while mentioned on a limited basis in our data, was sought out by some novice teachers to assist them in working with students possessing challenging behaviors. Some graduates also found it useful to have their administrators see what they were doing in their instructional time and give constructive *feedback on their practice*. Furthermore, administrators who *created a school culture* that was inclusive of socioemotional learning and was culturally responsive to the students' needs were also cited as a helping factor. One middle-school teacher described school-wide initiatives administrators promoted that she felt made a difference including building socioemotional learning, emphasizing Afrocentrism, and establishing literacy programs where students could self-select texts to read for 30 minutes a day.

How a Lack of Support Can Hinder Effectiveness

In contrast, some teachers felt their inability to be effective stemmed from a lack of support at the school or district level. One school and district factor the novice teachers in our study mentioned was that the *professional development* they were provided with was ineffective. Some new teachers felt the content of the professional development did not consider the context of the school or provide teachers with support for culturally responsive instruction. For instance, one middle-school teacher felt that if she had learned at the new teacher institute or from her school system how to take into account the specific background of the children at her school, she would have been more successful starting out. Teachers also commented on the content of professional development not being timely or accessible, with one saying, "I don't think the opportunities are always circulated very well to the schools." This teacher went on to express frustration at learning something in the spring that she would have found extremely beneficial the previous November. In addition, the novice teachers felt that the kind of professional development they needed to be successful in high-needs settings and in schools with large proportions of ESOL students was either not offered or offered too late to be useful for them to become culturally responsive.

Finally, as novice teachers, the *support of a mentor* within the school building was something the teachers in our study expressed a need for; however, they lacked systematic support at their school. Some graduates were never assigned a mentor, others had mentors who did not follow through with meetings, and one noted there was never time provided for mentors and mentees to meet. The desire for increased support was underscored by many graduates, as one explained:

> I just think that there wasn't a lot of support when I came to my school district for new teachers. We have a mentor program, but there wasn't ever really time to meet with our mentor. And there wasn't really a lot of like, preparation for new teachers and what to actually do for our population of students. I struggled with that a lot, like a feeling of lack of support.

Thus, novices experienced ineffective mentoring due to time constraints and conflicting schedules with their mentor or a misalignment in grade level or subject area with their mentor. Additionally, an unapproachable, intimidating mentor or no mentor at all caused novices to experience additional stress.

DISCUSSION

This study used novice teachers' descriptions of CI to understand their efforts to impact students' learning and development. This methodology has been used successfully to explore the effectiveness of K–12 programs (Andreou et al., 2015), to evaluate teacher preparation for in person and online instruction (Many et al., 2019; Tanguay & Many, 2022), and to identify positive and negative behaviors of teachers at the college level (Khandelwal, 2009). Flanagan (1954) noted descriptions of CI are to serve as "direct observations of human behavior in such a way as to facilitate their potential usefulness in solving practical problems and developing broad psychological principles" (p. 327). In a previous research study using CI techniques, however, Many et al. (2019) noted the need to carefully prompt interviewees for explicit descriptions of classroom experiences to avoid obtaining teachers' broad perceptions of their effectiveness and their teaching contexts. While the data collection in our present study focused interviewees' attention on providing detailed narratives of the incidents they had identified as critical in demonstrating their impact on students, our understanding of the impact of these novice teachers on students' learning and development is limited by not having either direct classroom observations or interviews with students or school personnel to triangulate the self-reported phenomena the educators discussed.

Participants in this study were graduates of educator preparation programs guided by a mission of social justice and advocacy. In relating their efforts to impact student learning and development, these novice urban teachers indicated that factors related to their teacher preparation programs contributed to their ability to be successful in high-need schools. Our findings underscored how culturally responsive preparation that focused on learners was important to teacher effectiveness in the classrooms. Successful urban education teachers are committed, as noted in previous literature, to using knowledge of their learners' development; academic knowledge; and personal, cultural, linguistic, and community assets to make connections to instruction to improve learning (Ladson-Billings, 2014, Muhammad, 2020). They recognize the criticality of building student relationships and establishing positive learning communities in order to impact student learning and development. Teacher preparation focused on culturally relevant, subject-specific pedagogy and on immersion in clinical experiences with diverse students were among the most impactful practices that helped our novice teachers succeed during induction (Bastian & Marks, 2017; Ingersoll et al., 2012).

These novice teachers were prepared within a program that emphasized cultural responsiveness and were currently teaching in schools with a high percentage of students of color from high poverty areas. To be effective, these young teachers explicitly expressed a need for induction support in certain areas (i.e., community building, classroom management, differentiated instruction for diverse learners, resource and administrative support). As can be seen from the analysis, the novice teachers established positive student relationships, created culturally responsive learning communities, and exhibited authentic care through advocacy while also demonstrating high expectations for their students and respect for their cultural identity and intellect (Muhammad, 2020). Although teachers in our study alluded to being warm demanders (Bondy & Ross, 2008), those who experienced a lack of support at the school or district level felt hindered at developing students' achievement, affective capacity, identity, and well-being. Such school-related constraints have also been shown to exacerbate stress and burnout in novice teachers (Tricarico et al., 2015).

Very few studies have investigated how teacher perceptions about the supports provided during their initial years can have implications for induction programs—specifically in terms of partnerships between universities and school districts. As seen from this data, a critical need exists for high-quality induction support for beginning teachers, specifically, in high-need and underfunded schools. This study provides recommendations for induction support based on the factors the novice teachers found helpful or hindering during their initial years in the teaching profession. University faculty should continue to support their inductees through their initial years of teaching by building upon the student teaching relationship, the knowledge of their graduates, and the knowledge of the context of the high-need schools where they will be teaching. Furthermore, these connections between universities and partner schools and districts allow for a reciprocal relationship and provide a strong incentive—that best practices from the field can come back to improve teacher education and university-based induction (Bastian & Marks, 2017). Such a collaboration between universities and P–12 partner schools could provide pathways for hiring graduates, provide feedback to teacher education programs, and extend teacher education beyond certification to provide scaffolding for in-service teacher development during induction (Bastian & Marks, 2017).

Novice teachers require several supports as they become acclimated to the rigors of being full-time educators; however, research has shown that new teachers are disproportionately placed in high-need schools with significant teacher attrition (Borman & Dowling, 2008). These schools serve large populations of students living in poverty who need systems-oriented, programmatic student support where school counselors and social workers identify students' needs and strengths and provide bridges between students, families, teachers, and service providers (Herberle et al., 2021). Many urban school districts are unable to provide these types of comprehensive, organizational supports, which teachers need to be effective and which buffer educator burnout (Bastian & Marks, 2017; Herberle et al., 2021; Ingersoll, 2012). Overwhelmed by the demands of the profession in the first two years, new teachers face mandates; a lack of autonomy; and an absence of systematic, high-quality support—all of which lead to teacher turnover (Ingersoll & May, 2011). Our work underscores the importance of comprehensive induction supports—such as an orientation program, instructional resource teachers, professional development, and opportunities to collaborate with colleagues and other school service providers. Such supports were critical components for developing new teachers' capacity to impact learning and development, and these are factors that research has shown also enhances job satisfaction (Kohli, 2019; Nielsen et al., 2007).

In closing, novice teachers' transition to the job and their perceived efficacy was impacted by three main factors evident also in teacher education literature: (a) preparation in teacher education to meet the needs of urban schools, (b) context-specific induction support offered by the school or district, and (c) personal characteristics of the teachers as professionals (DeAngelis et al., 2013; Nielsen et al., 2007; Tait, 2008; Tricarico et al., 2015). These factors were woven throughout our findings, interacting in a way that teachers felt empowered, and which enabled them to persist in the face of challenge (Ado, 2013; Gu & Day, 2007). Through

Factors Shaping Teacher Education Graduates' Abilities 151

the intertwined framework provided by programs, schools, and personal professional endeavors, novice teachers were able to effectively motivate students, engage in critical practices, and create positive learning environments for their students (Kohli, 2019). Should the educational community commit to providing such a network of collaborative support, more teachers who enter urban classrooms would be enabled to cultivate the genius of the students they serve (Muhammad, 2020) and become the caring, capable, professionals they were meant to be.

REFERENCES

Ado, K. (2013). Keeping them on the bus: Retaining early career teachers in a successful urban school. *The New Educator, 9*(2), 135–151. https://doi.org/10.1080/1547688X.2013.778761

Andreou, T. E., McIntosh, K., Ross, S. W., & Kahn, J. D. (2015). Critical incidents in sustain school-wide positive behavioral interventions and supports. *The Journal of Special Education, 49*(3), 157–167. https://doi.org/10.1177/0022466914554298

Bastian, K. C., & Marks, J. T. (2017). Connecting teacher preparation to teacher induction: Outcomes for beginning teachers in a university-based support program in low-performing schools. *American Educational Research Journal, 54*(2), 360–394. https://doi.org/10.3102/0002831217690517

Bhatnagar, R., Kim, J., Many, J. E., Barker, K., Ball, M., & Tanguay, C. (2016). Are we making our social justice framework salient?: Students' perceptions of urban teacher preparation program effectiveness. *National Teacher Education Journal, 9,* 27–39.

Bondy, E., & Ross, D. D. (2008). The teacher as warm demander. *Educational Leadership, 66*(1), 54–58.

Borman, G. D., & Dowling, N. M. (2008). Teacher attrition and retention: A meta-analytic and narrative review of the research. *Review of Educational Research, 78,* 367–409. https://doi.org/10.3102/0034654308321455

Butterfield, L. D., Borgen, W. A., Maglio, A.T., & Amundson, N. E. (2009). Using the enhanced Critical Incident Technique in counselling psychology research. *Canadian Journal of Counselling, 43*(4), 265–282.

Corbin, J., & Strauss, A. (2008). *Basics of qualitative research* (3rd ed.). SAGE.

DeAngelis, K. J., Wall, A. F., & Che, J. (2013). The impact of preservice preparation and early career support on novice teachers' career intentions and decisions. *Journal of Teacher Education, 64*(4), 338–355. https://doi.org/10.1177/0022487113488945

Feiman-Nemser, S. (2001). Helping novices learn to teach: Lessons from an exemplary support teacher. *Journal of Teacher Education, 52*(1), 17–30. https://doi.org/10.1177/0022487101052001003

Flanagan, J. (1954). The critical incident technique. *Psychological Bulletin, 51*(4), 327–358.

Freedman, S. W., & Appleman, D. (2009). "In it for the long haul": How teacher education can contribute to teacher retention in high-poverty, urban schools. *Journal of Teacher Education, 60*(3), 323–337.

Gu, Q., & Day, C. (2007). Teachers resilience: A necessary condition for effectiveness. *Teaching and Teacher Education, 23*(8), 1302–1316. https://doi.org/10.1016/j.tate.2006.06.006

Herberle, A. E., Sheanain, U. N., Walsh, M. E., Hamilton, A. N., Chung, A. H., & Eells Lutas, V. L. (2021). Experiences of practitioners implementing comprehensive student support in high-poverty schools. *Improving Schools, 24*(1), 76–93. https://doi.org/10.1177/1365480220943761

Ingersoll, R. (2012). Beginning teacher induction: What the data tell us. *Phi Delta Kappan, 93*(8), 47–51. http://www.kappanmagazine.org/content/93/8/47

Ingersoll, R., & May, H. (2011). *Recruitment, retention and the minority teacher shortage* (CPRE Research Report #RR-69). Consortium for Policy Research in Education. https://repository.upenn.edu/gse_pubs/226

Ingersoll, R., Merrill, L., & May, H. (2012). Retaining teachers: How preparation matters. *Educational Leadership, 69*(8), 30–34.

Kohli, R. (2019). Lessons for teacher education: The role of critical professional development in teacher of color retention. *Journal of Teacher Education, 70*(1), 39–50. https://doi.org/10.1177/0022487118767645

Khandelwal, K. A. (2008). Effective teaching behaviors in the college classroom: A Critical Incident Technique from students' perspective. *International Journal of Higher Education, 21,* 299–309.

Ladson-Billings, G. (2014). Culturally relevant pedagogy 2.0: a.k.a. the remix. Harvard Educational Review, 84(1), 74–84.

Many, J. E., Bhatnagar, R., & Tanguay, C. (2019). Learning from the experiences of novice urban teachers: Teacher education and induction program factors that influence effectiveness. *GATEways to Teacher Education, 30*(1), 16–30. https://issuu.com/gaate/docs/gateways_fall_2019/16

Maready, B., Cheng, Q., & Bunch, D. (2021). Exploring mentoring practices contributing to new teacher retention: An analysis of the beginning teacher longitudinal study. *International Journal of Evidence Based Coaching and Mentoring, 19*(2), 88–99. https://doi.org/10.24384/rgm9-sa56

Muhammad, G. (2020). *Cultivating genius: An equity framework for culturally and historically responsive literacy.* Scholastic.

Nielsen, D. C., Barry, A. L., & Addison, A. B. (2007). A model of a new-teacher induction program and teacher perceptions of beneficial components. *Action in Teacher Education, 28*(4), 14–24. https://doi.org/10.1080/01626620.2007.10463425

Ronfeldt, M., & McQueen, K. (2017). Does new teacher induction really improve retention? *Journal of Teacher Education, 68*(4), 394–410. https://doi.org/10.1177%2F0022487117702583.

Tait, M. (2008). Resilience as a contributor to novice teacher success, commitment, and retention. *Teacher Education Quarterly,* Fall, 57–75. http://www.jstor.org/stable/23479174

Tanguay, C. L., & Many, J. E. (2022). New teachers' perceptions of their impact on student learning while developing knowledge and skills to teach online.

International Journal of Technology in Education, 5(4), 637–653. http://dx.doi.org/10.46328/ijte.309

Tricarico, K. M., Jacobs, J., & Yendol-Hoppey, D. (2015). Reflection on their first five years of teaching: Understanding staying and impact power. *Teachers and Teaching*, 21(3), 237–259. https://doi.org/10.1080/13540602.2014.953821

Warsame, K., & Valles, J. (2018). An analysis of effective support structures for novice teachers. *Journal of Teacher Education and Educators*, 7(1), 17–42.

Yin, R. K. (2018). *Case study research and applications: Design and methods* (6th ed.). SAGE.

CHAPTER 7

THE FLUID CURRICULUM

Reinvigorating the Role of the Teacher as Curriculum Maker

Bradley Conrad
Capital University

Christy McConnell
University of Northern Colorado

Sarah Campbell
University of Northern Colorado

P. Bruce Uhrmacher
University of Denver

ABSTRACT

In this conceptual article the authors advocate for a "fluid curriculum," one that empowers teachers to create equitable, culturally relevant curriculum that is responsive to their students, relevant to their students' lives, and adaptable to the local context in which it is enacted. Because a fluid curriculum places the teacher as creator and students as engaged actors, encouraging, and implementing it may address both the teacher retention and equity issues in U.S. schools.

Curriculum and Teaching Dialogue,
Volume 25, Numbers 1 & 2, pp. 155–169
Copyright © 2023 by Information Age Publishing
www.infoagepub.com
All rights of reproduction in any form reserved.

Gloria Ladson-Billings (2016), forerunner of culturally responsive pedagogy, has called for education researchers to "defend the right for the curriculum to be fluid and changing rather than fixed and rigid" (p. 104). Ladson-Billings continued, "Perhaps it is time to once again reaffirm John Dewey's notion of a curriculum that emerges from the experiences of the learners. And such a curriculum will depend heavily on the skill of our nation's teachers" (p. 104).

Why call for a fluid curriculum now? For decades, educators have utilized many factors and filters to design and choose curriculum: input from subject matter experts (resulting in standards; Porter et al., 2011), influence from policymakers (Perna et al., 2014), the need to address issues in contemporary society (e.g., equity-focused approaches; Dover, 2009; Thompson & Thompson, 2018), and the needs and interests of students themselves (Buchanan et al., 2016; Muhammad, 2020; Tyler, 1949). The latter approach has more recently been overlooked and even intentionally ignored in contemporary curriculum, particularly in scripted and predetermined approaches written by anyone other than classroom teachers. It is urgent that educators heed calls like Ladson-Billings's (2016) for a fluid and changing curriculum for two salient reasons: to address the teacher retention crisis and to increase equitable access to learning for all students.

At first, it may seem surprising to connect fluid curriculum design to the teacher retention crisis, but teachers are leaving partly because they are frustrated by "low job control" (Chambers et al., 2019) and by a perceived inability to influence school policy (Dunn, 2015; Dunn et al., 2017; Ni & Rorrer, 2018). Teacher self-efficacy studies also point to a strong connection between teacher control and job satisfaction (Zee & Koomen, 2016). Although teachers are also concerned with salary potential and lack of administrative support (Carver-Thomas & Darling-Hammond, 2017; Ni & Rorrer, 2018), exiting teachers report a lack of flexibility and autonomy in their jobs as a primary cause for their stress (Diliberti et al., 2021; Dunn et al., 2017). Teachers trusted to design and implement their own curriculum could experience more control over their work, which could reduce their stress and risk of burnout.

Therefore, inviting school leaders to encourage and guide teachers to create fluid and responsive curriculum could stem the tide of departing teachers. It is particularly important to focus on those who are leaving in greater numbers in high need areas such as teachers in Title I schools, in certain subject areas (math, science, special education, foreign language, and English Language Development [ELD]), for Black and Latinx teachers (Walker, 2022), and for teachers in their first three years (Carver-Thomas & Darling-Hammond, 2019). This turnover of teachers is harming student achievement and well-being while concurrently creating instability in a profession that relies on institutional knowledge and mentorship (García

& Weiss, 2019). A school that supports teachers in designing and implementing a fluid curriculum will directly address these factors, possibly encouraging more teachers to stay in the profession.

As the teacher retention crisis has intensified, school leaders' awareness of the need to increase equitable access to learning for all students has also heightened. Darling-Hammond (2007) sounded the alarm that unequal funding for schools in the United States is negatively impacting the achievement of minority and low-income students. She argued that our system will only become more equal if reforms "alter the quality and quantity of learning opportunities [students] encounter," assuring, "access to high-quality teaching within the context of a rich and challenging curriculum supported by personalized schools and classes" (Darling-Hammond, 2007, p. 329). It is encouraging that, as of 2020, 44 of 50 states (plus the District of Columbia) mentioned "equity" in state-level education documents as a "concern or guiding principle" (Li et al., 2020). However, Muhammad (2020) argued that schools have focused too much since No Child Left Behind (NCLB) on the teaching of skills, and that an equitable system demands a more holistic approach—the cultivation of "identity, skills, intellectualism, and criticality" (p. 57). This culturally responsive curriculum better engages students in learning (Gay, 2010a; Larson et al., 2018). Therefore, Ladson-Billings's call for a fluid curriculum is a concrete solution to two urgent challenges currently facing K–12 education in the United States, as a curriculum that is responsive to particular students in particular classrooms could fuel teachers' commitment to stay in the profession even as it improves equity across our schools.

But how can we, as educators, guide teachers to resist the predetermined, external curriculum in favor of a fluid curriculum that will ensure all students receive an equitable education? We propose that guiding and then trusting teachers to implement a fluid curriculum will simultaneously nurture teachers—precisely by trusting their autonomy and their judgment—and build equity in classrooms, leading to even better learning outcomes than schools would have seen otherwise.

TEACHERS AS CURRICULUM MAKERS

The image and practice of the teacher as curriculum maker is not new (Alsubaie, 2016; Connelly & Clandinin, 1988; Kimwarey et al., 2014; Lee et al., 2011), but it demands a fresh examination after two decades of an NCLB-inspired trend toward scripted curricula, a practice that some have argued is undemocratic (Fitz & Nikolaidis, 2020). Students learning in classrooms where teachers control the curriculum outperform those whose teachers have little or no control (Sleeter, 2008). These teachers are more effective in implementing culturally responsive practices (Ladson-Billings, 1995), and are better situated to improve the success of immigrants, refugees, and students of color (Rojas & Liou, 2017; Trueba, 1988). Moreover, when teachers have more curricular autonomy, they experience a greater sense of efficacy and are thus less likely to leave the profession (Ingersoll et al., 2019; Wright, 2018).

Because a fluid curriculum is characterized by its responsiveness to the particular students in a classroom, its relevance to their lives, and its adaptability to a local context, such a curriculum can only come from one source—teachers. They bring their knowledge of their students. They bring their knowledge of content. They bring pedagogical content knowledge (Shulman, 1987). They bring who they are. Together, these elements converge to create a curriculum that can be significant to teach, meaningful to learn, and culturally and socially relevant and responsible.

A fluid curriculum moves the teacher from the role of *implementer/adaptor* to that of *creator*. For example, a high school English teacher handed a district preplanned unit on argumentative writing will receive a schedule of texts and writing prompts, as well as a pre-made summative assessment. The same teacher, trusted to take a fluid approach to curriculum, would center the unit design on the concept of argumentative writing, but then would choose texts and design learning and writing activities responsive to the needs, interests, and identities of the students in their classroom. A fluid curriculum, therefore, "[frees] the teacher to teach, with ingenuity, flexibility, and confidence" (Eisner, 2002, p. 368). The outcome—guiding students to learn how to write argumentatively—will be the same; the process will be different for both the teacher and the students.

DEFINING A FLUID CURRICULUM

Ladson-Billings (2016) called on researchers to defend a curriculum that is flexible instead of rigid, urging educators to prioritize students' experiences over standardized tests and curriculum. Our goal is to flesh out this appeal and to give form to Ladson-Billings's initial characterization. Staying focused on how teachers might attend to students' needs and interests, we call this type of curriculum a fluid curriculum. A *fluid curriculum* may be defined as the rich educational opportunities created by perceptive teachers (McConnell et al., 2020) and their students that connect content and pedagogical content knowledge; personalized meaning making; and engaged interactions with local, regional, and global communities. Stated differently, perceptive teachers engage in a fluid curriculum when they focus on students' individuality, cultural affiliations, and universal attributes and when they aim to provide meaningful educational experiences and evaluations. Furthermore, good teachers already attend to a fluid curriculum though they may not use that term.

Created by Perceptive Teachers

Teachers will be able to create a fluid curriculum by first becoming perceptive teachers. Perceptive teaching, as introduced in *Lesson Planning with Purpose: Five Approaches to Curriculum Design* (McConnell et al., 2020), describes the intersection of research on culturally responsive teaching and educational motivation. Perceptive teachers continually examine who they are, including their attributes of open-mindedness, awareness of culture and beliefs (of self and others), caring, and authenticity. A perceptive teacher reads deeply and widely, stays apprised of local current events, talks often to their students about the students' interests and identities, and embraces the attitude of a lifelong learner. Thus, perceptive teachers acknowledge the relationship between who they are—open minded, aware, caring, and authentic—with what they do—personalizing the educational experience, teaching the whole person, teaching with intention, and supporting the development of autonomy. Because perceptive teachers are deeply aware of themselves, their students, and their communities (McConnell et al., 2020), this awareness becomes the compass for how they design their curriculum. The perceptive teacher draws from this well and curates ideas and materials, intentionally designing a meaningful learning experience for their students.

Perceptive teachers also continually reflect upon what they do, including how they personalize each learning experience to the various cultural perspectives and identities present in the class. Perceptive teachers teach the whole person with intention and with the goal to inspire and nurture the skill of autonomy (McConnell et al., 2020). Lastly, perceptive teachers balance the needs of students by attending to their individual, group, and universal interests. As the anthropologists Clyde Kluckhohn and Henry Murray (1953) wisely asserted, "Every man [*sic*] is in certain respects like all other men, some other men, and no other men" (p. 53). At times, in order to understand and reach a student's interest, a teacher will attend to their productive idiosyncrasies (Eisner, 2002), the uniqueness of each child. At other times, teachers may attend to the student's primary group affiliations. Prevalent in today's discourse is a focus on culture, race, and gender, and even a regional way of life (Southern, Midwestern, etc.) may prevail. Further, attending to what we all share in common may also be informative in certain times and places.

Centered on Students' Individuality, Cultures, and Universality

A fluid curriculum is further characterized by the fact that teachers shape it in direct response to specific students in particular contexts. Even a formal state, district, or school curriculum can become fluid when teachers adapt, through their lesson and unit plans, the knowledge, concepts, and skills they are required to teach to meet the interests of their students. Such a curriculum is inherently culturally responsive, as it takes into consideration multiple perspectives, including the social, political, and cultural context in which it is being taught. A fluid curriculum will address concerns of equity because it will be tailored to individual students' identities and contexts (Castagno & McKinley, 2008; Gay, 2010b; Nieto, 2005) and will nurture teachers to stay in the profession because they are empowered to be curriculum makers rather than robotic deliverers of a canned curriculum designed for disembodied students (Fradkin-Hayslip, 2021; Worth & Van den Brande, 2020).

Focused on Meaningful Educational Experiences

Along with taking into consideration both students and the context in which learning takes place, a fluid curriculum places strong emphasis on the experience of students. Meaningful student experiences in education are not a luxury, but a necessity, and those experiences must be designed with the specific learners in mind (Dewey, 1938/1997). Such experiences increase engagement, encourage inquisitiveness, and foster meaning-making (Claxton, 2007; Dunleavy & Milton, 2009; Glenn, 2000). Well-designed, personalized experiences bring to life static academic content, connecting directly to the lives of the learners and to their past, present, and future experiences as members of a diverse society (Dewey, 1938/1997). As such, rather than focusing solely on educational outcomes, a fluid curriculum places a high level of importance on the experience of students in learning on their way to either predetermined or even unplanned "expressive" outcomes (Eisner, 1967, p. 17).

Context and Community-Oriented

Finally, a fluid curriculum will impact student learning the most if it is connected to the local community, both physically and socially (Oguilve et al., 2021), in balance and interplay with national and global concerns. The school walls must be permeable, expanding the notion of "classroom"

The Fluid Curriculum   161

to include community spaces and local environments. The playground, a local pond, or a nearby strip mall can all be sources of the fluid curriculum. Within those environments, family members, community leaders, and local businesspeople serve as important sources of wisdom that should be honored alongside the "official" knowledge that is taught through textbooks (Smith, 2014). This approach creates fertile ground for meaningful, relevant investigations that can span content areas and encourage critical thinking, collaboration, and problem solving among other skills while engaging students as "researchers, meaning-makers, and problem solvers" (Demarest, 2015, p. 1). By fostering connections with their local communities, students have an opportunity to act upon issues they care about and then watch that action lead to real, tangible change (Lane-Zucker, 2004). Developing this quality of place-based curriculum requires more time and effort than implementing a premade curriculum, but it will be the former that students remember, since it will be the former that inspires authentic, deep learning (Vander Ark et al., 2020, p. 65).

METHODS FOR IMPLEMENTING A FLUID CURRICULUM

For a fluid curriculum to be successful, teachers must be supported by teacher education programs, school administrators and district leaders. Referencing our own work (see McConnell et al., 2020) and the research of various educational theorists as indicated, we have identified four conditions for a fluid curriculum to succeed: (a) support for teachers to learn multiple approaches to curriculum design; (b) a focus on evaluation through reflection and the lens of the instructional arc; (c) a sustained process for gathering student input and feedback; and (d) administrative support through dedicated time and space for teacher collaboration.

Support for Teachers in Teacher Education Programs and at Schools

To be intentional in their curriculum planning, teachers need to not only know their students and understand the context in which they are teaching, but they must also fully comprehend the connection between theory and practice of the various approaches to curricular design (Good et al., 2009; Higgs, 2013). Apple (1979) pointed out long ago that teachers were being deskilled in curriculum design and little has changed since he made that assertion. The fluid curriculum requires a re-skilling and reinvigoration of the image of the teacher as curriculum maker (Connelly &

Clandinin, 1988) accomplished through the support described, including a new mastery of lesson planning.

While there are many models for lesson planning, we have discerned five major approaches that are grounded in theory and research but designed for practical application: behaviorist, constructivist, aesthetic, ecological, and integrated social-emotional (McConnell et al., 2020). The behaviorist approach to lesson planning focuses on efficiently developing certain skills and behaviors in students, such as comma usage or identifying parts of an insect. The constructivist approach is designed for individualized meaning-making and student-centered engagement. The aesthetic approach helps teachers create sensory-rich, memorable experiences for their students. The ecological approach brings real-world relevance to the curriculum while also helping students see and make connections to each other, their community, the environment, and beyond. The integrated social-emotional approach is most useful to aid in relationship building and holistic development. Understanding these different approaches empowers teachers by providing them with a menu of curricular approaches to meet their intended aims while attending to the interests of their students within the local context (McConnell et al., 2020).

With this variety of curricular approaches at their disposal, teachers can better design and implement engaging curriculum. While each of the five models has an intentional beginning, middle, and end, they are all quite different in how the experiences for students unfold. For example, a behaviorist lesson is generally centered on direct instruction (Hunter, 1984), including modeling and guided practice. An aesthetic lesson builds the experience from the center, focusing on the senses and direct experience of content and concepts rather than "drill and kill" methods. Both approaches have merit and can (and should, we argue) exist alongside each other to meet the needs of students and of the content at hand.

A Focus on Evaluation Through Reflection and the Instructional Arc

Administrators and district leaders, as well as teacher educators, will wonder—if teachers are creating the curriculum in response to the particular students in their classrooms, how do we know it is good? How do we know students are learning? With teachers at the heart of the curriculum design process, their role carries more responsibility and weight. Providing teachers with a reflective framework can help them consider their work individually, with other co-collaborators, and with administrators. We call this framework the Instructional Arc (see Figure 7.1; see Uhrmacher et al., 2017).

Figure 7.1

The Instructional Arc

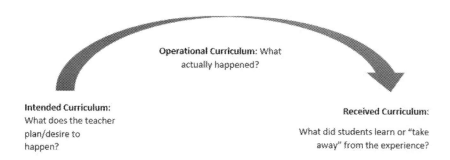

Intended Curriculum: What does the teacher plan/desire to happen?

Operational Curriculum: What actually happened?

Received Curriculum: What did students learn or "take away" from the experience?

The Instructional Arc is unique in that it explicitly attends to the relationship between what teachers intended, what actually happens, and what students experience and take away: the intended, the operational, and the received curriculum (Eisner, 2002). Note, however, that the Arc is not intended to simply align the three components for congruence. Rather, reflecting on the Arc ensures that teachers and students attend to surprise and unexpected learning, which are integral to a curriculum's fluidity and responsiveness. This Arc can be a way toward productive dialogue and evaluation. For example, a teacher could discuss their intentions with students and ask what else they wish they had learned, perhaps in an exit ticket or an online survey. An administrator could ask the teacher to expand upon their intentions and how they align with an equitable classroom. The teacher could share the students' reflections with colleagues in juxtaposition with their own beliefs about what students learned. These questions can all be supported by various data sources available to the teacher and school, including test scores, writing samples, a sustained process for gathering student input and feedback, and other windows into student learning. The Instructional Arc can also be used as a framework for student input and feedback.

A Sustained Process for Gathering Student Input and Feedback

In a fluid curriculum, students should be involved in as many aspects of planning and reflecting as possible. While student choice can drive motivation (Evans & Boucher, 2015), it also guides cultural responsiveness and inclusivity (Gay, 2010b; Ladson-Billings, 1995; Storz & Nestor, 2008). Students ought to have the opportunity to provide feedback at each point in the Instructional Arc. First, they should be brought in during the design phase to provide input into what they are learning and why. It is here in particular where matters of culture can be expanded. For example, in a lesson on the American Revolution, understanding the war through various cultural lenses would be beneficial and motivating. Next, students ought to have input and provide feedback during the operational curriculum. What is working? What needs improvement? Much like athletes who have a game plan (the intended curriculum) and then respond and modify their game plan during the course of a game (the operational curriculum), students can actively reflect on their immediate experiences to guide the process. At the end of the lesson, time ought to be allotted to reflect on the entire curriculum. What worked? What could have gone better? What cultural lenses were promoted? Which were left out? The goal is to spark new interests and further growth. Teachers cannot cover every aspect of any given subject, but they can ignite further desires to know more. Using student feedback, teachers can engage more deeply in the curriculum design process, which we suggest would benefit from dedicated time and space.

Administrative Support Through Dedicated Time and Space for Teacher Collaboration

The process of creating a fluid curriculum will require intentional conversation and practice over time. The process will also benefit from intentional spaces set aside for curriculum design. Such spaces can provide a variety of inspirational resources and materials, as well as access to others for sharing and brainstorming ideas. In contrast to a professional learning community focused on student data, a Curriculum Studio could be a space focused on experiences of the teacher as they create experiences for their students. Through our research we have found the process of collaborative and creative planning to be effective—even euphoric (Moroye & Uhrmacher, 2009).

Dedicated time and opportunities for effective collaboration and mentorship from colleagues or teacher leaders is particularly crucial in a teacher's first five years (García & Weiss, 2019; Sabina et al., 2023). Further, more veteran teachers will also benefit from consistent trust in their work to be responsive to particular students' needs. Schools that focus on increased administrative support retain more teachers (Kraft et al., 2016; Ni & Rorrer, 2018). Therefore, building-level choices that foster collaboration and support will contribute to student learning and to teacher sustainability.

CONCLUSION

Gloria Ladson-Billings (2016) urged educators to "use the study of curriculum as a vehicle for democracy, civic participation, and a more equitable and just society" (p. 102). A fluid curriculum that is created by perceptive teachers; that is centered on students' individuality, cultures, and universality; that is focused on meaningful educational experiences; and that is community oriented will lead to a deeper sense of both student and teacher engagement. Two decades of accountability reforms have pushed our most effective and most creative teachers to leave the profession (Dunn, 2015, 2017), and that exodus is harming vulnerable students the most (Carver-Thomas & Darling-Hammond, 2017). Most teachers enter the profession because they want to make a difference in the lives of children (Ni & Rorrer, 2018). A movement toward equitable and just classrooms that truly respond to students, their teachers, and their communities will entice those high-quality teachers to stay. In fact, when school leaders and teacher educators revitalize the image of the teacher as curriculum maker and provide the necessary support and resources, teachers will be able to meet the needs of their students with enthusiasm. Such renewed hope and energy will reenergize the profession.

REFERENCES

Alsubaie, M. A. (2016). Curriculum development: Teacher involvement in curriculum development. *Journal of Education and Practice*, 7(9), 106–107. https://doi.org/10.12698/cpre.2011.rr69

Apple, M. W., & Paul, K. (1979). *Ideology and curriculum*. Routledge.

Buchanan, S., Harlan, M., Bruce, C., & Edwards, S. (2016). Inquiry based learning models, information literacy, and student engagement: A literature review. *School Libraries Worldwide*, 22(2), 23–39. https://doi.org/10.29173/slw6914

Carver-Thomas, D., & Darling-Hammond, L. (2017). Teacher turnover: Why it matters and what we can do about it. *Learning Policy Institute*. https://doi.org/10.54300/454.278

Carver-Thomas, D., & Darling-Hammond, L. (2019). The trouble with teacher turnover: How teacher attrition affects students and schools. *Education Policy Analysis Archives*, 27(36). https://files.eric.ed.gov/fulltext/EJ1213629.pdf

Castagno, A. E., & McKinley, B. (2008). Culturally responsive schooling for indigenous youth: A review of the literature. *Review of Educational Research*, 78(4), 941–993. https://doi.org/10.3102/0034654308323036

Chambers Mack, J., Johnson, A., Jones-Rincon, A., Tsatenawa, V., & Howard, K. (2019). Why do teachers leave? A comprehensive occupational health study evaluating intent-to-quit in public school teachers. *Journal of Applied Biobehavioral Research*, 24(1), e12160. https://doi.org/10.1111/jabr.12160

Connelly, F. M., & Clandinin, D. J. (1988). *Teachers as curriculum planners. Narratives of experience*. Teachers College Press.

Claxton, G. (2007). Expanding young people's capacity to learn. *British Journal of Educational Studies*, 55(2), 1–20. https://doi.org/10.1111/j.1467-8527.2007.00369.x

Darling-Hammond, L. (2007). Third annual Brown lecture in education research— The flat earth and education: How America's commitment to equity will determine our future. *Educational Researcher*, *36*(6), 318–334. https://doi.org/10.3102/0013189x07308253

Demarest, A. B. (2015). *Place-based curriculum design: Exceeding standards through local investigations*. Routledge.

Dewey, J. (1997). *Experience and education* (Reprint ed). Simon and Schuster. (Original work published 1938)

Diliberti, M., Schwartz, H. L., & Grant, D. M. (2021). *Stress topped the reasons why public school teachers quit, even before COVID-19*. RAND Corporation. https://www.rand.org/pubs/research_reports/RRA1121-2.html

Dover, A. G. (2009). Teaching for social justice and K–12 student outcomes: A conceptual framework and research review. *Equity & Excellence in Education*, *42*(4), 506–524. https://doi.org/10.1080/10665680903196339

Dunleavy, J., & Milton, P. (2009). *What did you do in school today? Exploring the concept of Student Engagement and its implications for Teaching and Learning in Canada*. Canadian Education Association. https://education.alberta.ca/media/3069762/cea-2009-wdydist-concept.pdf

Dunn, A. H. (2015). The courage to leave: Wrestling with the decision to leave teaching in uncertain times. *The Urban Review*, *47*(1), 84–103. https://doi.org/10.1007/s11256-014-0281-x

Dunn, A. H., Farver, S., Guenther, A., & Wexler, L. J. (2017). Activism through attrition?: An exploration of viral resignation letters and the teachers who wrote them. *Teaching and Teacher Education*, *64*, 280–290. https://doi.org/10.1016/j.tate.2017.02.016

Eisner, E. W. (1967). *Instructional and expressive educational objectives: Their formulation and use in curriculum* (ED028838). ERIC. https://eric.ed.gov/?id=ED028838

Eisner, E. W. (2002). *The educational imagination: On the design and evaluation of school programs* (4th ed.). Macmillan.

Evans, M., & Boucher, A. R. (2015). Optimizing the power of choice: Supporting student autonomy to foster motivation and engagement in learning. *Mind, Brain, and Education*, *9*(2), 87–91. https://doi.org/10.1111/mbe.12073

Fitz, J. A., & Nikolaidis, A. C. (2020). A democratic critique of scripted curriculum. *Journal of Curriculum Studies*, *52*(2), 195–213. https://doi.org/10.1080/00220272.2019.1661524

Fradkin-Hayslip, A. (2021). Teacher autonomy, motivation, and job satisfaction: Perceptions of elementary school teachers according to self-determination theory. *Ilkogretim Online*, *20*(2). https://doi.org/10.17051/ilkonline.2021.02.25

García, E., & Weiss, E. (2019). *The teacher shortage is real, large and growing, and worse than we thought* (The Perfect Storm in the Teacher Labor Market Series 1). Economic Policy Institute. https://www.epi.org/163651

Gay, G. (2010a). *Culturally responsive teaching: Theory, research, and practice* (2nd ed.). Teachers College Press.

Gay, G. (2010b) Acting on beliefs in teacher education for cultural diversity. *Journal of Teacher Education*, *61*(1–2), 143–152. https://doi.org/10.1177/0022487109347320

Glenn, J. M. (2000). Teaching the Net Generation. *Business Education Forum*, 54(3), 6–14. http://www.ajhepworth.yolasite.com/resources/Teaching_and_Learning_with_the_Net_Generation.pdf

Good, T. L., Wiley, C. R., & Florez, I. R. (2009). Effective teaching: An emerging synthesis. In L, J. Saha & A. G. Dworkin (Eds.), *International handbook of research on teachers and teaching* (pp. 803–816). Springer. https://doi.org/10.1007/978-0-387-73317-3_51

Higgs, L. G. (2013, May 14–17). *Theory in educational research and practice in teacher education* [Paper presentation]. Annual International Conference of the Bulgarian Comparative Education Society, Plovdiv, Bulgaria. https://eric.ed.gov/?id=ED567134

Hunter, M. (1984). Knowing, teaching, and supervising. In P. Hosford (Ed.), *Using what we know about teaching* (pp. 169–195). Association for Supervision and Curriculum Development.

Ingersoll, R., May, H., & Collins, G. (2019). Recruitment, retention, and the minority teacher shortage. *Education Policy Analysis Archives*, 27(37), 1–42. https://doi.org/10.12698/cpre.2011.rr69

Kimwarey, M. C., Chirure, H. N., & Omondi, M. (2014). Teacher empowerment in education practice: Strategies, constraints and suggestions. *IOSR Journal of Research & Method in Education*, 4(2), 51–56. https://doi.org/10.9790/7388-04225156

Kluckhohn, C. K. M., & Murray, H. A. (1953). Personality formation: The determinants. In C. K. M. Kluckhohn & H. A. Murray (Eds.), *Personality in nature, society and culture* (pp. 53–70). Alfred A. Knopf.

Kraft, M. A., Marinell, W. H., & Shen-Wei Yee, D. (2016). School organizational contexts, teacher turnover, and student achievement: Evidence from panel data. *American Educational Research Journal*, 53(5), 1411–1449. https://doi.org/10.3102/0002831216667478

Ladson-Billings, G. (1995). Toward a theory of culturally relevant pedagogy. *American Educational Research Journal*, 32(3), 465–491. https://doi.org/10.3102/00028312032003465

Ladson-Billings, G. (2016). And then there is this thing called the curriculum: Organization, imagination, and mind. *Educational Researcher*, 45(2), 100–104. doi:10.3102/0013189X16639042

Lane-Zucker, L. (2004). Foreword in David Sobel, *Place Based Education*. Orion Society.

Larson, K. E., Pas, E. T., Bradshaw, C. P., Rosenberg, M. S., & Day-Vines, N. L. (2018). Examining how proactive management and culturally responsive teaching relate to student behavior: Implications for measurement and practice. *School Psychology Review*, 47(2), 153–166. https://doi.org/10.17105/spr-2017-0070.v47-2

Lee, J., Yin, H., Zhang, Z., & Jin, Y. (2011). Teacher empowerment and receptivity in curriculum reform in China. *Chinese Education and Society*, 44(4), 64–81. https://doi.org/10.2753/ced1061-1932440404

Li, A., Harries, M., & Ross, L. F. (2020). Reopening K–12 schools in the era of COVID-19: Review of state-level guidance addressing equity concerns. *The Journal of Pediatrics*, 227. https://doi.org/10.1016/j.jpeds.2020.08.069

McConnell, C., Conrad, B., & Uhrmacher, P. B. (2020). *Lesson planning with purpose: Five approaches to curriculum design.* Teachers College Press.

Moroye, C. M., & Uhrmacher, P. B. (2009). Chapter 12: Aesthetic themes of education. *Curriculum and Teaching Dialogue, 11*(1–2), 85.

Muhammad, G. (2020). *Cultivating genius: An equity framework for culturally and historically responsive literacy.* Scholastic Incorporated.

Ni, Y., & Rorrer, A. K. (2018). *Why do teachers choose teaching and remain teaching? Initial results from the educator career and pathway survey (ECAPS) for teachers.* University of Utah, Utah Education Policy Center. https://uepc.utah.edu/our-work/why-do-teachers-choose-teaching-and-remain-teaching-initial-results-from-the-educator-career-and-pathway-survey-ecaps-for-teachers/

Nieto, S. (Ed.). (2005). *Why we teach.* Teachers College Press.

Oguilve, V., Wen, W., Bowen, E., Abourehab, Y., Bermudez, A., Gaxiola, E., & Castek, J. (2021). Community making: An expansive view of curriculum. *Journal of Curriculum Studies Research, 3*(1), 69–100. https://doi.org/10.46303/jcsr.2021.8

Perna, L. W., Klein, M. W., & McLendon, M. K. (2014). Insights and implications for state policy-makers. *The ANNALS of the American Academy of Political and Social Science, 655*(1), 209–230. https://doi.org/10.1177/0002716214539895

Porter, A., McMaken, J., Hwang, J., & Yang, R. (2011). Common core standards: The new US intended curriculum. *Educational researcher, 40*(3), 103–116. https://doi.org/10.3102/0013189x11405038

Rojas, L., & Liou, D. D. (2017). Social justice teaching through the sympathetic touch of caring and high expectations for students of color. *Journal of Teacher Education, 68*(1), 28–40. https://doi.org/10.1177/0022487116676314

Sabina, L. L., Touchton, D., Shankar-Brown, R., & Sabina, K. L. (2023). Addressing teacher retention within the first three to five years of employment. *Athens Journal of Education, 10*(2), 345–364. https://doi.org/10.30958/aje.10-2-9

Smith, G. A. (2014). Place-based education: Learning to be where we are. *PDK International. 83*(8). https://doi.org/10.1177/00317217020830080

Shulman, L. S. (1987). Knowledge and teaching: Foundations of the new reform. *Harvard Educational Review, 57,* 1–22. https://doi.org/10.17763/haer.57.1.j463w79r56455411

Sleeter, C. (2008). An invitation to support diverse students through teacher education. *Journal of Teacher Education, 59*(3), 212–219. https://doi.org/10.1177/0022487108317019

Storz, M. G., & Nestor, K. R. (2008). It's all about relationships: Urban middle school students speak out on effective schooling practices. In F. P. Peterman (Ed.), *Preparing to prepare urban teachers* (pp. 77–101). Peter Lang.

Thompson, D. L., & Thompson, S. (2018). Educational equity and quality in K–12 schools: Meeting the needs of all students. *Journal for the Advancement of Educational Research International, 12*(1), 34–46. https://files.eric.ed.gov/fulltext/EJ1209450.pdf

Trueba, H. T. (1988). Culturally based explanations of minority students' academic achievement. *Anthropology & Education Quarterly, 19*(3), 270–287. https://doi.org/10.1525/aeq.1988.19.3.05x1565e

Tyler, R. W. (1949). *Basic principles of curriculum and instruction.* University of Chicago Press.

Uhrmacher, P. B., Moroye, C., & Flinders, D. J. (2017). *Using educational criticism and connoisseurship for qualitative research.* Routledge.

Vander Ark, T., Liebtag, E., & McClennen, N. (2020). *The power of place: Authentic learning through place-based education.* Association for Supervision and Curriculum Development.

Walker, T. (2022, Feb. 1). *Survey: Alarming number of educators may soon leave the profession.* NEA Today. https://www.nea.org/advocating-for-change/new-from-nea/survey-alarming-number- educators-may-soon-leave-profession.

Worth, J., & Van den Brande, J. (2020, January). *Teacher autonomy: How does it relate to job satisfaction and retention?* National Foundation for Educational Research. https://www.nfer.ac.uk/media/3874/teacher_autonomy_how_does_it_relate_to_job_satisfaction_and_retention.pdf

Wright, J. L. (2018). *A multiple-case study on the perceptions of teacher autonomy in a traditionally structured and a teacher powered school* [Doctoral Dissertation, Liberty University]. Digital Commons. https://digitalcommons.liberty.edu/doctoral/1757/

Zee, M., & Koomen, H. M. (2016). Teacher self-efficacy and its effects on classroom processes, student academic adjustment, and teacher well-being: A synthesis of 40 years of research. *Review of Educational research, 86*(4), 981–1015. https://doi.org/10.3102/0034654315626801

VOLUME 25, NUMBER 2

EDITORIAL REMARKS

THE TEACHER SHORTAGE AND RAPIDLY INCREASING VIRTUAL SCHOOLS

John L. Pecore
University of West Florida

The first warnings of a potential teacher shortage in the United States occurred in the mid-1980s. According to a Rand Corporation Report (Darling-Hammond, 1984; Antonucci, 2016) titled *A Coming Crisis in Teaching*, the main causes of an impending teacher shortage were poor working conditions, low pay, lack of decision-making input, and a prevalence of standardized testing. Of the impending teacher shortage, Linda Darling-Hammond (1984) wrote: "Unless major changes are made in the structure of the teaching profession, so that teaching becomes an attractive career alternative for talented individuals, we will in a very few years face widespread shortages of qualified teachers" (p. vi). Darling-Hammond's report cautioned that the least academically qualified people could become the teaching force for future generations of American schoolchildren. The predicted teaching shortage of the late 1980s, however, was averted because of a growing teaching force and consistent student enrollment (Antonucci, 2016) resulting in a lower overall pupil-teacher ratio (Ingersoll & Merrill, 2013).

Curriculum and Teaching Dialogue,
Volume 25, Numbers 1 & 2, pp. 173–176
Copyright © 2023 by Information Age Publishing
www.infoagepub.com
All rights of reproduction in any form reserved.

174   J. L. PECORE

After the Great Recession of 2007–2009, alarms sounded for another potential teacher shortage. Although slowed substantially because of the dropping demand for teachers due to budget cuts and consistent student enrollment, today's teacher shortage has been growing since 2016 (García & Weiss, 2019). The shortage is the result of a decade of significant decline in undergraduate students pursuing teaching degrees. According to the Pew Research Center, the number of bachelor's degrees in education has declined by 19% since the early 2000s with more than half of that decline occurring over the past five years (Schaeffer, 2023). The teacher shortage almost doubled, from 64,000 unfilled positions during the 2015–2016 school year to over 110,000 during the 2017–2018 school year (Walker, 2022).

The growing teacher shortage is most impactful in critical-need subject areas like science, mathematics, and special education, as well as in high-needs schools. According to Feder (2022), unless reversed, the precipitously dropping number of undergraduate teaching certificates awarded by universities in secondary STEM education will decrease from over 15,000 in 2019 to less than 5,000 by 2030. In high-poverty schools, the number of fully certified teachers is 3% less than in low-poverty schools.

Another interesting trend is the declining K–12 student enrollment in public and private schools and the substantial increase in charter and home school enrollments. In Florida, enrollment over the last three years has decreased almost 2% in public schools and over 4% in private schools. Charter schools have increased by over 9% and home schooling has increased by over 47% (PK–12 Public School Data Publications and Reports, n.d.). Nationally, the largest shift in student enrollment is occurring in virtual schools, with a 176% increase over the last three years (Lehrer-Small, 2022). In 2020 there were 691 virtual schools in the United States with Florida leading the way with 222 (Common Core of Data, n.d.). Teachers in smaller school settings (i.e., charter and virtual schools) have a more positive perception of working conditions, reporting more administrative support, more influence in school policies, more sense of community and collegiality, and more classroom autonomy (Ni, 2012). Considering the shifting K–12 student enrollment to charter and virtual schools and the ability of smaller schools to provide a perceived better workplace, specifically preparing K–12 teachers for careers in charter and virtual schools may help to address the teacher shortage.

Issue 2 of Volume 25 contains a keynote address and six articles that offer ideas for enhancing working environments for teachers. First is Jen Johnson's keynote address during the 2022 American Association for Teaching and Curriculum conference. This keynote explores Johnson's journey from a classroom teacher in Chicago Public Schools to leadership in the Chicago Teachers Union. In her talk, Johnson addresses the

The Teacher Shortage and Rapidly Increasing Virtual Schools 175

importance of solidarity, which is critical for reducing the teacher shortage by improving teaching conditions. Next, Sarah Campbell provides insight into the impact of administrative support on veteran teachers in the article "How Veteran Teachers Are Impacted by Administrators: A Case Study." Administrative support is a prominent factor in addressing the teaching shortage.

The two articles that follow provide suggestions for improving curriculum and consequently provide an opportunity for teachers to assist with providing decision-making input. In the conceptual essay "Ideological Foundations, Curricular Models, and the Path of Bilingual Education," Leah Davis considers the historical influence of ideological perspectives and policies on bilingual education. Davis proposes curricular models that practice translanguaging to support bilingualism. In the article "Bespoke Learning: Using the Evidence Continuum to Design Learner-Centered Curriculum and Teaching," Robyn Thomas Pitts considers the usefulness of the evidence continuum in creating learner-centered curricula and strengthening teachers' pedagogy while increasing their content knowledge.

The final three articles in this volume begin with co-authors Sarah Campbell, Rebecca Reinhardt, Mallori Sage, and Emily Strong's investigation of the impact of stressors that lead to burnout in veteran teachers. In their article "The Lived Experience of Female K–12 Teachers During the COVID-19 Pandemic: A Phenomenological Study," they stress the importance of administrative and instructional support along with a reevaluation of teaching as a profession. In "Ninth-Grade Students with Disabilities' Math Efficacy and Teachers' Instructional Efficacy, John Palladino conducts an analysis of secondary data to demonstrate both positive and negative relationships in math efficacy and instructional efficacy among ninth-grade students with disabilities. In the last article, "Narcissistic or Overwhelmed? Divergent Pathways to Academic Entitlement" by Elizabeth Pope, Monica Erbacher, and Lauren Pierce, the authors examine the connections between academic entitlement and narcissism, self-esteem, self-efficacy, and self-compassion. The authors surveyed 140 undergraduate students and suggested using mindfulness to lessen academic entitlement.

The six articles in Issue 2 represent a range of topics that provide insight into supporting teachers. Improving working conditions with supportive administrators and giving teachers input into curriculum decisions address two main causes of the current teacher shortage. Most states have resorted to providing temporary 5-year teacher certifications to individuals with their bachelor's degree, and, in Florida, to military veterans with their associate degree. These controversial alternatives assist with filling teacher vacancies, but also highlight the severity of the shortage of highly qualified teachers. Over 30% of teachers have no educational background in the main subject they teach. Traditional routes to becoming a teacher (that is, obtaining an education degree) account for 83% of those certified (García & Weiss, 2019). With the surge in enrollment in virtual learning, developing programs for teaching in virtual schools may help to address the teacher shortage by attracting students to the profession and thus increasing the number of undergraduate teaching certificates awarded by universities.

REFERENCES

Antonucci, M. (2016). *Analysis: New warnings of teacher shortage sound like déjà vu all over again*. The 74. https://www.the74million.org/article/analysis-new-warnings-of-teacher-shortage-sound-like-deja-vu-all-over-again/

Common Core of Data. (n.d.). *Table 3. Number of virtual schools, total state enrollment, total virtual school enrollment, and virtual school enrollment as a percentage of state total enrollment: School year 2019–20*. National Center for Educational Statistics. https://nces.ed.gov/ccd/tables/201920_Virtual_Schools_table_3.asp

Darling-Hammond, L. (1984). *Beyond the commission reports: The coming crisis in teaching*. The Rand Corporation. https://www.rand.org/content/dam/rand/pubs/reports/2007/R3177.pdf

Feder, T. (2022). The U.S. is in dire need of STEM teachers. *Physics Today, 75*(3), 25–27. https://doi.org/10.1063/PT.3.4959

García, E., & Weiss, E. (2019). *The teacher shortage is real, large and growing, and worse than we thought: The first report in "The perfect storm in the teacher labor market" series*. Economic Policy Institute. https://www.epi.org/publication/the-teacher-shortage-is-real-large-and-growing-and-worse-than-we-thought-the-first-report-in-the-perfect-storm-in-the-teacher-labor-market-series/

Ingersoll, R., & Merrill, L. (2013). *Seven trends: The transformation of the teaching force*. Consortium for Policy Research in Education. https://www.cpre.org/sites/default/files/workingpapers/1463_seventrendsupdatedoctober2013.pdf

Lehrer-Small, A. (2022). *Virtual school enrollment kept climbing even as COVID receded, new data reveal*. The 74. https://www.the74million.org/article/virtual-school-enrollment-kept-climbing-even-as-covid-receded-new-data-reveal/

Ni, Y. (2012). Teacher working conditions in charter schools and traditional public schools: A comparative study. *Teachers College Record, 114*(3), 1–26.

Schaeffer, K. (2023). *A dwindling number of new U.S. college graduates have a degree in education*. Pew Research Center. https://www.pewresearch.org/short-reads/2022/09/27/a-dwindling-number-of-new-u-s-college-graduates-have-a-degree-in-education/

Walker, T. (2022). *Average teacher salary lower today than ten years ago, NEA report finds*. NEA. https://www.nea.org/advocating-for-change/new-from-nea/average-teacher-salary-lower-today-ten-years-ago-nea-report-finds

PK–12 Public School Data Publications and Reports. (n.d.). *Students*. Florida Department of Education Home. https://www.fldoe.org/accountability/data-sys/edu-info-accountability-services/pk-12-public-school-data-pubs-reports/students.stml

KEYNOTE ADDRESS GIVEN AT AATC CONFERENCE
ON OCTOBER 7, 2022, IN CHICAGO, ILLINOIS

FINDING AND SUSTAINING SOLIDARITY

Jen Johnson
Chicago Teachers Union,
Chief of Staff

Thank you so much for inviting me to speak at this conference.

I am a high school history teacher, and I knew I wanted to be a high school teacher when I was a teenager. I guess I never wanted to leave high school. Somehow, I think because I was open to being a part of an educator community, I find myself now the Chief of Staff of Chicago Teachers Union (CTU) and someone who has to think about solidarity a lot.

Solidarity means a very particular thing now to me in my role as a CTU leader. Today, solidarity means being a part of a democratic and fighting union that seeks to preserve and transform public education that empowers our students and that helps members enforce and protect their rights, but both as part of a greater movement to achieve racial, social, and economic justice. Prior to working in organized labor, I had a vague notion of solidarity as loyalty created by participating in a shared struggle or in shared objectives.

My parents are baby boomers and were deeply shaped by their upbringing in the Civil Rights Movement Era. My white mother was 15 years old when my grandfather, an English teacher at the time at New Trier High School on the North Shore here in the Chicago area, took her on the last day of the Selma to Montgomery march. My white Christian ecumenical grandparents thought of themselves as being in solidarity with civil rights organizers and, more than many but less than some, found ways for their family to support the movement for racial justice.

My Black father, who was born in a factory town outside of Birmingham, Alabama and who came of age in the rust belt city of Cincinnati, eventually became a high school teacher at a public school in West Michigan, where I was subsequently born and raised. When he started teaching there, the school's student population was still mostly white and was integrating, but by the time he retired, the school's student body was almost entirely Black. Dad's solidarity showed up in his dedication to his school community and generations of students over a 30-plus-year career, in spite of the ways that gentrification and segregation actually increased in my hometown over that period of time.

What I did not know growing up was that my grandfather was at New Trier when they formed their Education Association and that my dad was a career-long member of the Michigan Education Association. He and I only talked about the fact that he was a career-long union member for the first time a few years before the pandemic. I asked him on a visit to see my husband and me in Chicago, why he did not talk about being a union member. He pulled out his retiree MEA membership card and said around I do not know so that it reads: He pulled out his retiree MEA membership card and said "I do not know."

While my grandfather was teaching at the height of unionization in this country's history, my father was teaching during unionization's escalating decline. Neither of them talked to me growing up about being a union member even though I became a teacher because of their example. Their political orientation was toward racial and economic justice, but they seemingly did not experience unions as a major part of their identity as justice-oriented educators.

I think my experience is not so uncommon among the ranks of people my age who became educators. Unions were something historical and not nearby or present, unless you were one of my colleagues who grew up in a deeply union family or were raised in or found a leftist political orientation and home. Some of my colleagues had this upbringing, but most did not. I knew I wanted to be a teacher from when I was a teenager, but those closest to me who had been in teachers' unions did not have the forethought to orient me to what that meant and what that could mean.

I received my first classroom in Chicago Public Schools when I was 21 years old and had no idea of what it really meant when I signed a union card a few months into the job. My educator preparation program at prestigious Northwestern University, near my grandparents' home, was completely inadequate at preparing me to be a Chicago educator and did not at all pretend to prepare me to be a Chicago Teachers Union member.

The only reason I became an active union member was because, a couple years in, I was noticed by our school librarian who was our union delegate. She thought I had potential as a union leader. As a result, I became an associate CTU delegate at my school and started going to the monthly CTU meetings with her. Then, I met a young teacher organizer at a history professional development (Professor Lois Weiner knows him) and he convinced me to start coming to some meetings. Those meetings eventually turned into the founding of the Caucus of Rank and File Educators and I was part of the team that won the leadership of the CTU in 2011. The young teacher organizer who recruited me is now the CTU Vice President.

This is where I think I am supposed to say, Chicago is a Union Town. I mean, that is true, and my initial union experiences as a CTU delegate, under the previous leadership, presented a very thin definition of what union solidarity looked like. The union was active, and there was a base layer of veterans who were involved and tried to get some of us newbies involved. Union solidarity then meant showing up to meetings to report back to your members. It meant voting in favor of the proposed contract and existing leadership. It meant you were supposed to agree to get on a bus when the union was going to do some lobbying or protesting. This presentation of union solidarity was composed of routine actions and tactics without a vision or a strategy or an explanation for the systemic challenges we faced in our school buildings. When schools were threatened with closure, the union said, get on a bus and come to a protest, but treated the fight as isolated and not part of a grander plan by the power structures.

On the other hand, the meetings that I went to that were organized by the young teacher organizer and veteran union dissenters challenged that simplistic view. I was intrigued by the ragtag group that he and others recruited to start meeting in union hall basements and public library social rooms around the city and I kept showing up. Over months, we formed a multi-racial, multi-generation group of experienced and not-so-experienced union dissidents, leftists, and unaffiliated educators wanting to stop racist policies harming our schools and city. We developed a platform that said that our union's existence is directly tied to the ways that white supremacy and capitalism are seeking to privatize and destroy urban public education. We understood that anti-Black racism combined with corporate greed were centrally responsible for the escalating attacks and disinvestment in our public schools and our neighborhoods. We envisioned a union that fought with and alongside our students, families, and community members, who are mostly Black and Brown, to make our schools better, but not just that—to challenge systems and power structures to give us a say in making our community better and more just as well.

With this message, we won leadership of the CTU and have been re-elected several times since. In 2011, we issued a platform called *The Schools Chicago's Students Deserve* and then, a couple of years later, we put out a platform called *A Just Chicago*, noting the ways that our school conditions are directly tied to the greater community conditions created by white supremacy and capitalism. We see the work to achieve both these things (the schools our students deserve and a just Chicago) as our long-term work.

Over the last decade plus, we have built a union where members are proud to wear their red CTU shirts in public and they mostly get high fives and kudos in response. By organizing member leadership building by building, we have demonstrated that we can strike, in spite of neoliberal forces passing legislation in 2011, which tried to make striking impossible by requiring a 75% affirmative strike vote of our entire membership. We have pushed the bounds of bargaining as constrained by law and then helped to elect legislators to repeal legislative limits on our bargaining rights in 2020. In order to exercise our collective solidarity, we have to push the limits and do the work to expose how legal barriers sought to hold us back because we are advocating for Black and Brown students and a union of women educators. Our students, their families and communities have seen that, and we have been able to build solidarity beyond our school buildings together.

Still, as the teaching force continues to whiten, because neoliberal education reform policies have pushed out Black educators, shrunk preservice teacher preparation programs, and exposed just how undervalued and challenging the teaching profession is, our union's solidarity is consistently tested by the conservative instincts of self-protection grounded in whiteness. We have to consistently challenge a minority of white members in particular, who would rather we put our heads back down into the sand and ignore the ways that racist city policy is leading to dramatic drops in enrollment in Chicago Public Schools, threatening our union existentially, but signaling the crisis faced by working people of color to continue to exist, work, and live in the city of Chicago at all.

As my CTU President Stacy Davis Gates says, we must recognize the holistic identities and needs of working people. In particular, the labor movement has this lesson to learn to grow our power and win on behalf of our communities. At the Labor Notes conference this summer, President Davis Gates said:

> Labor has got to be redefined to include the worker from sunup to sundown. Workers suffer from police brutality, workers have their children's

schools shut down, workers are facing eviction because housing is unafford-able, workers are suffering under unfair immigration policies.... We are workers and we are mothers, we are workers and we are daughters, we are workers and we are sisters.

Calling out racism and capitalism and paternalism and all the other isms and calling on our educators to see their union solidarity as extensive and intersectional is devastatingly hard work. It is particularly difficult as a Black woman, like myself, or like former President Karen Lewis and current President Stacy Davis Gates. We are required to defend our humanity and the humanity of people who look like us or are silenced and marginal-ized for other parts of their identities. We have to convince some of these members that the needs of our Black and Brown students, our LGBTIA+ students, their families, and colleagues like us require them to grow and listen. The last election in CTU this past spring was contentious, and a right-wing caucus with seeming ties to the mayor's office ran on a plat-form of sticking to the bread-and-butter union issues and not getting too political or adversarial with our bosses. And we still won. We have built a mandate for this vision of extending solidarity, but it is not easy or without challenges. Our union solidarity must extend to the intersectionality of our members, our students, and our labor movement.

As a labor union, we have to apply our expanded definition of soli-darity to how we do our bread-and-butter work. For example, we had to evolve our member defense policies to ensure that they are aligned to our anti-racist values. We must meet our legal obligation to the duty of fair representation, but how far do we defend a white teacher who alleg-edly doubled down when questioned by a Black colleague about hanging a stuffed Black football figurine toy by the neck in a classroom? How far do we defend a white teacher who allegedly said to immigrant students who refused to stand for the national anthem at an assembly, "Go back to your country?" We are part of a conversation in our state union about how to responsibly meet our obligations *and* increase internal controls. While we can extend grace to members who can learn and grow and change, we must be clear to members that our solidarity does not extend to remorse-less, racist or otherwise harmful patterns of behavior. Our union solidarity must extend to our students.

How do we as a labor union organize and better prepare more and more of our members to teach our students, who are 90% students of color, in ways that honor, celebrate, inspire, and empower them? A few years ago, parents exposed that one of our white members assigned Kindergarten students homework about African animals for Black History Month. In our members-only Facebook group just this week, a teacher member, who identified themselves as *European American*, asked for help because their

Black and Brown 7th-grade students were questioning how she taught them about the American Constitution. Particularly because she was talking about *the slaves* and *the treatment of the slaves*. Thankfully, several teachers responded quickly to the post to teach her the term *enslaved people* and seemingly gave her feedback she could hear. Our union solidarity must extend to our curriculum.

There are positive examples. Earlier this fall, the school district attempted to fire two white social justice teachers at a southeast side high school which is located in a school community where working-class white and Latinx protesters and organizers have been resisting the imposition by the mayor of a metal processing plant being built in their community. The project had the potential to further pollute an already industrially saturated working-class community. The two teachers taught their students about these issues. Some of these students were already connected to community-based organizations and were involved in protests against the mayor's decisions. After 36 hours of pitched protest by our union and the community, the board of education bucked the mayor and voted unanimously against firing the two teachers. As far as I can remember, this was the first or only time the board unanimously agreed to go against what was perceived to be the political will of the mayor. Educators must be able to tell the truth in their classrooms. The basic bread-and-butter member defense aligned with our vision for the kind of classroom and community our students deserve. Our solidarity was easily wielded in this instance.

I personally have been a part of supporting the development and implementation of a mandatory CPS curriculum called "Reparations Won" that was introduced in 2017. The curriculum was won as part of an historic, first ever in the nation, city ordinance and reparations package for survivors of police torture in 2015. The ordinance was won over the course of a decades-long fight by Black men incarcerated after being tortured by Chicago police. The curriculum requires middle and high school students to examine the ways that systemic racism in Chicago and in the police department caused the torture to be ignored for years, but also how the Black torture survivors, their families, and allies fought and fought and fought until they could no longer be ignored. I organized and led professional developments at the union with fellow CTU teachers to help prepare our members to teach it. Because, believe me, it is not being taught in all our schools as required. Some of our teachers are not yet capable of teaching it, and some of our families have actively resisted the implementation of the curriculum. The definition of solidarity that I have developed as a CTU member over the last decade requires us to continue to press our members to understand that they have to teach curricula that expose students to hard, local truths. We have to allow students to see how organizing and activism is required to destroy the systems attempting to hold them back.

Students have to see educators with their union shirts on saying, doing, and teaching in ways that recognize their identities, their communities, and the challenges they face. There is so much work to do to take the solidarity that we have built through school building organizing, community coalition and exercising our power through strikes, and extending it into the day-to-day teaching and learning. I am thankful that there are more and more educators, including white educators, that understand and are leading the work required. This is union work and is a critical part of our solidarity.

Today, we are in an exciting moment in history when it comes to union organizing. I think, in no small part, our CTU strike in 2012 on the platform of *The Schools Chicago's Students Deserve* helped rejuvenate recognition of what teachers' unions can do, be, and represent. On the heels of a red wave of teacher strikes around the country, including in states where the law does not provide access to collective bargaining, now Amazon and Starbucks workers are joining the unionization wave. Amidst these efforts, we have seen the pitched organizing and protest calling for police accountability; for immigrant, women, and LGBTQIA+ rights; and access to abortion. I am hopeful. But I know how much it has taken to stay steady at the helm at CTU. I have seen how difficult the conditions have gotten in schools and how the pandemic tried to wear down educators dedicated to this vision of union solidarity for justice. The perceived advances of workers and marginalized people continue to face a dangerous backlash in the forms of conspiratorial fascistic political candidates winning office by stoking racist fears and seeking to divide the working class racially. In education, we have seen states ban textbooks that teach true history; school districts ban books that reflect young people's diverse experiences; and the needs of students of color and LGBTQIA+ students—like protection from physical harm and school policies (like bathrooms and haircuts and uniforms) that do not punish them for being themselves—become controversies. Most recently, right-wing bigot governors are coercing asylum-seeking migrants, including school-age children, to board buses and planes to northern cities like Chicago in inhuman political stunts.

In Chicago, in the last few weeks, we have seen hundreds of migrants predominantly from Venezuela brought to our city adding to the needs in our schools for bilingual services—but perhaps even more critically, making the need for affordable housing in the city acute. Our mayor and school leaders "welcome" these newcomers with words, but our school and city infrastructure and policies are inadequate to actually meet their needs. The district cannot even track where the migrant students are enrolling. The CTU has been working with local immigrant rights and community-based organizations to collect supplies for families and identify gaps in services in the schools where our members find the new students in their classrooms. We have to be vigilant. We have to see our teacher's union as the tip of the spear. And that is exhausting for our members. It is definitely exhausting to me, and I have only been around for 20 years. Our most vocal CTU member on climate change, for example, is Bea Lumpkin, who just turned 104. She is at every major rally and union convention! We just issued *The Schools Chicago's Students Deserve 3.0*, an in-depth research report updating our platform and positions for this new phase of the work. Check it out on our website to see the breadth of the issues that we think as a union we must expose and fight for in order to achieve our goals. We need folks like you to do work that leads to a strong anti-racist curriculum that teaches labor and union history to our students—the good, the bad, and the ugly—so we can challenge unions to expand solidarity for justice. We need folks like you to do work that challenges teacher preparation programs to responsibly teach how to develop student and community centered anti-racist curriculum in partnership with students, parents, and community.

We need folks like you to do work that helps hone professional development curriculum that is effective and anti-racist for all, but particularly white educators. We need folks like you to do work that examines and points toward ways to eliminate barriers to teachers' unions building and exercising power for the common good. We need folks like you to do work that lifts up the voices of educators as women, as queer, as parents, as workers, as people of color and as unionists so that our intersectional identities are not pushed to the side and ignored. We need folks like you to examine the perniciousness of whiteness and anti-Blackness in curriculum and in school systems, structures, and culture to be able to stamp out every last bit of it. We need folks like you, who, when you are in town for a conference, to look for and show up to local organizing fights.

We have got healthcare workers here in Chicago at an LGBTQIA+ serving health care system called Howard Brown who almost went on strike last week who need our solidarity. We have got faculty at the community colleges who serve mostly Black and Brown students from low-income families in a hard contract fight that did an action downtown yesterday because the county is not bargaining in earnest with them. We have got Black and Brown students who rallied at their charter school yesterday because they feel the school is ignoring their needs. We have got CTU candidates running for office locally to show their solidarity to city hall who need support.

We have so many needs but so many exciting opportunities to put our solidarity in action and challenge the limits of what solidarity has meant. I will close with this. Since coming on to CTU staff in 2013, the year after the CTU went on strike in 2012 for the first time in 25 years, I have spoken to undergrad and graduate classes of preservice teachers at Chicagoland universities regularly. In fact, I spoke to a master's class at University of Illinois at Chicago this Wednesday night on the Yom Kippur holiday. The students' questions and understanding of unions and teachers' unions today sounds dramatically different from what I experienced myself as a preservice teacher. These social studies students were not at all turned off by my talk of white supremacy and how it necessitates our teachers' union to think and act big and demand that they be anti-racist educators. I do not get obviously anti-union questions so much anymore. I am grateful to be able to witness that change. I am thankful to the local university faculty, who are typically faculty union members themselves, who invite me to speak to their classes because they recognize that their future educators MUST have an understanding of what union membership and solidarity can mean, unlike my own experience. I left the class on Wednesday excited, knowing that the students I spoke to were future CTU members.

We have so much work to do. But if educators and workers can be won to seeing solidarity through an intersectional lens and as extending beyond the walls of our work sites, we will beat back our opponents and achieve more justice for more people. It is perhaps audacious. It is definitely necessary. And being audacious is the CTU way.

Thank you for having me.

Note: Jennifer Johnson is the current Deputy Mayor of Education, Youth and Human Services for the city of Chicago and can be reached at msjohnsonlphs@gmail.com.

CHAPTER 1

HOW VETERAN TEACHERS ARE IMPACTED BY ADMINISTRATORS

A Case Study

Sarah Campbell
University of Northern Colorado

ABSTRACT

In this study, the author examines six veteran teachers' perspectives on how administrative support has impacted their decision to stay in the same building. Three themes emerged from the interviews: (a) teachers feel administrators should leave them alone; (b) teachers want administrators to protect them; and (c) teachers want to be valued as professionals. In this article, the author argues that research on workplace grief helps explain this contradiction as a protective response.

Teachers are leaving American schools—and it has become an emergency, as 83% of superintendents reported teacher shortages in 2021 (Hanover Research, 2021), and when teachers leave, both student achievement and the stability of a profession that relies on institutional knowledge are threatened (García & Weiss, 2019; Katz, 2018). The problem is most severe in Title I schools and in certain subjects, including math, science, special education, foreign language, and English Language Development (ELD; Carver-Thomas & Darling-Hammond, 2019). Recent research and policy

Curriculum and Teaching Dialogue,
Volume 25, Numbers 1 & 2, pp. 187–201
Copyright © 2023 by Information Age Publishing
www.infoagepub.com
All rights of reproduction in any form reserved.

work has focused on why teachers leave, blaming low salary potential (Carver-Thomas & Darling-Hammond, 2019), high stress levels (Diliberti et al., 2021), and poor working conditions (Ansley et al., 2019; Geiger & Pivovarova, 2018).

However, teachers are most likely to leave the profession when they feel unsupported by their administrators (Burkhauser, 2017; Grissom & Bartanen, 2019; Johnson et al., 2012; Ni & Rorrer, 2018) or when the administrators themselves turn over frequently (DeMatthews et al., 2022). In fact, Carver-Thomas and Darling-Hammond (2019) found that lack of effective and positive administrative support ranked even above salary concerns for teachers who decided to leave. For novice teachers, administrative support ranked as the primary reason they chose to stay in or leave the profession (Cells et al., 2022). Becker and Grob (2021) identified improved administrative support as the most important change schools can make to retain teachers.

PURPOSE OF RESEARCH AND RESEARCH QUESTION

However, some teachers stay, and not just in the profession, but in the same schools. They stay for decades, weathering multiple administrators. Because schools that work to increase administrative support retain more teachers (Kraft et al., 2016; Ni & Rorrer, 2018; Reitman & Karge, 2019), the purpose of this study was to discover how relationships with administrators have impacted the decision of teachers who have chosen to remain in one building for at least the past nine years. The question that guided the study was the following: How do these veteran teachers characterize their relationships with administrators and how does that perception affect teachers' quality of life at work? This study approached the problem of teacher retention from a new angle—examining how relationships with administrators impact some teachers' choice to stay. This research may provide insight into moves schools can make to retain more teachers for the long term.

LITERATURE REVIEW

Reasons for the Increase in Teacher Turnover in the Past Decade

Enrollment in traditional teacher preparation programs has steadily decreased since 2010, and the COVID-19 pandemic has increased the number of certified teachers leaving the profession (Hanover Research,

2021). A 2018 report from the Utah Education Policy Center found that the same factors influenced teachers who stay in the same building for years, teachers who change schools but stay in the profession, and teachers who choose to leave: the presence or lack of strong relationships with colleagues and administrators in a school, and how ethically they were treated by those people (Ni & Rorrer, 2018). Most of the research on the teacher retention problem in the past decade has been conducted in triage mode as states and independent education policy institutes have scrambled to slow the bleed of teachers from schools. Therefore, the focus has been on the teachers who leave, on data collected from exit surveys, exit interviews, and even from teachers' public resignation letters (Dunn, 2018).

Why has this turnover increased in the past decade? Dunn (2018) identified the increased stress caused by the "neoliberal reforms" (p. 3) enacted since No Child Left Behind (NCLB, 2001) including the increase of teacher accountability measures, of standardized testing and associated school accountability measures, and of influence of private companies on public education. After all, teacher turnover has not increased worldwide; the Learning Policy Institute noted that countries like Finland and Singapore do not face this challenge at all (Carver-Thomas & Darling-Hammond, 2019). Teacher turnover is an *American* problem.

Aspects of Administrators that Impact Teacher Turnover

If Dunn (2015, 2018) was correct that teacher turnover has increased in response to the education policy shifts of the past two decades, then the studies that demonstrate administrative support as the most important factor in retaining teachers must be viewed in a new light. Dworkin and Tobe (2014) identified the two kinds of trust that exist in complex societies: "organic" and "contractual" (p. 122). They argued that "prior to externally-based accountability" (p. 122), teachers were trusted much more organically to work autonomously within their classrooms; the contractual trust was implemented only when there was "clear evidence of incompetence" (p. 122). The external measures implemented across states since NCLB (2001) have shifted schools away from organic trust and into more contractual trust, thus contributing to heightened teacher burnout (Dworkin & Tobe, 2014). Because administrators are responsible for communicating and enforcing this contractual relationship, they become the face of what are often viewed as punitive measures. This change in the nature of trust between administrators and teachers helps explain why teachers say they are most likely to leave the profession if they feel unsupported by their administrators (Burkhauser, 2017; Grissom & Bartanen, 2019; Johnson et al., 2012; Ni & Rorrer, 2018; Cells et al., 2022).

Conversely, teachers with "supportive school leadership and positive relationships with administrators and other personnel" (Ansley et al., 2019, p. 3) are more likely to stay in the profession, as teachers' perception of their quality of life at work depends on the principal more than upon any other factor (Burkhauser, 2017; Johnson et al., 2012). For this reason, some researchers have begun to advocate for principal residency programs that teach principals how to build trust and a sense of community with their teachers (Carver-Thomas & Darling-Hammond, 2019).

Many studies and policy reports have focused on how administrators can support novice teachers in their first five years through mentorship measures, professional development, and general support (Katz, 2018; Reitman & Karge, 2019; Cells et al., 2022). However, Jacob et al. (2012) argued that this focus misses "the real retention crisis" (p. 6), particularly in urban schools; effective experienced teachers are not choosing to stay. However, some teachers do stay—and some stay in the same building for decades. The question here is how relationships with administrators impact those veteran teachers' decisions to return each fall to the same school.

METHODOLOGY

As a current teacher in a large comprehensive public high school that has seen five principals in the past 12 years, I wanted to investigate whether relationships with administrators have been key to veteran teachers' decisions to stay, as the research has suggested with novice teachers. A qualitative case study methodology involved the collection of multiple sources of data, including semi-structured interviews of teachers, brief online questionnaires, and document analysis of annual teaching staff rosters. These data sources created a holistic picture of the impact of administrators on veteran teacher retention.

Study Participants and Data Collection

Six teachers who have taught at Park High School (pseudonym) for at least the past five administrators (since fall of 2015) participated in the study. All six completed a consent form and provided demographic information. I then interviewed each teacher in person; the interviews were recorded using a password-protected iPhone Voice Memo. Each teacher selected a pseudonym. The six teachers included a math teacher who ultimately asked their specific responses be removed from this manuscript, though they consented to remain in the count and overall analysis; a special education teacher, "Donnie Hakanson," who has taught at Park

High School for 9 years; a social studies teacher, "Ann Lawrence," who has taught at Park High School for 12 years; an English teacher, "Francesca Beaupre," who has taught at Park High School for 22 years; a business teacher, "Devin Smith," who has taught at Park High School for 24 years; and an art teacher, "Vincent Kline," who has taught at Park High School for 25 years. It was not possible to select anyone from the science or world language departments, as no teacher in those departments has worked at the school long enough to qualify for this study. The current principal of Park High School provided site permission in writing.

ANALYSIS

From the transcripts of the six interviews, I wrote "portraits" (Lawrence-Lightfoot, 2005, p. 6) of each teacher. This creative process helped me to distill three common themes from the portraits, using an analytic realism framework (Altheide & Johnson, 1994). This framework allowed me to analyze the relationship between the specific context of Park High School and these particular teachers.

SETTING AND RESEARCHER'S STANCE

Park High School, where all six teachers work each day, is a historic building constructed in 1926 with a current student population of 1,722. As of 2021, 54.4% of the student body identified as non-White and 43% of the students qualified for free or reduced lunch. As one of 57 high schools in this large urban area, Park High School employs approximately 90 full-time teachers each year.

As a White female teacher who has spent the past twenty years of my life working in public middle and high schools, I am inside this study as a participant as much as I am outside of it as a researcher. In twenty years of teaching in public schools, I have worked for ten principals. While I have considered leaving the profession at certain junctures, I have stayed. It is this direct experience that gives me unique insight.

FINDINGS

In the past 12 years, Park High School has seen five different principals, called Principal A, B, C, D, and E, and a dramatic shift in demographics, as more neighborhood families choose to send their children to the school and as national policy shifts have decreased our number of immigrant students. These changes in leadership and demographics combined with the chaos of the pandemic have created a deeply uncertain work environment. And yet, 22 teachers who worked at Park High School in fall of 2015 with Principal A still work at the school in the fall of 2022 with Principal E. Why? What could understanding these teachers' reasons for staying teach administrators and education policymakers about teacher retention?

Three common themes emerged in the analysis of the six interview transcripts. All six teachers either emphasized that they wish administrators would just leave them alone or that administrators really do not have an impact on teachers' quality of life at work. However, all six also expressed the wish that their administrators would guard or protect them, and they insisted that their quality of life at work increases when administrators actually recognize what they contribute to student learning and to the school environment.

Theme 1: Administrators Should Leave Us Alone; They Do Not Matter

Early-career teachers stay in the profession because of the support (or lack thereof) from their administrators (Burkhauser, 2017; Ni & Rorrer, 2018; Cells et al., 2022). However, all six veteran teachers defined their ideal principal as one who simply, in Vince's words, "leaves me alone." Donnie identified the most "terrifying" of administrators he has had in his career as one who made teachers "[sign] a book next to the principal's office every day," who, "[had] admin sit in their cars to see who walked out during their planning periods." For Ann, a good principal is one who creates a situation in which "I'm being trusted to do my job. And we as a staff are trusted to do our jobs." Devin liked leaders like his current one, Principal E, who is "taking the approach of hands off. I don't feel nitpicked." Francesca noted that her ideal principal does not lead from "top down" but from a place of trust of the teachers they have hired. Indeed, it seems that these six teachers, perhaps resistant to those "top-down policies" Dunn (2015) identified as a *push* factor that makes teachers want to leave the profession, have learned to value most the principal they do not ever see. Considering that too much administrative involvement with instructional leadership can actually harm student achievement (Sebastian & Allensworth, 2013), this instinct to be left alone makes sense.

All six of these veteran teachers insisted that, whether they micromanage or leave teachers alone, administrators do not matter much to their quality of life at work. Francesca noted that "administrators come and go, and especially at [Park High School]. So if you can wait it out long enough, usually, it's okay. And that has shown itself to be true over and over again." Devin admitted:

> The multiple times I've thought about quitting because of these people [administrators], I basically find my own way to calm down, and then continue forward, because I realized they leave every five years … I just have to wait for another one to see how it goes.

Ann has also learned "[administrators] come and go. My day-to-day job doesn't change all that much based on who's in charge, as long as I stay out of their hair." With a principal she disliked, she said, "I felt like I could stay away enough from him that I could stick it out," until the next principal came along. Donnie explained that "there's this bizarre canyon between administrators and teachers that is illogical," and that each administrator who passes through presents different challenges that must be weathered. For Vince, the intensified emphasis on standardized testing has "degraded" the administrative role, causing more turnover. He said, "I'm not hopeful for administrators in the current system, but I'm hopeful for teachers … because they will just do the work they've always done."

Theme 2: We Wish the Administrators Would Protect Us

The first theme indicates that, even though novice teachers require supportive and involved administrators in order to stay in the teaching profession (Carver-Thomas & Darling-Hammond, 2019), veteran teachers seem to require administrators who just ignore them and let them do their jobs. However, the other two themes that emerged in this study indicate a different perspective. Even as all six teachers insisted administrators do not matter, all six also said that their lives at work would be better if their administrators protected them. This desire for protection is in keeping with findings that teachers are more likely to stay in the profession if their administrators serve as a "bureaucratic shield" between teachers and outside pressures ranging from parents to the district, and if they promote safe working conditions, including discipline support (Becker & Grob, 2021, p. 14).

Ann said she has most liked the principals who made her "feel supported," but Principal D made her feel that it was never safe to express her ideas. She served for two years of Principal D's administration as an elected teacher on Park High School's School Leadership Team (SLT), which meets every other week to advise the principal on scheduling, instruction, and other building issues. Ann explained:

194   S. CAMPBELL

> I started to notice after a few months that [Principal D] took the other people on SLT who were men a lot more seriously ... I started to notice that like any time I said something or had an idea, he would either ignore it or disagree with it.... So I started texting one of the guys on SLT, like my thoughts ... because we both wanted to see whether he would respond if it was from a guy. It was fascinating. Shocking. Those comments were very well received.

This unsafe environment made Ann consider searching for a job elsewhere. It was only after she reminded herself that she could probably wait out this principal's tenure that she decided to stay.

On the other hand, Francesca felt supported by Principal D because "I got accused of something falsely under his watch, [and] he absolutely made sure I was not publicly persecuted." Principal D's support reassured her and kept her from quitting, a sharp contrast to the fact that Principal C "[did] not back me up" when some of Francesca's decisions were questioned by parents and students. Francesca also appreciated Principal A's willingness to defend and protect teachers. She said, "I didn't always agree with her. And she was [angry] at me a couple of times. But she listened, and she made positive change" because she protected teachers from district measures that did not work for Park High School. Francesca echoed Ann's belief that school leaders must create an environment in which all teachers feel safe to share their ideas; the best leadership, she explained, is "[when] they're asking for buy-in from the faculty; it's linked arms."

Donnie decided he would need to move to a different school after four years of Principal D had eroded his sense of safety, making him fear expressing any opinions. However, before he took a new job, he sent an email to the newest principal of Park High School, Principal E, and "the response was very positive ... and I was surprised in a good way. I was like, 'Okay, this is alright.'" He chose to stay at Park High School, and he said he has continued to feel reassured by Principal E's positivity.

Vince has learned in his 26 years of teaching to soothe each new principal into a connection that will ultimately protect Vince. He said he tries to "share positive things ... wonderful things I see happening. Because then later if I need to ask for something, I'm already sort of stereotyped as a nice person, which I generally am." Like the other teachers, Vince has learned to value a principal who keeps the environment safe and protected, but he has also learned how to nurture and elicit that response from the principal.

For Devin, the administrators that improve his quality of life at work are the ones who manage student behavior so teachers can do their jobs. Devin observed that he prefers administrators who are "seen in the building," who don't expect teachers to "do something you wouldn't do yourself." Although Principal A "bugged me in certain respects ... she was involved in everything. She was *running* the building. She wasn't the boss who delegated and sat back a little bit; she was *seen*."

For all six of the teachers, the best administrators are leaders who create a safe space for the teachers to do their jobs (Hanover Research, 2021) and to express their ideas (Ni & Rorrer, 2018). Why, then, did they also all say that they want administrators to leave them alone? Ann's perspective on Principal D provides insight here. When administrators make these teachers' daily lives feel less safe, teachers who are committed to staying try to endure until the next inevitable administrative turnover occurs.

Theme 3: The Best Administrators Value and Respect Us

Just as all six teachers actually want administrators who protect them, they also all said that their quality of life at work is far better when their administrators recognize what each teacher contributes and value them as individuals. Of course, the teachers' desire for positive recognition from their administrators is in line with what Ansley et al. (2019) found about "supportive school leadership and positive relationships with administrators" (p. 3), and it echoes what Becker and Grob (2021) discovered about the importance of administrators building "relational trust" (p. 10) with teachers.

Vince explained that in his long teaching career, he has only had two administrators who came close to ideal, because "they realized I was articulate or kind or both. And they started to use me in a way that would respect who I was." One of these administrators asked him to coach teachers and to become the art department chair. For Francesca, Principal D's choice to reach out to her in the summer before he started made her feel valued after a year of feeling unvalued by Principal C. She explained, "He said, 'I understand you're really valuable to the school. Let's see what can happen.'" That respectful encouragement convinced her not to quit, "to see what would happen with the new guy."

Devin discussed the ways in which his first principal at Park High School "empowered" him to experiment. Devin guided his students to open and then run a school store. He remembered, "We made $65,000 in revenue in the first year…. They all went to New York for free as part of our business program." Years later, Principal D trusted Devin to design and make the graduation ceremony video while the school was scattered into homes during the COVID lockdown. While Devin had been trusted to make such videos by previous principals, including Principals A, B, and C, Principal D paid him "a huge stipend … I'm happy he recognized what I did."

Every year in his evaluation, Donnie asks the administrator the same question: "Am I an important part of the community?" He explained, "If the answer is yes, then I have to decide if it's a choice I want to make to return or not. If the answer is no, I'm going to start looking for another job." Donnie wants to work in a place where he "[feels] part of what's happening." He said, "I don't understand why we aren't being utilized as the experts that we are ... so we can seek out real solutions as a community." He has taught for 25 years, and yet, "with all the different administrators I've had, I don't think I've ever been asked my opinion." This echoes Ann's wish that Principal D had valued her opinions. She appreciated Principal A and C primarily because she felt "supported" by them. Ann particularly felt that Principal C was good "at the 'recognizing we're humans' part of being a principal."

All six teachers emphasized that this level of administrative respect for what they contribute and for who they are as human beings is rare. Francesca, who has worked for eleven principals in her career so far, explained:

> It's just that [good leadership] really can change everything.... In schools, where you're asking people to do so much unpaid, unappreciated work that's thankless and challenging in ways you can't even imagine with so many factors we can't control—if you can control how you treat the people who work here, [you'll change everything]. And you do that not by shaming everyone all the time...Instead, start with the assumption that your faculty knows what they're doing and that they're excellent teachers.

DISCUSSION

The six teachers' discussion of times they have been valued and respected confirmed that teachers' perception of their quality of life at work depends on the principal more than upon any other factor (Burkhauser, 2017; Johnson et al., 2012). However, if they have not always gotten that respect, what has kept them teaching at Park High School? It seems the first theme—apathy about the impact of principals—has been caused by the frequent turnover of those principals, an instability that negatively affects school culture even more than teacher turnover (Hanselman et al., 2016). As Ann explained, by her fourth principal at Park High School, she had learned that "as soon as you get used to [a principal], they leave, and then you have to get used to a new person." Teachers want to be valued and respected, and when they experience that kind of treatment, their quality of life at work increases. As these veteran teachers have learned to weather constant changes in leadership and attitudes toward trust (Dworkin & Tobe, 2014), they have begun to protect themselves by expressing apathy toward administrators. It is easier to insist administrators do not matter than to express the longing to be protected and valued by each and every new one who walks through the front doors of Park High School.

Because these veteran teachers have endured so much change in leadership at Park High School, their conflicting responses about administrators may be a protective response to the continual and unpredictable change in leadership. In fact, Zell (2003) identified the loss of each leader—and the associated change—as a cause of grief in a workplace, a kind of "organizational death" (Bell & Taylor, 2011, p. 3). Zell (2003) argued that employees undergoing such loss exhibit the stages of grief identified by Kubler-Ross (1969, as cited by Zell, 2003, p. 75) in her research on death and dying, including denial, anger, bargaining, depression, and acceptance. In the acceptance stage, people "no longer fight the inevitable and prepare for their impending death" (Kubler Ross, 1969, as cited by Zell, 2003, p. 75) or, in a workplace, for the impending end of each leader's tenure (Zell, 2003). These six veteran teachers demonstrated that acceptance stage as they shrugged off the importance of administrators, even as they acknowledged that good administrators could vastly improve their quality of life at work.

LIMITATIONS OF THE STUDY

It is worth noting that my close involvement with this school and with these teachers creates as much internal bias as it does an enlightened perspective. In addition, as with any qualitative study, the relatively small number of participants can perhaps raise questions about generalizability. This was a site-focused study that pursued a research question about a specific school that has experienced frequent administrative turnover; for that reason, one veteran teacher from each department represented the school. However, future researchers could seek confirmation of these results by interviewing veteran teachers at other high schools.

CONCLUSION

In this study, I asked why veteran teachers stay in the same building that has experienced frequent administrative turnover, by focusing on six veteran teachers' perceptions of how administrators impact their quality of life at work. Coding of the six interviews yielded clear themes: teachers say administrators do not actually matter and should leave them alone, even as they also say they wish administrators would protect them and value them. This apparent contradiction between wanting administrators to disappear and wanting administrators to be consistent and positive figures can possibly be explained as a protective reaction to constant and unpredictable changes in leadership.

These findings reveal the urgency of current experiments with principal residency programs that teach principals how to build trust and a sense of community with their teachers (Carver-Thomas & Darling-Hammond, 2019). In addition, district-level leaders must pay careful attention to transitions when a school like Park High School shifts to a new principal. Finally, education policymakers must listen to what these veteran teachers identify as improvements in the workplace for teachers: protection, respect, and consistency. As Francesca observed, "[Good leadership] really can change everything."

REFERENCES

Altheide, D., & Johnson, J. (1994). Criteria for assessing interpretive validity in qualitative research. In N. Denzin & Y. Lincoln (Eds.), *Handbook of qualitative research* (pp. 485–499). SAGE.

Ansley, B. M., Houchins, D., & Varjas, K. (2019). Cultivating positive work contexts that promote teacher job satisfaction and retention in high-need schools. *Journal of Special Education Leadership*, *32*(1), 3–16, https://eric.ed.gov/?id=EJ1274904

Becker, J., & Grob, L. (2021). *The school principal and teacher retention*. Metropolitan Educational Research Consortium.

Bell, E., & Taylor, S. (2011). Beyond letting go and moving on: New perspectives on organizational death, loss and grief. *Scandinavian Journal of Management*, *27*(1), 1–10. https://doi.org/10.1016/j.scaman.2010.09.013

Burkhauser, S. (2017). How much do school principals matter when it comes to teacher working conditions? *Educational Evaluation and Policy Analysis*, *39*(1), 126–145. https://doi.org/10.3102/0162373716668028

Carver-Thomas, D., & Darling-Hammond, L. (2019). The trouble with teacher turnover: How teacher attrition affects students and schools. *Education Policy Analysis Archives*, *27*(36). https://files.eric.ed.gov/fulltext/EJ1213629.pdf

Cells, P., Sabina, L. L., Touchton, D., Shankar-Brown, R., & Sabina, K. L. (2022). Addressing teacher retention within the first three to five years of employment. *Athens Journal of Education, 10*(2), 345–364. https://doi.org/10.30958/aje.10-2-9

DeMatthews, D. E., Knight, D. S., & Shin, J. (2022). The principal-teacher churn: Understanding the relationship between leadership turnover and teacher attrition. *Educational Administration Quarterly*, *58*(1), 76–109. https://doi.org/10.1177/0013161x211051974

Diliberti, M., Schwartz, H. L., & Grant, D. M. (2021). *Stress topped the reasons why public school teachers quit, even before COVID-19*. RAND.

Dunn, A. H. (2015). The courage to leave: Wrestling with the decision to leave teaching in uncertain times. *The Urban Review*, *47*(1), 84–103. https://doi.org/10.1007/s11256-014-0281-x

Dunn, A. H. (2018). Leaving a profession after it's left you: Teachers' public resignation letters as resistance amidst neoliberalism. *Teachers College Record*, *120*(9), 1–34. https://doi.org/10.1177/016146811812000906

Dworkin, A. G., & Tobe, P. F. (2014). The effects of standards based school accountability on teacher burnout and trust relationships: A longitudinal analysis. In D. Van Maele, P. Forsyth, & M. Van Houtte (Eds)., *Trust and school life* (pp. 121–143). Springer. https://doi.org/10.1007/978-94-017-8014-8_6

García, E., & Weiss, E. (2019). *The teacher shortage is real, large and growing, and worse than we thought*. The First Report in "The Perfect Storm in the Teacher Labor Market" Series. Economic Policy Institute.

Geiger, T., & Pivovarova, M. (2018). The effects of working conditions on teacher retention. *Teachers and Teaching*, *24*(6), 604–625. https://doi.org/10.1080/135 40602.2018.1457524

Grissom, J. A., & Bartanen, B. (2019). Strategic retention: Principal effectiveness and teacher turnover in multiple-measure teacher evaluation systems. *American Educational Research Journal*, *56*(2), 514–555. https://doi.org/10.3102/0002831218797931

Hanover Research. (2021). *4 strategies to increase teacher retention*. https://www.hanoverresearch.com/reports-and-briefs/4-strategies-proven-to-increase-teacher-retention/?org=k-12-education.

Hanselman, P., Grigg, J., K. Bruch, S., & Gamoran, A. (2016). The consequences of principal and teacher turnover for school social resources. In *Family Environments, School Resources, and Educational Outcomes* (pp. 49–89). https://doi.org/10.1108/s1479-353920150000019004

Jacob, A., Vidyarthi, E., & Carroll, K. (2012). *The irreplaceables: Understanding the real retention crisis in America's urban schools*. TNTP.

Johnson, S. M., Kraft, M. A., & Papay, J. P. (2012). How context matters in high-need schools: The effects of teachers' working conditions on their professional satisfaction and their students' achievement. *Teachers College Record*, *114*(10), 1–39. https://doi.org/10.1177/016146811211401004

Katz, V. (2018). *Teacher retention: Evidence to inform policy*. EdPolicyWorks. https://curry. virginia. edu/sites/default/files/uploads/epw/Teacher% 20Retention% 20Policy% 20Brief. Pdf

Kraft, M. A., Marinell, W. H., & Yee, D. (2016). School organizational contexts, teacher turnover, and student achievement: Evidence from panel data. *American Educational Research Journal*, *53*, 1411–1449. https://doi.org/10.3102/0002831216667478

Lawrence-Lightfoot, S. (2005). Reflections on portraiture: A dialogue between art and science. *Qualitative Inquiry*, *11*(1), 3–15. https://doi.org/10.1177/1077800404270955

Ni, Y., & and Rorrer, A. K. (2018). *Why do teachers choose teaching and remain teaching? Initial results from the educator career and pathway survey (ECAPS) for teachers*. Utah Education Policy Center.

NCLB (2001). *No child left behind act of 2001*. Pub. L, (107-110).

Reitman, G. C., & Karge, B. D. (2019). Investing in teacher support leads to teacher retention: Six supports administrators should consider for new teachers. *Multicultural Education*, *27*(1), 7–18. d https://doi.org/10.1177/088840649501800204

Sebastian, J., & Allensworth, E. (2013). How do secondary principals influence teaching and learning. *Principal's Research Review, 8*(4), 1–5. https://doi.org/10.1086/688169

Zell, D. (2003). Organizational change as a process of death, dying, and rebirth. *The Journal of Applied Behavioral Science, 39*(1), 73–96. https://doi.org/10.1177/0021886303039001004

APPENDIX

Interview Questions

- What factors have contributed to your choice to remain at this school?
- What factors have challenged your commitment to stay at this school (and/or in the teaching profession)?
- Describe your ideal relationship with an administrator. To what extent would this ideal relationship make a difference to your quality of life at work? Have you experienced this or anything close to it?
- Describe your relationship with previous administrators. To what extent did that relationship affect your quality of life at work?
- Describe your perception of the current (new) administrators. How is your relationship with them affecting your quality of life at work?
- Is there anything else I should know about teacher/administrator relationships that I did not think to ask?

Online Survey Questions (Distributed Via a Link to Google Forms on Personal Email):

1. To what extent do you feel an administrator's relationship with you affects your quality of life at work? (1 = *Not at all.* 7 = *Quite a bit.*)
2. Please rank how the following aspects of an administrator affect your quality of life at work (1 = *affects my quality of life at work most*; 5 = *affects my QOL at work least*)? (Aspects listed for teachers to rank: positive support; fair evaluations; evident trust in teachers; the administrator's overall effectiveness; the administrator's teaching experience)
3. Please rank how the following aspects improve your quality of life at work (1 = *most important*; 6 = *least important*)? (Aspects listed

for teachers to rank: administrative support; administrative effectiveness; collegial support and connection; reasonable salary; reasonable number of responsibilities outside of my classroom; reasonable total number of students)

4. Please rank your overall quality of life at work under each of the past five administrators (1 = *low quality of life at work*; 7 = *high quality at life at work*):

Admin, 2011–15	Admin, Spring '16	Admin, '16–'18	Admin, '18–'22	Admin, Fall '22+
1 → 7	1 → 7	1 → 7	1 → 7	1 → 7

5. Have you ever considered leaving this building and/or this profession? Explain when and why. (open-ended response)
6. Please describe the administrator whom you have found most effective and supportive in your career so far. Please avoid names. (open-ended response)

Demographic Information

7. How many years have you been a teacher? ___
8. How many years have you taught in this building? ___
9. For how many principals have you worked? ___
10. What grades have you taught? (K, 1, 2, 3, 4, 5, 6, 7, 8, 9, 10, 11, 12, college)
11. In what departments have you taught (list all of them)? _____
12. How old are you? ___
13. With what gender do you identify? (male/female/other)
14. With what sexual orientation do you identify? _____
15. With what ethnicity do you identify? _____
16. What is your highest level of education? (bachelor's, master's, doctorate)
17. What is your marital status? (single/married/partnered/widowed/other)
18. Do you have children? (yes/no)
19. What pseudonym would you like us to use for you in writing up this study? _____

CHAPTER 2

IDEOLOGICAL FOUNDATIONS, CURRICULAR MODELS, AND THE PATH OF BILINGUAL EDUCATION

Leah Davis
Brigham Young University

ABSTRACT

This conceptual essay examines the historic, ideological foundations of bilingual education in the United States as influenced by various perspectives and policies related to multilingual learners. Additionally, past and current curricular models of bilingual education are analyzed through an ideological lens, illustrating connections between monoglossic and heteroglossic ideologies and the curricular models. The practice of translanguaging is discussed as a heteroglossic practice that supports bilingualism in current and future curricular models and recommendations for stakeholders are addressed.

Within the United States today, "language is weaponized for waging offensive and exclusionary politics against immigrant, refugee, and multilingual communities of color" (Hafner & Ortiz, 2021, pp. 145–146), and within classrooms, English language instruction can inflict harm on linguistically marginalized populations. Language weaponization is defined as "the process by which words, discourse, and language in any form have been used or are being used to inflict harm on others" (Herrera & Bryan,

---

Curriculum and Teaching Dialogue,
Volume 25, Numbers 1 & 2, pp. 203–216
Copyright © 2023 by Information Age Publishing
www.infoagepub.com
All rights of reproduction in any form reserved.

2022, p. 3). Language weaponization can be present in language education practices, policies, curriculum, and spaces where languages are taught and utilized. Bilingual education, including pedagogy and practice, is ever-changing and adapting as students whose first language is not English, here referred to as multilingual learners, continue to pour into public schools across the United States. Unfortunately, multilingual learners have historically become victim to language weaponization through bilingual education programs that have appeared well intended and designed to support the linguistic development of these students. Therefore, it is necessary to address bilingual education from historical and ideological perspectives to understand in what ways language has been weaponized in educational spaces and how to take steps to deweaponize language and instead empower multilingual learners through bilingual education.

Throughout the last half of a century, models of bilingual education have changed frequently and morphed as theories and assumptions regarding language, multilingualism, and the role of White Mainstream English (WME; Baker-Bell, 2020) have shifted.

Many studies have illustrated the value of bilingual education programs, programs aimed at the English language development of emergent multilingual students, in English acquisition both academically and socially (Bialystock, 2001; Portes & Hao, 2002). However, systems that promote WME and academic English, a form of WME, require multilingual learners to reject their home languages and home cultures, code-switch, and assimilate in order to prevent being subject to linguistic racism (Baker-Bell, 2020). To move away from monoglossic instructional systems and practices that only honor WME and academic English towards heteroglossic systems and practices that respect and honor multilingualism, it is necessary to understand how language ideology has informed programmatic and instructional design of bilingual education programs in the United States. By understanding the history of bilingual education and the progression of different instructional models for multilingual learners, educational leaders can reflect on their language ideologies and practices and take steps to deweaponize English education for multilingual learners.

HISTORICAL BACKGROUND OF BILINGUAL EDUCATION

A historical foundation of legislation is an essential starting point in illustrating shifts in bilingual education and associated ideologies. In 1968, during Lyndon B. Johnson's presidency, the Bilingual Education Act was passed to provide funding for educational resources for students living in language-minoritized communities (García, 2009a). Because this was a time of low U.S. immigration, this act was targeted toward students who were already citizens of the United States. Although the passage of this legislation illustrates a change in understanding of how policy should support educational equity for multilingual learners, the act was founded on a deficiency perspective of multilingual learners focused on remediating their weak English skills without regard to their diverse linguistic abilities (Petrzela, 2010). It also provided only $7.5 million to pilot bilingual education programs (Gándara & Escamilla, 2016). The passage of this legislation was controversial, and its intended purpose remained unclear as "bilingual education" was not defined and could be interpreted as instruction given in two languages or instruction meant to transition multilingual learners to English as soon as possible (Crawford, 2004).

In 1974, the Supreme Court ruled in *Lau v. Nichols* that "equal treatment of English-speaking and non-English-speaking students did not constitute equal educational opportunity and, therefore, violated non-English-speaking students' civil rights" (Ovando, 2003, p. 9). The ruling declared that school districts had to provide equal access to curriculum to English-speaking and non-English speaking students (Gándara & Escamilla, 2016). Although the ruling did not offer school districts a framework or guidance to achieve equal curriculum access, the ruling led the Office of Civil Rights to publish a plan in 1975 for school districts to use in identifying multilingual learners and testing their language proficiencies. The school districts' plan also stated that if a school had more than twenty multilingual learners, they should implement a bilingual education program and multilingual learners should be moved from pull-out English instruction classes to mainstream classes as soon as possible (Souto-Manning, 2016).

In 1978, Title VII of the Civil Rights Act was amended to allow multilingual learners to enroll in bilingual education programs. Title VII provided funding to schools "to develop and carry out new and imaginative elementary and secondary programs designed to meet the special educational needs of children of limited English-speaking ability" (Bilingual Education Act, 1968, Section 702). The Bilingual Education Act and Title VII did not include any clauses noting the home cultures and languages of multilingual learners, but it was a promising step to promote more equitable learning for multilingual learners and gave school districts power to design their own bilingual education programs.

In 2001, the Bilingual Education Act was repealed and replaced with Title III of the No Child Left Behind Act (NCLB). This legislation, also known as the Language Instruction for Limited English Proficiency and Immigrant Students, included nine purposes focused on assisting multilingual learners with standardized testing through the development of school programs aimed at "preparing limited English proficient children, including immigrant children and youth, to enter all-English instruction settings"

(NCLB, 2001). This law did not end bilingual education programs, but did promote English-only instruction focused on standardized testing preparation (Nieto, 2009). Additionally, in the last 20 years, all federal offices that included the term bilingual in their names have been renamed using the term "English Language Acquisition" (García, 2009b, p. 187).

MONOGLOSSIC IDEOLOGICAL FOUNDATIONS

Bilingual education policy and programs beginning in the 1960s illustrate a prevailing monoglossic ideology within the United States (Cenoz & Gorter, 2015; García, 2009a). Monoglossic language ideology, a form of standard language ideology, encompasses a rigid perspective that sets standard English as a norm and expectation (García, 2009a). It does not allow for flexibility and does not view multilingual learners on a continuum (García, 2009b). Within educational systems, monoglossic language ideology is common and instructional practices that promote monoglossia are frequently utilized by teachers (Cenoz & Gorter, 2015; Zúñiga et al., 2018). Teachers of multilingual learners often adopt a deficit perspective of multilingual learners which is founded in a belief in achievement gaps between multilingual learners and monolingual students (Zhao, 2016). This perspective, coupled with doubt regarding the academic value of allowing students to use languages other than English in the classroom, leads teachers to implement monoglossic practices (Zúñiga et al., 2018). From this linguistic and instructional stance, those in power dictate the standard version of the taught language. Students or others who diverge from standard language use are considered improper language users, and through this ideology and its associated practices, multilingualism is reduced to "two or more monolongualisms" (García, 2009a, p. 51). Additionally, within monoglossic ideology and practice, multilingual learners face unique obstacles that their monolingual peers do not face (Wiley et al., 2014) and the languages and associated cultures of these diverse multilingual learners are minimized (Anzaldúa, 1999). Within monoglossic systems, student academic achievement and success are centered around academic English and the attainment of traditional knowledge across content areas. Within these systems, achievement is measured in standard, academic English.

Historically, monoglossic language ideologies were introduced during European colonization as colonists used language as a tool of nationalistic power and assimilation. Monoglossic ideology was initially introduced in the Americas as European settlers colonized the region (Flores, 2014), but expanded in the early 1900s as the Naturalization Act of 1906 was passed, requiring immigrants to speak English in order to become U.S. citizens (Gándara & Escamilla, 2016). Although there were places and periods of time in which bilingualism was accepted and promoted, such as the implementation of German bilingual schools in the Midwest, French bilingual schools in Louisiana, and Spanish bilingual schools in the New Mexico Territory, economic recession and the passage of legislation that did not favor immigrant populations led to the promotion of monoglossic ideology (Kloss, 1977). Within the United States, a strong movement emerged, beginning with the work of Noah Webster, to create a standardized English language representative of a unified nation, not the growing numbers of linguistically diverse individuals contained within the nation's population (Flores, 2014).

The two solitudes perspective, a theory that emerged from monoglossia, has informed traditional English as a Second Language (ESL) programs in U.S. schools since its advent in 2007 (García, 2009a). The two solitudes perspective focuses on the development of the L2, standard English, while typically minimizing or disallowing classroom use of the L1, the student's first or home language (Cummins, 2017). The monoglossic focus of this perspective, which separates the home language and standard school language, is founded in Cummins's (2007) theory which called for a "rigid separation" (p. 221) of the L1 (first language) and L2 (second language) in L2 instruction. Although many researchers have since identified weaknesses in the two solitudes viewpoint and illustrated a need for multilingual instruction, preservice teacher programs and public schools often enact programming and practices that align with the two solitudes viewpoint (Meier & Conteh, 2014; Taylor & Snoddon, 2013).

PULL-OUT AND PUSH-IN MODELS OF ENGLISH AS A SECOND LANGUAGE

The most traditional model for educating multilingual learners is through ESL programming. ESL uses only English as the mode of instruction and does not regard the home languages of the students (García, 2009b). Because ESL instruction is only provided in English, the teacher is not required to be bilingual. ESL pull-out instruction is often used in elementary settings where multilingual learners are removed from the mainstream classroom daily for English instruction. At secondary levels, students usually attend a class period of ESL instruction (Rennie, 1993). Pull-in models of ESL instruction also exist where an ESL teacher supports a mainstream content teacher through co-teaching or providing in-class support for multilingual learners (Mabbott & Strohl, 1992).

TRANSITIONAL BILINGUAL EDUCATION MODEL

In alignment with monoglossic ideology, transitional bilingual education (TBE) programs are designed for students designated as English Language Learners (ELLs), and typically use the native language as a bridge towards English language acquisition (Gándara & Escamilla, 2016). These programs provide content area instruction in the student's home language and also provide a course of ESL. García (2011) expressed the temporary value of transitional bilingual programs: "We cannot destroy the transitional bilingual education 'safe houses' for students will need them, temporarily, before they come into the 'contact zone' of the mainstream classroom" (p. 144). Unfortunately, when classrooms include students of diverse language backgrounds, TBE models are difficult to implement (Gándara and Escamilla, 2016).

TBE programs provide opportunities for students to gain proficiency in English while using the home language as a support; however, this model is a form of subtractive bilingual education because it does not foster growth of the home language. Instead, the home language's only purpose is as a tool to acquire English (Baker, 2011). In addition to being subtractive, TBE programs are assimilationist because they do not develop bilingualism or biliteracy and can lead to students losing their home language. Also, within these models, multicultural perspectives are not included (Gándara & Escamilla, 2016).

A TRANSITION TOWARDS HETEROGLOSSIC IDEOLOGY

Monoglossic ideology is juxtaposed with heteroglossic language ideology, a perspective that focuses on the multifaceted nature of language and its uses. Bakhtin (1981), who established the concept of heteroglossia, explained that,

> at any given moment of its evolution, language is stratified not only
> into linguistic dialects in the strict sense of the word ... but also ...
> into languages that are socio-ideological: Languages of social groups,
> "professional" and "generic" languages, languages of generations, and so
> forth. (pp. 271–272)

Bakhtin noted an approach to language that is broader than monoglossic approaches, an approach founded on the idea that students must use their complete range of linguistic capacity to effectively build multiliteracy (Hornberger & Skilton-Sylvester, 2000). Heteroglossia focuses on the complete and fluid use of a language user's linguistic repertoire (Salaberry, 2020).

Weber (2009) expanded on this perspective by noting both pedagogical and social implications of heteroglossic language ideology. Weber stated that through this ideology, diverse linguistic and cultural resources are validated, even those that are not considered standard. However, heteroglossia should not be confused with double-monolingualism where languages remain separate and integration of language knowledge is not supported through additive approaches (García, 2009b; Heller, 2006). If teachers develop meta-ideological awareness of language ideology, they will be able to understand diverse communicative repertoires of students and support students as they traverse their own language learning (Rymes, 2010).

DUAL-LANGUAGE BILINGUAL EDUCATION PROGRAMS

Dual-Language Bilingual Education (DLBE) programs constitute two main models of additional language education. One-way DLBE consists of a homogeneous language group learning a partner language, such as English-speaking students learning Spanish. Two-way DBLE programs include English-speaking students and students already fluent in the partner language in the same classroom, such as Spanish-speaking multilingual learners and English-speaking students. In two-way DLBE classrooms, students from each language group learn the language of the other group. Within the United States, these programs are difficult to implement because they require sufficient enrollment from English-speaking and partner-language-speaking students. More often, one-way DLBE programs are implemented with English-speaking students only (García, 2009a). Two-way DBLE programs promote identity development, cross-cultural competence, and multicultural appreciation for students by connecting students across racial, cultural, and socioeconomic backgrounds (García, 2017; Howard et al., 2018).

Past research has shown that multilingual learners in DBLE programs academically outperform multilingual learners in non-DBLE programs and DBLE programs can maintain and develop the biliteracy of multilingual learners (García & Wei, 2009; Morita-Mullaney et al., 2020). However, DBLE programs can promote linguistic inequality between students if the minoritized student group is required to be a "language broker" for the English-dominant students instead of an equal partner (Oliveira et al., 2020, p. 573). When programs exacerbate already-existing inequalities between minority and majority language users, they create an equity trap (Morita-Mullaney et al., 2020). Additionally, Morita-Mullaney et al. (2020) highlighted that multilingual learners in DLBE programs often do not take advanced-level electives, specifically electives in math and science. Therefore, while DBLE programs show strengths in teaching English to multilingual learners, the model fails to limit all inequities faced by multilingual learners and illustrates that raising the status of minoritized languages cannot be accomplished through English instruction or instruction provided in an English-speaking environment (Oliveira et al., 2020). Dorner and Cervantes-Soon (2020) expressed:

> Equity in dual language bilingual education necessitates an understanding of the history and value of cultures, our elders, and students' already present plurilingualism and making sure our pedagogies provide minoritized language students with opportunities to grow and develop their full linguistic repertoire. (p. 536)

TRANSLANGUAGING AS A HETEROGLOSSIC INSTRUCTIONAL MODEL

Although past theories of bilingual education and multilingual education have viewed L1 and L2 as separate languages of instruction, new research has questioned the separation of languages of instruction and provided promising practices of heteroglossic methods implementation (García, 2014; May, 2017). Multilingual worlds in which language users communicate and interact require complex language practices (Pennycook, 2017). Complex communication includes "forms of hybrid language use that are systemically engaged in sensemaking" (García et al., 2011, p. 5). Translanguaging is an instructional practice that engages teachers and students within complex communication possible through full use of individuals' linguistic repertoires. Both teachers and students can translanguage by using all linguistic resources in their repertoire. For multilingual learners, this practice often appears as using their home language and English together. The term *translanguaging* first appeared as *Trawsieithu*—a Welsh term introduced by Cen Williams in her 1980s dissertation (Lewis et al., 2012). In this context, translanguaging referred to a strategy used across content areas for using two languages in the same lesson. García and Kleifgen (2020) argued that "translanguaging transforms our understandings of language, bi/multilingualism, and pedagogical approaches to support multilingual learners' use and further expansion of their unique meaning-making repertoire" (p. 553).

Translanguaging can be viewed as both an ideology and a practice. When put into practice, it normalizes multilingualism, does not functionally separate languages, and promotes an individual's use of their complete linguistic repertoire (Creese & Blackledge, 2018). Translanguaging occurs within spaces that allow for and promote translinguistic practice (Wei, 2011), and, when implemented, blurs the lines between dominant and non-dominant languages (Poza, 2017). Because the concept of translanguaging is evolving, it is difficult to accept a single definition of the practice. Baker (2011) defined translanguaging as "the process of making meaning, shaping experiences, gaining understanding and knowledge through the use of two languages" (p. 288). Furthermore, Cenoz and Gorter (2011) described translanguaging as "the combination of two or more languages in a systematic way within the same learning activity" (p. 359). Flores (2014) expanded on these definitions by noting that translanguaging is a political act.

Translanguaging is an exemplary heteroglossic practice. The goal of translanguaging practices, which is a visible enactment of heteroglossic ideology, is "to valorize students' diverse linguistic repertoires by positioning their skills in languages other than Standard English as valuable classroom assets to be built on rather than handicaps to be overcome" (Flores & Rosa, 2015). Although this approach can provide broader language-learning opportunities, it can be argued that schools and their structures fail to support broad, heteroglossic language development and dampen linguistic opportunities for students (Creese & Blackledg, 2010; Flores, 2014). Gándara and Escamilla (2016) outlined the following obstacles to the implementation of heteroglossic language education models: increasing populations of superdiverse students with diverse linguistic backgrounds; monolingual and monocultural Common Core standards; monolingual state and national standardized testing; and teacher shortages, specifically in areas with diverse students.

THE FUTURE OF BILINGUAL EDUCATION

Since the emergence of multilingual learners in U.S. public schools and the political recognition of their need for equality in public education, programmatic changes and adaptations have not kept pace with the continually changing identities of multilingual learners (Gándara & Escamilla, 2016). Bilingual programs, although each designed to help the language development of multilingual learners, often place greater value on the dominant language than the student's home language or focus on linguistic justice but face implementational obstacles. Umansky and Reardon (2014) conducted a longitudinal study of multilingual learners, following them from kindergarten through high school. Their findings illustrated that multilingual learners in transitional and dual-language bilingual programs outperformed their peers in English-only programs on all standardized measures and attained higher levels of English proficiency sooner. However, stakeholders must ask themselves how bilingual education programs can be improved if language barriers were removed, and students were allowed to access and build upon their full linguistic repertoire as they learn English and content area knowledge.

Bilingual education programs are built upon language ideologies and system policies that are far removed from the individual needs of multilingual learners (Flores & García, 2017; Valdés, 2018). The identity of multilingual learners is rapidly changing. In the past, these students were often immigrants to the United States. Today, many are simultaneous bilinguals who were born in the United States and speak a language other than English at home. Many multilingual learners have been exposed to English since birth (Escamilla et al., 2014). So, it is essential that stakeholders address what the goal of bilingual education is for their student population.

Imagining a new future of bilingual education can be difficult, especially when recent political events and research highlight continued hostility against immigrants and racially marginalized populations (Hafner & Ortiz, 2021; Orelus et al., 2020). Therefore, educational leaders and teachers must define goals for multilingual learners and implement changes to allow multilingual learners unbounded opportunities for success. If the goal of educational leaders and teachers is for multilingual learners to simply gain English proficiency, current bilingual education models may suffice. However, if the goal of bilingual education is to promote bilingualism and biliteracy and to promote complete linguistic development and expression of a student, stakeholders must readdress their language ideologies and associated policies in order to build opportunities for heteroglossic practices, such as translanguaging.

Accomplishing full implementation of heteroglossic practices, although promising, is not a simple or quick task. To do so, embedded language ideologies must shift. Meighan (2021) suggested transepistemic language education, a method of learning and understanding while engaging with people of diverse languages and cultures, as a method to "unlearn cognitive and linguistic imperialism in language learning and teaching" (p. 1). Flores and Rosa (2019) highlighted the importance of viewing racialized linguistic minorities from an asset-based perspective. De Costa et al. (2022) called upon organizations to publish position statements to denounce all forms of racism, including linguistic racism. These suggested steps have the potential power to help educational leaders and teachers shift their ideological positioning, but it must be added that preservice teacher education programs and professional development programming must also teach heteroglossic principles and practices, such as translanguaging. Educational stakeholders need education and tools in order to shift their practice as their perspective of language use and learning shift. Lastly, academic researchers must continue to explore methods to support the heteroglossic ideological development of teachers and educational leaders so that future educators enter the field equipped with the perspectives necessary to empower multilingual learners through linguistically relevant instruction and deweaponize language.

REFERENCES

Anzaldúa, G. (1999). Chapter 22: Putting Coyolxauhqui together: A creative process. *Counterpoints, 90*, 241–261. https://doi.org/ 10.1515/9780822375036-007

Baker, C. (2011). *Foundations of bilingual education and bilingualism*. Multilingual Matters.

Baker-Bell, A. (2020). *Linguistic justice: Black language, literacy, identity, and pedagogy*. Routledge.

Bakhtin, M. (1981). Discourse in the novel (M. Holquist, & C. Emerson, Trans.). In M. Holquist (Ed.), *The dialogic imagination* (pp. 259–422). University of Texas Press. https://www.scirp.org/(S(i43dyn45teexjx455qlt3d2q))/reference/referencespapers.aspx?referenceid=1989730

Bialystok, E. (2001). *Bilingualism in development: Language, literacy, and cognition*. Cambridge University Press.

Bilingual Education Act. (1968). http://www.congress.gov/

Creese, A., & Blackledge, A. (2010). Translanguaging in the bilingual classroom: A pedagogy for learning and teaching? *The Modern Language Journal, 94*(1), 103–115.

Cenoz, J., & Gorter, D. (2011). A holistic approach to multilingual education: Introduction. *The Modern Language Journal, 95*(3), 339–343. http://doi.org/10.1111/j.1540-4781.2011.01204.x

Cenoz, J., & Gorter, D. (Eds.). (2015). *Multilingual education*. Cambridge University Press.

Cummins, J. (2007). Rethinking monolingual instructional strategies in multilingual classrooms. *Canadian Journal of Applied Linguistics, 10*(2), 221–240.

Cummins, J. (2017). Teaching for transfer in multilingual school contexts. *Bilingual and Multilingual Education, 3*, 103–115. http://dx.doi.org/10.1007/978-3-319-02324-3_8-1

Crawford, J. (2004). *Educating English learners: Language diversity in the classroom*. Bilingual Education Services.

Creese, A., & Blackledge, A. (2018). *The Routledge handbook of language and super-diversity*. Routledge.

De Costa, P. I., Her, L., & Lee, V. (2022). Weaponizing and de-weaponizing antiracist discourse: Some things for language educators to consider. *International Journal of Literacy, Culture, and Language Education, 2*, 98–107. http://dx.doi.org/10.14434/ijlcle.v2iMay.34393

Dorner, L. M., & Cervantes-Soon, C. G. (2020). Equity for students learning English in dual language bilingual education: Persistent challenges and promising practices. *TESOL Quarterly, 54*(3), 535–547. http://dx.doi.org/10.1002/tesq.599

Escamilla, K., Hopewell, S., Butvilofsky, S., Sparrow, W., Soltero-González, L., Ruiz-Figueroa, O., & Escamilla, M. (2014). *Biliteracy from the start: Literacy squared in action*. Caslon Publishing.

Flores, N. (2014). Let's not forget that translanguaging is a political act. *The Educational Linguist*, 7. https://educationallinguist.wordpress.com/2014/07/19/lets-not-forget-that-translanguaging-is-a-political-act/

Flores, N., & García, O. (2017). A critical review of bilingual education in the United States: From basements and pride to boutiques and profit. *Annual Review of Applied Linguistics*, *37*, 14–29. http://dx.doi.org/10.1017/S0267190517000162

Flores, N., & Rosa, J. (2015). Undoing appropriateness: Raciolinguistic ideologies and language diversity in education. *Harvard Educational Review*, *85*(2), 149–171. http://dx.doi.org/10.17763/0017-8055.85.2.149

Flores, N., & Rosa, J. (2019). Bringing race into second language acquisition. *The Modern Language Journal*, *103*, 145–151.

Gándara, P., & Escamilla, K. (2016). Bilingual education in the United States. *Bilingual and Multilingual Education*, *12*(1), 439–452. https://doi.org/10.1007/978-3-319-02258-1_33

García, O. (2009a). *Bilingual education in the 21st century: A global perspective*. Wiley-Blackwell.

García, O. (2009b). Emergent bilinguals and TESOL: What's in a name? *TESOL Quarterly*, *43*(2), 322–326. https://doi.org/10.1002/j.1545-7249.2009.tb00172.x

García, O. (2017). Bilingual education. *The Handbook of Sociolinguistics*, 405-420.

García, O., & Kleifgen, J. A. (2020). Translanguaging and literacies. *Reading Research Quarterly*, *55*(4), 553–571. http://dx.doi.org/10.1002/rrq.286

García, O., Makar, C., Starcevic, M., & Terry, A. (2011). The translanguaging of Latino kindergarteners. *Bilingual Youth: Spanish in English-Speaking Societies*, *42*, 33–55.

García, O., & Wei, L. (2014). Language, bilingualism and education. *Translanguaging: Language, Bilingualism and Education*, 46–62. http://dx.doi.org/10.1057/9781137385765.0010

Hafner, A. H., & Ortiz, F. W. (2021). Toward transformative teaching for English language learners: Critical texts in sheltered English immersion courses. *Curriculum and Teaching Dialogue*, *23*(1/2), 145–160.

Heller, M. (2006). *Linguistic minorities and modernity: A sociolinguistic ethnography*. A&C Black.

Herrera, L. J. P., & Bryan, K. C. (2022). Language weaponization in society and education: Introduction to the special issue. *International Journal of Literacy, Culture, and Language Education*, *2*, 1–5. https://doi.org/10.14434/ijlcle.v2iMay.34380

Hornberger, N. H., & Skilton-Sylvester, E. (2000). Revisiting the continua of biliteracy: International and critical perspectives. *Language and Education*, *14*(2), 96–122. https://doi.org/10.1080/09500780008666781

Howard, E. R., Sugarman, J., Christian, D., Lindholm-Leary, K. J., & Rogers, D. (2018). *Guiding principles for dual language education* (3rd ed.). Center for Applied Linguistics.

Kloss, H. (1977). *The American bilingual tradition*. Newbury House Publishers.

Lewis, G., Jones, B., & Baker, C. (2012). Translanguaging: Origins and development from school to street and beyond. *Educational Research and Evaluation*, *18*(7), 641–654. http://dx.doi.org/10.1080/13803611.2012.718488

Mabbott, A., & Strohl, J. (1992). Pull-in programs–A new trend in ESL education. *MinneTESOL Journal*, *10*, 21–30. https://conservancy.umn.edu/bitstream/handle/11299/109062/TESOL-1992.pdf?sequence=1&isAllowed=y#page=30

May, S. (2017). Bilingual education: What the research tells us. In O. Garcia, S. May, A. Lin (Eds.), *Bilingual and multilingual education: Encyclopedia of language and education.* (3rd ed., pp. 81–100). Springer.

Meier, G., & Conteh, J. (2014). Conclusion: the multilingual turn in languages education. *The Multilingual Turn in Languages Education*, 292–299.

Meighan, P. J. (2021). *Transepistemic language education: Knowledge co-creation in English language teaching.* SSRN. https://dx.doi.org/10.2139/ssrn.4011394

Morita-Mullaney, T., Renn, J., & Chiu, M. M. (2020). Obscuring equity in dual language bilingual education: A longitudinal study of emergent bilingual achievement, course placements, and grades. *TESOL Quarterly*, *54*(3), 685–718. http://dx.doi.org/10.1002/tesq.592

No Child Left Behind Act. (2001, January). Title III: Language instruction for limited English proficient and immigrant students. In *107th Congress, 1st Session, December* (Vol. 13, p. 2001).

Nieto, S. (2009). *Language, culture, and teaching: Critical perspectives.* Routledge.

Oliveira, G., Lima Becker, M., & Chang-Bacon, C. K. (2020). "Eu sei, I know": Equity and immigrant experience in a portuguese-English dual language bilingual education program. *TESOL Quarterly*, *54*(3), 572–598. http://dx.doi.org/10.1002/tesq.589

Orelus, P. W. (2020). Other people's english accents matter: Challenging standard english accent hegemony. *Excellence in Education Journal*, *9*(1), 120–148.

Ovando, C. J. (2003). Bilingual education in the United States: Historical development and current issues. *Bilingual Research Journal*, *27*(1), 1–24. http://dx.doi.org/10.1080/15235882.2003.10162589

Pennycook, A. (2017). Language policy and local practices. *The Oxford Handbook of Language and Society*, 125–140. https://doi.org/10.1093/oxfordhb/9780190212896.013.11

Petrzela, N. M. (2010). Before the federal bilingual education act: Legislation and lived experience in California. *Peabody Journal of Education*, *85*(4), 406–424. https://doi.org/10.1080/0161956X.2010.518021

Portes, A., & Hao, L. (2002). The price of uniformity: Language, family and personality adjustment in the immigrant second generation. *Ethnic and Racial Studies*, *25*(6), 889–912. https://doi.org/10.1080/0141987022000009368

Poza, L. (2017). Translanguaging: Definitions, implications, and further needs in burgeoning inquiry. *Berkeley Review of Education*, *6*(2), 101–128. https://doi.org/10.5070/B86110060

Rennie, J. (1993). *ESL and bilingual program models.* (ED362072). ERIC Digest. https://eric.ed.gov/?id=ED362072

Rymes, B. (2010). 19. Classroom discourse analysis: A focus on communicative repertoires. In N. H. Hornberger & S.L. McKay (Eds.), *Sociolinguistics and language education* (pp. 528–546). Multilingual Matters.

Salaberry, M. R. (2020). The 'transformative' potential of translanguaging and other heteroglossic educational practices. *Journal of Multilingual Theories and Practices, 1*(2), 266–289. http://dx.doi.org/10.1558/jmtp.16459

Souto-Manning, M. (2016). Honoring and building on the rich literacy practices of young bilingual and multilingual learners. *The Reading Teacher, 70*(3), 263–271. http://dx.doi.org/10.1002/trtr.1518

Taylor, S. K., & Snoddon, K. (2013). Plurilingualism in TESOL: Promising controversies. *TESOL Quarterly*, 439–445. http://dx.doi.org/10.1002/tesq.127

Umansky, I. M., & Reardon, S. F. (2014). Reclassification patterns among Latino English learner students in bilingual, dual immersion, and English immersion classrooms. *American Educational Research Journal, 51*(5), 879–912.

Valdés, G. (2018). Analyzing the curricularization of language in two-way immersion education: Restating two cautionary notes. *Bilingual Research Journal, 41*(4), 388–412. http://dx.doi.org/10.1080/15235882.2018.1539886

Weber, J. J. (2009). *Multilingualism, education and change* (Vol. 9). Peter Lang.

Wei, L. (2011). Multilinguality, multimodality, and multicompetence: Code-and modeswitching by minority ethnic children in complementary schools. *The Modern Language Journal, 95*(3), 370–384. http://dx.doi.org/10.1111/j.1540-4781.2011.01209.x

Wiley, T. G., & Rolstad, K. (2014). The common core state standards and the great divide. *International Multilingual Research Journal, 8*(1), 38–55. http://dx.doi.org/10.1080/19313152.2014.852428

Zhao, Y. (2016). From deficiency to strength: Shifting the mindset about education inequality. *Journal of Social Issues, 72*(4), 720–739. https://doi.org/10.1111/josi.12191

Zúñiga, C. E., Henderson, K. I., & Palmer, D. K. (2018). Language policy toward equity: How bilingual teachers use policy mandates to their own ends. *Language and Education, 32*(1), 60–76. https://doi.org/10.1080/09500782.2017.1349792

CHAPTER 3

BESPOKE LEARNING

Using the Evidence Continuum to Design
a Learner-Centered Curriculum

Robyn Thomas Pitts
University of Denver

ABSTRACT

The evidence continuum is a five-domain model for building evidence through needs assessment, program theory, process evaluation, outcomes and impact evaluation, and optimization studies. In this conceptual article, the first two domains of the evidence continuum are used to design a learner-centered course on advanced research methods, and strategies for adapting a conventional curriculum for learner-centeredness are provided. Implications are discussed regarding praxis, pedagogical content knowledge development, and learner-centered assessment and evaluation.

It is November. Course enrollments are in, and my teaching load for January is changing. I will be picking up a section of a class that I have never taught before, and it needs to be comparable to the sections being taught by other instructors. Unfortunately, the course is not designed in a way that reflects my praxis, and the class starts soon. The instructional style of the course is "sage on the stage" with lectures and slides, and the assignments feel rote. In adapting the course to center learners' needs and

Curriculum and Teaching Dialogue,
Volume 25, Numbers 1 & 2, pp. 217–231
Copyright © 2023 by Information Age Publishing
www.infoagepub.com
All rights of reproduction in any form reserved.

interests, there are so many parallels with how the evaluation knowledge base supports the development of people-serving programs. The evidence continuum is helpful for quickly centering learners' needs and desired outcomes in this single course and across many courses to take stock of students' holistic learning.

In this article, the evidence continuum, which is well-known in the field of evaluation, is used to design a learner-centered curriculum. The continuum is a five-domain tool for building high-quality evidence for program evaluation across key phases of a program lifecycle (i.e., design, implementation, and evaluation). The first two domains of the evidence continuum provide a heuristic for adopting a learner-centered approach by using needs assessment (Domain 1) and program theory (Domain 2) methods. By embedding these strategies into the teaching and learning model, the continuum provides a strategy for applying Weimer's (2013) framework for learner-centered teaching through learner engagement, skill development, intentional reflection, shared control, and collaboration. A *need* represents a gap between what learners should accomplish and where they start. While typical approaches establish learners' needs relative to content-related outcomes, a broader view acknowledges the desired outcomes that learners have based on their prior experience, interest in the topic, and motivation for learning.

As a result of using the evidence continuum to design curriculum, instructors craft learning experiences that flexibly accommodate learners' needs and desired outcomes. They do so by incorporating *adaptive elements* into a learning experience to create space for learners to identify and engage with their own interests. Some strategies for converting conventional course elements into adaptive ones are illustrated in Table 3.1. These strategies provide multiple means of engagement, representation, and expression (CAST, 2018) and facilitate bespoke learning experiences. In the same way that bespoke goods like clothing are tailored for a particular consumer, *bespoke learning* refers to learning that is customized for a particular learner. The term *bespoke* will be used to describe learning experiences that prompt learners to identify and engage with their own needs and desired outcomes.

A graduate course on survey design and analysis is used to illustrate how to use the evidence continuum to design a learner-centered course. Reflections on using the evidence continuum in this way center on balancing conventional and adaptive elements of learning; implications for learner-centered assessment and evaluation; and deepening praxis through reflection and critical analysis. Importantly, the continuum does not replace conventional strategies for planning—it augments them by creating a strategy for analyzing holistic learning (i.e., learning occurring across many learning experiences). Holistic learning occurs within a

Table 3.1

Adapting Courses to Center Learners' Needs and Desired Outcomes

Course Element	Description
Course Syllabus □ Learning Agreements	The *instructor creates space* for learners to identify their core values, collaborate to develop a core set and description, and use the agreement for mutual accountability.
Reading List □ Self-Selected Readings	The *instructor creates space* for learners to select some readings. Using a sign-up sheet, learners select a reading for which they will facilitate a class discussion.
Assignments □ Task Menus/Rubrics	The *instructor creates space* for learners to select a final project from a menu of options. Learners may contract for a grade (A, B, C) by selecting a task/s (e.g., portfolios). A single rubric is used for all tasks.
Grading Scheme □ Developmental Grading	The *instructor creates space* in feedback to focus on what matters most. Instead of points and partial credit, criteria-based grades are assigned (e.g., missing, approaches, meets, or exceeds expectations).
New Element: Learner Intake Survey	The *instructor creates space* for learners to articulate their needs, interests, and aspirations. Learners are prompted to revisit these personal anchors and consider how their learning is consolidating over time.
New Element: Active Learning to Leverage Prior Learning	The *instructor creates space* within discussions and active learning exercises to leverage learners' contributions. Prior experiences contribute to a culture of shared learning, deepen learning by exploring tricky aspects of prior experiences, and expand learning by sharing among learners.
Homework Questions □ Reflection Journal	The *instructor creates space* for learners to apply learning to a problem or project of their own choosing and to reflect on that experience. Prompts focus on critical analysis and reflection.
Article Analysis Task □ Self-Selected Article	The *instructor creates space* for learners to select studies that are relevant to their interests. The quality of the critique is assessed with a rubric on identifying the merits and weaknesses of the study.
Written Assessments □ Project-Based Learning	The *instructor creates space* for learners to engage in through-course assessment by demonstrating learning through a project that is relevant to their interests. The project is chunked across multiple tasks, some of which are procedural and others of which are assessed for learning quality. Feedback is incorporated across the project.
Instructor Selects Discipline □ Learners Select Disciplines	Outcomes remain unchanged (see Figure 3.4) with the exception that learners engage in project-based learning within their own disciplinary contexts. The *instructor creates space* for learners to select examples to position assignments within a discipline of their own choosing. Rather than analyzing instructor-defined examples and datasets, learners engage in exploratory assignments that position their learning in authentic spaces of interest to them, thus enabling deeper, more significant learning.

220   R. T. PITTS

single course (e.g., learning across sessions or units of curriculum), across a sequence of multiple courses in a particular area of study (e.g., a sequence of courses on statistics), or across a program of study (e.g., across many courses, course sequences, and co-curricular requirements).

RELEVANT LITERATURE

In the latter half of the 20th century, a boon of government-funded initiatives to improve Americans' quality of life catalyzed a growing need for systematic approaches to evaluate the quality of human service programs (Cronbach, 1980). Initially conceived of as a transdisciplinary practice (Scriven, 2008), evaluation is a complex form of stakeholder-centered (Centers for Disease Control and Prevention [CDC], 2011) mixed methods research (Creswell & Plano Clark, 2018) with its own unique knowledge base (Coryn et al., 2017), theory (Mertens & Wilson, 2012), and methodology (Davidson, 2005). One of the key contributions of evaluation as a discipline and burgeoning profession (Ayoo et al., 2020) is the evidence continuum (Rossi et al., 2018), a framework that illuminates the interrelationships among various evaluation activities and provides a coherent model for systematically judging the merit, worth, value, or significance (Scriven, 1991) of people-serving programs. Even though evaluation is often viewed as occurring after programs have been implemented, its frameworks support the earliest stages of program planning.

The Evidence Continuum

The continuum depicts a sequential process for building evidence across five domains to ensure a program achieves social change. The five domains are:

1. *Evidence of need* defines the nature, scale, and scope of social needs.
2. *Evidence of theory and logic* depicts how a program is designed to meet social needs. The feasibility, sufficiency, and necessity of its elements are assessed by aligning its outcomes, outputs, activities, and inputs using tools like logic models (CDC, 2011; Taylor-Powell & Henert, 2008) and program theory (Funnell & Rogers, 2011).
3. *Evidence of process* assesses program implementation, services, and participant experiences.

4. *Evidence of outcomes and impact* assesses changes in outcome levels over time. Studies of participants' longitudinal changes in outcomes are known as outcome evaluations. When outcome level changes are compared between participants and a robust counterfactual (i.e., a group that has been constructed to be equivalent on key variables of interest), this is known as an impact evaluation (Rossi et al., 2018).
5. *Evidence of efficiency* addresses the optimal use of resources (e.g., costs, benefits).

Relationships Between the Five Domains

Akin to matryoshka dolls (nesting dolls), the five domains of the evidence continuum are expressed as a Bronfenbrenner model (see Pitts, 2021, for visual). The need for a program (Domain 1) provides the basis for its design (Domain 2). Evaluating the quality of program implementation (Domain 3) is inherently connected to understanding why the program was needed (Domain 1) and how it was intended to be delivered (Domain 2). Evaluating program effectiveness in terms of outcomes or impact (Domain 4) is ill-advised without evidence that the program was implemented well (Domain 3), and expensive impact studies (Domain 4) and cost analyses (Domain 5) should not be undertaken without evidence of positive outcomes (Domain 4). While it is not necessary to start each evaluation in Domain 1, evidence in each domain must be of sufficient quality to enable evaluative work in subsequent domains (e.g., a program must be well implemented (Domain 3) for meaningful outcomes evaluation (Domain 4; see Rossi et al., 2018). Furthermore, evidence-building does not always proceed linearly: needs assessment and logic models are developed concurrently because they are closely linked. As needs are determined, they are integrated into the logic model and vice versa.

For example, to evaluate an after-school literacy program, an evaluator must understand the specific needs for the program (e.g., supporting readers near versus far below grade-level expectations; providing bilingual support for English language learners) and how the program is structured to meet its goals (e.g., curricular approaches and expected duration/dosage). Upon implementation of the program, evidence of need and program theory is used to determine the extent to which the program is delivered and received as intended (e.g., participation rates, fit with learners' needs) and the extent to which the expected outcomes are achieved (e.g., growth on a pre- or post-assessment). If the program demonstrates success, additional studies are warranted to determine if the success can be

Using the Evidence Continuum to Center Learners in Curriculum and Teaching

Curriculum and teaching in higher education are often evaluated, yet many foundational evaluation concepts (e.g., the evidence continuum, needs assessments, logic models, and evaluation matrices) are not regularly applied in the design, implementation, and assessment of curriculum and teaching (Rickards & Stitt-Bergh, 2016). Since evaluation is often viewed as a service industry rather than a unique discipline or profession (Gullickson et al., 2019), instructors who might benefit from using evaluation concepts within their praxis may not be aware of its knowledge base. The term "program evaluation" may be misleading because evaluation is a systematic process for judging the quality not only of programs but of any evaluand (e.g., an intervention, curriculum, training, course, or policy). The term "program" is often used in a broad sense to describe the subject of an evaluation study.

The evidence continuum is useful for centering learners with curriculum and teaching because the continuum centers peoples' needs and social issues within programs (Rossi et al., 2018). Nearly a century ago, Dewey (1938) first introduced the idea that students are unique learners and that their interests should provide the basis for instructional design. Teaching and learning are constructivist, sociocultural processes (Kolb, 1984). Centering learners within pedagogy involves understanding learners' motivations, interests, and prior learning (Santi & Gorghiu, 2017), and these learner variables are addressed within contemporary frameworks for instructional design (e.g., see *Understanding by Design* [Wiggins & McTighe, 2005], Universal Design for Learning [CAST, 2018]). According to Fink (2013), high-quality learning experiences are the result of four elements: backward design; alignment of curriculum, teaching, and assessment; emphasis on the long-term value of learning; and promoting inclusion and access through differentiation. The first two elements of high-quality learning focus on an instructor's need to articulate their underlying model for teaching and learning, which aligns with Domain 2 of the evidence continuum on program theory. The latter two elements of high-quality learning focus on honing that initial model using the needs assessment methods of Domain 1.

Instructors further center learners' needs and desired outcomes by positioning learning experiences within authentic, real-world settings via experiential and place-based learning that emphasizes "learning by doing" (Santi & Gorghiu, 2017; Williams, 2017). Since the learner landscape changes over time, instructors must pay attention to potential drift in content, audience, and program settings over time (Pitts, 2021). However, centering learners in the curriculum does not mean attempting to meet the individual learning needs of every possible learner. Rather, learners should be prompted to identify and engage with their own needs and desired outcomes. Research on learner-centered models for teaching (Agustini et al., 2021; Lencastre et al., 2020; Matriano, 2020) and preparing instructors to adopt a learner-centered approach (Uygur & Yelken, 2021; Withers, 2016) suggests that learner-centered approaches are more effective than instructor-centered approaches in terms of learning outcomes attainment, students' depth of learning, and instructors' perceived self-efficacy.

DESIGNING BESPOKE LEARNING

The purpose of this article is to use a well-known model from evaluation to design a learning experience that is sensitive to learners' needs and desired outcomes. The premise for using the evidence continuum to center learners is threefold: curriculum and teaching are enhanced when instructors unearth and respond to learners' needs; Domains 1–2 of the evidence continuum are a heuristic for thoughtfully developing a model for learner-centered curriculum; and instructors who use the evidence continuum engage with their praxis and deepen their pedagogical content knowledge (PCK). PCK is an instructor's specialized understanding of how to convey content area expertise to learners (Shulman, 1986). Using the evidence continuum involves two steps: the instructor develops an initial model for teaching and learning (Domain 2), then hones the model using needs assessment (Domain 1). This process is illustrated using a graduate-level survey design and analysis course. The course was selected for its broad applicability since research methods are studied in most university programs, and surveys are used in all research approaches (i.e., quantitative, qualitative, and mixed methods research).

Step 1: Articulating an Initial Model

As seen in Table 3.2, there are six common elements of a logic model: inputs, activities, outputs, and three types of outcomes. As with backward planning, it is often helpful to start with the end in mind by identifying outcomes. *Outcomes* provide an anchor for the vision of a successful learner in the short term (i.e., desired changes in knowledge, skills, attitudes, and mindsets within learning objectives), intermediate term (i.e., desired changes in behaviors and actions within the *so that* of learning objectives), and long term (i.e., changes in perspectives or life conditions within the *why* of learning). Although intermediate- and long-term outcomes are often not able to be assessed and may be aspirational in nature, they ensure alignment of learning with what matters most (i.e., essential questions and enduring understandings).

Table 3.2

Guiding Questions for Developing a Logic Model

Element	Examples of Guiding Questions
Outcomes	
Long term	What are the ultimate reasons why learners need this learning experience?
Intermediate	What main behavioral changes should learners experience?
Short term	How will learners know they have had a successful learning experience and are well-positioned to achieve intermediate outcomes?
Activities	How will learners and instructors engage in the learning experience?
Outputs	What evidence will be tracked to see how learning is progressing?
Inputs	What wisdom and resources will contribute to a successful learning experience?

Outcomes are closely related to the core program *activities*, which are the means through which learners will achieve the intended outcomes. Learning activities produce *outputs*, or measurable evidence that learners were provided with the "opportunity to learn" (Moss et al., 2008, p. 1) as well as data learning activities (e.g., test results or rubric ratings). For educational programs, it is helpful to organize participants and activities underneath outputs because they are closely connected. Finally, *inputs* indicate the resources needed to implement activities, produce outputs, and achieve outcomes (e.g., staff, volunteers, facilities, or funding). Guiding questions for developing each component of a logic model are also included in Table 3.2.

Table 3.3 depicts a conventional logic model for a typical graduate-level course on survey design and analysis. Program-level learning outcomes, assessment plans, curriculum map, a previous course syllabus, and other teaching materials for the course (i.e., textbook, Canvas course, rubrics) were used to develop this logic model. The inputs for this course include a syllabus, textbook, readings list, course schedule, assignments, answer keys, grading schemes, and policies and procedures. The participants (i.e., the learners and the instructor) engaged in various learning activities that produce evidence of learning via four assignments: (a) homework on assigned reading; (b) a midterm article critique to analyze the methodological quality of an assigned survey research study; (c) a survey design assessment on item design, instrument development, and sampling procedures; and (d) a survey analysis assessment using an instructor-provided dataset. The quality of learning is assessed using answer keys that determine the extent to which learners have achieved the three short-term outcomes: obtaining a fundamental awareness of a breadth of survey research topics, critiquing the quality of an assigned survey research study, and designing and analyzing survey data. Intermediate outcomes include the ability to ethically apply survey methods and complete technical tasks. Long-term outcomes relate to literacy and the application of survey research methods. The scope of this course is limited in that it does not adequately prepare learners to conduct scale development and validation studies, lead survey research, or innovate survey methodology.

Step 2: Honing the Model for Bespoke Learning

By articulating a logic model, instructors engage in a thoughtful process of connecting goals with activities, outputs, and inputs. However, learning experiences are not one-size-fits-all. In Step 2, instructors hone their initial models by incorporating strategies that prompt learners to identify and engage with their own needs and desired outcomes (Domain 1). This is achieved by embedding needs assessment strategies within the model. Needs assessment methods are typically facilitated through three phases including pre-assessment, assessment, and post-assessment (Altschuld & Watkins, 2014; Rossi et al., 2018). Methods for pre-assessment are most well-suited to action-oriented classroom settings and include reviewing research literature and extant data (e.g., records, databases, reports, and marked assignments), interviewing former learners, and conducting observations.

Table 3.4 depicts a learner-centered logic model for a bespoke version of the graduate-level methods course. The starting resources, or inputs, are the same as the first logic model but they have been modified to create space for learners' needs, interests, perspectives, and aspirations (see Table 3.1) and a learner intake survey is added to create space for learners and instructors to engage with learners' needs. The participants in the course are the same for both logic models, and they engage in the same types of learning activities that produce evidence of learning. However, in the second logic model, learners articulate their needs and desired outcomes and instructors actively engage with their praxis. The most significant changes to the logic model can be seen in the activities; the nature of the assignments has shifted significantly to create space for learner exploration of the content through project-based learning and receive responsive feedback via through-course assessment (see Table 3.1).

Table 3.3

A Logic Model of a Typical Graduate-Level Survey Design and Analysis Course

	Outputs			Outcomes	
Inputs	Participants	Activities □ Products	Short-Term	Intermediate	Long-Term
Course Syllabus Course Schedule with Text & Other Readings Assignments and Answer Keys Grading Scheme Policies/Procedures	Learners Instructor(s) Teaching Assistant(s)	Class Sessions • Didactics • Active Learning HW Questions (20%) HW Questions (20%) Survey Design Assignment (30%) Survey Analysis Assignment (30%)	Fundamental awareness of the breadth of survey research topics Ability to critique the quality of studies/ findings A limited, general experience of the precursor content and skills needed for behavioral outcomes using a predefined example	Ethical use of surveys methods: (1) design items, instruments, and samples to (2) administer surveys, monitor response rates, and collect data Technical ability: clean data, check error sources, assess survey quality, and interpret findings	Enhanced survey methodology literacy Enhanced survey research methodology usage and findings Reduction of specious survey research and/ or spurious findings
				Not	
			Ability to conduct measurement scale development and validation studies	Preparation sufficient to be an expert/ authority (e.g., to lead survey research)	A reasonable dose or duration for innovating survey methodology

Table 3.4

A Learner-Centered Logic Model of the Graduate-Level Survey Design and Analysis Course

		Outputs	Outcomes		
Inputs	**Participants**	**Activities □ Products**	**Short-Term**	**Intermediate**	**Long-Term**
Course Syllabus *as Instructor-Learner Agreement*	Learners/Their Self-Reported: • *Needs* • *Interests* • *Perspectives* • *Aspirations*	Class Sessions • Didactics • *Active Learning that Leverages Learners' Prior Experiences*	Fundamental awareness of the breadth of survey research topics	Ethical use of surveys methods: (1) design items, instruments, and samples, and (2) administer surveys, monitor response rates, and collect data	Enhanced survey methodology literacy Enhanced survey research methodology usage and findings
Course Schedule: Textbook & *Learner-Selected* Readings		*Reflection Journal (20%)*	Ability to critique the quality of studies/ *findings in a chosen discipline*		
Assignment *Menus and Rubrics*	Instructor(s) • *Praxis* • *PCK* • *Motivation*	Critique of a *Self-Selected Article (20%)*		Technical ability: clean data, check error sources, assess survey quality, and interpret findings	Reduction of specious survey research and/ or spurious findings
A Developmental Grading Scheme (e.g., specs grading; Nilson, 2014)		Learner Survey Project • *IRB Application for Class Project (5%)* • *CITI Research Certificate (5%)*	A limited, general experience of the precursor content and skills needed for behavioral outcomes *in a chosen discipline*		
Policies/Procedures	Instructor(s) • *Interests* • *Preferences* • *Praxis* • *PCK*	• *Specifications Table and Précis (10%)*			
Learner Intake Survey		• *Survey Form and Analysis Plan (20%)* • *Analysis Report (20%)*		**Not**	
			Ability to conduct measurement scale development and validation studies	Preparation sufficient to be an expert/ authority (e.g., to lead survey research)	A reasonable dose or duration for innovating survey methodology

Note. Changes are noted in italics. Shaded cells are unchanged from the conventional logic model (see Table 3.1).

DISCUSSION

Domains 1 and 2 of the evidence continuum provide a heuristic for designing learning in a way that creates space for learners' needs and desired outcomes. There are two important constraints to this notion. Learning should not hinge solely on the perceived needs of learners; rather there should be a balance between conventional and adaptive model elements (Grant, 2002). The professional education of medical practitioners (e.g., physicians or nurses) would be unsuccessful if its educators developed a curriculum that was wholly responsive to learners' needs and desired outcomes. Like medical trainees, most learners are not well-positioned to understand the fullness of their learning needs because learners are, by their very nature, new to a discipline. Learning experiences are maximized using a balance of conventional and adaptive elements. Neither is inherently better than the other; aligning elements with learning goals is key.

Additionally, learning cannot be differentiated for every possible learner. Since it is neither reasonable nor fruitful for an instructor to attempt to unearth and respond to every possible need of a learner audience, it is helpful to draw a distinction between models that are *sensitive* to learners' needs from those which are *responsive* to them. Each learner is capable of unearthing and responding to their own needs when learning experiences include adaptive elements that create space for learner choice through the universal design of learning for multiple means of engagement, representation, and expression (CAST, 2018). Another strategy for limiting the potential complexity of differentiated learning comes from reflecting on learners' typical needs across years of teaching experience. While Earley (2014) has proposed the need for instructors to address disparate learning needs of research producers and consumers, I have found it helpful to delineate further the learning needs of advanced research methods learners: consumers (who need methods literacy), technicians (who need methods proficiency), and designers (who need methods mastery). Combined with an understanding of the typical disciplinary settings of learners, this framework increases learner engagement and motivation by attuning instructors to the various needs and desired outcomes of their typical learner audience.

Though the focus of this article is on using Domains 1 and 2 of the evidence continuum to design a learner-centered curriculum, the continuum can be extended through all five domains for learner-centered assessment and evaluation. Process evaluation (Domain 3) assesses the design, delivery, and reception of learning experiences. These three dimensions of the "instructional arc" (McConnell et al., 2020, p. 3) recognize the importance of considering multiple perspectives to provide high-quality learning experiences. Learning outcomes assessment (Domain 4) is a robust, practitioner-oriented discipline with a burgeoning knowledge base of its own (see https://www.learningoutcomesassessment.org). Impact evaluation (Domain 4) and efficiency studies (Domain 5) are useful when evidence is needed for administrative purposes (e.g., conducting cost-benefit analyses).

Using the evidence continuum to design curriculum and teaching enables instructors to deepen their praxis by articulating and examining their PCK (Shulman, 1986). A specialized form of deep knowing, PCK is developed as seasoned instructors refine their praxis over many teaching and reflection cycles. PCK research has been limited because it requires instructors to make their PCK explicit, and there are limited known strategies for facilitating this type of reflection (Nind, 2020). Viewing PCK development as a product of experiential learning (Kolb & Kolb, 2005), instructors need structured reflection strategies to make sense of their experiences and guide future actions. The evidence continuum is a heuristic that illuminates PCK, thus enabling reflection, praxis development, and PCK research.

CONCLUSION

In this article, the evidence continuum is used to design a learner-centered curriculum. The first two domains of the continuum provide a heuristic for operationalizing learners' needs (Domain 1) and depict how needs will be addressed in the learning experience (Domain 2). Using the evidence continuum to design a learner-centered curriculum begins by articulating a model for teaching and learning using conventional approaches (Domain 2), then honing that model to create spaces for learners to engage in bespoke learning (Domain 1). Strategies for centering learners in curriculum and teaching are not new; rather, the contribution of this article is a heuristic for focusing instructors' thinking on their conventional and adaptive elements. This heuristic creates a strategy for instructors to deepen and intentionally develop their PCK.

REFERENCES

Agustini, K., Wahyuni, D. S., Mertayasa, I. N. E., Wedhanti, N. K., & Sukrawarpala, W. (2021). Student-centered learning models and learning outcomes: Meta-analysis and effect sizes on the students' thesis. *Journal of Physics: Conference Series, 1810*(1), 012049. https://doi.org/10.1088/1742-6596/1810/1/012049

Altschuld, J. W., & Watkins, R. (2014). A primer on needs assessment: More than 40 years of research and practice. *New Directions for Evaluation, 2014*(144), 5–18. https://doi.org/10.1002/ev.20099

Ayoo, S., Wilcox, Y., LaVelle, J. M., Podems, D., & Barrington, G. V. (2020). Grounding the 2018 AEA evaluator competencies in the broader context of professionalization. *New Directions for Evaluation*, *2020*(168), 13–30. https://doi.org/10.1002/ev.20440

CAST (2018). *Universal design for learning guidelines version 2.2.* http://udlguidelines.cast.org

Centers for Disease Control and Prevention. (2011). *Introduction to program evaluation for public health programs: A self-study guide*. U.S. Department of Health and Human Services. https://www.cdc.gov/evaluation/guide/index.htm

Coryn, C. L. S., Wilson, L. N., Westine, C. D., Hobson, K. A., Ozeki, S., Fiekowsky, E. L., Greenman, G. D., & Schröter, D. C. (2017). A decade of research on evaluation: A systematic review of research on evaluation published between 2005 and 2014. *American Journal of Evaluation*, *38*(3), 329–347. https://doi.org/10.1177/1098214016688556

Creswell, J. W., & Plano Clark, V. L. (2018). *Designing and conducting mixed methods research* (3rd ed.). SAGE.

Cronbach, L. J. (1980). *Toward reform of program evaluation* (1st ed.). Jossey-Bass.

Davidson, E. J. (2005). *Evaluation methodology basics: The nuts and bolts of sound evaluation*. SAGE.

Dewey, J. (1938). *Experience and education*. Macmillan.

Earley, M. A. (2014). A synthesis of the literature on research methods education. *Teaching in Higher Education*, *19*(3), 242–253. https://doi.org/10.1080/13562517.2013.860105

Fink, L. D. (2013). *Creating significant learning experiences: An integrated approach to designing college courses*. John Wiley & Sons.

Funnell, S. C., & Rogers, P. J. (2011). *Purposeful program theory: Effective use of theories of change and logic models*. Jossey-Bass.

Grant, J. (2002). Learning needs assessment: Assessing the need. *British Medical Journal*, *324*(7330), 156–159.

Gullickson, A. M., King, J. A., LaVelle, J. M., & Clinton, J. M. (2019). The current state of evaluator education: A situation analysis & call to action. *Evaluation & Program Planning*, *75*, 20–30. https://doi.org/10.1016/j.evalprogplan.2019.02.012

Kolb, D. A. (1984). *Experiential learning: Experience as the source of learning and development*. Prentice Hall.

Kolb, A., & Kolb, D. A. (2005). Learning styles & learning spaces: Enhancing experiential learning in higher education. *Academy of Management Learning & Education*, *4*(2), 193–212. https://doi.org/10.5465/amle.2005.17268566

Lencastre, J. A., Morgado, J. C., Freires, T., & Bento, M. (2020). A systematic review on the flipped classroom model as a promoter of curriculum innovation. *International Journal of Instruction*, *13*(4), 575–592. https://doi.org/10.29333/iji.2020.13436a

Matriano, E. A. (2020). Ensuring student-centered, constructivist and project-based experiential learning: Applying the exploration, research, interaction and creation (ERIC) learning model. *International Online Journal of Education and Teaching*, *7*(1), 214–227. https://eric.ed.gov/?id=EJ1244245

McConnell, C., Conrad, B., Uhrmacher, P. B. (2020). *Lesson planning with purpose: Five approaches to curriculum design*. Teachers College Press.

Moss, P. A., Pullin, D. C., Gee, J. P., Haertel, E. H., & Young, L. J. (Eds.). (2008). *Assessment, equity, and opportunity to learn*. Cambridge University Press.

Mertens, D. M., & Wilson, A. T. (2012). *Program evaluation theory and practice: A comprehensive guide*. Guilford Press.

Nilson, L. B. (2014). *Specifications grading: Restoring rigor, motivating students, and saving faculty time*. Stylus.

Nind, M. (2020). A new application for the concept of pedagogical content knowledge: Teaching advanced social science research methods. *Oxford Review of Education, 46*(2), 185–201. https://doi.org/10.1080/03054985.2019.1644996

Pitts, R. T. (2021). Pinpointing where to start: A reflective analysis on the introductory evaluation course. *Canadian Journal of Program Evaluation, 35*(3), 437–449. https://doi.org/10.3138/cjpe.69697

Rickards, W. H., & Stitt-Bergh, M. (2016). Higher education evaluation, assessment, and faculty engagement. *New Directions for Evaluation, 2016*(151), 11–20. https://doi.org/10.1002/ev.20200

Rossi, P. H., Lipsey, M. W., & Henry, G. E. (2018). *Evaluation: A systematic approach* (8th ed.). SAGE.

Santi, A. E., & Gorghiu, G. (2017). The student-centered learning model in John Dewey's progressive conception. *Studia Universitatis Babeş-Bolyai Psychologia-Paedagogia, 62*(2), 77–86. https://doi.org/10.24193/subbpsyped.2017.2.04

Scriven, M. (1991). *Evaluation thesaurus*. SAGE.

Scriven, M. (2008). The concept of a transdiscipline: And of evaluation as a transdiscipline. *Journal of Multi-Disciplinary Education, 5*(10), 65–66. https://doi.org/10.56645/jmde.v5i10.161

Shulman, L. S. (1986). Those who understand: Knowledge growth in teaching. *Journal of Education (Boston, Mass.), 193*(3), 1–11. https://doi.org/10.1177/002205741319300302

Taylor-Powell, E., & Henert, E. (2008). *Developing a logic model: Teaching and training guide*. University of Wisconsin-Extension. http://www.uwex.edu/ces/pdande

Uygur, M., & Yelken, T. Y. (2021). Trainer training program developed for instructors about student-centered teaching-learning processes and its effects: A study of a curriculum development in higher education. *International Journal of Curriculum and Instruction, 13*(3), 2981–3000. https://ijci.globets.org/index.php/IJCI/article/view/361

Weimer, M. (2013). *Learner-centered teaching: Five key changes to practice* (2nd ed.). Wiley.

Wiggins, G., & McTighe, J. (2005). *Understanding by design* (2nd ed.). ASCD.

Williams, M. K. (2017). John Dewey in the 21st century. *Journal of Inquiry & Action in Education, 9*(1), 91–102. https://digitalcommons.buffalostate.edu/jiae/vol9/iss1/7/

Withers, M. (2016). The college science learning cycle: An instructional model for reformed teaching. *CBE—Life Sciences Education, 15*(4), 1–12. https://doi.org/10.1187/cbe.15-04-010

CHAPTER 4

THE LIVED EXPERIENCE OF FEMALE K–12 TEACHERS DURING THE COVID-19 PANDEMIC

A Phenomenological Study

Sarah Campbell, Rebecca Reinhardt, Mallori Sage, and Emily Strong
University of Northern Colorado

ABSTRACT

This study examined the lived experiences of veteran female K–12 teachers who taught during the COVID-19 pandemic. The participants emphasized relationship building, the reevaluation of teaching as a career, the importance of administrative and systemic support, and both positive and negative experiences of teaching during the pandemic. This study offered space for female educators to reflect on their unique experiences, providing insight into the cathartic process of sharing lived experiences in general.

Feelings of stress and burnout are not new to K–12 teachers. Even prior to the COVID-19 pandemic, teachers reported experiencing high rates of stress and burnout at work (Ferguson et al., 2012). In 2014, a national

---

Curriculum and Teaching Dialogue,
Volume 25, Numbers 1 & 2, pp. 233–248
Copyright © 2023 by Information Age Publishing
www.infoagepub.com
All rights of reproduction in any form reserved.

Gallup poll found that an estimated 46% of teachers reported "high daily stress," a rate only matched by nurses and physicians (Bottiani et al., 2019). Teachers are most stressed by high workloads, difficult student behavior, and accountability policies like No Child Left Behind and Race to the Top (Brasfield et al., 2019).

Therefore, when the COVID-19 pandemic struck in 2020, new stressors—for example, teaching online, managing students' deteriorating mental health, and balancing high expectations with empathy—only exacerbated the existing stressors (Pressley, 2021). These new stressors are negatively impacting teachers' own mental health (Correa & First, 2021). As a result, a staggering 55% of educators are now considering leaving the profession earlier than initially planned (Walker, 2022).

PURPOSE OF RESEARCH AND RESEARCH QUESTION

Recent studies have focused on the increased stress on teachers during COVID-19, including the fact that female teachers have experienced significantly more stress at work during the pandemic than their male counterparts (Klapproth et al., 2020). Therefore, this study sought to explore the lived experiences of female educators who taught in the years before the pandemic began and who have continued to teach as the world has encountered COVID-19. In an attempt to understand the impact of the pandemic on these teachers' existing stresses in their work, this question framed the study: What are the lived experiences of female K–12 teachers through COVID-19 in regard to their overall quality of experience in the profession?

LITERATURE REVIEW

Factors of K–12 Teacher Burnout Prior to COVID-19

In K–12 teachers, burnout has been a growing research interest as accountability pressures have heightened and class sizes and total student load have burgeoned in the past decade (Dworkin & Tobe, 2014). Ferguson et al. (2012) found that "occupational stress" (p. 29) is a significant reason for teachers' anxiety and depression, and that this stress has decreased teachers' job satisfaction. However, this stress is primarily worsened not by teaching itself, but by non-teaching-related workload and pressures such as parent communication, meetings, emails, documenting accountability measures, and non-teaching roles (Lawrence et al., 2019). In addition, some factors increase the likelihood that a teacher will be stressed, such as being female, having less experience, or working as a teacher in an urban school with fewer resources (Bottiani et al., 2019).

In addition to these demands of teaching, teachers have increasingly been expected to be trained to handle trauma, as 25% of American children experience at least one traumatic event by the age of 16 (Lang et al., 2015). Teachers are on the front lines, teaching students dealing with trauma, yet little attention has been paid to the needs of those teachers (Hydon et al., 2015). This proximity to and care of children suffering from trauma increases educators' propensity to suffer from secondary traumatic stress, leading to increased emotional burden, stress, and anxiety (Blitz et al., 2016).

Systematic Attempts to Mitigate K–12 Teacher Stress

When Brasfield et al. (2019) studied teachers' wellness habits and stress levels, they found that promoting resiliency and wellness has the potential to increase teacher satisfaction and retention. They also discovered that teachers who took steps for their own physical and mental health were better able to cope with the daily stressors involved with teaching (Brasfield et al., 2019). In addition, teachers who have access to social-emotional support in their school buildings show lower levels of stress and exhaustion (Camacho et al., 2021).

Teachers' stress can also be lowered when teachers have affiliations with colleagues, and when they have more resources (Bottiani et al., 2019). However, Yin et al. (2019) argued that while job autonomy and authentic administrative support can improve teachers' job satisfaction, job demands negatively affect that satisfaction and even outweigh the potential positives. In particular, the demands posed by legislative policies on school accountability and high-stakes testing have increased teachers' stress in the past decade (Brasfield et al., 2019).

How COVID-19 Has Exacerbated K–12 Teacher Stress and Burnout

Recent studies from around the world have confirmed teachers' steeply rising stress levels during the pandemic. Two studies found that stress levels rose in teachers who had to teach online (Jakubowski & Sitko-Dominik, 2021; Palma-Vasquez et al., 2021); another study identified higher stress levels in female teachers (Matiz et al., 2020); and a British study concluded that COVID-19 has heightened teachers' level of burnout (Kim et al., 2021).

In the United States, studies have confirmed that educators are experiencing secondary trauma symptoms and compassion fatigue (which Pembroke [2015] defined as "significant depletion or exhaustion of the [person's] store of compassion" [p. 120]) as a result of the pandemic (Etchells et al., 2021). In addition, COVID-19 is increasing the number of teachers leaving the profession (Pressley, 2021) and the increasing mental health issues (especially anxiety and depression) that students have experienced since the start of the pandemic have increased those issues for teachers, as well (Correa & First, 2021).

The Impact of the COVID-19 Pandemic on Female Teachers

Although the literature has already begun to address the impacts of COVID-19 on teachers and students, it has not addressed the unique concerns of female teachers. Viewing female teachers' experiences of COVID-19 through the lens of liberal feminism, which Crotty (2020) defined as a "humanism ... [that demands] a significant measure of economic reorganization and resource redistribution and rather profound changes in consciousness" (pp. 163–164), could illuminate realities the literature has not yet examined. Female teachers experience higher job satisfaction (Toropova et al., 2021) and are less likely to leave the profession than male teachers (Räsänen et al., 2020). However, they feel higher levels of stress and burnout (Bottiani et al., 2019; Smetackova, 2017).

THEORETICAL STANCE

This study used the qualitative method of phenomenology with a feminist interpretative framework. Phenomenology seeks to understand a common concept or a phenomenon (Creswell & Poth, 2018). Feminist research strives to create "collaborative and nonexploitative relationships, to place the researcher within the study so as to avoid objectification and to conduct research that is transformative" (Creswell & Poth, 2018, p. 28). Further, the aim of utilizing a liberal feminist perspective in seeking the experiences of women is to reduce or eliminate injustices and unfreedom that women experience (Crotty, 2020).

A liberal feminist stance allowed us to examine the specific experiences female teachers have had teaching during the pandemic. Recent studies have confirmed that female teachers have experienced significantly *more* stress during the pandemic than their male counterparts (Klapproth et al., 2020; Matiz et al., 2020). Why? How did teaching during the COVID-19 pandemic exacerbate those aspects or create new challenges for female teachers? This study seeks to fill that gap in the literature.

METHODOLOGY, STUDY PARTICIPANTS, AND SETTING

This phenomenological study (Creswell, 2018) sought to understand the lived experiences during the COVID-19 pandemic of experienced (five or more years of teaching) female private and public-school K–12 teachers' mental health. Four K–12 teachers in Illinois and Colorado private and public schools were selected based on the following criteria: female teachers with more than five years of experience who actively taught in a classroom (virtual, hybrid, or in-person) during COVID-19. Interviews took place in four different geographic locations in Illinois and Colorado based on the residency of the researcher.

METHOD FOR DATA COLLECTION

In each semi-structured in-person interview, each of the four participants was interviewed once, by one researcher, for 45 minutes. Participants chose pseudonyms before the interviews began. Participants were then asked questions about their experience of teaching in general and about their experience of teaching during the pandemic (see Appendix). The participants were also asked demographic questions in a paper survey provided at the end of the interview. Each interview was audio recorded utilizing a password-protected iPhone Voice Memo.

Four female teachers were interviewed in March 2022. All names are pseudonyms. "Eve," age 43, is a white, public school special education transition teacher who has 18 years of teaching experience and holds a master's degree. She is married and has two elementary-aged children. "Alice," a 42-year-old, white, single, female teacher with some graduate school, has been teaching for 14 years, and she currently teaches English in a comprehensive public high school. "Emma" is a 34-year-old, white, single, public-school teacher who teaches elementary school in an urban-emergent school district. She has been teaching for seven years and has recently graduated with her master's degree. "Katie," age 34, is a white, independent school teacher and co-chair of Diversity, Equity, and Inclusion, who has been teaching for 12 years and holds a master's degree.

ANALYSIS

The interviews were transcribed using Otter, and then our group met to establish an intercoder agreement (Creswell, 2018). We developed a preliminary code list, applied the codes to our transcripts, and then met again to discuss our re-coded transcripts. After coding and re-coding, we utilized the interpretative phenomenological analysis (IPA) technique (Merriam,

2009) to analyze and interpret our coded data, distilling it for themes. IPA enables understanding of participants' lived experiences acknowledging the psychological and social constructs they live within (Smith & Nizza, 2022).

Finally, for consistency with the feminist approach and to keep the research participants as active members of the study, the researchers had brief individual conversations with each participant to verify the common themes. These conversations served to confirm the findings of the study and to provide room for additional feedback from the participants. These conversations allowed the researchers to actively analyze the data while collecting it (Merriam, 2009). Furthermore, sharing the themes had the potential to validate the experiences of each educator.

RESEARCHERS' STANCE

All members of our research team identify as white females connected to education through our professions, which include high school teacher, elementary school teacher, occupational therapist, and psychotherapist. Through our connection to education we witness, and at times personally experience, the effects of stress and burnout related to teaching. When the COVID-19 pandemic began in March 2020, the two teachers taught online and in hybrid models; the occupational therapist shifted to teaching and job coaching remotely; and the psychotherapist conducted disaster mental health for the Red Cross remotely. This personal connection to both the general stress and burnout of the education profession and to the particular stresses posed by COVID-19 gave us unique insight into our research study.

FINDINGS

Four common themes emerged in the analysis of the four interview transcripts. All four interviewees emphasized their value of relationship building with students, their reevaluation of teaching as a career, the importance of administrative and systemic support, and that teaching during the pandemic had both negative and positive aspects.

Relationship Building

Interviews with these four teachers showed relationships to be one of the most important and meaningful aspects of teaching. Given that "it is a

The Lived Experience of Female K–12 Teachers   239

basic psychological need for relatedness that can explain the importance of personal relationships within the classroom for teachers" (Split et al., 2011, p. 465), it makes sense that teachers' value of connection with their students emerged as a significant theme. Emma illustrated this fundamental bond when she shared, "I've been called mom."

Teachers' job satisfaction is positively related to teachers' perceptions of their relationships with students (Veldman et al., 2013). Therefore, more intentional relationship building with students may explain why female teachers experience higher job satisfaction than male teachers (Toropova et al., 2021). Katie recalled her own relationships with her teachers as one of the reasons she chose teaching as a profession, since "helping young ones to feel seen, heard, and valued for who they are, and who they could be," and "to give them the love that I received as a student myself," brings meaning and purpose to her work. Alice described her teaching style as "relationship-based," explaining, "I do present to the students that I'm open for more meaningful, more significant relationships should they need that from an adult." Emma also ensures her students know she is someone they can connect with. She explained:

> I think they, at least I hope they would see me as someone they can go to.
> Someone who is going to help them out when they are having a problem
> and let me know things that are going on. Whether it's personally, at home.
> Or when they're out of my classroom.

Katie captured this same sentiment by saying, "You can be an important part of people's lives."

Re-evaluation of Teaching as a Career

Even though all four interviewees emphasized how much they value the possibility of relationship building in the teaching profession, all four also reported that they have considered leaving the profession entirely. Although female teachers are less likely to actually leave the profession than male teachers (Räsänen et al., 2020), they feel higher levels of stress and burnout (Bottiani et al., 2019; Smetackova, 2017). Even though experienced female teachers like the four interviewees in this study will probably continue teaching, they are also likely to reassess their role within education, such as moving to a different school or moving into a different role (Hall et al., 2022).

For Eve, this mostly occurred in her first couple of years of teaching. She said, "There were times where I really questioned…. 'How am I going to get through this?' I was so overwhelmed." Emma described her first teaching job similarly, saying, "Just so much stress … I was working all the time through the whole weekend. I didn't have time to go see my family … all the nitpicking in the coaching (from administration). I just never felt like I was ahead." Alice confessed that, even after 14 years of teaching, she still considers leaving the profession "every year. Some years more than others. But every year, there's at least one point in the year, where I'm like, 'uhh, there's got to be an easier way.'" Katie is actively looking for options outside of education. She explained, "The current system I'm in is too flawed. And I've been trying to be a part of the movement for positive change for the last many years and that hasn't happened, so I need something fresh."

However, none of these four women have left the profession yet. Instead, they have each attempted to change or reframe their situation within education. Emma shifted her situation early in her career, moving from a charter school to a traditional public school. In August, as she attended an in-service at the charter school where she first worked, she decided:

> If I didn't have a job by the time school started, I was going to quit and go to a store to work. You know, retail … I worked so hard that summer, I was going on a whole bunch of interviews.

For Eve and Alice, the decision to reframe their roles within education came later. For example, Eve explained,

> I got decision fatigue, I got compassion fatigue … I was constantly problem solving. So after about seven, eight years, I didn't want to do this anymore. And then I switched to transition [from high school level] because that's where my passion really is. I had to make a change for my sanity.

Alice suddenly reached a point nine years into her career in which she needed to make a change. She decided to stay in the same teaching role as an English teacher at a large comprehensive high school, but "about five years ago," she decided, "I've got to find a way to stay in or I've got to find a new place to go, and … that's when I shifted it all to more relationship-based." Katie has not yet made a change, but wants to. She said:

> I still love being around kids. That hasn't changed. I definitely care about the belonging, love, and justice, DEI concepts as being the most important kind of education that anybody can receive. So whether that would mean I'd go to a nonprofit, I don't know. I'm still trying to process that. If nothing else, I feel like a change in our organization needs to happen. I might not be ready to give up on education itself yet.

All four women expressed the tension between believing in what they are doing as teachers and often feeling too exhausted and burned out to stay much longer. However, as Alice explained, each day can be a recommitment to the profession: "On the worst days ... [I think], I can't handle another one of these, but then I come home, and I walk Lucky [her dog], and I get some good sleep, and I decide I can do it again."

Administrative and Systemic Support Makes a Significant Difference

Part of the tension between what these teachers said they value (relationship building) and the frustration that has pushed each of them to reevaluate teaching as a career lies in the quality of administrative support each teacher experiences. The importance of administrative and systemic support was the third theme that emerged from the four interviews.

Teachers with supportive administrators are more likely to feel equipped to handle the stressors of teaching (Camacho et al., 2021; Ferguson et al., 2012). Emma described feeling like she can go to her building principal for advice and support. She feels that her principal genuinely cares about her as a human inside and outside of the school building. Eve has similar feelings about her administration. She said, "We have a really good relationship where we can both be really open and honest with each other. And so I'm very grateful for my relationship with my supervisor. He's been wonderful."

Unfortunately, other educators do not feel comfortable with or supported by their administration. In fact, lack of administrative support is one of the top stressors in the teaching profession (Haydon et al., 2018). Alice explained, "It's insulting for administrators to say 'I'm going to let you go from this meeting an hour early on Thursday to practice your self-care,' when you've just spent the last four days trying to break me." This often-tone-deaf lack of support drives some teachers away from the teaching profession, as discussed above.

Other teachers trying their best to meet the needs of their students often find themselves pitted against an administration that perpetuates poor policy and practices. These teachers often feel like they are at battle. Emma described having to "fight tooth and nail" to get her student the individualized education program he needed and requiring the personal "courage" to enter that battle.

If teachers lack administrative support, they are forced to find or create their own support systems. Alice reflected:

> I don't think I receive any official structural support from the district or from my building administration. I think all the support that I get is the support I have created for myself, or that others have allowed me to create with them.

Katie attributed poor experiences with administration to a systemic issue—the unwavering pressure from the top down in education. Katie said:

> I think I'm very aware that the people who, quote-unquote, should be of-fering support aren't receiving support themselves, so it's part of a systemic thing. And, again, the fact that my supervisors are all women, I think there's a lot there, too. They're taking care of their families, and they're try-ing to take care of other people's families, and then they're taking care of everything at school, and then they're just giving, giving, giving, and then they don't have anything left to give to them, the rest of us.

Although the theme of administrative support is not a surprising com-monality, it is a poignant one. The stress involved in the teaching field is undeniable, but facing those stressors in a healthy, collaborative, and supportive environment makes all the difference (Camacho et al., 2021; Ferguson et al., 2012).

The Experience of Teaching in a Global Pandemic

When the COVID-19 pandemic began to shut down the world in March of 2020, these four experienced teachers had already encountered some of the factors that can lead to burnout for teachers, including the "occu-pational stress" (Ferguson et al., 2012) of trying to build relationships with students amid a burgeoning workload (Lawrence et al., 2019) and with shaky administrative support. Then, schools had to shift online. Teachers like these four interviewees experienced the loss of routine and normalcy and the challenges of abruptly transitioning to remote learning. However, not all of this change was negative.

Change of Routine

Each participant discussed the significant changes in routine that she experienced as a result of the COVID-19 pandemic. Eve described the abrupt change in normalcy: "There was a routine that we were used to, we were comfortable with, and COVID just threw all that out the window." For Emma, there was no longer any routine—she found herself taking it "day by day." Alice was surprised to discover an increase in autonomy and control that stemmed from the new normal. She explained, "I had control not just over my classroom and my curriculum; I had control over how I managed my day." Eve, who experienced relief from "professional responsibilities simmering down" at the start of the pandemic, lamented that things still do not feel "normal" now, even after two years. She explained, "COVID just changed everything. [It] is still not back to the way it was ... I feel like I'm rebuilding my program."

From Classroom to Remote Learning

The shift to remote learning impacted not only how each teacher created and executed lesson plans, but also how each one interacted with her students. Emma, an experienced teacher of seven years, admitted, "Being virtual, I felt like a first-year teacher." Eve, another experienced teacher, reflected:

> I think, as a first- or second-year teacher, it must have been an absolute nightmare. Maybe it's because I've been in my role long enough, I've kind of got a pretty good handle on what I'm doing. That made it easier than some people's experiences.

However, despite the difficulty that teachers reported with moving to online teaching, they also viewed it as an opportunity to pause, reflect, and re-prioritize. Alice reflected, "We pulled back from so much and just focused on the essentials, it really was an opportunity to stop and reflect and re-prioritize what we were doing and why."

Not only were lesson plans taking longer to convert for remote learning, but each teacher also reported feeling a disconnect from her students and coworkers. Alice explained, "The *worst* was the isolation from the students and the isolation from my peers." Emma echoed these feelings of isolation: "It was very isolating ... mentally, being there for the kids was hard ... I didn't have that personal connection with them." For each of our participants, the shift to remote learning meant a loss of relationships with students and an increase in feelings of isolation and bitterness. Katie spoke to this, "How do we acknowledge all that we have gone through? And all that we've had to maneuver? And then also still be able to show up for the kids 100%? It's hard to feel like anything but bitter."

LIMITATION OF THE STUDY

The sample size was small; this was intentional so the researchers could focus deeply on each teacher's lived experiences, which is a core aspect of IPA methodology. However, a limitation of a small sample size is lack of representation, in this case, of the teaching population at large. An

CONCLUSION

Female teachers were already experiencing high levels of stress and burnout prior to the COVID-19 pandemic. However, the pandemic further intensified these feelings, disproportionately affecting female teachers due to their personal and professional roles (Rawal, 2021). The four themes that emerged in the in-depth interviews of these four female teachers revealed that the pandemic was less a catalyst for the challenges female teachers experience and more of a spotlight—illuminating the reality that female teachers have long been struggling with stress and burnout in this profession. As Emma said, "I think the pandemic definitely showed where holes are in education—how the system is just not good. Not that I didn't know it had issues before, but now it really has stood out."

The analysis of these four interviews demonstrates that future research should examine ways in which administrative support can reduce burnout and stress for all teachers, but with a dynamic lens that specifically acknowledges the lived experience of female teachers. Additionally, because the teachers interviewed shared their gratitude for the opportunity to share their experiences, future research should explore the cathartic and transformative possibilities of bearing witness to others' struggles.

Given that 76% of public-school teachers are female (National Center for Education Statistics, 2021), it is crucial that school leaders become aware of the particular lived experiences of the female teachers in their buildings. Although they are more likely to stay in the profession than their male counterparts (Räsänen et al., 2020), female teachers who receive more administrative and systemic support as they work to teach and build meaningful relationships with students are more likely to experience a higher quality of life at work. Intentionally supporting female teachers in this way could lead to greater job satisfaction, instead of the stressful reevaluation of roles or jobs. Then, in another extreme situation like the COVID-19 pandemic, these teachers will possess more of a reservoir from which to provide the first response such trauma requires.

Today, a few years past the initial outbreak of COVID-19, schools are beyond the policies mandating masking, remote learning, and social distancing. However, teachers are still experiencing unsustainable pressure. COVID-19 did not so much add to that pressure as it highlighted pre-existing deficits in our educational system. This study unsurfaced the need to pause and actively listen to the lived experiences of educators, not merely for their sake, but for the betterment of education as a whole.

REFERENCES

Blitz, L. V., Anderson, E. M., & Saastamoinen, M. (2016). Assessing perceptions of culture and trauma in an elementary school: Informing a model for culturally responsive trauma-informed schools. *The Urban Review, 48*(4), 520–542. https://doi.org/10.1007/s11256-016-0366-9

Bottiani, J. H., Duran, C. A., Pas, E. T., & Bradshaw, C. P. (2019). Teacher stress and burnout in urban middle schools: Associations with job demands, resources, and effective classroom practices. *Journal of School Psychology, 77,* 36–51. https://doi.org/10.1016/j.jsp.2019.10.002

Brasfield, M. W., Lancaster, C., & Xu, Y. J. (2019). Wellness as a mitigating factor for teacher burnout. *Journal of Education, 199*(3), 166–178. https://doi.org/10.1177/0022057419864525

Camacho, D. A., Hoover, S. A., & Rosete, H. S. (2021). Burnout in urban teachers: The predictive role of supports and situational responses. *Psychology in the Schools, 58*(9), 1816–1831.

Correa, N., & First, J. M. (2021). Examining the mental health impacts of COVID-19 on K–12 mental health providers, school teachers, and students. *Journal of School Counseling, 19*(42), 1–26. https://eric.ed.gov/?id=EJ1328847

Creswell, J. W., & Poth, C. N. (2018). *Qualitative inquiry & research design: Choosing among five approaches* (4th ed.). SAGE.

Crotty, M. (2020). *The foundations of social research.* Routledge.

Dworkin, A. G., & Tobe, P. F. (2014). The effects of standards-based school accountability on teacher burnout and trust relationships: A longitudinal analysis. In *Trust and School Life* (pp. 121–143). Springer.

Etchells, M., Brannen, L., Donop, J., Bielefeldt, J., Singer, E., Moorhead, E., & Walderon, T. (2021). Synchronous teaching and asynchronous trauma: Exploring teacher trauma in the wake of covid-19. *Social Sciences & Humanities Open, 4*(1), 100197. https://doi.org/10.1016/j.ssaho.2021.100197

Ferguson, K., Frost, L., & Hall, D. (2012). Predicting teacher anxiety, depression, and job satisfaction. *Journal of Teaching and Learning, 8*(1), 27–42. https://doi.org/10.22329/jtl.v8i1.2896

Hall, K. S., Kingsville, T. X., Gilles, M. A., & Cumberland, M. D. (2022). Reasons for teacher attrition: Experience matters. *Editorial Review Board, 8,* 8–13. https://doi.org/10.1016/s0742-051x(21)00338-3

Haydon, T., Leko, M. M., & Stevens, D. (2018). Teacher stress: Sources, effects, and protective factors. *Journal of Special Education Leadership, 31*(2), 99–108. https://eric.ed.gov/?id=EJ1275350

Hydon, S., Wong, M., Langley, A. K., Stein, B. D., & Kataoka, S. H. (2015). Preventing secondary traumatic stress in educators. *Child and Adolescent Psychiatric Clinics, 24*(2), 319–333. https://doi.org/10.1016/j.chc.2014.11.003

Jakubowski, T. D., & Sitko-Dominik, M. M. (2021). Teachers' mental health during the first two waves of the COVID-19 pandemic in Poland. *PloS One, 16*(9), e0257252. https://doi.org/10.1371/ journal.pone.0257252

Kim, L. E., Oxley, L., & Asbury, K. (2021). "My brain feels like a browser with 100 tabs open": A longitudinal study of teachers' mental health and well-being during the COVID-19 pandemic. *British Journal of Education Psychology*, *92*(1), 299–318. https://doi.org/10.31234/osf.io/cjpdx

Klapproth, F., Federkeil, L., Heinschke, F., & Jungmann, T. (2020). Teachers' experiences of stress and their coping strategies during COVID-19 induced distance teaching. *Journal of Pedagogical Research*, *4*(4), 444–452. https://doi.org/10.33902/jpr.2020062805

Lang, J. M., Franks, R. P., Epstein, C., Stover, C., & Oliver, J. A. (2015). State-wide dissemination of an evidence-based practice using Breakthrough Series Collaboratives. *Children and Youth Services Review*, *55*, 201–209. https://doi.org/10.1016/j.childyouth.2015.06.005

Lawrence, D. F., Loi, N. M., & Gudex, B. W. (2019). Understanding the relationship between work intensification and burnout in secondary teachers. *Teachers and Teaching*, *25*(2), 189–199. https://doi.org/10.1080/13540602.2018.1544551

Merriam, S. (2009). *Qualitative research: A guide to design and implementation*. John Wiley & Sons.

Matiz, A., Fabbro, F., Paschetto, A., Cantone, D., Paolone, A. R., & Crescentini, C. (2020). Positive impact of mindfulness meditation on mental health of female teachers during the COVID-19 outbreak in Italy. *International Journal of Environmental Research and Public Health*, *17*(18), 6450. https://doi.org/10.3390/ijerph17186450

National Center for Education Statistics. (2021). *Characteristics of public school teachers*. The condition of education. https://nces.ed.gov/programs/coe/indicator/clr

Palma-Vasquez, C., Carrasco, D., & Hernando-Rodriguez, J. C. (2021). Mental health of teachers who have teleworked due to COVID-19. *European Journal of Investigation in Health, Psychology, and Education*, *11*(2), 515–528. https://doi.org/10.3390/ejihpe11020037

Pembroke, N. (2015). Contributions from Christian ethics and Buddhist philosophy to the management of compassion fatigue in nurses. *Nursing and Health Sciences*, *18*(1), 120–124. https://doi.org/10.1111/nhs.12252

Pressley, T. (2021). Factors contributing to teacher burnout during COVID-19. *Educational Researcher*, *50*(5), 325–327. https://doi.org/10.3102/0013189x211004138

Räsänen, K., Pietarinen, J., Pyhältö, K., Soini, T., & Väisänen, P. (2020). Why leave the teaching profession? A longitudinal approach to the prevalence and persistence of teacher turnover intentions. *Social and Psychological Education 23*, 837–859. https://doi.org/10.1007/s11218-020-09567-x

Rawal, D. M. (2021). Work-life balance among female school teachers [K–12] delivering online curriculum in Noida [India] during COVID: Empirical study. *Management in Education*, 089202062199430. https://doi.org/10.1177/0892020621994303

Smetackova, I. (2017). Self-efficacy and burnout syndrome among teachers. *The European Journal of Social & Behavioral Sciences*, *20*(3), 229–241. https://doi.org/10.15405/ejsbs.219

Smith, J. A., & Nizza, I. E. (2022). *Essentials of interpretative phenomenological analysis*. American Psychological Association. https://doi.org/10.1037/0000259-001

Split, J. L., Koomen, H. M., & Thijs, J. T. (2011). Teacher wellbeing: The importance of teacher-student relationships. *Educational Psychology Review*, *23*(4), 457–477. https://doi.org/10.1007/s10648-011-9170-y

Toropova, A., Myrberg, E., & Johansson, S. (2021). Teacher job satisfaction: the importance of school working conditions and teacher characteristics. *Educational Review*, *73*(1), 71–97. https://doi.org/10.1080/00131911.2019.1705247

Veldman, I., Van Tartwijk, J., Brekelmans, M., & Wubbels, T. (2013). Job satisfaction and teacher–student relationships across the teaching career: Four case studies. Teaching and *Teacher Education*, *32*, 55–65. https://doi.org/10.1016/j.tate.2013.01.005

Walker, T. (2022, February 1). *Survey: Alarming number of educators may soon leave the profession.* NEA News. https://www.nea.org/advocating-for-change/new-from-nea/survey-alarming-number-educators-may-soon-leave-profession

Yin, H., Huang, S., & Chen, G. (2019). The relationships between teachers' emotional labor and their burnout and satisfaction: A meta-analytic review. *Educational Research Review*, *28*, 100283. https://doi.org/10.1016/j.edurev.2019.100283

APPENDIX

Interview Questions

- Why did you become a teacher?
- What does teaching mean to you?
- How would you describe your teaching style with students? To what extent does your gender affect that style?
- What is your relationship with your students? In what ways does your gender affect that relationship?
- Describe your relationship with your current supervisors. To what extent does your gender affect that relationship?
- How would you describe your experience as a female educator?
- What was your experience at work before COVID-19?
- What were your responsibilities outside of school before COVID-19?
- During COVID-19, in what ways did those outside-of-school responsibilities change?
- Describe your experience at work now. To what extent has COVID-19 affected that experience?
- What personal self-care practices and/or professional support have you accessed during COVID-19?
- What support have you received from your school and/or district?

- Tell me what motivated you to come to work in the first years of your career.
- Tell me what currently motivates you to come to work.
- Have you ever thought about leaving the teaching profession? If so, when and why?
- What else would you like to say about how COVID-19 has impacted you as a female teacher?

CHAPTER 5

NINTH-GRADE STUDENTS WITH DISABILITIES' MATH EFFICACY AND TEACHERS' INSTRUCTIONAL EFFICACY

John M. Palladino
Eastern Michigan University

ABSTRACT

This secondary data analysis of the High School Longitudinal Study of 2009 (HSLS) examined math efficacy among 9th-grade students with disabilities ($n = 2,065$), as well as the instructional efficacy among the mathematics teachers to whom they were assigned ($n = 1,478$). Follow-up tests showed both positive and negative relationships between each of the measures and certain educational conditions that HSLS addressed. Implications for policy and practice are provided, as are limitations and future research suggestions.

The national proliferation of science, technology, engineering, and math (STEM) initiatives and the Common Core State Standards throughout the past two decades have coincided with increased high school mathematical expectations (Morales-Chicas & Agger, 2017; Stoker et al., 2018). In their analysis of high school graduation requirements, the Education Commission of the States (2019) reported that most states require at least three, if

---

Curriculum and Teaching Dialogue,
Volume 25, Numbers 1 & 2, pp. 249–262
Copyright © 2023 by Information Age Publishing
www.infoagepub.com
All rights of reproduction in any form reserved.

not four years of mathematics courses (see Table 5.1). The standard aims to prepare students for multiple postsecondary opportunities, such as college entry, college graduation, and gainful employment, to name a few (Lee, 2012). Scholars stress how students' performance in freshman mathematics courses determines if their trajectory through all of high school mathematics and into postsecondary settings will be successful. Thus, students with disabilities (SWDs) and their known unpreparedness to begin high school with ample mathematical proficiency should sound a warning bell. Myers et al. (2021), for example, conducted an analysis of national test scores and found that less than 10% of 9th-grade SWDs have basic mathematical proficiency. The authors likewise report that the phenomenon worsens as the proficiency rate drops to 7% by the time SWDs reach senior year. The deleterious reality explains the numerous mathematics course failures high school SWDs will experience (Boaler, 2016; Mazzotti, 2021).

Table 5.1

Number of Years of High School Mathematics Requirements in the United States

Years of mathematics requirements	Number of states requiring	Specific states requiring
Four years of mathematics requirements	15 and the District of Columbia	Alabama, Arizona, Arkansas, Delaware, District of Columbia, Florida, Georgia, Louisiana, Michigan, Mississippi, New Mexico, North Carolina, Ohio, Rhode Island, Tennessee, West Virginia
Three years of mathematics requirements	28	Alaska, Connecticut, Hawaii, Idaho, Illinois, Indiana, Iowa, Kansas, Kentucky, Maryland, Minnesota, Missouri, Nebraska, Nevada, New Hampshire, New Jersey, New York, North Dakota, Oklahoma, Oregon, South Carolina, South Dakota, Texas, Utah, Virginia, Washington, Wisconsin, Wyoming
Two years of mathematics requirements	2	California, Montana
Mathematics requirements set by local decision	5	Colorado, Maine, Massachusetts, Pennsylvania, Vermont

Note. Cited from the Education Commission of the States (2019, February). *High school graduation requirements*. https://reports.ecs.org/comparisons/high-school-graduation-requirements-01

The likelihood SWDs cannot launch a successful start to their high school mathematics requirements defies the postsecondary educational intentions 75% of these students will declare at the start of 9th grade (Lipscomb et al., 2017) and for which the ever-increasing mathematics standards strive to address. The irony that the mathematical standards match SWDs' long-term pursuits, but appear unattainable because of mathematical shortcomings, exposes the need to enhance 9th-grade SWDs' math efficacy (e.g., Allsopp, et al., 2017). The literature is not silent about how efficacious individuals can overcome obstacles through positive beliefs about themselves (e.g., "I can and want to go to college even though I have a disability") and the execution of behaviors that goal attainment requires (e.g., completing courses and earning a diploma; Bandura et al., 2003). Examples include Kalaycioglu's (2015) secondary data analysis about the socioeconomic status, math efficacy, anxiety, and mathematics achievement among 8,800 students throughout six different nations: "For all six countries, the most important predictor of mathematics achievement is math self-efficacy" (p. 1391). Likewise, in their study of 1,163 upper elementary students' self-reports of perceived math efficacy, Fast et al. (2010) reported "higher levels of math self-efficacy positively predicted math performance" (p. 729). While these and other studies offer hope for the ameliorative nature of students' math efficacy, a need exists to identify specific conditions associated with 9th-grade SWDs' math efficacy (King-Sears & Strogilos, 2020; Love et al., 2020).

The study responded to the gap with attention on four conditions known to relate to students' efficacious behaviors, but not yet confirmed relative to 9th-grade SWDs' math efficacy. First, grade retention occurs in 29 states and Washington, D.C. (Wright, 2021) and use of the practice among SWDs often occurs (Lipscomb, 2017). Descriptions throughout the literature report retention as one of life's most stressful and stigmatizing experiences (e.g., Boaler, 2016). Although retention has a negative relationship with high school success (Hughes et al., 2018), a comparable relationship with 9th-grade math efficacy remains unknown. Second, findings about the relationship between students' math efficacy and the evaluations they receive for their mathematical performances (e.g., Siegle & McCoach, 2007) have not accounted for a similar relationship between incoming 9th-grade SWDs' math efficacy and the most recent and formal mathematics evaluation they received for their 8th-grade mathematics course. Third, the relationship between students' efficacious behaviors and their perceptions of academic settings (Fast et al., 2010; Siegle & McCoach, 2007) has yet to be established between 9th-grade SWDs' math efficacy and perceptions of 9th-grade mathematics teachers. Last, a relationship exists between students' overall efficacy and teachers' (a) instructional efficacy (e.g., Anderson & Olivier, 2022; Donohoo et al., 2018), (b) pedagogical decision-making (Powell et al., 2022), and (c) resolve to engage all students in daily instruction (Wang et al., 2017), but one that has yet to be explored within the context of 9th-grade SWDs and the mathematics teachers to whom they are assigned.

In response to the aforementioned gaps, the study ensued with a twofold purpose for a secondary analysis of publicly available High School Longitudinal Study of 2009 (HSLS) (Ingels et al., 2011) data. The first purpose was to determine if the math efficacy measure Middleton (2013) established based on the entirety of the HSLS 9th-grade student population ($n = 21,000$) would maintain when retested with an extrapolated HSLS sample composed of just SWDs. No other scholar since Middleton has repeated the testing of the measure with such a configuration. Included with this first purpose was the intent to also conduct follow-up tests for a correlation coefficient to determine any relationships between 9th-grade SWDs' math efficacy and the previously discussed conditions: (a) grade retention, (b) 8th-grade mathematics report card grades, and (c) perceptions about 9th-grade mathematics teachers. The additional testing included a control for different disability types and the status of 9th-grade SWDs' access to special education programs and services. The second purpose was to then discuss 9th-grade SWDs' math efficacy in tandem with their 9th-grade HSLS mathematics teachers' instructional efficacy. Doing so required the establishment of a newly formed HSLS instructional efficacy measure and tests for a correlations coefficient to determine the measure's relationship with mathematics teachers' pedagogical decision-making and resolve to engage all students in daily instruction.

Two research questions guided the study's analyses:

1. Does Middleton's previously established HSLS 9th-grade math efficacy measure maintain its reliability when tested with an extrapolated homogenous SWDs sample, as well as relate to other HSLS variables?
2. Can a reliable measure of instructional efficacy be established based on responses from HSLS mathematics teachers who taught the SWDs, as well as relate to other HSLS variables?

The rigor of the HSLS, prior HSLS and efficacious behavior scholarship, and the present study's large sample sizes, informed the hypothesis that both measures would prove to be reliable and relate to other HSLS variables, and thereby broaden the awareness about 9th-grade SWDs' math efficacy.

METHODS

Participants

The HSLS public-use policy allows scholars access to its 21,000 freshman participants' data for secondary analysis purposes, as well as the survey data of their parents or guardians, mathematics and science teachers, school administrators, and school counselors. A purposeful selection of HSLS students and mathematics teachers comprised the present study's samples. The first sample included the 9th-grade HSLS students for whom parents or guardians provided an affirmative response ("yes") when asked if their adolescents had one or more of the following disabilities or disorders ($n = 2,065$): learning disability, development disability, intellectual disability, and attention-deficit/hyperactivity disorder (ADD/ADHD). The parent or guardian survey did not seek responses for other disabilities or disorders, such as hearing impairments and deaf blindness, to name a few. Furthermore, how parents or guardians interpreted *intellectual disability*, a catchall for various disorders, remains unknown. A follow-up parent or guardian survey question inquired about whether or not the SWDs *were currently receiving special education services* in 9th grade and aided the present study's division of the first sample into two subgroups based on "yes" ($n = 806$) and "no" ($n = 1,259$) responses. The second sample included the HSLS teachers to whom the SWDs were assigned for their 9th-grade mathematics course ($n = 1,478$). The reader should note that the HSLS mathematics teacher survey did not probe for answers specific to any one HSLS student participant, but rather about teaching experiences in general. Therefore, the mathematics teacher sample includes educators who may have taught (a) more than one HSLS student in any one or more freshman courses; (b) HSLS, non-HSLS, general education, and special education learners in any one freshman course; and (c) additional content subject areas besides mathematics, such as science courses.

Measures

The measures conducted in this study resulted from two established HSLS protocols. First, previous studies have confirmed the validity of HSLS surveys and questions necessary for subsequent secondary analysis studies. For example, Ingels et al. (2011) provided a review of HSLS psychometrics and explained how designers conducted field tests for each variable's effectiveness and order of placement within HSLS surveys:

> Where Bayesian estimation procedures were applied, the estimate of the error variance was computed as the mean of the variances of the posterior

254   J. M. PALLADINO

> distributions of ability for each test-taker in the sample [and] the IRT-esti-
> mated reliability was 0.92 after sample weights were applied. (p. 32)

The National Center for Education Statistics (2011) houses additional reports about HSLS psychometrics and further validates the variables' reliability. Second, the paring-down process of HSLS's voluminous 5,800 variables pursuant to answering specific research questions and synthesizing results is common practice for secondary analysis research projects (e.g., Champion & Mesa, 2018).

Math Efficacy Measure

Middleton (2013) was the first scholar to establish a HSLS 9th-grade student motivational measure comprised of five subscales (identity, interest, utility, effort, and self-efficacy), each proven to have a reliable Cronbach alpha and composite reliability: "The results show that the scales have moderate to very high internal consistency" (p. 87). Of particular importance to the present study was the self-efficacy subscale (α = .90; composite reliability = .93) Middleton established based on four HSLS survey questions and a 4-point Likert scale with ranges from *strongly agree* to *strongly disagree*. The four self-efficacy subscale statements are (a) I am confident that I can do an excellent job on math assignments; (b) I am confident that I can do an excellent job on math tests; (c) I am certain that I can understand the math textbook; and (d) I am certain that I can master skills in this math course. The present study used Middleton's self-efficacy measure to answer the first part of research question one: Does Middleton's previously established HSLS 9th-grade math efficacy measure maintain its reliability when tested with an extrapolated homogenous SWDs sample? The replicated testing was based on a reliability threshold set at a .70 Cronbach alpha (see Lin et al., 2019; Sezer & Yilmaz, 2019, for arguments about alpha thresholds).

The present study then conducted follow-up tests for a correlation coefficient to determine the self-efficacy measure's relationship with specific HSLS variables and to answer the second part of research question one: Does Middleton's previously established HSLS 9th-grade math efficacy measure relate to other HSLS variables? The testing was based on a significance threshold set at .05. Chosen demographic variables for the present study's SWDs sample (n = 2,065) included 8th-grade mathematics report card letter cards and the grade levels at which any retention may have occurred. Additional variables included five HSLS questions about the sample's perceptions of the 9th-grade mathematics teachers to whom they were assigned and a 4-point Likert scale with ranges from *strongly agree* to *strongly disagree*. The survey statements were as follows: My math teacher treats some kids better than other kids; my math teacher makes math interesting; my math teacher makes math easy to understand; my math teacher wants students to learn and not just memorize things; and my math teacher does not let people give up when the work gets hard.

Instructional Efficacy Measure

The present study set out to establish an instructional efficacy measure based on the mathematics teachers' sample and their responses to five questions about student qualities that limit how they teach using a 4-point Likert scale ranging from *A Lot* to *Not at All*. The five qualities are as follows: Students with different academic abilities in the same class; students with special needs; uninterested students; low morale among students; and disruptive students. The present study tested the measure's reliability to answer the first part of research question two: Can a reliable measure of instructional efficacy be established based on responses from HSLS mathematics teachers who taught the SWDs? The test was based on a reliability threshold set at a .70 Cronbach alpha.

The present study then conducted follow-up tests for a correlation coefficient to determine the instructional efficacy measure's relationship with specific HSLS variables and to answer the second part of research question two: Does the measure of instructional efficacy relate to other HSLS variables? The testing was based on a threshold set at .05. The first set of variables included nine HSLS questions about the sample's pedagogical decisions to stress certain mathematical concepts and a 4-point Likert scale with a range from *heavy emphasis* to *no emphasis*. The nine concepts were as follows: Math concepts; algorithms and procedures; computational skills; problem solving skills; mathematical reasoning; logical structure of mathematics; math ideas; speedy and accurate computations; and standardized test preparation.

The second set of variables included three HSLS questions about the sample's steadfastness and a 4-point Likert scale with a range from *strongly agree* to *strongly disagree*. The three questions were as follows: I know how to increase student retention of information from lesson to lesson; I know techniques to redirect disruptive students quickly; and I can get through to even the most difficult or unmotivated students.

RESULTS

Research Question One: The Study's SWDs Sample and Math Efficacy

The null hypothesis for the first research question was rejected. Middleton's (2013) 9th-grade HSLS math efficacy measure proved to be reliable when tested with the present study's 9th-grade SWDs' sample ($\alpha = .882$) and maintained when controlling for the sample's specific mathematics courses (e.g., Algebra I, geometry) and special education status. Noteworthy is that those with a learning disability yielded lower math efficacy scores compared with those with a developmental disability, intellectual disability, and attention-deficit hyperactivity disorder ($p < 0.00$). Each of the three follow-up tests for a correlation coefficient between the measure and other HSLS variables yielded and maintained significance when controlling for the sample's 9th-grade access to special education programs and services. First, within the sample, those who had been retained at any point throughout their K–9 education had lower scores on the math efficacy measure compared to those who had never been retained ($p < 0.02$). Among all who had been retained, those who were in their second attempt of passing 9th grade had the lowest math efficacy scores ($p < 0.00$). Second, those who self-reported having earned an *A* and *B* letter grades for their 8th-grade mathematics report cards had significantly higher 9th-grade math efficacy than those who had reported having earned a *C* letter grade or below ($p < 0.00$). Third, those who responded with *strongly agree* or *agree* about their mathematics teachers' abilities to make instruction *interesting* and *easy to understand* had higher math efficacy scores than those who responded with *disagree* or *strongly disagree* ($p < 0.001$ for both measures). No significance was found among the responses for the remaining three perception questions: My math teacher treats some kids better than other kids; my math teacher wants students to learn and not just memorize things; and my math teacher does not let people give up when the work gets hard.

Research Question Two: The Study's 9th-Grade Mathematics Teacher Sample and Instructional Efficacy

The null hypothesis for the second research question was rejected. The establishment of the instructional efficacy measure proved to be reliable when tested with the present study's mathematics teacher sample ($\alpha = .751$). Each of the two follow-up tests for a correlation coefficient between the measure and other HSLS variables yielded significance. First, the results about the sample's pedagogical decisions to stress certain mathematical concepts for their 9th-grade mathematics teaching showed that a *heavy emphasis* on six of the nine concepts yielded higher instructional efficacy scores compared to those who had reported a *moderate emphasis*, *minimal emphasis*, or *no emphasis* ($p < 0.05$ for each of the six variables). The six variables were (a) computational skills; (b) problem solving skills; (c) mathematical reasoning; (d) logical structure of mathematics; (e) math ideas; and (f) standardized tests preparation. No significance was found for any of the remaining three variables: Math concepts; algorithms and procedures; and speedy and accurate computations. Second, those in the sample who responded with *strongly agree* or *agree* for all three questions about steadfastness had higher instructional efficacy scores than those who responded with *disagree* or *strongly disagree* ($p < 0.05$ for each of three questions). The three questions were (a) I know how to increase student retention of information from lesson to lesson; (b) I know techniques to redirect disruptive students quickly; and (c) I can get through to even the most difficult or unmotivated students.

DISCUSSION

This study confirmed the conditions related to math efficacy among an extrapolated HSLS 9th-grade SWDs sample. Three specific findings offer generalizable implications for enhancing 9th-grade SWDs' math efficacy in particular and for the greater likelihood of diploma attainment and successful post-secondary pursuits in general. First, lower math efficacy reported among SWDs with grade retention histories compared to those never retained ($p < 0.02$) expands upon Bandura et al.'s (2003) and others' arguments about how repeated negative experiences thwarts efficacious development. The present study illustrates how time throughout elementary and middle school years and any positive mathematical experiences that may have occurred along the way could not mitigate the findings about diminished 9th-grade math efficacy. Grade retention occurrences as far back as 1st grade and all grades thereafter established or at least sustained a negative relationship with the SWDs' math efficacy at the onset of 9th grade. The finding sounds a rallying call for legislators, school administrators, teachers, and parents and guardians in states where retention policies exist to contextualize retention beyond a short-term, quick-fix solution and consider the negative ramifications associated with compromised 9th-grade math efficacy. Since HSLS did not inquire about the academic discipline deficits associated with students' prior grade retention, the conclusion cannot be made that mathematical shortcomings were the cause. Deficits in other disciplines may have resulted in the grade retentions and yet could have established the negative relationship with SWDs' 9th-grade math efficacy reported in this study.

Second, the study's report card finding offers new insights about how 9th-grade SWDs perceive their mathematical competency and confidence at the start of high school, which then informs a sense of 9th-grade math efficacy. The results pinpoint SWDs' 8th-grade mathematics report card letter grades lower than a *B* as the cutoff between enhanced and weakened 9th-grade math efficacy ($p < 0.00$). A tenable interpretation suggests the connotation of average mathematical performance inferred from a *C* letter grade was not enough to instill a sense of mathematical competence and confidence, let alone a *D* or *F* letter grade. A related possibility accounts for dismissive comments others (e.g., peers, teachers, counselors, parents, guardians) might have made about the *C* letter grade and that the sample interpreted as indicative of poor performance. Regardless, the finding points out how SWDs may benefit from broader discussions about their mathematical performances beyond formal report card letter grades. Other findings from the study reinforce the recommendation. For example, broadened self-evaluations could bolster SWDs' confidence and mitigate instances of *low morale among students*—a concern that, when present, had a negative relationship with the instructional efficacy among this study's mathematics teacher sample ($p < 0.02$). Consistent performance feedback could also facilitate discussions about mathematical content and result in 9th-grade SWDs' perceptions of mathematics teachers as *easy to understand*, the affirmation of which related to 9th-grade math efficacy in the present study ($p < 0.00$). Furthermore, ongoing dialogues with SWDs about their mathematical performance could inform 9th-grade mathematics teachers' future pedagogical decision-making. The study's instructional efficacy findings point out the positive relationship among teachers who place a *heavy emphasis* on multiple components of mathematical instruction ($p < 0.05$). The potential final outcome of enhanced 9th-grade SWDs' math efficacy in tandem with their 9th-grade mathematics teachers' enhanced instructional efficacy adds an additional layer to the already existing discourse about how teacher efficacy influences student achievement.

Third, the study spotlights how individuals in the SWDs sample with verified *learning disabilities* had the worse math efficacy compared to the rest of the sample ($p < 0.00$). The finding was an outlier because no other tests exposed any significant differences among students with *learning disabilities*. Therefore, the study considered the arguments throughout the literature about how students with learning disabilities necessitate continuous metacognition guidance (e.g., Allsopp et al., 2017) in order to interpret the finding. Metacognitive skills include an awareness about and understanding of one's own thought process and, if compromised, could have influenced responses to HSLS math efficacy questions. The finding does not clarify if the students with learning disabilities in the present study had skewed perceptions about their mathematical performances and/or their expectations for a mathematical competency threshold. Regardless, although all 9th-grade SWDs could benefit from the prior discussed findings about grade retentions and report card grades, particular attention should be afforded those with learning disabilities and whose math efficacy appears most at risk.

LIMITATIONS

The study's unique findings come with five inherent limitations. First, the study only addressed SWDs' math efficacy at the 9th-grade level and bound the generalizability of the findings to freshman year mathematics. Second, the selection of specific HSLS variables for the study's follow-up tests for a correlation coefficient based on the cited literature was a subjective process. Third, HSLS's research design and survey questionnaires did not allow for a direct comparison between any one SWD in the present study and their assigned 9th-grade mathematics teacher. The inability to study 9th-grade SWDs' math efficacy as a dependent variable and mathematics teachers' instructional efficacy as an independent variable could not be rectified. Fourth, HSLS did not query about the specific 8th-grade mathematics course (e.g., pre-algebra) the 9th graders had completed. The lack of information prevented the present study from determining if a relationship exists between specific 8th-grade mathematics classes and SWDs' 9th-grade math efficacy. Finally, perceptions about mathematics teachers' abilities to make mathematics *interesting* and *easy to understand* proved relatable to the SWD's 9th-grade math efficacy, but specific instructional approaches that garnered the SWDs' accolades could not be addressed.

FUTURE RESEARCH

A need exists for additional scholarship to broaden the present study's findings. HSLS includes additional data collection waves that occurred when the freshmen participants were in 11th and 12th grades, as well as three years after high school graduation. An examination of SWDs' math efficacy beyond the present study's 9th-grade focus could illustrate potential changes over time and as enrollment into new high school mathematics courses occurs. Further research could determine if non-mathematical HSLS variables (e.g., science course questions) relate to 9th-grade SWDs' math efficacy and thereby illustrate how another academic discipline may need to be considered for math efficacy enhancement efforts. Additional non-mathematical HSLS variables that could enhance the present study's findings include demographics, such as students' race and gender. Follow-up studies could replicate the present study's use of Middleton's (2013) math efficacy measure and the established mathematics teacher instructional efficacy measure, but with samples outside of HSLS and that account for all special education disability types. The design could position SWDs' math efficacy as a dependent variable and math teachers' instructional efficacy as an independent variable in a way that cannot be accomplished with original HSLS data.

CONCLUSION

This study was a first-ever known attempt to measure the math efficacy of 9th-grade SWDs with a secondary data analysis of the High School Longitudinal Study of 2009 (HSLS). The significant results it procured reinforce the need to establish SWDs' math efficacy throughout elementary and middle school and ahead of high school. They also spotlight the potential threat towards math efficacy growth that retention policies and practices create when imposed on this population. Finally, the findings reinforce claims throughout the social and behavioral sciences literature about how students' perceptions of themselves, their academic performances, and of their teachers inform their own efficacious behaviors.

REFERENCES

Allsopp, D., Lovin, L. H., & van Ingen, S. (2017). Supporting mathematical proficiency: Strategies for new special education teachers. *Teaching Exceptional Children, 49*(4), 273–283. https://doi.org/10.1177/0040059917692112

Anderson, S. G., & Olivier, D. F. (2022). A Quantitative study of schools as learning Organizations: An examination of professional learning communities, teacher self-efficacy, and collective efficacy. *Research Issues in Contemporary Education, 7*(1), 26–51. http://www.leraweb.net/ojs/index.php/RICE/article/view/91

Bandura, A., Caprara, G., Barbaranelli, C., Gerbino, M., & Pastorelli, C. (2003). Role of affective self-regulatory efficacy in diverse spheres of psychosocial functioning. *Child Development, 74*(3), 769–782. https://doi.org/10.1111/1467-8624.00567

Boaler, J. (2016). *Mathematical mindsets: Unleashing students' potential through creative math, inspiring messages and innovative teaching.* Jossey-Bass.

Champion, J., & Mesa, V. (2018). Pathways to calculus in U.S. high schools. *PRIMUS: Problems, Resources, and Issues in Mathematics Undergraduate Studies, 28*(6), 508–527. https://doi.org/10.1080/10511970.2017.1315473

Donohoo, J., Hattie, J., & Eells, R. (2018). The power of collective efficacy. *Educational Leadership, 75*(6), 40–44. https://www.ascd.org/el/articles/the-power-of-collective-efficacy

Education Commission of the States. (2019, February). *High school graduation requirements.* https://reports.ecs.org/comparisons/high-school-graduation-requirements-01

Fast, L. A., Lewis, J. L., Bryant, M. J., Bocian, K. A., Cardullo, R. A., Rettig, M., & Hammond, K. A. (2010). Does math self-efficacy mediate the effect of the perceived classroom environment on standardized math test performance? *Journal of Educational Psychology, 102*(3), 729–740. https://doi.org/10.1037/a0018863

Hughes, J. N., West, S. G., Kim, H., & Bauer, S. S. (2018). Effect of early grade retention on school completion: A prospective study. *Journal of Educational Psychology, 110*(7), 974–991. http://dx.doi.org/10.1037/edu0000243

Ingels, S.J., Pratt, D.J., Herget, D.R., Burns, L.J., Dever, J.A., Ottem, R., Rogers, J.E., Jin, Y., & Leinwand, S. (2011). *High School Longitudinal Study of 2009 (HSLS:09). Base-Year Data File Documentation* (NCES 2011-328). U.S. Department of Education. National Center for Education Statistics. https://nces.ed.gov/pubsearch/pubsinfo.asp?pubid=2011328

Kalaycioglu, D. B. (2015). The influence of socioeconomic status, self-efficacy, and anxiety on mathematics achievement in England, Greece, Hong Kong, the Netherlands, Turkey, and the USA. *Educational Sciences: Theory and Practice, 15*(5), 1391–1401. https://doi.org/10.12738/estp.2015.5.2731

King-Sears, M., & Strogilos, V. (2020). An exploratory study of self-efficacy, school belongingness, and co-teaching perspectives from middle school students and teachers in a mathematics co-taught classroom. *International Journal of Inclusive Education, 24*(2), 162–180. https://doi.org/10.1080/13603116.2018.1453553

Lee, J. (2012). College for all: Gaps between desirable and actual P–12 math achievement trajectories for college readiness. *Educational Researcher, 41*(2), 43–55. https://doi.org/10.3102/0013189X11432746

Lin, W., Mayer, C., & Lee, B. (2019). Validity and reliability of the teamwork evaluation of non-technical skills tool. *Australian Journal of Advanced Nursing, 36*(3), 29–38. https://www.ajan.com.au/archive/Vol36/Issue3/4Lee.pdf

Lipscomb, S., Haimson, J., Liu, A., Burghardt, J., Johnson, D., & Thurlow, M. (2017). *Preparing for life after high school: The characteristics and experiences of youth in special education* (NCEE 2017-4017; Findings from the National Longitudinal Transition Study 2012, Vol. 1.). United States Department of Education, Institute of Education Sciences, National Center for Education Evaluation and Regional Assistance. https://ies.ed.gov/ncee/pubs/20174016/pdf/20174017.pdf

Love, A. M. A., Findley, J. A., Ruble, L. A., & McGrew, J. H. (2020). Teacher self-efficacy for teaching students with autism spectrum disorder: Associations with stress, teacher engagement, and student IEP outcomes following COMPASS consultation. *Focus on Autism and Other Developmental Disabilities, 35*(1), 47–54. https://doi.org/10.1177/1088357619836767

Mazzotti, V. L., Rowe, D. A., Kwiatek, S., Voggt, A., Chang, W. H., Fowler, C. H., Poppen, M., Sinclair, J., & Test, D. W. (2021). Secondary transition predictors of postschool success: An update to the research base. *Career Development and Transition for Exceptional Individuals, 44*(1), 47–64. https://doi.org/10.1177/2165143420959793

Middleton, J. (2013). More than motivation: The combined effects of critical motivational variables on middle school mathematics achievement. *Middle Grades Research Journal, 8*(1), 77–95. https://www.infoagepub.com/mgrj-issue.html?i=p54c3b12e96247

Morales-Chicas, J., & Agger, C. (2017). The effects of teacher collective responsibility on the mathematics achievement of students who repeat algebra. *Journal of Urban Mathematics Education, 10*(1), 52–73. https://jume-ojs-tamu.tdl.org/JUME/article/view/287/209

Myers, J. A., Brownell, M. T., Griffin, C. C., Hughes, E. M., Witzel, B. S., Gage, N. A., Peyton, D., Acosta, K., & Wang, J. (2021). Mathematics interventions for adolescents with mathematics difficulties: A meta-analysis. *Learning Disabilities Research & Practice, 36*(2), 145–166. https://doi.org/10.1111/ldrp.12244

National Center for Education Statistics. (2011). *High School Longitudinal Study of 2009* [Data file and code book]. https://nces.ed.gov/surveys/hsls09/

Powell, S. R., Mason, E. N., Bos, S. E., Hirt, S., Ketterlin-Geller, L. R., & Lembke, E. S. (2021). A systematic review of mathematics interventions for middle-school students experiencing mathematics difficulty. *Learning Disabilities Research & Practice, 36*(4), 295–329. https://doi.org/10.1111/ldrp.12263

Sezer, B., & Yilmaz, R. (2019). Learning management system acceptance scale (LMSAS): A validity and reliability study. *Australasian Journal of Educational Technology, 35*(3), 15–30. https://doi.org/10.14742/ajet.3959

Siegle, D., & McCoach, D. B. (2007). Increasing student mathematics self-efficacy through teacher training. *Journal of Advanced Academics, 18*(2), 278–312, 330–331. https://doi.org/10.4219/jaa-2007-353

Stoker, G., Mellor, L., & Sullivan, K. (2018). *Trends in Algebra II completion and failure rates for students entering Texas public high schools* (REL 2018–289). U.S. Department of Education, Institute of Education Sciences, National Center for Education Evaluation and Regional Assistance, Regional Educational Laboratory Southwest. https://ies.ed.gov/ncee/rel/Products/Region/southwest/Publication/90140

Wang, L., Li, J., Tan, L., & Lee, L. (2017). Contextualizing teacher efficacy in a high-performing system: A research agenda. *British Journal of Educational Studies, 65*(3), 385–403. http://dx.doi.org/10.1080/00071005.2016.1277016

Wright, A. (2021, Jun 07). *Pandemic prompts some states to pass struggling third graders.* TCA Regional News. https://www.pewtrusts.org/en/research-and-analysis/blogs/stateline/2021/06/07/pandemic-prompts-some-states-to-pass-struggling-third-graders

CHAPTER 6

NARCISSISTIC OR OVERWHELMED?

Divergent Pathways to Academic Entitlement

Elizabeth J. Pope
University of Arizona

Monica K. Erbacher
Independent Scholar

Lauren Pierce
Northern State University

ABSTRACT

Academic entitlement (AE) is expecting favorable academic outcomes regardless of performance. This study tests relationships between AE, narcissism, self-esteem, self-efficacy, and self-compassion to identify pathways for reducing AE. Results revealed two divergent pathways to AE, narcissism and over identifying with negative emotions (OI). OI, holding onto negative emotions, is the opposite of mindfulness, further supporting AE as a maladaptive coping response. Mindfulness, a component of self-compassion, should be explored in interventions reducing AE.

Curriculum and Teaching Dialogue,
Volume 25, Numbers 1 & 2, pp. 263–281
Copyright © 2023 by Information Age Publishing
www.infoagepub.com
All rights of reproduction in any form reserved.

Academic entitlement (AE) is the perception that one deserves favorable academic outcomes regardless of performance. AE is a pervasive problem related to undergraduate cheating (Stiles et al., 2017) and noncompliance (Kopp & Finney, 2013). Previous claims have been made that AE may be the result of low self-esteem or connected to narcissism (Baer, 2011; Brummelman et al., 2016; Chowning & Campbell, 2009; Greenberger et al., 2008; Stronge et al., 2016). The purpose of this study was to further explore the relationships of self-esteem and narcissism as underlying characteristics leading to AE and to include self-efficacy as a possible contributing characteristic of AE. Relationships between AE and self-esteem, narcissism, and self-efficacy may lead to interventions addressing self-efficacy and self-compassion to mitigate AE.

Today's undergraduate students bring widely "different attitudes, expectations, preparation, strengths, and shortcomings into the college classroom" (Mazer & Hess, 2016, p. 356). Behavioral differences identified in the literature leading to uncivil behaviors such as engaging with technology, materials, or conversations unrelated to coursework during class or interactions with instructors that are characterized as disrespectful or demanding meet the definition of academic entitlement (Chowning & Campbell, 2009). Research has shown that AE is pervasive among undergraduate students and can lead to problematic behaviors such as cheating (Stiles et al., 2017) and noncompliance with academic standards or expectations of behavior (Kopp & Finney, 2013). These negative behaviors can have deleterious consequences for students and can cause distress among teaching faculty. For example, noncompliant behaviors such as cheating in the form of plagiarism can create additional meetings for teaching faculty that require them to demonstrate a burden of proof and place students under intense disciplinary action. These types of stressful situations can contribute to increased feelings of strain and burnout in teaching faculty (Jiang et al., 2017).

Underlying Characteristics and Pathways to Academic Entitlement

Prior studies have examined the relationship between behaviors associated with AE to identify underlying characteristics that may contribute to AE. Individual characteristics among learners such as self-esteem, narcissism, and gender have produced mixed results in relationship to AE. Baer (2011) found that students who had high levels of self-esteem were more likely to exhibit behaviors linked to AE. Previous research has shown links between increased levels of narcissism and behaviors associated with AE

(Chowning & Campbell, 2009; Greenberger et al., 2008; Whatley et al., 2019); however, results have also indicated that narcissism is not the only characteristic leading to AE.

The relationship between self-esteem and narcissism is somewhat inconclusive and complex (Bosson et al., 2008; Stronge et al., 2016). Results from some studies indicate that those who show narcissistic personality traits have a high level of self-esteem (Brummelman et al., 2016). Other studies have shown the opposite and propose that narcissism is related to low self-esteem (Bosson et al., 2008; Kohut, 1966). Further exploration of the relationships between AE and self-esteem, narcissism, and other potential contributing characteristics is needed to identify clear pathways leading to AE.

Identifying pathways to AE is one way that researchers can begin to think about potential interventions to reduce AE and improve outcomes for students and faculty. Previous research suggests that it is essential to identify pathways to academic entitlement to effectively design interventions (Sohr-Preston & Boswell, 2015). Specifically identifying pathways that result in entitlement and subsequently using these pathways to design interventions that address students' lack of ability to cope with failure in a way that does not threaten their self-efficacy or self-esteem could provide students with healthier and more productive strategies. The use of pathway-based interventions may reinforce student agency by allowing students to take an active role in their learning rather than relying on entitled behaviors to gain their desired outcomes.

CURRENT STUDY

This study was designed to provide additional clarity around the relationship between narcissism and self-esteem as they relate to AE. To further explore underlying characteristics of AE, measures of self-efficacy and self-compassion were included. Specifically, this study was designed to answer the following research questions:

1. What is the relationship between AE, narcissism, self-esteem, self-efficacy, and self-compassion?
2. Which relationships show pathways with potential for reducing AE?

To provide further rationale for the use of these specific characteristics as they relate to AE, definitions and related literature on self-esteem, self-efficacy, and self-compassion are provided in the following sections.

Self-Esteem

Self-esteem is defined in the literature as the evaluation of one's abilities, qualities, and characteristics as good or bad (Baumeister et al., 2003; Leary, 1999; Levine & Munsch, 2014). For this study, using the Rosenberg Self-Esteem Scale (RSE), self-esteem was defined as a global evaluation of one's own self-worth (Rosenberg, 1965). In academic settings, researchers initially thought that high self-esteem in students led to improved academic outcomes; however, further research has indicated that self-esteem is likely a product of academic achievement (Baumeister et al., 2003). For students who may not be achieving in ways they expect, behaviors related to AE could potentially be an attempt to protect self-esteem in academic settings (Kernis et al., 2008; Neff et al., 2005). Given the inconclusive relationship between self-esteem and narcissism and AE in prior research, including self-esteem as a potential pathway to AE was necessary.

Self-Efficacy

Self-efficacy is defined as one's belief that they will or will not be successful at a given task (Bandura, 1977). The more successful experiences one has, the greater the sense of efficacy in that area and, potentially, the higher one's sense of self-esteem. A mastery experience occurs when a learner attempts a new or challenging task and is successful. By definition, mastery experiences place a great deal of agency in the hands of the learner. It may take a learner multiple attempts before they master a new skill, making it likely they will encounter failure along the way. In the case of AE, episodes of failure can cause increased stress, leading to entitled behaviors (Chowning & Campbell, 2009). Rather than continue with the struggle of learning, academically entitled students resort to less-than-desirable behaviors that will hopefully yield their desired outcome of a perceived good grade (Chowning & Campbell, 2009). While self-efficacy is the belief in one's ability to be successful in a specific domain (Bandura, 2002), general self-efficacy refers to a tendency to view oneself as capable in a variety of situations. Increased general self-efficacy should result in decreased AE, because individuals with high self-efficacy tend to set high goals, persist at tasks, and attribute failure to their own efforts or lack thereof (Devonport & Lane, 2006). If general self-efficacy hinders academic entitlement, accurate understanding and measurement may offer insights for reducing academic entitlement. Thus, a measure of general self-efficacy was also included in the study design.

Self-Compassion

Using Neff's (2003) model of self-compassion as a framework for learners to cope with failure in a positive way may be the key to helping students who exhibit AE. Self-compassion is defined as "being open to and moved by one's own suffering, experiencing feelings of caring and kindness toward oneself, taking an understanding, nonjudgmental attitude toward one's inadequacies and failures, and recognizing that one's own experience is part of the common human experience" (Neff, 2003, p. 224). Self-compassion is often associated with one's psychological well-being and fosters emotional resilience (Neff, 2009). Neff (2003) proposed that there are three components of self-compassion: self-kindness, common humanity, and mindfulness. Self-kindness is described as treating oneself with care instead of harsh self-judgment (Neff, 2003). Common humanity is defined as recognizing that imperfection is a common and human shared experience rather than feeling isolated by one's failures (Neff, 2003). Neff (2003) defined mindfulness as it relates to self-compassion, as viewing one's experience in a balanced perspective instead of exaggerating the dramatic storyline of suffering.

Taken together, we designed this study to further examine the relationships of narcissism, self-esteem, self-efficacy, and self-compassion to AE. Understanding these relationships will provide a more refined model of potential pathways leading to AE and inform interventions designed to reduce AE.

METHODS

Participants

In fall of 2018, 140 students across one general education and one social science course at a public, southwestern university anonymously completed an online survey designed to take one hour or less. Both courses included undergraduate general education courses and most students were either in their first or second year at the university. The average age of participants was 19.95 years ($SD = 2.65$). Detailed demographic information for participants is presented in Table 6.1. Students in the two cooperating courses had the option to participate in various research studies of their choosing or to complete an alternative assignment as a research engagement component of the course (5% of their final grade in each class). Participants received partial credit towards the research engagement component. All procedures were approved by the institution's IRB, including the determination that the minor credit towards the final grade was not considered coercive.

Table 6.1

Demographics of Participants

Descriptor	n	%
Gender		
Female	96	71.11
Male	38	28.14
Non-binary	1	0.74
Total	135	99.99
Race/ethnicity		
White	70	51.85
Latinx	41	30.37
Black	11	8.14
Asian	9	6.67
Native American	1	.74
Prefer not to respond	3	2.22
Total	135	99.99

Note. Participants were on average 19.95 years old ($SD = 2.65$)

Reading speed greatly varied by participant. Participants who spent less than 10 minutes to complete the entire survey and who demonstrated any evidence of patterned responding (i.e., choosing 4 = *Agree* for all items on one page of the survey) were removed from all data analyses for satisficing (Barge & Gehlbach, 2012; Hamby & Taylor, 2016), leaving $n = 135$.

Materials and Measures

Participants completed a variety of attitudinal, behavioral, and demographic self-report measures. Of interest in this study were five measures: the Academic Entitlement Questionnaire (AEQ; Kopp et al., 2011), the Rosenberg Self-Esteem scale (RSE; Rosenberg, 1965), the shortened 16-item version of the Narcissistic Personality Inventory (NPI; Ames et al., 2006), the General Self-Efficacy Scale (GSE; Chen et al., 2001), and the Self-Compassion Scale (SCS; Neff, 2003). The SCS was developed to have 6 subscales measuring the 6 poles of 3 continuums which include: self-kindness versus self-judgment, common humanity versus isolation, and mindfulness versus over identification with emotion. All other scales were developed to be unidimensional. Only the RSE contained reverse-scored items (half of the items). Item responses on appropriate items of the RSE were reverse scored so that higher RSE scores indicated higher self-esteem. For all other scales and subscales, higher scores indicated more of that construct.

The study takes a two-step approach to build a structural equation model (SEM) that examines pathways to academic entitlement through the aforementioned factors. While the Academic Entitlement Questionnaire (AEQ), Rosenberg Self-Esteem scale (RSE), Narcissistic Personality Inventory (NPI), and General Self-Efficacy Scale (GSE) are all considered unidimensional, exploratory factor analysis (EFA) and confirmatory factor analysis (CFA) were done on each scale to examine the underlying factor structure prior to application in the structural equation model and as a data reduction technique to determine the strongest relationships within each factor. Table 6.2 illustrates the survey measures of interest resulting from the EFA and CFA two-step approach and Table 6.3 illustrates the factor model fit by measure prior to determining the final structure of the SEM.

Table 6.2

Survey Measures of Interest

Measure	Example item	Response scale anchors
Academic entitlement (AEQ; Kopp et al., 2011)	If I don't do well on a test, the professor should make tests easier or curve grades.	1 = *strongly disagree* 7 = *strongly agree*
Self-esteem (RSE; Rosenberg, 1965)	On the whole, I am satisfied with myself.	1 = *strongly disagree* 4 = *strongly agree*
Narcissism (NPI; Ames et al., 2006)	Pick the statement that best describes you:	1 = *I think I am a special person.* 0 = *I am no better or no worse than most people.*
General self-efficacy (GSE; Chen et al., 2001)	I will be able to achieve most of the goals I have set for myself.	1 = *strongly disagree* 5 = *strongly agree*
Self-compassion scale (SCS; Neff, 2003)		
Self-judgment (SCS-SJ)	When I see aspects of myself that I don't like, I get down on myself	1 = *Almost never* 5 = *Almost always*

Table 6.3

Factor Model Fit by Measure

Measure and model (*N* items)	χ^2(df)	*p*	TLI CFI	RMSEA	SRMR	ev > 1adj. or |r| > .100	Model comparison χ^2(df), *p*
			AEQ (8)				
EFA						1	
1-factor	44.396(20)	.001	.910	.098	.061		
2-factorH	28.834(13)	.007	.910	.099	.043		15.562(7), .029
3-factorH	10.857(7)	.145	.959	.068	.025		17.977(6), .006
CFA							
1-factor	45.889(20)	.001	.934	.098	.049	2	
			RSE (10)				
EFA						2	
1-factor	154.144(35)	<.001	.765	.163	.098		
2-factor	42.062(26)	.024	.957	.072	.035		112.080(9), <.001
3-factor	16.912(18)	.529	1.004	.000	.023		25.150(8), .001
CFA							
1-factor	160.796(35)	<.001	.816	.163	.082	11	
2-factor	104.656(34)	<.001	.897	.124	.064	9	56.139(1), <.001
SE, Method	63.202(30)	<.001	.951	.091	.048	4	41.455(4), <.001
			GSE (8)				
EFA						1	
1-factor	63.177(20)	<.001	.920	.130	.051		
2-factorH	28.979(13)	.007	.954	.099	.025		34.198(7), <.001
3-factorH	10.547(7)	.160	.981	.066	.016		18.432(6), .005
CFA							
1-factor	63.121(20)	<.001	.945	.126	.040	1	

(Table continued on next page)

Table 6.3 (Continued)

Factor Model Fit by Measure

Measure and model (N items)	χ^2(df)	p	TLI			ev > 1adj. or $|r| >$ .100	Model comparison χ^2(df), p
			CFI	RMSEA	SRMR		
NPI (12)							
EFA						1	
1-factor	87.468(44)	<.001	.762	.089	.082		
2-factorL	48.612(34)	.050	.896	.050	.055		38.856(10), <.001
3-factor	29.241(25)	.254	.959	.041	.042		19.371(9), .022
CFA							
1-factor [a]	80.535(44)	.001	.902	.079	.120	--	
1-factor [a], with 1 error	47.045(43)	.310	.989	.026	.094	--	22.558(1), <.001
SCS (26)							
EFA						3	
1-factor	923.787(299)	<.001	.493	.136	.137		
2-factor	623.381(274)	<.001	.688	.108	.082		300.410(25), <.001
3-factor	492.181(250)	<.001	.762	.095	.062		131.200(24), <.001
4-factor	405.016(227)	<.001	.806	.087	.051		87.165(23), <.001
5-factor	345.477(205)	<.001	.829	.083	.044		59.539(22), <.001
6-factor	293.358(184)	<.001	.851	.078	.039		52.119(21), <.001
7-factor	251.590(164)	<.001	.865	.075	.034		41.768(20), .003
8-factorH	194.692(145)	.004	.913	.064	.029		56.898(19), <.001
CFA							
6-factor	570.483(284)	<.001	.809	.087	.079	79	
6-factor, 2 super factors	589.724(292)	<.001	.802	.088	.089	95	19.241(8), .014
super factors							

(Table continued on next page)

Table 6.3 (Continued)

Factor Model Fit by Measure

Measure and model (N items)	χ^2(df)	p	TLI CFI	RMSEA	SRMR	ev > 1adj. or |r| > .100	Model comparison χ^2(df), p
			SCS – Negative Subscales (SJ, IS, OI; 13 items)				
CFA							
3-factor	123.099(62)	<.001	.915	.086	.061	11	
3-factor, 1 super factor	123.099(62)	<.001	.915	.086	.061	11	Equivalent (cannot test)

Note. TLI = Tucker-Lewis index; CLI = comparitive fit index; RMSA = root-mean-square error of approximation SRMR = standardized-root-mean residual.

HSolution included one or more Heywood cases. Guidelines from Hu and Bentler (1999) were used to evaluate model fit. Number of eigenvalues > adjusted cut-offs from parallel analysis given in EFA rows. Number of \|correlation residuals\| > 0.100 given for CFA solutions.

[a] Satorra-Bentler scaled test statistics and WLSMV used. Only two items loaded on the second factor. Correlated errors were a better solution.

AEQ,[1] GSE,[2] and NPI[3] responses were unidimensional. Four NPI items were removed for trivial loadings in all models, and two remaining NPI items were permitted correlated residuals due to the fact that factor structure is not of primary interest in relation to the hypotheses of this study. The unidimensional measure of narcissism allows for an understanding of the relationship between general narcissism and self-esteem. For this reason, a two-factor model was tested for RSE (Hunter & Gerbing, 1979). RSE items loaded on one self-esteem factor, with reverse-scored items cross-loaded on one method factor as shown in Table 6.3. The cross-loading onto the method factor is likely attributed to the variance of the reverse-coded items. RSE items were uncorrelated with self-esteem items. Of the six SCS factors, self-judgment (SJ), isolation (IS), and over identification with emotion (OI) were retained for hypothesized relationships with AE. To reduce additional models, only the three anti-self-compassion factors previously referenced were kept after running a separate 3-factor model with just these subscales due to hypothesized positive relationships to AE.

Structural Model

Next, a structural equation model with 8 factors (AEQ; GSE; RSE-self-esteem; RSE-method factor; NPI; and the SJ, IS, and OI subscales from

Narcissistic or Overwhelmed? 273

the SCS measure) was fit to the data using lavaan and WLSMV estimation, given the mix of binary and Likert scale responses. Item loadings and residual variances were fixed to the values obtained in the independent factor models and thus were not estimated (Steiger, 2002). Fifteen factor correlations and six regression weights for factors were freely estimated. Factor variances were fixed to one. Correlations were included between the GSE, self-esteem, NPI, and three anti-self-compassion factors. The AEQ factor was regressed on these six factors. Regression coefficients that were not statistically significant ($\alpha = .05$) and not practically significant ($sr2 > .02$) were fixed at 0. Final correlations, regression coefficients, and fit statistics from this structural equation model are presented in Table 6.4.

Table 6.4

Factor Correlations and Regression Weights from the 8-Factor SEM

			Factor Correlations			
Factor	RSE	GSE	NPI	SCS-SJ	SCS-IS	SCS-OI
RSE-Method	-- [a]	-- [a]	-- [a]	-- [a]	-- [a]	-- [a]
RSE	1.000					
GSE	0.690	1.000				
NPI	0.243	0.195	1.000			
SCS-SJ	-0.574	-0.065	-0.136	1.000		
SCS-IS	-0.462	-0.258	-0.225	0.793	1.000	
SCS-OI	-0.427	-0.187	-0.191	0.740	0.679	1.000

			Factor Regressions			
AEQ ~	β	B	z	p	CI	sr^2
RSE	-- [a]	-- [a]				-- a
GSE	-- [a]	-- [a]				-- a
NPI	0.218	0.226	1.933	.053	-0.003, 0.455	.048
SCS-SJ	-- [a]	-- [a]				-- a
SCS-IS	-- [a]	-- [a]				-- a
SCS-OI	0.207	0.215	2.182	.029	0.022, 0.409	.043

Note. RSE = Rosenberg Self-Esteem scale; GSE = General Self-Efficacy scale; NPI = Narcissistic Personality Inventory; SCS-SJ = Self-Compassion Scale - Self Judgement; SCS-IS = Self-Compassion Scale- Isoloation; SCS-OI = Self-Compassion Scale - Over identification with emotion; AEQ = Academic Entitlement Scale.

Model Fit: cSB2(1258) = 1347.391, p = .040, CFI = .920, RMSEA = .023, SRMR = .104. Correlation residuals unavailable for WLSMV estimation.

[a] -- = fixed to 0.

Only two constructs with both statistical and practical significance predicted academic entitlement: narcissism ($sr2 = .048$) and over identification with emotion ($sr2 = .043$), the opposite of mindfulness. Figure 6.1 shows the final model with corresponding correlations among predictors with statistically ($p < .05$) and practically significant regression paths.

Figure 6.1

Pathways to Academic Entitlement

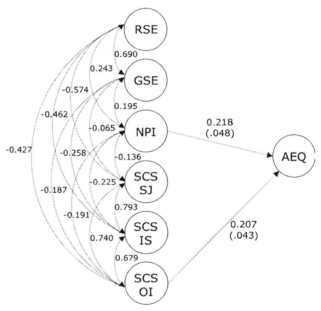

Note. Final SEM containing all correlations among predictors with statistically ($p < .05$) and practically ($sr^2 > .02$) significant regression paths. Parameters provided are correlations and raw regression weights (with variance uniquely explained or semipartial r^2 noted in parentheses).

Overview of Results

When considered holistically, results indicate that self-esteem and AE are not related as suggested in previous research and would not be an effective intervention pathway (Baer, 2011; Chowning & Campbell, 2009). Additionally, no relationship between self-efficacy and AE was found in the current model, suggesting self-efficacy interventions may not be effective in the context of AE.

The model does suggest two pathways to AE that may be helpful to understanding plausible and applied interventions. A positive relationship exists between narcissism and AE ($sr2 = .048$) and over identification with emotion ($sr2 = .043$), the opposite of mindfulness. The statistical and practical significance of these pathways indicate a potential area for future meaningful interventions.

DISCUSSION

Self-Esteem, Self-Efficacy, and Academic Entitlement

The lack of relationship between self-esteem and AE could be attributed to the fact that the model used for data analysis was designed to separate out unique effects contributing to AE. It is plausible that the portions of global self-esteem that relate to AE overlapped with characteristics from other measures used in this study. If the part of self-esteem related to AE overlaps with the narcissism measure, then the relationship could be attributed to narcissism rather than self-esteem which would correspond with previous studies' results examining narcissism, self-esteem, and AE (Baer, 2011; Brummelman et al., 2016; Chowning & Campbell, 2009; Greenberger et al., 2008; Stronge et al., 2016; Whatley et al., 2019). The lack of relationship between self-efficacy and AE could be because a general self-efficacy measure was used rather than examining self-efficacy as a context-specific construct within an academic context or in relation to a student's perceived most difficult or easiest course. Using a measure of self-efficacy that is tied to challenging academic situations or general academic beliefs may yield additional useful information as to whether there is or is not a relationship between self-efficacy and AE.

Two Pathways to Academic Entitlement

Results did provide support for two possible pathways to AE. The first pathway is similar to results from previous studies where students who scored high on the NPI (Chowning & Campbell, 2009; Greenberger et al., 2008; Whatley et al., 2019) also scored high in AE. Students in this sample who scored higher on the NPI were more likely to endorse items such as "I think I am a special person" and "I am more capable than other people." If these students view themselves as superior to their classmates, it is likely that they also believe that they are more deserving of good grades and special treatment from faculty.

The other pathway leading to AE was among students who scored high on the measure of self-compassion, specifically related to over-identifying with negative emotions. Students who are more likely to over identify with negative emotions may ruminate on negative emotions associated with perceived failure creating a sense of self-doubt and questioning their place in the college or university community. Both groups of students may feel as though their place within the higher education community is somewhat fragile. As pressures have continued to mount for students through increased tuition, increasingly competitive scholarships and financial aid, and increased performance expectations, maintaining a sense of belongingness and making sure their place in the community is secure has become a central concern for students (Kuh et al., 2006; Twenge, 2017). When faced with information and experiences that students view as a threat to their belongingness, the need to defend their position within the academic community increases. Research has shown that the response of individuals who possess high levels of narcissism when presented with information or feedback that they view as threatening or contradictory to their grandiose views of themselves is often anger (Bushman & Baumeister, 1998). Students who experience anger related to criticism and who are high in AE may resort to confrontational and hostile behaviors when experiencing struggle or failure (Chowning & Campbell, 2009; Kopp & Finney, 2013; Stiles et al., 2017).

Students who score high on the NPI may be more likely to use aggressive behaviors to refute the information they see as incorrect and reaffirm their place within the academic environment. Students who score high on the measure associated with over-identifying with negative emotions may be more likely to exhibit more covert or internalized behaviors to solidify their place within the academic environment when faced with failure. Results also support a positive relationship between over identifying with negative emotions and self-judgment.

Which Relationships Identify Pathways With Potential for Reducing AE?

In consideration of the second research question, the two pathways leading to AE provide potential avenues for intervening and decreasing the presence of AE. Helping students develop self-compassion (Neff, 2003) with particular emphasis on developing mindfulness practices may prove effective as an intervention for reducing AE among students on either pathway leading to AE. Students who tend to over identify with negative emotions may turn to negative self-judgment as a coping mechanism when experiencing failure. Practices aligned with self-compassion may serve as a useful tool to help reframe failure from negative self-judgment to healthier attributions supporting a mastery orientation. Neuroscience research has shown that engaging in self-criticism triggers the fight or flight response in the brain and causes cortisol levels to increase. Engaging in self-compassion triggers the hormones associated with belongingness, connectedness, and love such as oxytocin (Brackett, 2019). Replacing self-criticism with compassionate self-talk is one way to express self-compassion when dealing with undesirable outcomes. Compassionate self-talk could potentially help students move from the fight or flight response of engaging in behaviors of AE to a more mindful and more productive response. Using ERP and fMRIs, Moser et al. (2017) found that using compassionate self-talk in the third person allows one to regulate their emotions rather than having to exert cognitive control. By using the third person perspective it often becomes easier to express ideas of compassion as many students are well versed in expressing compassion for others. By making themself the "other" using third person language, compassionate self-talk becomes much less effortful and could potentially allow the student to regulate their emotions in a more positive way, as opposed to engaging in self-judgment or behaviors associated with AE.

Another suggestion to decrease AE worth exploring is to incorporate low stakes opportunities for students, allowing them to make mistakes or experience failure as a part of the learning process without jeopardizing outcomes in their higher education careers. Incorporating low stakes opportunities for feedback and assessment of student learning may help reaffirm student beliefs that they belong in the institution and assist in reframing mistakes as a part of the learning process rather than a signal that they do not belong in higher education classrooms.

LIMITATIONS AND FUTURE RESEARCH

One major limitation of this study is that the measure of self-efficacy used was for general self-efficacy. Bandura (2002) proposed that self-efficacy was much more reliant on context and environment and varied within these contexts. While there may be a global concept of self-efficacy, in practice, levels of self-efficacy vary widely. Using the measure of global self-efficacy in this study did not yield any statistically significant results in relation to AE which could be the result of using a general measure of self-efficacy for the very specific context of the academic classroom. A better match that may have provided a more precise measure of the relationship between AE and self-efficacy would have been utilizing a measure related to self-efficacy within the specific subject area that each participant was reporting on throughout the survey. It seems plausible that low levels of self-efficacy in a specific subject area may lead to over-identifying with negative emotions when faced with failure, given Bandura's (1997) findings that it is

278 E. J. POPE, M. K. ERBACHER, and L. PIERCE

difficult for those with low levels of self-efficacy to perform because they often dwell on potential failure and have more self-doubt. Future research should explore the relationship of AE and self-efficacy in these specific contexts using more precise measures of self-efficacy to determine if self-efficacy truly does impact AE or not.

Another limitation of the present study is the use of self-report measures as the main source of data. Self-report measures are inherently problematic for a variety of reasons including but not limited to social desirability bias, response bias, and the use of rating scales that may not accurately capture each participant's most precise response to each item.

Future research should also be focused on the development and implementation of mindfulness practices such as the third-person self-talk to examine whether these kinds of skills are useful in decreasing behaviors associated with AE. It would also be useful to know whether interventions such as these are equally as effective in decreasing AE for students who are high in over-identifying with negative emotions and those who scored high on the narcissism scale. While this study provided useful insight into these two pathways that result in AE, it is unknown whether similar interventions would be effective or if differing interventions would be necessary.

REFERENCES

Ames, D. R., Rose, P., & Anderson C.P. (2006). The NPI-16 as a short measure of narcissism. Journal of Research in Personality, 40(4), 440-450. https://doi.org/10.1016/j-jrp.2005.03.002

Baer, J. C. (2011). Students' distress over grades: Entitlement or a coping response? *Journal of Social Work Education*, 47(3), 565–577. https://doi.org/10.5175/JSWE.2011.200900127

Bandura, A. (1977). Self-efficacy: Toward a unifying theory of behavioral change. *Psychological Review, 84*(2), 191–215. https://doi.org/10.1037/0033-295X.84.2.191

Bandura, A. (1997). *Self-efficacy: The exercise of control*. W.H. Freeman and Company.

Bandura, A. (2002). Social cognitive theory in cultural context. *Applied Psychology: An International Review, 51*, 269–290. https://doi.org/10.1111/1464-0597.00092

Barge, S., & Gehlbach, H. (2012). Using the theory of satisficing to evaluate the quality of survey data. *Research in Higher Education, 53*(2), 182–200. https://doi.org/10.1007/s11162-011-9251-2

Baumeister, R. F., Campbell, J. D., Krueger, J. I., & Vohs, K. D. (2003). Does high self-esteem cause better performance, interpersonal success, happiness, or healthier life styles? *Psychological Science in the Public Interest, 4*(1), 1–44. https://doi.org/10.1111/1529-1006.01431

Bosson, J. K., Lakey, C. E., Campbell, W. K., Zeigler-Hill, V., Jordan, C. H., & Kernis, M. H. (2008). Untangling the links between narcissism and self-esteem: A theoretical and empirical review. *Social and Personality Psychology Compass, 2*, 1415–1439. https://doi.org/10.1111/j.1751-9004.2008.00089.x

Brackett, M. (2019). *Permission to feel: Unlocking the power of emotions to help our kids, ourselves, and our society thrive*. Celadon Books.

Brummelman, E., Thomaes, S., & Sedikides, C. (2016). Separating narcissism from self-esteem. *Current Directions in Psychological Science, 25*(1), 8–13. https://doi.org/10.1177/0963721415619737

Bushman, B.J. & Baumeister, R.F. (1998). Threatened egotism, narcissism, self-esteem, and direct and displaced aggression: Does self-love or self-hate lead to violence? *Journal of Personality and Social Psychology, 75*(1), 219–229. https://doi.org/10.1037/0022-3514.75.1.219

Chen, G., Gully, S. M., & Eden, D. (2001). Validation of a new general self-efficacy scale. *Organizational Research Methods, 4*(1), 62–83. https://doi.org/10.1177/109442810141004

Chowning, K., & Campbell, N. J. (2009). Development and validation of a measure of academic entitlement: Individual differences in students' externalized responsibility and entitled expectations. *Journal of Educational Psychology, 101*(4), 982–997. https://doi.org/10.1037/a0016351

Devonport, T. J., & Lane, A. M. (2006). Relationships between self-efficacy, coping, and student retention. *Social Behavior and Personality, 34*, 127–138. https://doi.org/10.2224/sbp.2006.34.2.127

Greenberger, E., Lessard, J., Chen, C., & Farruggia, S. P. (2008). Self-entitled college students: Contributions of personality, parenting, and motivational factors. *Journal of Youth and Adolescence, 37*(10), 1193–1204. https://doi.org/10.1007/s10964-008-9284-9

Hamby, T., & Taylor, W. (2016). Survey satisficing inflates reliability and validity measures: An experimental comparison of college and amazon mechanical turk samples. *Educational and Psychological Measurement, 76*(6), 912–932. https://doi.org/10.1177/0013164415627349

Hu, L., & Bentler, P. M. (1999). Cutoff criteria for fit indexes in covariance structure analysis: Conventional criteria versus new alternatives. *Structural Equation Modeling, 6*(1), 1–55. https://doi.org/10.1080/10705519909540118

Hunter, J. E., & Gerbing, D. W. (1979). *Unidimensional measurement and confirmatory factor analysis* (Occasional Paper No. 20). Institute for Research on Teaching, Michigan State University. https://edwp.educ.msu.edu/research/wp-content/uploads/sites/10/2020/11/op020.pdf

Jiang, L., Tripp, T. M., & Hong, P. Y. (2017). College instruction is not so stress free after all: A qualitative and quantitative study of academic entitlement, uncivil behaviors, and instructor strain and burnout. *Stress and Health, 33*(5), 578–589. https://doi.org/10.1002/smi.2742

Kernis, M. H., Lakey, C. E., & Heppner, W.L. (2008). Secure versus fragile high self-esteem as a predictor of verbal defensiveness: Converging finding across three different markers. *Journal of Personality, 76*(3), 477–512. https://doi.org/10.1111/j.1467-6494.2008.00493.x

Kohut, H. (1966). Forms and transformations of narcissism. *Journal of the American Psychoanalytic Association, 14*(2), 243–272. https://doi.org/10.1177/000306516601400201

Kopp, J. P., & Finney, S. J. (2013). Linking academic entitlement and student incivility using latent means modeling. *The Journal of Experimental Education*, *81*(3), 322–336. https://doi.org/10.1080/00220973.2012.727887

Kopp, J. P., Zinn, T. E., Finney, S. J., & Jurich, D. P. (2011). The development and evaluation of the academic entitlement questionnaire. *Measurement and Evaluation in Counseling and Development*, *44*(2), 105–129. https://doi.org/10.1177/0748175611400292

Kuh, G. D., Kinzie, J., Buckley, J. A., Bridges, B. K., & Hayek, J. C. (2006). *What matters to student success: A review of the literature*. National Postsecondary Cooperative. https://nces.ed.gov/npec/pdf/kuh_team_report.pdf

Leary, M. (1999). Making sense of self-esteem. *Current Directions in Psychological Science*, *8*, 32–35. https://doi.org/10.1111/1467-8721.00008

Levine, L. E. & Munsch, J. (2014). *Child development: an active learning approach*. SAGE.

Mazer, J. P., & Hess, J. A. (2016). Forum: Instructional communication and millennial students. *Communication Education*, *65*(3), 356–376. https://doi.org/10.1080/03634523.2016.1173715

Moser, J.S., Dougherty, A., Mattson, W.I., Katz, B., Moran, T.P., Guevarra, D., Shablack, H., Ayduk, O., Jonides, J., Berman, M.G., & Kross, E. (2017). Third-person self-talk facilitates emotion regulation without engaging cognitive control: Converging evidence from ERP and fMRI. *Sci Rep 7*, 4519. https://doi.org/10.1038/s41598-017-04047-3

Neff, K. D. (2003). The development and validation of a scale to measure self-compassion. *Self and Identity*, *2*(3), 223–250. https://doi.org/10.1080/15298860309027

Neff, K. D., Hsieh, Y., & Dejitterat, K. (2005). Self-compassion, achievement goals, and coping with academic failure. *Self and Identity*, *4*(3), 263–287. https://doi.org/10.1080/13576500444000317

Neff, K. D. (2009). The role of self-compassion in development: A healthier way to relate to oneself. *Human Development*, *52*(4), 211. https://doi.org/10.1159/000215071

Rosenberg, M. (1965). *Society and the adolescent self-image*. Princeton University Press.

Sohr-Preston, S., & Boswell, S. S. (2015). Predicting academic entitlement in undergraduates. *International Journal of Teaching and Learning in Higher Education*, *27*(2), 183–193. https://files.eric.ed.gov/fulltext/EJ1082877.pdf

Steiger, J. H. (2002). When constraints interact: A caution about reference variables, identification constraints, and scale dependencies in structural equation modeling. *Psychological Methods*, *7*(2), 210–227. https://doi.org/10.1037/1082-989X.7.2.210

Stiles, B. L., Pan, M., LaBeff, E. E., & Wong, N. (2017). The role of academic entitlement in college cheating: A comparison between China and the United States. *Research in Higher Education Journal*, *33*, 1–15. https://www.aabri.com/manuscripts/172744.pdf

Stronge, S., Cichoka, A., & Sibley, C. G. (2016). Narcissistic self-esteem or optimal self-esteem? A latent profile analysis of self-esteem and psychological entitlement. *Journal of Research in Personality*, *63*, 102–110. http://dx.doi.org/10.1016/j.jrp.2016.06.016

Twenge, J. M. (2017). *iGen: Why today's super connected kids are growing up less rebellious, more tolerant, less happy- and completely unprepared for adulthood and what that means for the rest of us.* Atria Books.

Watley, M., Wasieleski, D.T., Breneiser, J. E., & Wood, M. M. (2019). Understanding academic entitlement: Gender classification, self-esteem, and covert narcissism. *Educational Research Quarterly, 42*(3), 49–71. https://tinyurl.com/mvjck88y

NOTES

1. 1-factor CFA: $\chi2(20) = 45.889$, $p < .001$, CFI = .934, RMSEA = .098, SRMR = .049, 2 of 28 correlation residuals slightly $> |.10|$, additional factors resulted in Heywood cases.
2. 1-factor CFA: $\chi2(20) = 63.121$, $p < .001$, CFI = .945, RMSEA = .126, SRMR = .040, 1 of 28 correlation residuals slightly $> |.10|$.
3. 1-factor CFA with 1 residual correlation: $\chi2(43) = 47.054$, $p = .310$, CFI = .989, RMSEA = .026, SRMR = .094, no correlation residuals $> |.10|$.

OUTTAKE

THE TENSIONS AND INTENTIONS OF RESEARCHING ONGOING HOLOCAUST EDUCATION LEGISLATION

Rebecca C. Christ
Florida International University

Brandon J. Haas
University of North Georgia

As two researchers interested in Holocaust and genocide education—yet coming from different research backgrounds and philosophical orientations—we approached our scholarship with *intention* and a lot of *tension* about how to move forward productively. We were interested in investigating state legislation, particularly the flurry of it arriving since 2016, about teaching Holocaust and genocide education (and we both worked in states that were discussing or revising legislation). Through conversation, and initial inquiry and review of literature, we decided on the research question: What are the underlying assumption(s)/purpose(s)/power dynamic(s) of such legislation?

OUTTAKE INCIDENT: WHAT HAPPENED?

We "began" our inquiry by reading all the legislation requiring or recommending Holocaust and genocide education that we could find in the

Curriculum and Teaching Dialogue,
Volume 25, Numbers 1 & 2, pp. 283–286
Copyright © 2023 by Information Age Publishing
www.infoagepub.com
All rights of reproduction in any form reserved.

United States, including legislation that had passed and bills that were in process. Our initial document collection included legislation passed within the previous year, which we found interesting and exciting. In some states, proposed bills failed to pass, and we removed them from the list, even if we had read them. Thus, over the few months of initial analysis, we regularly updated our list of legislation, sometimes weekly. These changes led to a constant state of uncertainty about what we would find during each of our meetings.

Because of this ever-changing legislative landscape—and in order to complete the analysis for a potential manuscript—we then narrowed our focus to the 15 states listed at the time on the United States Holocaust Memorial Museum (USHMM) website of states requiring Holocaust education, genocide education, or a combination of the two. In September 2020, these states were: California, Colorado, Connecticut, Delaware, Florida, Illinois, Indiana, Kentucky, Michigan, New Hampshire, New Jersey, New York, Oregon, Rhode Island, and Virginia. We used USHMM's list because USHMM is a leader in Holocaust and genocide education in the United States, where these mandates are being passed and implemented. They maintained a webpage with an up-to-date list of states with legislation, which became the basis of how we located states with these policies.

Unfortunately, the legislative landscape was changing both too fast to move from analysis to writing and too slow to have a clear cut-off point to submit for publication. One criticism we received from our initial submission of the manuscript for publication was that we should have included all legislation passed between September 2020 and January 2022 when we focused on presenting the study and writing the manuscript. Our timeline was also well past our initial goals due to the COVID-19 pandemic consuming much of our emotional and cognitive energy. This situation was further complicated by the illusive nature of policy in some states, such as California and New York. As noted in our previous article (Haas & Christ, 2020), for our analysis of the legislation from California and New York, we utilized "the section of the Education Code that maintains the Holocaust and genocide education requirements of that state ... [because] [t]he original bill could not be located and/or the state's education code ha[d] been updated since the original bill passed" (p. 23). Another reality we had to grapple with included the various forms the legislation took. Some were mandates, some were suggestions, some were directed at particular stakeholders (Haas & Christ, 2020), and the form and format of legislation (as well as how it was tracked) varied between states.

Related to the flurry of legislation, and possibly caused by it, the USHMM changed how their website tracked state legislation about Holocaust and genocide education. What began as a focus on legislation that impacted secondary education moved to general legislation. It also shifted toward putting the responsibility to report new legislation on the states, and the links provided no longer always pointed directly to the legislative materials. A new trend in legislation had also begun in education spheres: anti-critical race theory or "divisive concepts" laws began to pass state legislatures at a dizzying pace. Many of these laws had elements contradicting the legislation related to Holocaust and genocide education or at least raised crucial questions for teacher implementation, which is a topic for our future work.

IMPACT AND RESOLUTION

Because of all the incidents discussed above, we have yet to publish the complete study; at various times, we have had to pause, revamp, and even pivot, and sometimes more than once over the last few years. These impacts and their consequent (potential) resolutions led us to think more deeply about how our scholarship is framed and how it can be advanced. One of our decisive pivots was to write about this experience as this research outtake—so others may also be able to consider and hopefully learn from this experience. Another important pivot is to reframe our work as a policy/ curricular investigation or think piece rather than a traditionally empirical piece, which we hope to publish in the near future.

REFLECTION

The impacts and (potential) resolutions also helped us reflect on what this situation could mean for research in our field. Our predominant reflection revolves mainly around the question (for ourselves and the field at large): How do education researchers conduct policy investigations when those policies are "in the midst"/ever-changing/in flux? We have been thinking about how this means that it is easier to research something that is *done/ finished/enacted* as opposed to *in process/in motion*, which can be counterproductive to our goals of trying to enact change when these types of policies are being proposed (or perhaps this is out of the scope of our "job"/role as educational researchers?—which would be disheartening). As researchers and on a scholarship front, are we forced to be *reactive* instead of *proactive*? In our project overall, we *were* able to write quickly about one state's legislation that was passed (Oregon; see Haas & Christ, 2020). We hope to have had some impact on practice via our writing on that legislation. However, we still could not change the legislation (or the parts of it that may have been concerning to us). We could not leverage a direct counter through our scholarship (if we wanted to do so).

Through our pivots to writing about these incidents as this research out-take and our plan to (hopefully) publish a policy/curricular investigation or think piece, we hope that our scholarship informs education researchers about the difficulties of doing this type of investigation, while not discouraging them from researching because we need to stay on the cutting edge of policies that affect education locally and nationally. We also hope our scholarship reaches teachers in the field, whom the legislation will directly impact, and that our writings help them think through how to navigate the requirements of these bills, as well as form better curricular and pedagogical practices for their students who ultimately are the most affected by the legislation. Especially now, education is a rapidly changing landscape, and we must do our best to interrogate the legislation that impacts education as quickly as possible so we might be better prepared to respond.

REFERENCE

Haas, B. J., & Christ, R. C. (2020). "Relating to instruction in public schools about genocide": An analysis of Oregon's Senate Bill 664. *Oregon Journal of Social Studies, 8*(2), 4–24.

OUTTAKE

GRAPPLING WITH THE EXIT FROM A COMMUNITY OF RESEARCH PARTICIPANTS

Juan Manuel Gerardo
University of Cincinnati

In the research community, everyone talks about access and entry when working with target research populations. I have posed this question to assistant and associate professors: "Well, what about exit?" I have never had a satisfying response. I usually hear "That's a good question, never thought about that!" or "That's such a good question, let's write about it." While I feel validated in my question, I am still waiting to receive a satisfactory response. Admittedly, my positive experience of immersing myself in Spanish-speaking immigrant communities is counterbalanced by my failed "exit" from the families and youth I befriended. So, in the hopes of initiating a thought-provoking conversation—even asynchronously—I pose to you, reader: how do we ethically, personally, and professionally "exit" from a person or group of people who participated in our research?

INTEGRATING MYSELF INTO A LATINO[1] COMMUNITY IN SOUTHERN CALIFORNIA

As a doctoral student, I wanted to intertwine my passion for working with Latino youth and families and my research interest in mathematics

---

Curriculum and Teaching Dialogue,
Volume 25, Numbers 1 & 2, pp. 287–290
Copyright © 2023 by Information Age Publishing
www.infoagepub.com
All rights of reproduction in any form reserved.

education. My search for a Latino community began soon after arriving at Urbana-Champaign. Initially, I was concerned with finding a community, specifically a Spanish-speaking community. Eventually, I found one at a local Catholic Church that provided a Spanish mass. Perfect. I chose this route since it was an approach I used while living in Southern California. While in California, I volunteered as a youth minister and developed friendships with families and youth. My approach to engaging with families and youth extends back to my years as a classroom teacher. I lived in the school's neighborhood and would drop off assignments, pick up completed assignments, lend dictionaries, and conduct parent conferences in my students' homes. I soon developed a way to measure how successfully I gained the trust of parents and youth: being invited over for a *carne asada* (a grilled skirt steak cookout) or invited to a former student's *quinceañera* (coming-of-age birthday for 15-year-old Latinas). When either of these invitations occurred, I knew I had gained enough credibility and trust with families. To this day, I remain in contact with some of these youth and families and have seen them move on to college and begin their professional careers. Furthermore, I have written many letters of recommendation and provided educational and professional career advice.

So, what "exit?" After all, I had befriended some parents and youth; some even became *comp/madres* and even godchildren. As a burgeoning researcher, I knew the measure of success. Having moved to a new state and starting anew in Urbana-Champaign, I felt I knew how to approach gaining entry with a new community of Spanish-speaking immigrants. I could not have predicted that my "exit" would be a failure this time. I did not soften the separation or maintain contact with families and youth as I had during my time in Los Angeles.

INTEGRATING MYSELF INTO A LATINO CATHOLIC COMMUNITY IN URBANA-CHAMPAIGN

When starting graduate school in Urbana-Champaign, I was warned about the challenges of gaining entry to the Spanish-speaking immigrant community. I did not meet the gatekeeper during my first semester since her husband was on sabbatical, but everyone told me about her. She was the de facto leader of the Latino Ministry at the local Catholic parish. It seemed that she was the one who would have to provide the stamp of approval to work with the Latino families of this Catholic parish. At that point, I was not conducting research but seeking to become a part of the Spanish-speaking immigrant community. So to gain entry, I volunteered at this church. I took on the following volunteer roles during Mass: lector, acolyte, greeter, usher, and sometimes all of these roles during the same mass. I was usually there every Sunday for my first two years, except when traveling to conferences or back home during holidays. Through my actions, I wanted to let parishioners know I was fully committed to them. Soon after, not purposefully at first, I became a catechist (a teacher for Sunday school but held on Saturdays) and then organized a performance of the Passion (the crucifixion of Christ) with some of the older youth of the parish.

I engaged in this kind of volunteer work for about two years at the parish. Soon after her return for the second semester of my graduate program, I got to know the gatekeeper. We became friends. She would remind me often about all the previous graduate students who came into the community, obtained their data, and just left. She felt compelled to protect the community and warn graduate student researchers to be ethical when working with Latino families. I realized that I needed to prove that I would not exploit community members and instead contribute to the community. One part of my community contribution was my church volunteering. The second contribution was the mathematics tutoring I did. I tutored countless youth, from elementary to college-aged students. I made numerous home visits and sometimes provided mathematical enrichment activities for children. At the request of the gatekeeper, for three consecutive summers, I led GED mathematics review sessions in Spanish. I wanted to ensure that the gatekeeper would not label me as just another academic who exploits the community and leaves.

I did and did not meet this expectation.

The families and youth I befriended and worked with did not become the focal point of my research. But I successfully recruited some of the youth to participate in an after-school mathematics program I coordinated for three years. The preservice secondary mathematics teachers they worked with ended up being my unit of analysis for my dissertation as I explored how the preservice teachers worked in solidarity and grappled with their own and the youths' mathematical concepts while playing mathematical games and puzzles. But I felt indebted to the parents and youth who—for three years—also participated in the math club, some later becoming members of the leadership team and volunteering at family mathematics community events.

Meanwhile, I met the criteria for gaining the trust of some families. I was, after two years of volunteering, invited for some carne asada and a quinceañera.

A FAILURE TO EXIT

But other life events also happened. I married. We had a child. I accepted my first academic position out of state. And I exited discreetly into the night. I told some families and youth that I was leaving the Urbana-Champaign area but not the parish or community. The "45" presidency was about to begin, and the community was going to be affected by mandates regarding the treatment of immigrants, especially undocumented immigrants. I was not there to support them.

Perhaps it is a flawed personality trait. I tend to communicate less with family and friends over long stretches of time. I lean on the belief that family is not going anywhere and true friends will understand. But this situation was different. These families and youth were not family or longtime friends I could take for granted. I foresaw and hoped for a mini celebration, a show of gratitude for how open the parish was to my presence and how it provided moral support as I worked to earn a PhD. But alas, it did not happen. The least I could have done was to write a letter of thanks in the weekly bulletin to express my gratitude. I would graduate years later, so too late for this idea.

LESSONS LEARNED REGARDING "EXIT"
FROM LATINO COMMUNITIES

The next time, in my new academic position in a different state and city from my first academic position, I will remain in contact with or perhaps befriend Latino families and youth research participants. I plan to be more communicative about the progress of my research and more vocally appreciative of my participants' engagement in my research. Ideally, my future research is (youth) participatory action research where my role as researcher and the role of participants blurs and they have an increased degree of engagement with the research, writing, and conference presentations. In this manner, we work in solidarity to communicate struggles, insight, and possible positive contributions to the community.

So, dear reader, how have you successfully "exited," or am I asking an existential question, and there never truly is an "exit?"

NOTE

1. I use the terminology of Latinx, which takes the political stance that gender is fluid and rejects that in Spanish the plural form privileges the masculine suffix. However, in the context of this manuscript, I use Latino because the families and youth I worked with did not identify themselves as Latinx but as Latino.

OUTTAKE

MAMA SCHOLARSHIP

Tackling the Motherlode

Robyn Thomas Pitts
University of Denver

On Christmas Eve in 2018, I sat in a local coffee shop, grading final exams in two-hour chunks. That fall, I planned lessons for others to facilitate during my upcoming maternity leave. I started a typical day with an early morning faculty meeting, ended it with a night class, and went into labor only a few hours later. Abruptly, I was no longer one foot in and one foot out—no longer maintaining my typical, aggressive work ethic as an early career scholar, but tackling that steep learning curve that faces anyone transitioning into the role of mama. Long, sleepless weeks had passed, and grades were due—an altogether reasonable yet daunting deadline to meet. I had passed the little one off to a grandparent (shout out to that village it takes to raise a child!) and carefully metered out my time, so I could get out of the house, get some grading done, get back before I was needed, and then repeat. That afternoon, stepping one foot back into my professional world felt like an alien activity. I was uncertain how to juggle my way into a new normal with such demanding new responsibilities.

SCHOLAR LIFE

As new researchers in the areas of curriculum and teaching, we watch our academic brands and identities unfurl across our early career years, often

---

Curriculum and Teaching Dialogue,
Volume 25, Numbers 1 & 2, pp. 291–295
Copyright © 2023 by Information Age Publishing
www.infoagepub.com
All rights of reproduction in any form reserved.

answering questions about a research agenda, manuscript pipeline, funding docket, and curriculum vitae of productivity in that delightful currency known as the illustrious "peer-reviewed article." We struggle to stuff myriad professional responsibilities into the small windows of time available to work. We also spend a healthy chunk of time on tasks that one would not readily identify as fitting into the royal triumvirate of research, teaching, and service. Such tasks include faculty governance meetings, mentoring conversations, and crafting a career trajectory. Notably, women in the academy are often subject to issues of workload equity, a phenomenon that scholar KerryAnn O'Meara et al. (2017) have described as a function of inequitable allocations of service, student support, and so-called "institutional housekeeping" (p. 1159). Mentors and coaches are available to help, including *Scholar's Voice* (https://scholarsvoice.org) and the *National Center for Faculty Development and Diversity* (https://www.facultydiversity.org).

MAMA LIFE

Early parenthood is an incredibly physically and emotionally demanding season of life with its ever-expanding roles, new rhythms and routines, and a slew of new identities that come with taking on legal responsibility for another human being (or a few). Sleep-deprived, full of love, and most of the time entirely bewildered, parents of young children are often described as *engaging in a demanding season of life*. This dynamic is universal, a human experience that affects both members of the parenting partnership—and yet, this season is also inevitably more demanding of those who give birth, provide round-the-clock caregiving for young ones, or slowly end up bearing the brunt of what is known as the *mental load*. The mental load is a popular term for describing the invisible labor that women take up to run households and manage children, even in partnerships where tasks are progressively split almost 50–50. The mental load is never static (the only constant is change!) as it slowly shifts across the day-to-day, eventually morphing into something almost unrecognizable across the various seasons of life with young, adolescent, and then adult children—and with aging parents.

LESSONS LEARNED ABOUT THE MAMA SCHOLAR LIFE

Since I chose to have children as I launched my career, it is unsurprising that I draw many parallels between my roles and responsibilities as a scholar and a mama. Here is some advice I received as a new mama scholar:

New Mama Advice: Sleep when the baby sleeps.

New Academic Advice: Develop a writing habit and be consistent. Write every day.

New Mama Advice: Ugh, daycare viruses are the worst—but they will be healthy in elementary!

New Academic Advice: Focus on the parts of your role that bring you joy. Learn to say no.

New Advice for Mama Scholars: Do not fret. Somehow, it all comes together.

This well-meaning advice can be challenging for mama scholars to adopt. Early on, new mamas are attempting to survive the short sleep cycles of their newborns for eight grueling weeks while also recovering from the physical exertion of pregnancy, kin keeping, and childbirth. New scholars are attempting to adjust to the unstructured nature of academic life, carve out space for that which brings them into the academy, and develop an identity as a scholar. No amount of will or force can help when unavoidable clashes between scholarship and motherhood ruin well-laid plans. This breakdown between "the planning" and "the doing" is amplified for early-career mama scholars who are establishing their careers (publish or perish!) while figuring out how to parent (children do not come with instructions!).

Like most academics who learn on the fly, my experience of becoming a mama scholar has been one of "learning by doing." Slowly and by blundering, I learned to tame the tasks that keep my family and academic lives flowing and create space for my ambitious, community-engaged scholarship. However, if we accept this learning curve as typical and something that everyone who has a child goes through, we miss the opportunity to learn from our challenges, reflect on our hard-earned lessons learned, and share them with the world through (you guessed it) a publication! So how does it all come together for mama scholars? Here are three lessons I learned about the motherlode.

The motherlode is a rich source of something, in this case, of mama scholarship. It involves two forms of mental load. The *maternal mental load* is steeped in the routine of the mundane. We wash kids' laundry, label each garment so it is not lost at school, buy bigger shoes, clothes, and sports gear, make meal plans and grocery lists, schedule medical and dental appointments, and make sure to pack those outfits the kids' auntie gave them when we travel to visit friends and family. Engaging in the "thinking about doing" of our scholarly work is a different mental load—an *academic mental load*. It is a family of process-based thinking and organizing tasks that are poorly understood or described and often invisible in the academy. We track our service, non-course teaching and mentoring, and scholarly productivity using tables, charts, and metrics that fuel our dossiers, manuscript pipelines, funding dockets, and annual performance reviews. We develop habits, routines, and boundaries to carve out time for research and writing since these tasks are often essential considerations in our long-term career success but have the least built-in accountability.

The motherlode leads mama scholars to be mentally partitioned—not only across but within the professional and personal aspects of our lives. The professional contributions of mama scholars are apportioned to research, scholarship, service, and other professional identities (such as a clinician who sees patients). We often overlook the time and energy it takes to plan and juggle our professional contributions. Our personal contributions are also partitioned—across roles of *doing* (e.g., mother, partner, daughter, sibling, friend) as well as the roles of *thinking* (e.g., household management, kin keeping, caregiving).

After writing a popular text on ensnaring people's attention using social media (Eyal & Hoover, 2014), Nir Eyal (2019) later published *Indistractable: How to Control Your Attention and Choose Your Life*. Attention is undoubtedly the currency of the mama scholar: we will always have more to do than we can do. There will be more interesting conferences than we can afford to attend and more calls for proposals by journals with special volumes and books than we can address. Clarity about priorities, agency to craft one's career, and a strategy for holding boundaries is necessary to become *indistractable* about what matters most. Viewing attention as currency is a powerful strategy for embracing the motherlode.

CONCLUSION

A mama scholar's life is real, robust, unique, demanding, and wonderful. There is always a lot going on and a great deal to do. Yet, we are not merely engaged in the doing. We are also inundated with the need to think about the doing—drawing our signal from the noise, managing cross-project and cross-family timelines and schedules, and ensuring that time reflects our priorities. While I will not attempt to speak for other mama scholars—in all the bold and confusing complexity and intricacy of their unfolding lives—drawing parallels between maternal and academic mental loads has helped me. I have learned that everything counts, including time spent juggling the mental load. Embracing the motherlode has enabled me to make sense of my time, responsibilities, and priorities, and perhaps this view might help others who are engaged in this season of life or who partner professionally or personally with someone who is.

If I had to whittle down this outtake to a single critical reflection, it would be this: As a mama scholar, I exert much effort to pull back from the humdrum of the day-to-day doing to peek at the skyline, the forest, the mountain range in the distance. I pause to think about the doing. I take a beat. Invariably, my focus dives below the clouds again. I am along for the ride.

I dive. I rise again.

REFERENCES

Eyal, N. (2019). *Indistractable: How to control your attention and choose your life*. BenBella Books.

Eyal, N., & Hoover, R. (2014). *Hooked: How to build habit-forming products*. Portfolio.

O'Meara, K., Kuvaeva, A., Nyunt, G., Waugaman, C., & Jackson, R. (2017). Asked more often: Gender differences in faculty workload in research universities and the work interactions that shape them. *American Educational Research Journal, 54*(6), 1154–1186. https://doi.org/10.3102/0002831217716767

OUTTAKE

"EVERYONE IS A MATH PERSON"

How Findings of Positive Math Identity Derailed My Study but Enhanced My Teaching

Stephanie B. Purington
Marist College

I am a math teacher-educator focusing on elementary preservice teachers (PSTs). In my previous life, I provided mathematics professional development to many elementary teachers in my area. I found that most teachers had severe math anxiety, which impacted their confidence in teaching math. As a high school teacher, I knew that my students had often been affected by the math avoidance of their elementary teachers, which was a driving force for me to leave the classroom and pursue my PhD. I wanted to teach elementary education majors before they arrived at the point of interacting with students; I wanted to improve both their content knowledge and their math identities.

On the path to my dissertation, I needed to conduct a pilot study to show proof of concept and research skills. Wanting to tackle the issue of math anxiety in teachers and how it affected students, I planned to study how PSTs thought their math anxiety might impact their teaching and their students. My dissertation would then involve developing an intervention

Curriculum and Teaching Dialogue,
Volume 25, Numbers 1 & 2, pp. 297–299
Copyright © 2023 by Information Age Publishing
www.infoagepub.com
All rights of reproduction in any form reserved.

to reduce math anxiety and educate the PSTs on the negative impact that anxiety could have on future students.

For my sample, I chose a group of students enrolling in an elementary certification program at a large university in New England. I had worked with the prior cohort in their Mathematics Methods course and noted that most students reported having math anxiety, so this cohort seemed like an excellent group to investigate. Previous research has also shown that elementary PSTs have the highest levels of math anxiety among college majors (Hembree, 1990), so I was expecting that at least half of the group would have math anxiety that would rise to the level of concern. During the week of their orientation for the program, I presented my study to the group and asked for volunteers. Twelve of the 13 cohort members agreed to be part of the study.

In the initial interview, the first participant expressed no math anxiety and felt ready to teach math. The same happened with the second participant and then the third. Concerned that I was not getting the expected results, I added some questions to the interview about what had led them to not have math anxiety given its prevalence in society. Still, I was sure the next participant would express math anxiety. I was wrong.

To my surprise, none of the participants indicated having math anxiety. They all reported feeling comfortable teaching math, believed that everyone was a "math person," and that every student could learn math. In fact, they were much more nervous about teaching literacy. I worked with the participants in their Mathematics Methods course the following semester, and they did not show signs of math anxiety.

With those results, the second part of my questioning—how they thought their anxiety would affect their teaching and their students—became moot. Thankfully, I had pivoted quickly to asking questions about what they believed to be the source of their self-efficacy in mathematics. I also conducted further interviews with a few students who had expressed that they used to have math anxiety, to explore more deeply how they came to have more positive math identities. Asking these additional questions allowed me to have findings that went beyond discovering that no one had math anxiety.

I found that all but two participants had taken the same two required math content courses from the same professor during their undergraduate program at the university. These courses are intended to review elementary math concepts while also giving students the opportunity to look at the material from a teacher's perspective. What are common errors and misconceptions? What are multiple strategies for solving a type of problem? What manipulatives or representations might help address different mathematical concepts?

The students credited the professor of these courses with allowing them to reconstruct their mathematical experiences and understandings in a way that made them feel much more confident in their abilities. They worked collaboratively, did a plethora of hands-on activities, and were expected to explain their thinking and reasoning at every step. The professor relentlessly stated that everyone could be a *math person*, and the students began to believe it for themselves. While several of them still had gaps in their mathematical knowledge, they were confident that they could work to fill those gaps before needing to teach those topics.

My pilot study was, in some ways, a total failure, as I no longer had a group of students with math anxiety that I could study. It was too late to try to recruit another group, ascertain their math anxiety, and gain access to their courses—so I had to pivot. In the end, my dissertation focused on math knowledge for teaching, which was a study also motivated through my work with the methods classes.

While my pilot study did not lead where I had intended, it was successful in other ways. I could report that a group of students who said they used to have math anxiety had been given an experience that allowed them to overcome it. This finding gave me hope as someone who planned to teach math content and methods courses to elementary PSTs. I met with the professor who made such a difference to the math identities of my participants, and we talked through his syllabus, methods, and beliefs. As I have started my college teaching journey, I use those resources as inspiration for my courses. I focus on helping my students to build new positive math identities by having them work collaboratively, create concrete and drawn representations, and explain their thinking. Through this process, my students are able to gain stronger conceptual understanding, which gives them more confidence in their readiness to teach math in the future.

While I may have grumbled about how the math professor my participants worked with had derailed my study, I am glad that I was able to meet with him and learn about how he made such an impact on his classes. I hope that I am making the same kind of difference for my students.

REFERENCE

Hembree, R. (1990). The nature, effects, and relief of mathematics anxiety. *Journal for Research in Mathematics Education*, *21*(1), 33–46.

OUTTAKE

THE METACOGNITION OF A READER

An Unexpected Co-Journey Towards Growth and Self-Discovery

Mallori Sage
University of Northern Colorado

In the fall of 2022, I was enrolled in a Social Justice course for my educational doctorate program. This course highlighted many critical topics through interviews, articles, and books. While discussing race and equity we read the book *We Can't Teach What We Don't Know: White Teachers, Multiracial Schools* by Gary Howard. I dutifully prepared myself to read and reflect on the book for the course. I gathered the necessary materials—the book, an orange highlighter, a notebook, a hot-pink flair pen (I am an elementary teacher, after all), and a cup of tea—and found a comfortable spot in my living room to embark on what I assumed would be a straightforward assignment. However, that was far from the case.

I had an unexpected experience while reading Howard's book. I was expecting to deepen my knowledge of white privilege and critical self-awareness. I expected to critically examine my practices, thoughts, and growth in this area. I first went through this internal process of awareness about five years ago while earning my master's degree in urban education. Doing the internal work of reckoning with my biases and privileges and how that impacts my day-to-day life was a life-changing and liberating

---

Curriculum and Teaching Dialogue,
Volume 25, Numbers 1 & 2, pp. 301–303
Copyright © 2023 by Information Age Publishing
www.infoagepub.com
All rights of reproduction in any form reserved.

experience. As a white female educator, I know this journey will be ongoing, as there is no finish line in change and growth. So, I went into the book with what I thought was an open mind and expected to learn some new, useful information and review some that I already knew. I was not expecting to experience someone else's journey through this book.

I purchased this book online from a second-hand bookstore. Therefore, there were signs of wear and tear, including highlighting and notes in the margins from the previous owner. It began as simple highlighted information but changed into handwritten notes in the margins where the individual felt conflicted. The notes started as passive or annoyed with phrases like "ugh" or "I think that is a stretch." These were found in areas that talked about white hegemony in history. The comments then turned to anger when the connection between white domination and protestant exploitation arose. Gary Howard (2006) explained that he was not criticizing the Bible but the way the Bible has been used historically to further white domination. On these pages, the notes stated, "Evangelism as dominance ... ridiculous" and "Are Christians not respectful to women?" A few pages later, when Howard pointed out the criticism Obama faced as the first Black president, the note read, "WOAH. WOAH. WOAH. What about Trump?? Every president gets crap."

At this point, I was completely judging the writer of these notes. I felt indignant that someone was missing the whole point of this book. How could this person be an educator? How could this person not see their privilege? How could this person not understand, or even try to understand, the complexities of race and history? How could this person who appeared to take pride in being Christian not see the need for justice, equity, and restoration? The notes in the margins stopped for a bit. I wondered if the previous owner had given up on the book.

But then, the underlining and the highlighting began again. It centered on quotes about students and connecting with students. Then the notes picked back up and said, "I see this with my students" and "How can I apply this to help my students?" I began to feel bad for judging this individual so harshly. Based on the notes, it appeared they were softening and changing.

Then I hit the section of the book that highlighted empathy. If the previous owner had not highlighted that whole section, I would have myself. I teach empathy to my students, and always use the phrase "walk in someone else's shoes." I use that phrase because that is how empathy was taught to me. But Howard has a more encompassing definition. Howard (2006) says, "Empathy means to feel with" (p. 79). He describes empathy as the ability to let go of ego. It is not the ability to fully understand someone else's experience but to be with them in that experience. This is beautiful and powerful and changes how I will describe empathy in the future.

The Metacognition of a Reader   303

This empathy section hit me because I had not applied it to the book's previous owner. I judged and even felt disgusted at their struggle with what I now realize was probably an inherited narrative of their white, conservative, Christian ideology (I realize these are also assumptions based on the contents of the notes, and I could be wrong about those identities). I also realized I did not have to try too hard to be empathetic because those were the same identities I inherited. These were identities that I had to work hard at deconstructing and reconstructing in a healthier fashion. These are areas I strive to remain conscious of because our process of expanding the arc of humanity is never complete.

The last handwritten note left in the book was in the action section on page 84. In the margin, the previous owner wrote, "What do I need to acknowledge?" Howard (2006) discusses the important "act of acknowledgment" and that "acknowledgment in itself was a source of enlightenment and healing" (p. 84).

That simple yet powerful question was then being asked by not just one but two individuals—the previous owner of the book and myself. I do not know who the previous owner is. I do not know how long ago they wrote those notes. I do know that we went on a journey together. It happened at different times and in different places, but, together, we underwent the critical and continual process of self-discovery and growth. Now, dear reader, I invite you to accompany us on this metacognitive journey. What do you need to acknowledge?

REFERENCE

Howard, G. R. (2006). *We can't teach what we don't know: White teachers, multiracial schools* (2nd ed.). Teachers College Press.

OUTTAKE

IT'S NOT ALWAYS BLACK AND WHITE

Reflections on Research Design, Participant Recruitment, and Data Collection

Ryan B. Warren
Georgia State University

I began working on my dissertation research in early 2022. My goal was to find participants to interview regarding their experiences with changes in the schools and the broader community of South Memphis, Tennessee. South Memphis is a predominantly Black community adjacent to the city's downtown core. Over the past 25 years, residents of South Memphis have faced several public-school closures and the demolition of public housing complexes, drastically changing the landscape. In preparing my research design, it was essential to center the voices of those marginalized community members who have been at the receiving end of policies and practices that have since made their neighborhoods unrecognizable.

When developing a plan for conducting my research, I was inspired by a CBS documentary entitled *Rising Tide: Priced Out in Miami* (Yamaguchi, 2020). This short film investigates the convergence of climate change and gentrification in Miami, Florida. In the film, host Adam Yamaguchi provides various perspectives on the issue by interviewing community members from Miami's Little Haiti community who are experiencing rising rents as their inland homes are becoming attractive to investors as well as the real

---

Curriculum and Teaching Dialogue,
Volume 25, Numbers 1 & 2, pp. 305–307
Copyright © 2023 by Information Age Publishing
www.infoagepub.com
All rights of reproduction in any form reserved.

estate investors who look to *reinvent* the community and attract wealthier residents. The documentary showcases a striking contrast between the vision for a new community that markets *innovation* and *arts* by investors compared to the reality of the culture and history of residents that is disappearing, much like the Miami coastline.

Inspired by the impression *Rising Tide* left on me, I set out to implement a similar strategy. My original goal was to recruit four community members and four people involved in charter school reform and housing redevelopment to participate in interviews. I was anticipating comparing the viewpoints of people who were at opposite ends of a spectrum. I was surprised to find out how much my participants' statements would overlap, complicating the issues of schools and housing.

For instance, my first four participants included two longtime community members from South Memphis, a charter school founder, and the charter school's executive director (principal). When asked about important places in South Memphis that needed to be preserved, all four participants discussed many of the same historical landmarks. Moreover, after discussing the fact that several area elementary and middle schools have been closed and demolished, a community member told me that her grandson attends a charter school (the same school that my other two participants are affiliated with) and that she likes the school compared to the traditional schools in the area. I expected to hear education reformers from outside of the community demonstrate a lack of knowledge of or concern for the culture and history of South Memphis. Additionally, I suspected community members would have negative views toward their traditional public schools being closed in favor of charter schools operated by outsiders.

After conducting interviews, I noticed the two participants from the charter school were well-informed about the culture and history of the surrounding community—though they fall short of making that culture and history visible to their students through the curriculum used at the school. The charter school founder obviously researched the community before opening a school there, but his responses to my questions sometimes came across as general rather than sentimental. To further complicate my understanding of the community's dynamics, community members often echoed the rhetoric from education reformers and redevelopers in the area more generally. After interviewing only four of my eight participants, I realized that my study was not turning out to feature the glaring dissimilarities I witnessed in *Rising Tide*, as much of the dialogue was overlapping.

After my first round of interviews, I had to understand my study from a new perspective. One avenue I explored was the use of language. Wealthy white elites have long been known to co-opt the language of Black movements for justice (Allen, 1969/1990; Buras, 2015). In the case of my study, the charter school reformers represent outside forces that have leveraged their knowledge of the community to promote their school. Further, I attended a neighborhood meeting held by people involved in redevelopment at a South Memphis community center. Community members who attended the meeting were regularly invited to these types of gatherings to listen to speakers share their plans for future development and ask for input from the community. Through these meetings, community members begin to take on the language of redevelopers regarding how they speak about the issues of the community.

The responses of my first four interviewees challenged me to reimagine my study. I felt a great deal of relief to have the opportunity to visualize my research with a fresh outlook. I was no longer confined to a strict recruitment strategy of four people from one side of the issue and four people from the opposing side. Instead, I understood the issues of education reform and gentrification to be more nuanced than a black-and-white issue. I was free to find participants from various backgrounds who had experience with schools and the surrounding community of South Memphis.

The adjustments I had to make helped me more than simply understanding my study as profoundly nuanced. It was a valuable lesson for an aspiring researcher. It challenged me to dig deeper and consider all available arguments and perspectives before jumping to conclusions. It also proved that a design that works well for one study might take more work to replicate. I continued recruiting participants and conducting interviews. However, I was not looking for responses that opposed those of other participants. Instead, I carefully listened to interviewees to understand why people think what they think, believe what they believe, and say what they say. In the end, my study was better off with an examination of education reform and gentrification that is not so black-and-white.

REFERENCES

Allen, R. L. (1990). *Black awakening in capitalist America*. Africa World Press. (Original work published 1969)

Buras, K. L. (2015). *Charter schools, race, and urban space: Where the market meets grassroots resistance*. Routledge.

Yamaguchi, A. (Executive Producer & Host). (2020, March 19). *Rising tide: Priced out in Miami* [TV Episode]. In *REVERB CBS Reports*. CBS Productions. https://www.cbsnews.com/video/cbs-reports-rising-tide-priced-out-in-miami/

OUTTAKE

TIME ZONES, PANDEMIC, AND WAR, OH MY!

The Challenges of Conducting an International Virtual Exchange

Jie Zhang
State University of New York Brockport

Mariana Sokol
Ternopil Volodymyr Hnatiuk
National Pedagogical University, Ukraine

Cynthia Boyer
Institut National Universitaire Champollion, France

As the world becomes more interconnected, it is paramount that college graduates are prepared to become global citizens. Studying abroad provides college students with opportunities to develop intercultural competence when immersing themselves in a different country. However, there are barriers that prevent students from participating in study abroad programs, such as cost, language, schooling, work, family, health, safety concerns, low priority, or fear of the unknown (Vernon et al., 2017). Since the outbreak of the pandemic in early 2020, the number of students studying abroad has decreased due to physical mobility restrictions (NAFSA, 2021).

Curriculum and Teaching Dialogue,
Volume 25, Numbers 1 & 2, pp. 309–313
Copyright © 2023 by Information Age Publishing
www.infoagepub.com
All rights of reproduction in any form reserved.

International virtual exchanges (IVE) enable students to learn anytime and anywhere with anyone in a global context using online platforms and technology. When students from different cultures, languages, and countries collaborate in teams on the same projects, they build a learning community, overcome challenges, and work toward shared goals. During the process, they learn not only about the content but also about themselves, their peers, cultures, diversity, teamwork, and more. IVE is a cost-effective solution to provide students with great opportunities to develop communication skills and intercultural competence and to prepare them for globalization without traveling abroad (Fowler et al., 2014; Zhang & Pearlman, 2018).

However, cross-country collaboration may present challenges, including different time zones, schedules, languages, class sizes, disciplines, cultures, and technology preferences. In addition, when collaboration occurs across disciplines, the participants may encounter challenges related to different course expectations and student learning outcomes (Zhang & Pearlman, 2021). Furthermore, unexpected obstacles may occur, such as the pandemic and war. In this outtake, three professors across the United States, Ukraine, and France co-planned and co-taught a three-way IVE project for three semesters. We share how we overcame challenges and implemented this project collaboratively, making education sustainable.

THE PROJECT, CHALLENGES, AND RESOLUTIONS

After months of co-planning, in the fall 2021 semester, we co-taught our first three-way interdisciplinary IVE project across three countries of the United States, Ukraine, and France. In the recent three semesters from fall 2021 to fall 2022, students enrolled in an English course in France, students in the Parallels of Intercultural Communication course in Ukraine, and students in the Assessment for Special Education course in the United States participated in this three-way IVE project. The goal of the project was to establish intercultural communication through the creation of virtual exchange modules, to integrate global collaboration into specific components of the educational and professional programs at various higher education institutions, to open the perspectives of communication between students of different countries, and to promote the principles of humanity and tolerance with an example of online international academic cooperation.

In each semester, the English course in France was offered in person with an average of 50 students, the Intercultural Communication course in Ukraine was offered online with 15–20 students, and the Assessment for Special Education course in the United States was offered online with an average of 25 students and ranged from 23 to 30 students. The unequal number of students among these three classes led to this three-way collaboration. The students could work in teams to support each other, and each team member could have a more evenly distributed workload.

Because of its unique feature of interdisciplinary collaboration across three countries, it was essential to develop common assignments so that learning could be relevant, meaningful, and beneficial to all students engaged in this project. The IVE project asked the students to (a) participate in an ice-breaker activity to introduce themselves and gain a better understanding of their peers, including their partner peers' cultures and countries; (b) make a team presentation, comparing the development of technology and its use in education in the United States, Ukraine, and France; and (c) reflect on learning through this interdisciplinary collaboration across cultures, languages, and countries. It was also critical to establish shared learning outcomes so all students would be motivated to work towards them. The participating students were supposed to reach the following student learning outcomes: (a) to gain cross-cultural, crosslinguistic, and cross-disciplinary diverse experiences; (b) to develop knowledge regarding the development of technology and its use in education across the United States, Ukraine, and France; (c) to demonstrate communication skills across cultures, disciplines, and countries using technology; and (d) to improve intercultural competence. We worked closely to co-plan and implement this three-way IVE project, support student learning, and assess their performance.

In addition to the imbalanced number of students and different disciplines, there were other challenges that we had to overcome when implementing this IVE project. The participants spoke English, French, Ukrainian, and other languages. Since the practice of the English language was one additional learning objective for French and Ukrainian participants, English was chosen as the common language used in this IVE project.

The participants were from locations across three time zones, which presented another challenge. Albi, France and Ternopil, Ukraine are six and seven hours ahead of Brockport (Eastern Standard Time [EST]) in the United States, respectively. The college students had obligations other than this project, such as work, family, and other classes, to name a few. Considering students' desire to find a common time to do their teamwork, we checked students' availability and set up 8–9 A.M. (EST, U.S.; i.e., 2–3 P.M. Albi, France and 3–4 P.M. Ternopil, Ukraine, respectively) on five Tuesdays for students to meet "face-to-face" online. Students also met outside these scheduled synchronous meetings on Zoom, FaceTime, Google Hangouts, or other jointly agreed upon platforms. Discussion continued via email, WhatsApp, or other technology tools for teamwork.

The pandemic also presented significant challenges. Some students had to miss the scheduled synchronous meetings or ask for extensions because they were sick, they had to take care of sick family members, or they experienced the death of their loved ones. Furthermore, Russia's invasion of Ukraine impacted the IVE project significantly. It was essential for the participants, including the professors and students, to keep communication open and remain flexible and supportive when encountering the unexpected. Despite all the difficulties and uncertainties, the dedication and persistence of the participants made the project possible. Emotional bonds and friendships were established beyond the academic project by working together to tackle difficulties, find solutions, and complete tasks.

REFLECTIONS AND IMPLICATIONS

Communication has proven to be a key element in the success of the collaboration and fostered a foundation of cooperation among us. We worked closely together, made timely communications, analyzed the challenges, and found the most appropriate solutions that mutually benefited all our students. By doing so, we overcame the obstacles and moved forward to complete the project despite all the unexpected difficulties. The triptych of communication, cooperation, and collaboration is based on the understanding and flexibility of each professor. Indeed, we were all identified from the beginning as a unit by our students, allowing shared teaching and a replacement of colleagues. For example, when one or two members of the co-teaching team could not take part in the synchronous videoconference, the rest of the team member(s) could run the meeting seamlessly. This collaborative teamwork allowed the project to be carried on without interruption. The trinomial format made the collaboration more accountable and reliable, especially when the pandemic and war caused the situation to be unexpected and unpredictable. Beyond the teaching aspect, the team, through its fluid and respectful communication, has united towards friendship. The collaboration thus extends to research.

A successful interdisciplinary virtual exchange project across languages, cultures, and countries comprises features such as the essence of foreign language in intercultural communication, the ability to carry out interlingual and intercultural mediation, and the need to implement various communication models to ensure mutual understanding. Another essential feature of an IVE collaboration is the formation of intercultural communicative competence of the acquirers, which includes intercultural knowledge, skills, and personal qualities (e.g., linguistic, sociocultural observation and sensitivity, empathy, and the ability to anticipate intercultural misunderstandings and avoid them).

In summary, it is essential to co-plan and co-teach shared interdisciplinary topics to make an IVE project interesting, meaningful, and profitable for all students across specific disciplines. The joint assignments helped the professors measure student learning outcomes and allowed professors to adjust based on student performance. IVE projects are a cost-effective means to prepare students for a globalized world while extending collaboration among professors from teaching to scholarship.

REFERENCES

Fowler, J. E., Pearlman, A. M. G., LeSavoy, B., & Hemphill, D. (2014). Opening SUNY to the world: Implementing multi-cultural curricular internationalization through the COIL network case studies from SUNY Oswego and College at Brockport. Cornell University, Ithaca, NY, May 27–30, 2014. *The 23rd SUNY Conference on Instruction and Technology.*

NAFSA: Association of International Educators. (2021). *Trends in U.S. Study Abroad.* https://www.nafsa.org/policy-and-advocacy/policy-resources/trends-us-study-abroad

Vernon, A., Moos, C., & Loncarich, H. (2017). Student expectancy and barriers to study abroad. *Academy of Educational Leadership Journal, 21*(1), 1–9. https://www.abacademies.org/articles/student-expectancy-and-barriers-to-study-abroad-6694.html

Zhang, J., & Pearlman, A. (2018). Expanding access to international education through technology enhanced collaborative online international learning (COIL) courses. *International Journal of Technology in Teaching and Learning, 14*(1), 1–11.

Zhang, J., & Pearlman, A. (2021). Adapting technology in a virtual exchange project across the U.S. and China. *Curriculum and Teaching Dialogue, 23*(1 & 2), 277–280.

BOOK REVIEW

REIMAGINING SCHOOL DISCIPLINE FOR THE 21ST CENTURY STUDENT: ENGAGING STUDENTS, PRACTITIONERS, AND COMMUNITY MEMBERS

By John A. Williams III & Chance W. Lewis

Reviewed by Lizette Burks
University of Houston Downtown

Although student discipline has become synonymous with the *role* of the principal or the assistant principal in most P–12 schools, student discipline or "rules, policies, and practices that exist in schools so school practitioners can manage student behavior to promote positive academic outcomes" lies in the practice of many, encompassing a wide range of education stakeholders including often ignored support staff that can collectively enact change to reduce and eliminate school discipline disparities (Williams & Lewis, 2022, p. xi). John A. Williams III and Chance W. Lewis' edited book *Reimagining School Discipline for the 21st Century Student: Engaging Students, Practitioners, and Community Members* not only challenges educators to understand why students face discipline the way they do in the U.S. school system but does so through a timely, unique, and necessary lens, exploring the dynamics of how power and privilege shape identities and access in society to unpack the disparities in school discipline for historically marginalized

---

Curriculum and Teaching Dialogue,
Volume 25, Numbers 1 & 2, pp. 315–318
Copyright © 2023 by Information Age Publishing
www.infoagepub.com
All rights of reproduction in any form reserved.

students. Williams and Lewis (2022) bring to light the "positionality of certain students in P-12 schooling environments," that, "place them in the direct cross-hairs of exclusionary and discriminatory school discipline practices and policies" (p. xi). Inequitable school discipline practices in the United States that historically and pervasively penalize students based on economic, racial, ethnic, cultural, sexual, gender, and national background identities and intersectionality are explored. The book is unique in that the chapters are written by scholars whose positionality aligns with the student group or affiliated topic they write about, providing more genuine, richer insights. In light of serious social and political issues confronting issues of diversity, equity, and inclusion in education throughout the 21st century, John A. Williams III, Assistant Professor of Multicultural Education at Texas A&M University at College Station, and Chance W. Lewis, Carol Grotnes Belk Distinguished Professor of Urban Education at the University of North Carolina at Charlotte, provide an opportunity to view school disciplinary issues in the context of more authentic discourses and aim to support education practitioners to be "cognizant of their position within the school discipline paradigm" (Williams & Lewis, 2022, p. xv).

Approaches and models connected to school discipline practices range from, but are not limited to, culturally responsive teaching practices (Ladson-Billings, 1995), restorative practices (Zehr, 2002), culturally responsive classroom management (Weinstein et al., 2003), and positive behavioral interventions support (Bradshaw et al., 2008). Williams and Lewis (2022) focus less on ambiguous models and more on the effectiveness of individual members enacting strategies within various frameworks, reigniting "asset-framed discussions, advocacy, and action around school discipline" (p. xv). *Reimagining School Discipline for the 21st Century Student* is organized into two sections that aim to reengineer how education practitioners, researchers, students, and the community collaborate through an interdisciplinary lens in support of reducing school discipline disparities for students. The first section (Chapters 1–4) focuses on historically marginalized students through first-hand experiences concerning school discipline. Cases include the importance of humanizing African American children, Latinx youth push-out and exclusion from traditional public schools, the infliction of harm for LGBTQ+ students and the impact of intersecting marginalized identities, and the continued colonization of American Indian students in K–12 public schools. The second section (Chapters 5–9) examines the importance of educators critically analyzing their identity to understand how and why discipline practices are disproportionate for historically marginalized students. Here, authors stress the importance of employing a critical conscious framework to address the consciousness gap between students of color and their white teachers; transforming how social workers are engaged in school discipline

Reimagining School Discipline For the 21st Century Student   317

through a critical framework; the reversal of using school counselors as disciplinarians and instead as a connector for intersecting stakeholders to reshape school discipline practices; and alternative proactive, rather than reactive, disciplinary approaches for diverse student bodies to be utilized by principals and assistant principals.

A significant component of *Reimagining School Discipline for the 21st Century Student* focuses on engaging a range of education stakeholders to consider what is at stake when inequitable school discipline causes students to "disengage from the education process entirely" (Williams & Lewis, 2022, p. 121). This disengagement has a ripple effect and, "our work in schools shapes lives and can propel students into careers which ultimately alter the course of their lives, the lives of their current and future family, and the ethos of the communities they come from" (Williams & Lewis, p. 122). This book would be valuable for students to read in undergraduate teacher education interdisciplinary seminars while exploring school discipline theory and practice. All preservice educators should have the opportunity to learn from firsthand experiences within the book's first section focusing on school discipline for historically marginalized students. For example, Chapter 4 provides seminal information about neocolonial structures in today's schools and the historical roots of school discipline structures. Other historically marginalized student groups discussed in this book connected clearly to the information shared in this important historical chapter. This book would also support graduate courses in instructional leadership, educational leadership, school social work education, and counselor education, as the second section of the book targets specific frameworks, strategies, and implications for these areas. Much like the authors state in their epilogue, the need to include additional "student groups and practitioners who are equally impacted by school discipline" is an area for future expansion (Williams & Lewis, p. 130). In the meantime, readers interested in other areas of access, equity, and achievement not presented in this volume should look to other books, numbering over 20, in this series (noted in the front matter). Overall, *Reimagining School Discipline for the 21st Century Student* situates the reader on critical disciplinary issues for historically marginalized students and reframes supporting students from an asset-based lens.

REFERENCES

Bradshaw, D. P., Koth, C. W., Bevans, K. B., Ialongo, N., & Leaf, P. J. (2008). The impact of school-wide positive behavioral interventions and supports (PBIS) on the organizational health of elementary schools. *School Psychology Quarterly, 23*(4), 462. https://doi.org/10.1037/a0012883

Ladson-Billings, G. (1995). Toward a theory of culturally relevant pedagogy. *American Educational Research Journal, 32*(3), 465–491. https://doi.org/10.3102/00028312032003465

Weinstein, C., Curran, M., & Tomlinson-Clarke, S. (2003). Culturally responsive classroom management: Awareness into action. *Theory Into Practice, 42*(4), 269–276. https://doi.org/10.1207/s15430421tip4204_2

Williams, J. A., & Lewis, C. W. (2022). Introduction and epilogue. In J. A. Williams & C. W. Lewis (Eds.), *Reimagining school discipline for the 21st century student: Engaging students, practitioners, and community members* (pp. xi–xxi). Information Age Publishing.

Zehr, H. (2002). *The little book of restorative justice.* Good Books.

BOOK REVIEW

LOOKING LIKE A LANGUAGE, SOUNDING LIKE A RACE

By Jonathan Rosa

Reviewed by Derek Gottlieb
University of Northern Colorado

I find it most useful, or apt, to think of Jonathan Rosa's *Looking Like a Language, Sounding Like a Race* (2019) first and foremost as a gift. Generosity characterizes every aspect of the book—its methodological attention and formal construction; its interdisciplinary range; and its ability and willingness to examine children, families, institutions, and educational personnel in a variety of settings and perspectives. When I say, in the context of a review for *Curriculum and Teaching Dialogue*, that this book is a gift, I mean that it offers readers something special and somewhat unexpected, a spectacular kind of permission to pursue customary interests in unaccustomed directions, along unfamiliar routes, with newly attuned ears and eyes to which interests might address themselves.

Looking Like a Language, Sounding Like a Race is a work in the field of linguistic anthropology, exploring what Rosa (2019) calls "the co-naturalization of language and race [as] a key feature of modern governance, such that languages are perceived as racially embodied and race is perceived as linguistically intelligible" (p. 2). However, the principal site of governance in and around which Rosa explores these dynamics is a public school in Chicago. Through observations, interactions, and interviews with children, family members, teachers, administrators, resource officers, Rosa explores

---

Curriculum and Teaching Dialogue,
Volume 25, Numbers 1 & 2, pp. 319–323
Copyright © 2023 by Information Age Publishing
www.infoagepub.com
All rights of reproduction in any form reserved.

320   D. GOTTLIEB

the sometimes contradictory and sometimes unexpected forms that this co-naturalization can take, and the unbelievably wide variety of ways that individuals within and around the institution negotiate the process. The ultimate effect of his work—for me, at least—has been to destabilize my somewhat ossified perspectives on a variety of issues within education. Destabilization is the right word, I think; it has been less a matter of coming around to the opposite side of some argument than it has been a revitalization of a capacity for "responding anew," in Richard Eldridge's (2008, p. 15) words, to a previously foregone conclusion.

Rosa divides his book into two parts, namely, as might be expected, one that focuses on the racialization of language and another that focuses on the lingualizing of race. Each part consists of three chapters, and each chapter seems to be taking off from one resonant quotation or event. Each trilogy of chapters examines the imbrications of race and language from the perspective of administrators navigating policy; from the perspective of students formulating and reformulating identities in response to family, peers, and institutions; and from the perspective of the elements of material culture through which all this navigation proceeds. Bringing these perspectives into conversation and confrontation with one another allows people—perhaps compels people—to step outside the habitual ways in which people tend to grasp a variety of topics:

> Seemingly superficial issues such as uniforms played crucial roles in ensuring students' safety. Seemingly problematic figures such as police officers became supportive community members. Seemingly conservative discourses of teacher accountability contributed to unprecedented graduation rates. Seemingly damaging mainstreaming practices provided students with access to high-level courses from which they would typically be excluded. (Rosa, 2019, p. 47)

It is a truism almost too banal to mention, but, as Ani DiFranco (1993) has said, "every tool is a weapon if you hold it right." It is worth underscoring that the relationship between weapon and tool extends in the other direction, as well. Rosa's work allows readers to see both sides of this dynamic, and it allows them to stand shoulder to shoulder with his participants, facing constraints that are also affordances, following narrow directives that are also expansive invitations, and adhering to social and institutional norms while also improvising upon them in acts of something like aspirational projection toward a desirable future.

The adventure of reading into which Rosa's book invites readers militates especially against the seemingly irresistible temptation to adopt strong stances on "solutions" to social—even existential—problems that run through particular policy formulations to be supervised and interpreted by particular institutions. Policies and institutions are at most worldly mediators, as Steven Klein (2020) calls them, through which and with which people organize socially and individually, pursuing visions of the good life that are at once personal and collective. Policies and institutional forms are at best points of departure; they can never be construed as the end of the line *if* the thing that people want is an ongoing mode of living well together. Policies and institutions are things to be worked on, worked against, worked through, and worked with; but they are not the kinds of things that can, even in the most utopian formulation, just do the work for people.

In thinking about "the work," the greatest gift in Rosa's book has less to do with anything like his "findings," and much more to do with the reminder of the goals of scholarly activity, of scholarly life, that readers can glimpse in the book. It allows readers to see—and even demands seeing—social research as a profoundly reflexive activity that is fully integrated with other modes of living together with others and perpetually on the lookout for further ways to understand, formulate, and organize around the facts of human lives. That readers can stand in need of this reminder is a kind of testament to the success of "modern governance" as an ideological formation, one that functions first and foremost through partition and distinction, as figured especially by the bright lines of international borders (Ndaliko, 2023; Sakai, 2021). Under this ideological formation—as under any ideological formation—the facts of human lives can both sit there in plain view and be also chronically misunderstood or even violently misrecognized. Coming to know facts like these is not very like the definitive (and, again, violent) operations of discovery or proof. Knowing, here, bears more of an affinity to remembering, reconfiguring, rearranging, resituating, reviewing, returning. And research has less of a monopoly on knowing than people might think. Research sits among a family of practices that also includes listening, reading, organizing, collaborating, bullshitting, attending, and so on. To read Rosa's book is to encounter a practice of scholarship that defies compartmentalization, even into categories as large as the humanities and the social sciences, to say nothing of the qualitative-quantitative spectrum, and that aspires to something more like fullness than completeness.

In reading *Looking Like a Language, Sounding Like a Race*, I am thrown back upon myself in a variety of ways. I have already mentioned the way that the work destabilizes and opens up phenomena that I, for one, have become all too habituated to treating as though they are well known and well defined—phenomena like race and language, obviously, but also research methods and research findings, thinking and doing, policy and practice, schooling and policing. I remember and grimace inwardly at the kinds of questions I habitually ask during dissertation proposal defenses, not because there is no value (obviously) in getting clear about the connection between the wording of a question and the way of pursuing an answer, but because of the way that such questions reify the idea that the world and the things of the world *just are* essentially clear a priori, that any messiness and indistinctness amounts to problematic contingency to be discounted if not eradicated entirely. It is all too easy to forget that a clearing is one thing and clarity another; it is all too easy to forget that clarity is often imposed upon the world, and that a clearing, by contrast, occurs within one.

This rigorous attention to the production of clarity, and costs of achieving it, is also something to be grateful for in Rosa's work. One can see it especially in the degree of recurrent attention Rosa pays to participants like Dr. Baez and Yesi, who exercise agency within overlapping structures that they do not exactly control, structures that also only incompletely govern them. Rosa's attention and descriptions are oriented by his wide reading within and across disciplines, but the facts of the matter are only incompletely illuminated by his erudition and therefore require his sustained attention. The learning, of which his book is a record and a vehicle, begins with questions that arise from the unexpected words of his participants— "I heard that Mexicans are Hispanic and Puerto Ricans are Latino" is the title and departure point of Chapter 2, for instance—but the learning on display ultimately outpaces its questions themselves, which is a worthy aspiration for scholarship as a whole.

Precisely for these reasons—that Rosa's work is explicitly drawing upon and in conversation with multiple disciplinary fields (including linguistics, anthropology, and anthropology), while simultaneously working within and speaking back to a wide range of social-theoretic traditions, as well— it is difficult to compare *Looking Like a Language, Sounding Like a Race* with other scholarly books. For instance, I might be tempted to say that the experience of reading it is like the experience of reading Savannah Shange's (2019) *Progressive dystopia: Abolition, Antiblackness, and Schooling in San Francisco*: both books use ethnographic methods to put the shortcomings of center-left policymaking in schools on full display. But Shange's book, while also brilliant, is more content to work within theoretical and disciplinary traditions; one might say that, like Rosa's, her book is asking readers to see the ground-level impacts of certain policies on traditionally marginalized populations differently. But Rosa's book extends the discussion further than Shange's by inviting readers to change the *way* that they see the interactions between school systems and traditionally marginalized students. That distinction also applies to the majority of books focused on (a) the experiences of Latinx/e/o students in particular and (b) issues of race in education in general. So much of that work examines and critiques the way that schools shape student experiences *for* a certain category of student. Rosa's book does this, too, but it also emphasizes that these "categories of students" are constantly in formation and under negotiation in interactions with peers, through contact with disciplinary structures (principals and law enforcement), and by responding to definition by policy.

In order to find other, similarly attentive work, readers should look at the work of Rosa's frequent collaborators, including Nelson Flores (2020, e.g.) and Vanessa Díaz. In the former case, Flores has not published a solo-authored book, which does not make his contributions less valuable, but which means that readers looking for a similar book to Rosa's will not find one authored by Flores yet. And in the latter case, Díaz (2020), while focused on similar dynamics, is not looking at schools, but at the changing racial and relational dynamics in the paparazzi, with a more direct critique of racial capitalism than one finds in Rosa. Rosa's particular attention to examining the interplay of social theories, academic fields, qualitative research methodologies, and the lived experiences of real people attending and working in schools is, so far, unique in the education literature.

Looking Like a Language itself is something of a clearing—as of the clouds, or as in the midst of a forest. It is an opening within which the familiar world might appear in a new light, revealing new possibilities. It is in that sense that the book might stand as an example, both in the kind of opening that it shows possible to make and in the further work in which it invites readers to engage.

REFERENCES

Díaz, V. (2020). *Manufacturing celebrity: Latino paparazzi and women reporters in Hollywood.* Duke University Press.

DiFranco, A. (1993). My I.Q. [Song]. On *Puddle dive*. Righteous Babe Records.

Eldridge, R. (2008). *Literature, life, and modernity.* Columbia University Press.

Flores, N. (2020). From academic language to language architecture: Challenging raciolinguistic ideologies in research and practice. *Theory into Practice, 59*(1), 22-31. https://doi.org/10.1080/00405841.2019.1665411

Klein, S. (2020). *The work of politics: Making a democratic welfare state.* Cambridge University Press.

Ndaliko, C. R. (2023). *To be Nsala's daughter: Decomposing the colonial gaze.* Duke University Press.

Rosa, J. (2019). *Looking like a language, sounding like a race: Raciolinguistic ideologies and the learning of Latinidad.* Oxford University Press.

Sakai, N. (2021). *The end of Pax Americana: The loss of empire and Hikikomori nationalism.* Duke University Press.

Shange, S. (2019). *Progressive dystopia: Abolition, antiblackness, and schooling in San Francisco.* Duke University Press.

BOOK REVIEW

TEACHING AS A HUMAN ACTIVITY: WAYS TO MAKE CLASSROOMS JOYFUL AND EFFECTIVE

By J. Amos Hatch

Reviewed by Katherine Perrotta
Mercer University

I am a former middle school teacher who began her career amid No Child Left Behind and am currently an assistant professor of teacher education who taught throughout challenging times, including the Great Recession and the COVID-19 pandemic. I reflected upon the complexities of teaching and how difficult it feels at times to hold onto the joy of teaching, while reading J. Amos Hatch's (2021) *Teaching as a Human Activity: Way to Make Classrooms Joyful and Effective*. Hatch suggests that teachers promote a love of learning by fostering authentic human relationships with students. By centering joy and care in the classroom, Hatch contends that teachers can build pedagogical resilience to cope with the uncertainty and stresses that impact education.

Teaching as a Human Activity is organized into five parts. Hatch (2021) provides "a rationale for why the described approach is important to teaching that can ignite a shared joy of learning" (p. xiii). Part 1 highlights the necessity of establishing connections with students through the implementation of democratic principles that provide students with a purpose

Curriculum and Teaching Dialogue,
Volume 25, Numbers 1 & 2, pp. 325–328
Copyright © 2023 by Information Age Publishing
www.infoagepub.com
All rights of reproduction in any form reserved.

326   K. PERROTTA

for their schooling. Part 2 provides some historical context to factors that contributed to teacher dissatisfaction over the past 40 years, and how the theoretical tenets of Vygotsky and Maslow can support teachers in being "warm demanders" (p. 55) when promoting engaged learning in K–12 classrooms. Part 3 addresses classroom management through teaching self-respect and creating rules that engage students in moral decision making. Part 4 presents specific instructional approaches to promote engaged learning through scaffolding; thinking and reasoning skills; critical analysis of texts, visuals, and digital media; and mindfully using technology to support learning. Part 5 offers advice for new teachers to prevent burnout through frequent self-reflection and fostering relationships and collaboration with colleagues, mentors, and school communities. Hatch shares in the postscript that this book was not intended "to be about teaching during a crisis" (p. 191). Hatch summarizes the thesis of this book by calling for compassion, kindness, honesty, trustworthiness, integrity, humility, and responsibility as essential elements of human interaction in the wake of the January 6th U.S. Capitol insurrection, which can "make things better for students and teachers" (p. 198).

Hatch's (2021) sharing of his experiences as a veteran, elementary school teacher, and professor in teacher education is a strength of this book. His advocacy for teaching based on human interaction, compassion, and joy is derived from his love of teaching and the numerous lessons he learned about the importance of democracy and relationships in education throughout his 45-year career. His candidness was refreshing to read, demonstrating his humanity as an educator. Such self-reflection can be a model for other teachers to overcome imposter syndrome and focus on life-long learning as part of their professional and personal growth.

A discussion of how Hatch's principles of creating effective classrooms apply to middle and secondary teachers would strengthen this book. Hatch's experiences are couched in his experiences teaching primary grades, which may make this book difficult for middle and high school teachers to relate to for application in their classrooms. Moreover, deeper analysis of the role of empathy (Davis, 2001; Endacott & Brooks, 2018; Perrotta, 2018a, 2018b; Wineburg, 2001; Yilmaz, 2007), care theory (Noddings, 2005), and democracy (Parker, 2001) as philosophical and pragmatic purposes of schools would bolster Hatch's (2021) thesis. While Hatch acknowledges that this book was scheduled for publication eight weeks prior to the 2021 Capitol riots, he does not address how the school closures due to the pandemic caused immense stress and tribulation for teachers, students, and educational stakeholders. As a result, Hatch misses the opportunity to support new and preservice teachers who face significant challenges that include delivering scripted curriculum, being evaluated based on how closely they follow a district pacing map, giving rote and high-stakes assessments,

Teaching as a Human Activity   327

avoiding so-called "controversial issues" for fear of retribution, and coping with low wages in light of historically high inflation rates and a looming recession.

Addressing diversity, equity, and inclusion as elements of humanizing the teaching profession would further strengthen this book. Hatch (2021) states that "expecting to make a difference in the life of just one student is aiming way too low" (p. 4). However, he needs to provide practical suggestions for fostering relationships with adolescents in 6–12 settings where teachers may have over 100 students. Hatch provides an example of how an action plan focused on assisting preservice teachers "code switch in professional settings" (p. 6) undermines decades of research aimed at decolonizing the curriculum and promoting culturally-relevant pedagogy (Ladson-Billings, 1995), especially in urban areas where Hatch taught (Muhammad, 2020). Discussion of linguistic justice, counternarratives, and empathy would strengthen his arguments on how teachers can model prosocial and moral behavior through emancipatory teaching, particularly when the majority of the teaching force is white and the majority of the public-school student body is Black, Indigenous, and people of color (BIPOC).

Now is a time in human history when experiencing joy seems fleeting, particularly for educators and students. *Teaching as a Human Activity* provokes the reader to reflect on their practice as a professional and a human. Such reflection is important for all educators at the beginning, middle, and end of their careers to contemplate their philosophies on the purpose of education and teaching to bring out every student's joy and potential.

REFERENCES

Davis, O. L., Jr. (2001). In pursuit of historical empathy. In O. L. Davis Jr., E. A. Yeager, & S. J. Foster (Eds.), *Historical empathy and perspective taking in the social studies* (pp. 1–12). Roman and Littlefield.

Endacott, J. A., & Brooks, S. (2018). Historical empathy: Perspectives and responding to the past. In S. A. Metzger, & L. McArthur-Harris (Eds.), *The Wiley international handbook of history teaching and learning* (pp. 203–226). John Wiley & Sons.

Hatch, J. A. (2021). *Teaching as a human activity: ways to make classrooms joyful and effective*. Information Age Publishing.

Ladson-Billings, G. (1995). Toward a theory of culturally relevant pedagogy. *American Educational Research Journal 32*(3), 465–491. http://doi.org/10.3102/00028312032003465

Muhammad, G. (2020). *Cultivating genius: An equity framework for culturally and historically responsive literacy*. Scholastic.

328 K. PERROTTA

Noddings, N. (2005). *Educating moral people: A caring alternative to character education.* Teachers College Press.

Parker, W. C. (2001). Toward enlightened political engagement. In W. B. Stanley (Ed.), *Critical issues in social studies research for the 21st century* (pp. 97–118). Information Age Publishing.

Perrotta, K. A. (2018a). A study of students' social identities and a historical empathy gap in middle and secondary social studies classes with the instructional unit "The Elizabeth Jennings Project." *Curriculum and Teaching Dialogue 20*(1&2), 53–69.

Perrotta, K. A. (2018b). Pedagogical conditions that promote historical empathy with "The Elizabeth Jennings Project." *Social Studies Research and Practice 13*(2), 129–146. https://www.emerald.com/insight/content/doi/10.1108/SSRP-11-2017-0064/full/html

Wineburg, S. (2001). *Historical thinking and other unnatural acts: Chartering the future of teaching the past.* Temple University Press.

Yilmaz, K. (2007). Historical empathy and its implications for classroom practices in schools. *The History Teacher 40*(3), 331–337. https://www.jstor.org/stable/30036827

BOOK REVIEW

TEACHING RESILIENCE AND MENTAL HEALTH ACROSS THE CURRICULUM

By Linda Yaron Weston

Reviewed by Naomi Jeffery Petersen
Central Washington University

As I prepared to teach a course in adolescent development and learning to secondary teacher candidates, I was looking for current texts incorporating social and emotional learning (SEL) and brain research. The title of this book, *Teaching Resilience and Mental Health Across the Curriculum,* held great promise, and Routledge is a prominent publisher. Its *Eye on Education* division tends to be practitioner-oriented in content and tone while less turgid than many scholarly publications. Regarding readability, it did not disappoint because Weston's (2022) breezy, chipper voice was infused throughout, as were her personal experiences and feelings. However, this level of readability also contributed to why this book was disappointing in nearly all other aspects.

I hoped for clear explanations of the many factors contributing to students' struggling and needing resilience and mental health support. I was expecting specific applications "across the curriculum." Wading through reflections on her somewhat dated classroom experience, it is possible to find some superficial summaries of hot topics, but the overall approach can be reduced to a simplistic and compassionate positive attitude with mediation exercises. This strategy was introduced in her 2020 book, also

Curriculum and Teaching Dialogue,
Volume 25, Numbers 1 & 2, pp. 329–332
Copyright © 2023 by Information Age Publishing
www.infoagepub.com
All rights of reproduction in any form reserved.

330 N. J. PETERSEN

published by Routledge, *Mindfulness for Young Adults: Tools to Thrive in School and Life*. Both books recommend exercises in forgiveness and strive for a mystic inner calm.

While she makes a passionate case for students needing opportunities to reflect on their values and engage in meditation, she does not help teachers, or teacher candidates understand how this exercise can be a part of their role and responsibilities to teach across the curriculum. Weston offers examples of curriculum units, but they need the context of what courses they could be taught in as well as how they align with the academic standards that teachers are held accountable for preparing their students to demonstrate. In secondary schools, an integrated curriculum is increasingly challenging to achieve, given that accountability has truncated the curriculum to focus on mandated tests.

There is a missed opportunity here—it is possible to integrate mindfulness and the host of critical pedagogical concepts she briefly mentions. For instance, in Chapter 5, she provides a list of 10 types of resilience which does not include the one type—stress resilience—she already introduced in the previous chapter on mental health. This chapter is problematic for being a superficial tour of topics that focuses on mindfulness, stress management, and self-care. This agenda reveals Weston's primary identity as a yoga instructor and her profound weakness in the mental health profession.

Missing are any helpful checklists to identify students in crisis needing referral to counseling. Missing are helpful guidelines for normative development at different ages. Missing are any insights to decode behaviors, especially any microaggressions between students. There are no criteria for checking one's implicit biases regarding neurodivergence and common dysfunctions. Missing are practical tips for communicating with families, working with other stakeholder agencies, and facilitating positive interactions among students that are appropriate in all classes.

All example curriculum units are humanities based and assume teachers are skilled in teaching and assessing reflective writing. That alone is a helpful topic she could have guided the non-humanities teachers in her audience to appreciate. Worse than omitting a helpful skill, she includes one that might backfire. She suggests a StoryCorps project of interviews with a breezy title of "Great Questions for Anyone," which are not great at all; in fact, several could be counterproductive because they might trigger traumatic associations that a young interviewer would be ill-equipped to navigate. An effective interview assignment would have a few focused questions on a particular topic, and should not encourage quasi-counseling interrogations.

I found the book frustrating. Educators teach entire courses in assessment that Weston reduces to a page of trite advice. The section on trauma-sensitive instruction was five pages of narrative with only one set

Teaching Resilience and Mental Health Across the Curriculum   331

of bullet points: personalization, pervasiveness, and permanence. These are wonderfully descriptive concepts, but she does not offer clear instructional techniques. She provides occasional lists of suggested activities that seem to trivialize what it takes to implement them. Each one requires some thoughtful awareness of context, which she discusses elsewhere but does not apply. Anecdote after anecdote concludes that a safe, supportive environment makes all the difference. It would be helpful to provide teachers with ways to perceive or develop that environment in order to identify points of intervention.

My primary disappointment is the organization of the entire book is inconsistent in its pace and function. There is no index. There are citations at the end of each chapter but not a comprehensive bibliography. While the title suggests integrating concepts across the curriculum, the book concludes with Weston's syllabus for an undergraduate two-credit course in mindfulness. Occasionally there are reflective questions but no criteria for success in any approach.

While she does include many current popular topics, like culturally responsive teaching and emotional literacy, Weston should acknowledge many established approaches and theoretical frameworks such as mindfulness (Langer, 1989), student-centered pedagogy (Dewey, 1897), and even the developmental neuroscience of adolescence (e.g., Center for Law, Brain, & Behavior, 2022). She cites statistics from the Centers for Disease Control and Prevention (CDC). However, Weston does not address its well-known acronym ACEs (Adverse Childhood Experiences; CDC, 2022) and fails to emphasize the recommended ways to help prevent adverse experiences and their effects. The CDC organizes its instructional materials as focused, practical, and optimistic. I was surprised she did not include better definitions and a scope and sequence for developing emotional competence, for instance, using Saarni's (1999) landmark model that identified the sequence of skills for emotional competence.

It is worth noting that some states, such as Washington (Washington Office of the Superintendent of Public Instruction, 2020), have developed academic standards for social and emotional learning. I live in the state of Washington. Every other school year, school districts must use one of the professional learning days funded under state law to train staff on SEL or SEL-related topics. All students are expected to be taught six standards: self-awareness, self-management, self-efficacy, social awareness, social management, and social engagement. Each has indicators for four levels of development (early elementary, late elementary, middle school, high school/adult). The indicators are written from a student's perspective, for example, "I can explain the different intensities of my emotions."

There is no doubt that a general disposition of caring (Noddings, 1991) and mindfulness is valuable—for teachers and their students. *Teaching*

Resilience and Mental Health across the Curriculum might be helpful to cultivate that discussion. However, it is insufficient to the task promised by its title. Teaching across the curriculum implies a rigorous analysis of opportunities to insert instructional techniques for achieving clear learning outcomes. An outcome as significant and elusive as resilience is worth a more effective resource (e.g., Bashant, 2020; Sadin, 2022).

REFERENCES

Bashant, J. (2020). *Building a trauma-informed, compassionate classroom: Strategies & activities to reduce challenging behavior, improve learning outcomes, and increase student engagement.* PESI Publishing.

Center for Disease Control and Prevention. (2022, April 6). *Help youth at risk for ACEs.* https://www.cdc.gov/violenceprevention/aces/help-youth-at-risk.html

Center for Law, Brain & Behavior at Massachusetts General Hospital. (2022, January 27). *White paper on the science of late adolescence: A guide for judges, attorneys, and policy makers.* https://clbb.mgh.harvard.edu/white-paper-on-the-science-of-late-adolescence

Dewey, J. (1897, January 16). My pedagogic creed. *The School Journal, 54*(3), 77–80.

Langer, E. J. (1989). *Mindfulness.* Addison-Wesley.

Noddings, N. (1991). Caring and Continuity in Education. *Scandinavian Journal of Educational Research, 35*(1), 3–12. https://doi.org/10.1080/0031383910350101

Saarni, C. (1999). *The development of emotional competence.* Guilford Press.

Sadin, M. (2022). *Trauma-informed teaching and IEPS: Strategies for building student resilience.* Association for Supervision & Curriculum Development.

Washington Office of the Superintendent of Public Instruction. (2020). *Social emotional learning (SEL).* https://www.k12.wa.us/student-success/resources-subject-area/social-emotional-learning-sel

Weston, L. (2022). *Teaching and mental health across the curriculum: A guide for high school and college teachers.* Taylor & Francis Group.

BOOK REVIEW

RECONSTRUCTING CARE IN TEACHER EDUCATION AFTER COVID-19: CARING ENOUGH TO CHANGE

Edited by Melanie Shoffner and Angela W. Webb

Reviewed by Jess Smith
Baylor University

The significant impact of COVID-19 on education is well documented (Paudel, 2021; Pokhrel & Chhetri, 2021; Sintema, 2020), but more work is needed as educators decide what changes are worth keeping and how teaching can and must be different moving forward through and past the realities of COVID-19. *Reconstructing Care in Teacher Education After COVID-19: Caring Enough to Change*, edited by Melanie Shoffner and Angela W. Webb, gathers 22 chapters around the central theme of reimagining Nel Noddings's (1984) work in crafting pedagogies of care in contemporary, pandemic-informed times. Each chapter presents its imagining of care in light of student, preservice teacher (PST), or educator needs that arose from teaching during COVID-19.

The introduction includes a relatable framing story of receiving contradictory course evaluations, with different students praising and criticizing the same teaching qualities. This relational tone is echoed in the collection of

---

Curriculum and Teaching Dialogue,
Volume 25, Numbers 1 & 2, pp. 333–335
Copyright © 2023 by Information Age Publishing
www.infoagepub.com
All rights of reproduction in any form reserved.

334   J. SMITH

research that follows. The book features more than 50 diverse international authors, ranging from current education graduate students and tenured and tenure-track teacher educators to in-service K–12 educators teaching and administrating schools, programs, and grants. Another strength is its readability and explicit connection to its central idea; the editors define care as "manifested in our relationships with, acceptances of, and responses to preservice teachers as individuals with specific needs" (Shoffner & Webb, 2022, p. 5). The subsequent chapters elaborate and riff on this idea. Some chapters more explicitly tie to Noddings than others—citations spanned articles from 1984 to 2014—which might confuse those new to her work, such as those reading this text as part of coursework without intentional scaffolding. However, as someone more familiar with her writing, I found these variations refreshing as they adapted and expanded seminal and newer works into the contemporary teacher education environment.

The editors organize the chapters into four parts—this division, in a few places, feels forced. While the first and third sections have clear boundaries and obvious definitions for inclusion, the second and fourth could have been combined and renamed. Part one, "Programmatic Approaches to Care," takes a broad approach, describing efforts of teacher education programs in terms of preservice teacher needs, accreditation responsibilities, and self-care. These chapters, while general, would serve department chairs or program directors well as they craft policies, curricula, and programming.

Part two, "Care in the Content Areas," endeavors to offer more precise details regarding implementation of the practices in more specific contexts. However, the three chapters leave a noticeable gap—they feature only TESOL teacher education, mathematics methods, and a capstone course that meets during the terms that PSTs engage in student teaching. This section would be helpful to teacher educators in these content areas, but I found myself looking for examples from other disciplines or from courses in different stages of clinical experience or teacher preparation to present a more robust exploration.

Part three, "Care and Teacher Educators," features a collection of self-reflective examinations. This section includes a chapter from one of the editors, looking at lessons learned during the COVID-19 pandemic, as well as chapters exploring ideas for building community, providing authentic care through Buddhist principles, and attending to expressed PST needs. This section in particular would serve well in a teacher education course, perhaps read by small groups of students and discussed in class among students who had read different chapters. The imaginings on the theme shared common ideas with varied and creative deviations.

Part four, "(Re)Framing Care," is the second course-specific section and again has some prominent gaps. This section features work on supporting Asian American PSTs and PSTs serving Black students in rural

Reconstructing Care in Teacher Education After COVID-19 335

environments as well as ideas for explicitly supporting PSTs through harboring, the methodology of which uses found poetry in the PSTs' words. Yomantas (2022) presents a complementary definition to the editors I found most relevant. She writes:

> As a teacher educator, my definition of care builds upon Noddings' [*sic*] (1984, 1988) work and extends to include the creation of authentic, humanized learning communities, situated in the context of care, as an ongoing pursuit and area of continual self-study. (p. 211)

This definition takes the additional steps of encompassing the reflexivity obvious in this work's chapters and tying Noddings (1984) to the humanizing language of Freire (1968/2021), a necessary nod in a contemporary, critical teacher education classroom.

Across chapters throughout the text, I found an emphasis on transparency in teaching and in the research itself—sometimes called forthrightness or honesty by the authors—the idea that invoking care in teacher education involves explicitly modeling and explaining the strategies educators hope to see PSTs apply in their teaching. I similarly noticed an emphasis on reflection and self-care in the chapters. I suspect that the level of reflexivity in this text is deeply tied to its authors' dedication to reconstructing care and considering their identities as part of doing so. The editors build a robust reimagining of care in teacher education. *Reconstructing Care* would be a great jumping-off point for discussion, whether for a faculty book study or in a graduate course exploring philosophies of teacher education.

REFERENCES

Freire, P. (2021). *Pedagogy of hope: Reliving pedagogy of the oppressed*. Bloomsbury. (Original work published 1968)

Noddings, N. (1984). *Caring: A feminine approach to ethics and moral education*. University of California Press.

Paudel, P. (2021). Online education: Benefits, challenges and strategies during and after COVID-19 in higher education. *International Journal on Studies in Education, 3*(2), 70–85. https://doi.org/10.46328/ijonse.32

Pokhrel, S., & Chhetri, R. (2021). A literature review on impact of COVID-19 pandemic on teaching and learning. *Higher Education for the Future, 8*(1), 133–141.

Shoffner, M., & Webb, A. W. (2022). *Reconstructing care in teacher education after COVID-19: Caring enough to change*. Routledge.

Sintema, E. J. (2020). Effect of COVID-19 on the performance of grade 12 students: Implications for STEM education. *Eurasia Journal of Mathematics, Science and Technology Education, 16*(7). https://doi.org/10.29333/ejmste/7893

Yomantas, E. (2022). Harboring teacher candidates: Care during COVID. In M. Shoffner, & A. W. Webb (Eds.), *Reconstructing care in teacher education after COVID-19: Caring enough to change* (pp. 211–224). Routledge.

BOOK REVIEW

BRINGING HISTORY AND CIVICS TO LIFE

By Karalee Wong Nakatsuka and Laurel Aguilar-Kirchoff

Reviewed by Aubrey Brammar Southall
Aurora University

Bringing History and Civics to Life by Karalee Wong Nakatsuka and Laurel Aguilar-Kirchoff is a timely collection of resources, ideas, and lesson plans written by educators for educators. As a former social studies teacher and current teacher educator, I found myself jotting down many notes to share with students. The authors state the book can be used outside of the social science discipline, and I agree. As a professor of secondary education who teaches all disciplines, I plan to add this book to my course texts. *Bringing History and Civics to Life* is organized so that research is quickly related to practice. This book pairs well in a methods class with Walter Parker's (2015) edited book, *Social Studies Today: Research into Practice*. The pragmatic nature of *Bringing History and Civics to Life* would help teacher candidates and veteran teachers turn theory into hands-on instruction.

The book is divided into two sections: the why and the how. Throughout the chapters, I found "thought-provoking ideas and resources" (Nakatsuka & Aguilar-Kirchoff, p. 18). The first three chapters of the book explore pedagogy connections to educational technologies. The text offers plenty of space for readers to reflect on a teacher's practice and to be able to "foster historical inquiry, build community, and help your students connect

---

Curriculum and Teaching Dialogue,
Volume 25, Numbers 1 & 2, pp. 337–338
Copyright © 2023 by Information Age Publishing
www.infoagepub.com
All rights of reproduction in any form reserved.

to civic action" (p. 19). The book's second half gives the reader the opportunity to apply all the knowledge they have gained along with companion edtech tools. Additionally, there are many practical lesson plan ideas.

The authors offer ways to use their pedagogical approaches to make classrooms more inclusive. Their goal is to end the "celebration of some imaginary glorious past" (p. 3). The resources provided help to make history more relevant and culturally responsive to students. The writers remind us, "as educators, we need to guide our students into an understanding that history happened to real people (just like them)" (p. 8).

The text shows examples of how to build community and collaboration within classrooms and schools. The authors share examples of icebreakers, warm-ups, websites, and content-based activities to assist teachers in this monumental task. Resources are provided to help students experience working with others who are different from themselves. Additionally, the authors offer ideas and suggestions on making the resources they provide accessible to all students. Personal vignettes are shared and help the reader visualize the authors' ideas.

Furthermore, there are ideas for promoting student exploration without ever leaving their classroom. Ideas for virtual field trips, explorations, simulations, and suggestions for guest speakers are provided. The authors share how to use "edtech to help history come to life" (p. 82) through gamification, timelines, online libraries and archives, and podcasts.

The lesson-planning checklist and questions toward the book's end help educators to find how to fit their newly acquired skills and knowledge into their classroom and district practices. The questions help teachers benefit from time restrictions, lesson plan structures, learning objectives, and various grade levels and bands. The materials needed for lessons, national standards, assessment ideas, adaptations, and suggested edtech tools make for a more practical application of the text.

Lastly, each chapter concludes with resources and applicable QR codes. Authors encourage readers to take part in the #tryonenewthingchallenge. The featured websites help teachers find project-based learning opportunities, historical empathy resources, and content-based professional development. Examples of resources shared include *The Elizabeth Jennings Project*, *PenPal Schools*, *Global Read Aloud*, and *The Living Room Project*. Veteran and new teachers alike could benefit from this informative read.

REFERENCES

Parker, W. C. (Ed.). (2015). *Social studies today: Research and practice*. Routledge.

Nakatsuka, K. W., & Aguilar-Kirchhoff, L. (2022). *Bring history and civics to life: Lessons & strategies to cultivate informed, empathetic citizens*. International Society for Technology in Education.

ABOUT THE AUTHORS

Adu-Gyamfi, Mary
Mary Adu-Gyamfi is an assistant teaching professor of elementary education in the College of Education and Human Development at the University of Missouri-Columbia.

Allaire, Franklin S.
Franklin S. Allaire is an associate professor of science education at the University of Houston-Downtown. His interests and publications focus on issues impacting the success of underrepresented minorities in STEM-related fields and the innovative use of technologies and pedagogies in science teaching and teacher preparation.

Allweiss, Alexandra
Alexandra Allweiss is an assistant professor of Teacher Education at Michigan State University. Her work critically explores how coloniality is maintained in and through various educational and social processes and centers decolonial efforts and possibilities.

Baker, Sheila F.
Sheila F. Baker is a professor and Director of the School Library and Information Science Program at the University of Houston-Clear Lake.

Bhatnagar, Ruchi
Ruchi Bhatnagar is a clinical associate professor in the College of Education & Human Development at Georgia State University.

339

340 ABOUT the AUTHORS

Bohan, Chara Haeussler
Chara Haeussler Bohan is a professor of Educational Policy Studies at Georgia State University and the current editor of *Curriculum and Teaching Dialogue*. She has authored and edited more than 100 publications, including books, journal articles, book chapters, book reviews, and encyclopedia entries. Her most recent book (with H. Robert Baker and LaGarrett King) is *Teaching Enslavement in American History: Lesson Plans and Primary Sources*.

Boyer, Cynthia
Cynthia Boyer is a professor of Anglo-American studies at Institut National Universitaire Champollion, France.

Burks, Lizette
Lizette Burks is an assistant professor of educational leadership in the Department of urban education at the University of Houston-Downtown.

Campbell, Sarah
Sarah Hahn Campbell is a doctoral student at the University of Northern Colorado and an English teacher in Denver Public Schools.

Castro, Antonio J.
Antonio J. Castro is an associate professor of social studies education at the University of Missouri-Columbia.

Christ, Rebecca C.
Rebecca C. Christ is an assistant professor in the department of teaching and learning at Florida International University.

Conn, Daniel R.
Daniel Conn is an associate professor and incoming department chair of teacher education and kinesiology at Minot State University.

Conner, Caroline J.
Caroline J. Conner is an associate professor of history education and history in the History and Philosophy Department at Kennesaw State University.

Conrad, Bradley
Bradley Conrad is the Cotterman Distinguished Endowed Chair and an associate professor at the Capital University School of Education.

Davis, Leah
Leah Davis is a doctoral candidate at Utah State University and a Clinical Faculty Associate at Brigham Young University.

About the Authors

Erbacher, Monica
Monica Erbacher is a consultant and independent scholar who specializes in quantitative methodologies and academic entitlement.

Farver, Scott
Scott Farver is an assistant professor of Teacher Education at Michigan State University. He uses Critical Whiteness Studies as a framing for examining and pushing against whiteness within educational spaces.

Gerardo, Juan Manuel
Juan Manuel Gerardo is an assistant professor at the University of Cincinnati, where he researches how pre- and in-service mathematics teachers work in solidarity with students and grapple with multiple conceptions of mathematics in both formal and informal settings.

Gottlieb, Derek
Derek Gottlieb is an associate professor at the University of Northern Colorado.

Haas, Brandon J.
Brandon J. Haas is an associate professor of social foundations and leadership education at the University of North Georgia.

Halvorsen, Anne-Lise
Anne-Lise Halvorsen is an associate professor of social studies education at Michigan State University. Her scholarship focuses on curriculum reform in social studies education, specifically exploring project-based learning, culturally sustaining pedagogy, and historical inquiry.

Johnson, Jennifer
Jennifer Johnson is the current Deputy Mayor of Education, Youth and Human Services for the city of Chicago. She is formerly the Chief of Staff of the Chicago Teachers Union, a role she held at the time of the keynote address published therein.

Kim, Yeji
Yeji Kim is an assistant professor of social studies education at the University of Missouri-Columbia.

Lastrapes, Renée E.
Renée E. Lastrapes is a professor and Education Program Director at the University of Houston-Clear Lake.

Many, Joyce E.
Joyce E. Many is a professor of Teaching and Teacher Education at the College of Education & Human Development at Georgia State University.

McConnell, Christy
Christy McConnell is a professor of Curriculum Studies and Educational Foundations at the University of Northern Colorado (she formerly published under the name Moroye).

Miskewicz, Andrea
Andrea Miskewicz is the Head of Museum Education at the Museum of History and Holocaust Education and an EdD candidate at Kennesaw State University.

Palladino, John M.
John M. Palladino is a professor of Special Education at Eastern Michigan University who specializes in emotional-behavior disorders, secondary methods, and special education administration.

Pecore, John
John L. Pecore is a professor and Askew Institute Research Fellow in the School of Education in the College of Education and Professional Studies at the University of West Florida. His scholarly interests focus on experiential learning in authentic and virtual STEM-related teaching and teacher preparation.

Perrotta, Katherine A.
Katherine A. Perrotta is an assistant professor of Middle Grades and Secondary with an emphasis on social studies education Education at Mercer University Tift College of Education

Petersen, Naomi Jeffery
Naomi Jeffery Petersen is a professor of teacher education in the Department of Curriculum, Supervision, and Educational Leadership at Central Washington University. She is also the founder and director of the Accessibility Studies Program.

Pierce, Lauren
Lauren Pierce is an assistant Professor at Northern State University. She researches co-regulation of motivation and identity relating to proactive coping and emotional regulation.

Pitts, Robyn Thomas
Robyn Thomas Pitts is an assistant professor at the University of Denver who studies methods education and praxis.

Pope, Elizabeth J.
Elizabeth J. Pope is an associate professor of practice at The University of Arizona. Her research focuses on social-emotional development and well-being.

Purington, Stephanie B.
Stephanie B. Purrington is a professional lecturer of education at Marist College in Poughkeepsie, New York, where she teaches STEM methods courses.

Reinhardt, Rebecca
Rebecca Reinhardt is a doctoral student at the University of Northern Colorado and an occupational therapist at Colorado State University.

Sage, Mallori
Mallori Sage is a doctoral student at the University of Northern Colorado and a third-grade teacher in Rockford Public Schools.

Samuels, Amy
Amy Samuels is an associate professor of instructional leadership at the University of Montevallo, who researches critical multiculturalism and cultural responsiveness.

Samuels, Gregory
Gregory Samuels is an associate professor of secondary education and Chief Diversity and Inclusion Officer at the University of Montevallo.

Shulsky, Debby
Debby Shulsky is an associate professor and Coordinator of Curriculum and Instruction at the University of Houston-Clear Lake.

Smith, Jess
Jess Smith is an affiliate clinical assistant professor at Baylor University and researches the intersection of mentorship and teaching reading and writing.

Sokol, Mariana
Mariana Sokol is a professor and head of the foreign languages department at Ternopil Volodymyr Hnatiuk National Pedagogical University, Ukraine.

Southall, Aubrey Brammar
Aubrey Brammar Southall is an associate professor and chair of secondary education at Aurora University.

Strong, Emily
Emily Strong is a doctoral student at the University of Northern Colorado and a school counselor at a Denver Lab School.

Tanguay, Carla L.
Carla L. Tanguay is a clinical associate professor and the assistant dean for educator preparation and accreditation in the College of Education and Human Development at Georgia State University.

Uhrmacher, P. Bruce
P. Bruce Uhrmacher is a professor at the University of Denver Morgridge College of Education.

Warren, Ryan B.
Ryan B. Warren is a doctoral student in Educational Policy Studies at Georgia State University.

Weiner, Lois
Lois Weiner is a former career teacher and Professor Emerita of education at New Jersey City University, Dr. Lois Weiner researches and writes about teachers' work, urban education, and labor, focusing on teacher unionism. She is currently writing a follow-up to her book *The Future of Our Schools: Teachers Unions and Social Justice* (Haymarket Press, 2012) about how the pandemic and informational technology have hastened capitalism's transformation of work globally, creating new, intense dangers and challenges for workers, including teachers, and teachers unions

Zhang, Jie
Jie Zhang is a professor of special education at the State University of New York (SUNY) Brockport.

Printed in the United States
by Baker & Taylor Publisher Services